THE UNITED IRISHMEN

Republicanism, Radicalism and Rebellion

EDITED BY DAVID DICKSON,
DÁIRE KEOGH AND
KEVIN WHELAN

THE LILLIPUT PRESS

First published in 1993 by
THE LILLIPUT PRESS LTD
4 Rosemount Terrace, Arbour Hill,
Dublin 7, Ireland.

A CIP record for this
title is available from
The British Library.

ISBN   0 946640 95 5 (cased)
        1 874675 19 8 (paper)

Jacket design by Jarlath Hayes
Set in 10 on 12 Janson by
                                turbulence
m e r m a i d
Printed in Dublin by ßetaprint

THE UNITED
IRISHMEN

CONTENTS

ILLUSTRATIONS

Between pages 196 and 197

Charles Lucas (1713–71), celebrated Dublin radical leader of the mid-century (*National Gallery of Ireland*)

Sir Edward Newenham (1732–1814), MP, reformer and outspoken supporter of the American Revolution (*NGI*)

Rev. John Thomas Troy (1739–1823), Archbishop of Dublin and intellectual leader of the Irish Catholic episcopacy in 1790s (portrait by T.C. Thompson, *NGI*)

Rev. Samuel Barber (1738–1811), leading Presbyterian minister, Moderator of the General Synod of Ulster 1792, and United Irishman (*Ulster Museum*)

John Giffard (1745–1819), editor of *Faulkner's Dublin Journal*, High Sheriff of Dublin, leading Orangeman and the radicals' *bête noire* under the sobriquet 'The Dog in Office' (*NGI*)

John FitzGibbon, Earl of Clare (1749–1802), Attorney-General and Lord Chancellor, member of the inner circle of government policy-makers, and leading conservative in the 1790s (*NGI*)

Theobald Wolfe Tone (1763–98), founder member of the United Irishmen, diplomat and French army officer (*National Library of Ireland*)

Archibald Hamilton Rowan (1751–1834), President of the first Society of United Irishmen in Dublin (*NGI*)

PREFACE

The 1991 bicentenary of the founding of the United Irishmen followed closely the bicentenary of the French Revolution of 1789. That event had been marked in Dublin by a major conference, whose proceedings were subsequently published as *Ireland and the French Revolution* (H. Gough and D. Dickson [eds]). It seemed equally appropriate to organise a conference commemorating the United Irish bicentenary in 1991. A novel feature was the decision to bilocate it in Belfast and Dublin, replicating the almost simultaneous founding of the United Irish societies in those cities in 1791. The conference, enthusiastically supported and very well attended in both locations, generated a high level of interest and debate.

The organising committee (T. Bartlett, P. Collins, D. Dickson, D. Keogh and K. Whelan) was especially indebted to the supporters of the conference: financial help came from the Cultural Relations Commission, the Electricity Supply Board, and Royal Insurance (Ireland); the Ulster Museum and Trinity College, Dublin were welcoming venues, while the Linen Hall Library and the Tailors' Hall hosted lively receptions. Special mention should be made of Peter Collins, who was the principal organiser of the Belfast leg of the conference.

The current volume is an edited collection of the conference proceedings. In producing it, we are especially indebted to the support of the Department of Modern History, TCD, the Institute of Irish Studies, Queen's University Belfast, Hugh Gough (for expert maintenance of the French connection), Brian MacDonald (for reformatting a heterodox collection of disks), and the Ulster Museum and, especially, the National Gallery of Ireland (for help with illustrations). We are also grateful to The Lilliput Press for their customary efficiency.

The United Irishmen: Republicanism, Radicalism and Rebellion rep-

resents the current lively state of study of the late 1790s in Ireland, but it also anticipates an accelerating interest in the period
as the bicentenary of the insurrection itself approaches. This
volume maps the terrain as it now appears, and signposts the
major areas of research to be addressed if we are to further our
understanding of this dynamic and formative decade in the evolution of modern Irish history.

CONTRIBUTORS

THOMAS BARTLETT
University College, Galway

ALLAN BLACKSTOCK
Public Records Office of Northern Ireland, Belfast

JOHN BRIMS
Central Archives, Stirling, Scotland

MARTIN BURKE
University of Chicago

W.H. CRAWFORD
Ulster Folk and Transport Museum

L.M. CULLEN
Trinity College, Dublin

NANCY J. CURTIN
Fordham University, New York

DAVID DICKSON
Trinity College, Dublin

MARIANNE ELLIOTT
Birkbeck College, London

THOMAS GRAHAM
Trinity College, Dublin

JACQUELINE HILL
St Patrick's College, Maynooth

ANN C. KAVANAUGH
Trinity College, Dublin

JAMES KELLY
St Patrick's College, Drumcondra, Dublin

DÁIRE KEOGH
Trinity College, Dublin

GILLES LE BIEZ
Université de Paris IV

DEIRDRE LINDSAY
Trinity College, Dublin

CLAUDE MAZAURIC
*Institut de Recherches et de Documentation en Sciences Sociales,
Université de Rouen*

IAN McBRIDE
Institute of Historical Research, University of London

R.B. McDOWELL
Trinity College, Dublin

JIM SMYTH
Trinity Hall, Cambridge

PIETER TESCH
Trinity College, Dublin

KEVIN WHELAN
Royal Irish Academy

1

THE BURDEN OF THE PRESENT: THEOBALD WOLFE
TONE, REPUBLICAN AND SEPARATIST[1]

Thomas Bartlett

Was Wolfe Tone a republican? Was he a separatist? At one time
to have posed such questions one ran the risk of being labelled
'revisionist', accused of wilfulness, and denounced as anti-national.
Tone's separatism and his republicanism seemed so much a
matter of historical record (and folk memory) that probing them
could scarcely be seen as anything other than an entirely redun-
dant, impishly impertinent, or positively perverse project. After
all, his claim that his objects had been 'to subvert the tyranny of
our execrable government, to break the connection with England,
the never-failing source of all our political evils and to assert the
independence of my country' spoke out so categorically as to pre-
clude all further discussion.[2]

In the 1980s, however, Tone studies received a much-needed
boost with the publication of two very different works. In 1982
Tom Dunne published a sharply written and provocative essay on
Tone's political philosophy entitled *Theobald Wolfe Tone, Colonial
Outsider*, and in 1989 Marianne Elliott's finely crafted full-scale
biography of Tone, *Wolfe Tone, Prophet of Irish Independence*,
appeared: for the first time, Tone's political views were subjected
to close examination.[3] Both authors found little that was novel or
sustained in Tone's thinking; both agreed that Tone was not a
systematic thinker. The union of creeds as a necessary pre-requi-
site for reform, wrote Tom Dunne, 'had become a commonplace
in the decades before 1791', and he swiftly dismissed Tone's claim
to have been a separatist 'from my earliest youth'. Instead, casting
him as an unanchored misfit longing 'to find an acceptable career,
a meaningful role, some fulfilment of the expectations natural to a
member of the colonial elite', Dunne argued that 'alienation and
despair finally made him a separatist and a revolutionary'.[4] While

Marianne Elliott sees Tone as a much more purposeful individual
than that portrayed by Dunne, she too describes Tone's progress
to republicanism as, variously, 'a case of necessity as much as
choice', or 'as an accident of character as much as of timing'.[5]
Again, like Dunne, she considers Tone's writings to have 'owed
much to ideas then in general circulation' and is at pains to deny
them any element of novelty.[6] So far as the intellectual context for
Tone's ideas is concerned, both authors offer different perspectives: Dunne sees Tone as representing the climax of a colonial
nationalist tradition, while Elliott sets Tone squarely in the context of eighteenth-century 'classical' republicanism.[7] These are
valuable insights, best regarded as complementary rather than
contradictory, and it may be worthwhile to explore some of their
implications. Accordingly, this paper seeks to examine the sources
of separatism and republicanism in Tone's thought. Such an
examination may show that there was in theory – and perhaps in
fact – a lively tension between Irish republicanism and separatism
in the late eighteenth century; and that the frequent assumption
that there was a necessary connection between the two has no
foundation. It may also be found that Tone's claims to novelty as
well as to consistency and modernity are rather stronger than
either Elliott or Dunne maintains.

'It has always been the political craft of courtiers and court government to abuse something which they called republicanism; but
what that republicanism was, or is, they never attempt to explain.'[8]
So Tom Paine protested: but it could be claimed that 'republicans' had only themselves to blame for these attacks, for they
themselves were notoriously vague as to what the word meant.
John Adams, an ardent republican in 1776, confessed in 1807 that
he had 'never understood' what a republic was and 'no other man
ever did or ever will', and he added for good measure that a
republic 'may signify anything, everything or nothing'.[9] It is not
difficult to find evidence to substantiate this point.

Montesquieu, reflecting on the classical republican model of
the city-state, maintained that a republic was suitable only for
small countries; by contrast Alexander Hamilton, writing in the
Federalist Papers, maintained that a large republic would in fact
thrive where a small one would assuredly collapse.[10] James Harrington, author of the seventeenth-century republican treatise

Oceana, claimed that in a republic, sovereignty could not be shared; notwithstanding which, Alexander Hamilton advocated nothing less than 'a Confederate Republic...an association of two or more states into one state'.[11] Montesquieu believed that the age of republics was over; the Federalists claimed that it had just begun.[12] Would a republic be at peace with her neighbours? Paine claimed that wars were caused by kings and he pointed to the example of Holland which 'without a king hath enjoyed more peace for this last century than any of the monarchical governments in Europe'.[13] On the other hand, Machiavelli's model of a republic was that of republican Rome which had armed the people and mobilised their disciplined *virtu* to dominate all around them; while Harrington stressed the desirability of republican expansionism – a policy speedily implemented in the New World in the century after independence.[14] Should a republic be based on land or on commerce, on real or on personal property? Again, contradictory viewpoints were voiced. Most republican theorists appear to have been hostile to commercial growth, seeing in it the seeds of future corruption; nor would it be difficult to portray eighteenth-century republicans as anti-capitalists, seekers after a lost or at least endangered communitarian society. For example, colonial pamphleteers in the 1770s declared that 'the bane of patriotism was commerce' and instead extolled the agrarian nature of the New World. Some republicans like Harrington and the authors of *Cato's Letters* even urged an agrarian law to prevent extremities of wealth.[15] On the other hand, Scottish republicans were anything but anti-capitalist and were very commercially minded – David Hume claimed that 'it is under republican government that commerce and culture initially flourish' – and among American republicans, Alexander Hamilton looked forward to the creation of a commercial empire in North America.[16] What did republican writers mean by equality? What did they mean by representation? Machiavelli claimed that in a republic *aequum ius* and *aequa libertas* – equality before the law and equality of access to office – should prevail, but he also assumed that the wisest and most honourable citizens would become the first magistrates; and later commentators have found in republicanism a strain 'which admires the aristocracy and admires wealth'.[17] Gordon Wood, for example, has concluded from his study of the relevant literature that 'for all its emphasis on equality, republi-

canism was still not considered by most to be incompatible with
the conception of a hierarchical society of different gradations and
a unitary authority to which deference from lower to higher
should be paid'.[18] As for representative institutions, Rousseau denounced them as 'a mockery of republican freedom' but, for their
part, the Federalist writers saw them as central to a republican
form of government.[19]

Perhaps the most striking aspect of the republican position in
the eighteenth century is its manifest lack of consensus on the
question of whether a republic had to adopt a specific form of
government. Provided the common weal was pursued, and 'commonwealth' was for a long time the usual translation from the
Latin *republica*, there was much scope for discussion. 'What the
republicans take themselves to be describing', writes Skinner, 'is
any set of constitutional arrangements under which it might justi-
fiably be claimed that the *res* (the government) genuinely reflects
the will and promotes the good of the *publica* (the community as a
whole). Whether a *res publica* has to take the form of a self-gov-
erning republic is not therefore an empty definitional question
but rather a matter for earnest enquiry and debate.'[20]

Viewed in this light it is clear that a republic was by no means
incompatible with monarchy. Machiavelli the republican and
author of the *Discourses* was also Machiavelli the monarchist and
author of *The Prince*; and the classic republican texts since his time
had been – to the twentieth-century mind – equally ambivalent on
this question. Sir Thomas Smith's *De Republica Anglorum* (1565)
was little more than a stagey defence of the Tudors; More's
Utopia allowed for an elective king, as did Sir Philip Sydney's
Arcadia (1580); Harrington's *Oceana* had provision for kingly government; and while Algernon Sydney (Sir Philip's great-nephew)
denounced the Stuarts in his *Discourses concerning Government*
(1681), he was careful to add that 'nothing is further from my
intention than to speak irreverently of kings'.[21] Admittedly, Montesquieu argued that republican virtue and monarchical government were incompatible, and Tom Paine in *Common Sense* (1776)
ridiculed monarchy, especially hereditary monarchy: an hereditary king made as much sense as an hereditary mathematician, he
wrote.[22] But most republican writers considered that a monarchical component would figure in every republican form of government – Adams considered the United States 'a monarchical

republic' – and their main concern was to ensure that in that blend of 'the one, the few, and the many' which constituted true republican government, 'the one' did not dominate.[23] In this respect, England represented for many republican writers the way forward, for they considered England to be in all but name a republic, 'a democracy disguised as a monarchy', with her constitution 'the best, the most equal, the freest in the world'.[24] Moreover, republicans everywhere were agreed that, as Paine put it, if a nation 'chose a monarchial form [of government], it had a right to have it so'.[25] Viewed in this light, it is no surprise that Blair Worden in his study of the development of English republican thought has pronounced it to be 'an over-simplification and in important respects an error to equate republicanism with opposition to kingship'.[26]

Republicanism in the early modern period was 'more a language than a programme' and the vocabulary was one of protest, of resistance to tyrants, combining an obsession with corruption and a search for virtue.[27] It was generally assumed that political virtue and civic virtue would be found most readily, though not exclusively, in a country whose citizens had the predominant part in the election or selection of their magistrate, prince or king. For this reason republicans everywhere sought to give a preponderant role to the people. 'Whenever I use the word republic with approbation', wrote John Adams, 'I mean a government in which the people have collectively or by representation an essential share in the government.'[28] Where the people had little or no say – either because of despotism or corruption – republicans were generally found seeking a return to some golden age or, more often, advocating parliamentary reform. Republicans did not concern themselves overly with precise forms of government: hereditary monarchies were least preferred – the chances of a patriot king like Alfred coming along were too remote – and their ideal government 'derived from the great body of society, not from an inconsiderable proportion or favoured class of it'.[29] Beyond that, republicans differed in their emphases and in their prescriptions. 'Of republics', wrote Adams, 'there is an inexhaustible variety because the possible combinations of the powers of society are capable of innumerable variations.'[30]

If there was little agreement among republicans on the precise *form* of republican government, there was universal recognition of

the *spirit* which ought to infuse it. Central to republican government was virtue. From Machiavelli to Paine, and including
Milton, Harrington, Montesquieu and Gibbon, republican writers
agreed that 'public virtue is the only foundation of republics'
(John Adams) and that a republic rose and fell by its store of
virtue or civic patriotism.[31] This moral dimension to republicanism came before everything else: with it, the common good was
promoted and liberty protected; without it, chaos and corruption
reigned. Republicanism therefore constituted a moral challenge to
its adherents, placing a heavy burden on them to live up to its
promise.

Where does Tone stand in this brief examination of republican
thought in the late eighteenth century and earlier? Tone never
claimed to be an ideologue: he wrote, 'I confess I dislike abstract
reasoning on practical subjects. I am buried in matter. When I
feel a grievance pinch me sorely I look neither for the major nor
minor of a proposition or syllogism but merely for the proximate
cause and the possibility of removing it'.[32] As both Dunne and
Elliott have noted, he was far from being a systematic thinker.
Dunne even warns against any attempt at 'over-systematising the
scattered polemics and autobiographical fragments addressed to
different audiences for a variety of purposes by a young man who
was more an activist than a thinker'.[33] Despite these caveats, there
are grounds for arguing that Tone was a thoroughgoing republican from an early date; at least, he was as much a republican as
those whose credentials in that respect have never been questioned.

Tone's language was unmistakably republican, filled with
notions of resistance to tyrants, opposition to hereditary aristocra-
cies, and replete with aspirations to end corruption and install
virtue. In these respects we can see Tone's indebtedness to that
eighteenth-century commonwealthman or republican rhetoric
associated with Jonathan Swift, Robert Molesworth, Francis
Hutcheson, and especially John Toland, the 'Donegal heretic' and
editor of Harrington's works published in Dublin in 1737. As
Caroline Robbins has shown and, more recently, as Sean Murphy
has confirmed, there was a republican coterie in Dublin in the
mid-eighteenth century which was vital in transmitting commonwealthman ideas to a new generation.[34] Tone's faith in parliamentary reform – 'with a parliament thus reformed everything is easy'

– was quintessentially republican and recognisably within the commonwealthman tradition.[35] His social conservatism was equally in keeping with republican thought as it had developed since the renaissance: the references in his writings to the men of no property were few and far between; he grew indignant at the charge that the United Irishmen aimed at 'a distribution of property and an agrarian law'.[36] Nor does Tone's preference for 'strong' government call into question his republicanism. His determination that while there would be 'just and reasonable liberty of the press', 'libels and calumny' on the government would be severely punished was unexceptional, for libel laws (and price controls, and sumptuary laws) were part of the republican agenda at that date.[37] Equally, Tone's admiration for martial virtues, even to the extent of proposing a military colony in the South Seas, should best be seen not as the negation of republicanism but (as Marianne Elliott notes) rather as evidence of 'a continuing mesmerisation with the military vigour of ancient Rome'.[38]

In his attitude towards religion, Tone also followed orthodox republican thought. Certainly he was no friend to an established religion, but it was Paine with his attack on all revealed religion who was out of step in this matter and Tone, like Machiavelli, believed that religion had a role to play in a republic. Again, like Machiavelli, and indeed like Montesquieu and Paine himself, Tone was bitterly critical of the Catholic church and saw republicanism with its emphasis on independence and virtue as the perfect antidote to clerical thraldom in Ireland and Europe.[39] Even Tone's far from hostile attitude towards kings in general, and George III and Louis XVI in particular, ought to be seen as in keeping with conventional republican ambivalence where monarchy was concerned, rather than as evidence of a lukewarm commitment to republicanism itself.[40] While Tone's republicanism may have been eclectic, this was because republicanism was itself eclectic at that time. It is only when twentieth-century criteria of republicanism are applied to Tone that he is found wanting. Freed from the burden of the present, Tone is seen for what he was – an instantly recognisable eighteenth-century republican.

Republicanism was, however, being redefined at the end of the eighteenth century. Under the impact of the American Revolution, republicanism came more and more to be associated with separatism and with national independence. Paine's *Common Sense* was a plea for American separatism as much as for republicanism; and on occasion, especially in the late 1790s, Tone himself uses the word republicanism to mean separatism.[41] But separatism and republicanism were not identical: there was a republican tradition in eighteenth-century Ireland but until the 1790s there was little trace of separatism. It may be argued that Tone's separatism stemmed from his growing realisation that only through separatism could republicanism flourish in Ireland.

The prehistory of the separatist impulse in Ireland – the conviction that Ireland could exist as an independent state separate from England or any other country – has yet to be written. None of the sixteenth-century or seventeenth-century rebels appear to have adopted a truly separatist stance. Tone's remark that Lord Edward Fitzgerald's ancestor 'Lord Thomas...lost his head on Tower Hill for a gallant but fruitless attempt to recover the independence of Ireland' would find little favour among historians today.[42] Even when Irish rebels conceived of Ireland as separate from England, it was merely in order to seek protection under the crown of France or Spain. In 1569, for example, Maurice MacGibbon, Archbishop of Cashel, journeyed to Spain to offer the kingdom of Ireland to a Spanish prince; and the offer of the Irish crown was made several times to Spanish kings over the next hundred years.[43] The idea that Ireland could exist on her own – both *independent of* and *separate from* England – seems to have been largely unthinkable. The independence that was sometimes demanded from the mid-fifteenth to the late eighteenth century was purely legislative and in no way aimed at denying royal authority over Ireland. Conversely, the demand for separation that was sometimes raised did not envisage an Ireland independent of other European countries. Admittedly, there was the intriguing plan put forward in 1627 by Irish exiles in the Low Countries, probably influenced by the example of the Dutch, to set up 'The Republic and Kingdom of Ireland';[44] in 1640 Conor Mahony in his *Disputatio Apologetica*, again published abroad, called on his countrymen to choose a native Catholic king;[45] and in 1641 in what has been described as 'one of the most extreme statements of Irish war aims' a few of the rebels in Limerick were reported to have demanded 'a free state to themselves as they had in Holland and not to be tied to any prince or king whatsoever'.[46]

At the same time, in all of these cases it was clearly envisaged that the King of Spain would have ultimate authority over Ireland. In any event, such mildly separatist sentiments as these were quite rare: more common by far was a fulsome declaration of loyalty to the English crown from those who rose in arms, and an outraged denial that separation was proposed. Owen Roe O'Neill, for example, found himself denounced in 1648 by his former colleagues in the Confederation of Kilkenny for allegedly seeking 'to alienate them ['his majesties faithful subjects'] from the crown of England', a charge he indignantly denied.[47] And whatever was at issue in the Williamite wars, it was certainly not the cause of Irish separatism.

Nor did Irish separatism figure in the opposition literature of the early eighteenth century. Tone later claimed that his 'great discovery' that the 'influence of England was the radical vice of our government' and that 'Ireland would never be either free, prosperous or happy...whilst the connection with England lasted' could have been found in the works of Swift and Molyneux.[48] This was flat nonsense; neither Swift nor Molyneux demanded more than that those English who were born or who lived in Ireland ('the true English people of Ireland') should be accorded the rights of Englishmen, and chief among these was the right to be bound only by laws to which one's consent had been given. In this respect their claim for legislative independence was designed to reform, and perhaps even strengthen, the connection between England and Ireland, not break it. Both writers argued against the proposition that Ireland was a depending or dependent kingdom, and both denied that Ireland was a colony or a conquered province. None of this, it is clear, can be construed as a desire to break the link: Ireland without England, Ireland without the English connection, was literally unthinkable for them and no trace of separatism can be found in their writings.[49] On the other hand, their probing of the bases of the link between Ireland and England; their resolute refusal to allow England to define unilaterally the Anglo-Irish relationship; and their unremitting hostility to English ministerial pretensions where Ireland was concerned, together fuelled English fears that the Protestants of Ireland were 'foolishly and seditiously...everyday aiming at independency'.[50] Not the least of the ironies in the story of Irish separatism is that its origins are to be found in England.

Throughout the eighteenth century, English politicians of all shades suspected that there was a significant body of opinion in Ireland which aimed at separatism. When the Anglo-Irish claimed that their parliament was, or ought to be, equal to that at Westminster, when they voiced their resentment at English commercial restrictions on Irish trade, and when they criticised English plunder of Irish patronage, none of them was in fact making a separatist plea. The subtleties of their arguments, however, were almost totally lost on their English audience. As Tone wryly commented, 'the bare mention of a doubt on the subject [of Ireland's dependency on England] had an instantaneous effect on the nerves of the English government here'.[51] Archbishop Boulter, chief representative of the 'English interest' in Ireland in the 1720s, claimed that some of those opposed to Wood's halfpence sought to 'propagate a notion of the independencey [*sic*] of this kingdom on that of England'.[52] Thirty years later, at the height of the Money Bill dispute, Archbishop Stone reluctantly conceded that he did not believe his opponents 'mad enough to entertain thoughts of separating from England', but avowed that 'some of them do certainly mean an emancipation from the English legislature and from English administration'.[53] To perennially suspicious English ministers such distinctions seemed specious. Queen Anne summed up the general view when she exclaimed that the Anglo-Irish 'had a mind to be independent if they could: but they should not'.[54] For the remainder of the eighteenth century, English ministers always heard the separatist note in the opposition rhetoric of the Anglo-Irish.[55]

Quite why English observers should have considered separatism to be an element within Irish patriotism is something of a puzzle. Perhaps the explanation lay in the fact that, as one commentator put it, 'unfortunately for this kingdom, it still bears the name of Ireland and the Protestant inhabitants the denomination of Irish with old ideas annexed to them of opposition to the interest of England'.[56] Again, it may be suggested that English concern at reputed separatist tendencies within the Anglo-Irish community reflected unease that the proper basis of connection between Ireland and England – colony, conquered province or sister kingdom – had never been mutually agreed or satisfactorily resolved. Lack of clarification on this score further fuelled English anxiety about the existence among Irish patriots of a 'hidden agenda' which included separatism. The periodic squalls which beset Anglo-Irish relations especially in the 1740s and 1750s did nothing to allay the strong suspicions of the English that some Irishmen nurtured separatist thoughts.[57] Finally, the answer may be found in the personalised terminology frequently employed in the eighteenth century to describe the Anglo-Irish connection. English politicians were accustomed to view the relationship between Ireland and England as identical to that between a child and its mother, with Ireland being cast in the role of dependent child. However, implicit in this child-colony/mother-country relationship was the threat that 'the child' would one day grow up and seek independence and separation. With the English locked into this colonial paradigm, it seemed almost natural that, as Walpole put it, the Irish 'both friends and foes' would wish one day to 'shake off' their 'dependency' on England.[58]

By the 1760s, that day when Ireland might seek independence did not appear to be all that far off. It was still possible to claim in the 1740s that 'we are come too late into the world to set up for ourselves' but growing Irish prosperity, the apparent extinction of the Catholic menace and the concurrent growth of Protestant nationalism threatened to undermine Ireland's continuing subordination to England.[59] The American example, too, might prove contagious: the furious constitutional debate of the 1760s and '70s culminated in Paine's *Common Sense*, and the logic of that clarion call to separatism could conceivably apply to Ireland (as Joseph Pollock in his *Letters of Owen Roe O'Nial* [1779] illustrated).[60] The separatist moment, however, had not yet arrived; although Irish patriot politicians seized the opportunity offered by England's difficulty to establish Ireland's legislative independence, Ireland remained resolutely loyal during the American War of Independence. The 'Constitution of 1782' represented the major achievement of eighteenth-century Protestant nationalism in that it defined the Anglo-Irish relationship in terms in accord with patriot rhetoric of earlier decades. But the arrangement was fundamentally flawed, and Tone was not the only commentator to consider it 'a most bungling imperfect business'.[61] It was far from being a final settlement, rather opening than closing the discussion on Ireland's constitutional status. Moreover, the departure of the American colonies from the empire helped shape the terms of the debate; after 1782 the only realistic options were union or separation.

Union, unlike separation, had been put forward at various times since the 1650s. Until the early eighteenth century, while Irish opinion had appeared to be in favour of this solution, seeing economic and commercial benefits from it, the English attitude had tended to be unenthusiastic, largely on the grounds that the Irish would take everything but could give nothing. As James Kelly has shown, these perceptions of advantage and disadvantage underwent a reversal in the decades after 1720: Irish opinion turned hostile – a reflection, among other things, of the growth of Protestant nationalism, while English opinion became increasingly favourable, a response in part to the same phenomenon.[62] By the 1750s, there was a distinct constituency in English politics which saw union, on financial and political grounds, as the only satisfactory solution to the problem of Anglo-Irish relations. Predictably, those English politicians in favour of union received an additional strength when the many shortcomings of the 'Constitution of 1782' were realised. Soon after, an Irish unionist coterie could be identified, for unionism, whether in Ireland or in England, fed on the fear of separation; that fear, already aroused by the concession of legislative independence, was further heightened in both countries by rejection of the essentially unionist commercial propositions in 1785. Unionism bred separatism, for the more talk there was of union, and the more that option was couched in the Manichaean terms of 'union or separation', then the more the idea of separation came to be discussed. As yet, separatism was muted: McDowell has found evidence that 'as early as the 1780s a section of Irish public opinion was playing with the idea of effecting separation from England by means of foreign assistance'. In 1784 the *Volunteer Journal* called for 'a total separation from England and Englishmen', but these were very much minority viewpoints and, as McDowell himself comments, 'their exponents may not always have meant quite what they said'.[63] Ironically, it was the arch-unionist John Fitzgibbon, Earl of Clare, who did most to propagate the separatist idea in the 1780s through his scaremongering tactics during the campaign for parliamentary reform and the regency crisis. Years later, Tone warned Clare that 'stirring the question' of separation publicly might be unwise as 'public opinion is an uncertain thing [and…it is therefore possible that the investigation may not serve his side of the argument'.[64]

Where then does Tone stand in the separatist tradition? Clearly he did not invent the idea: English nervousness, the growth of unionism and, latterly, Clare's utterances had kept the notion in the public domain; separation was, if not implicit, then buried somewhere in the colonial nationalism espoused in Ireland in the eighteenth century. In any case, separatism as a political concept was in the air; when the American colonies had successfully claimed their independence, it had received its greatest boost since the setting up of the Dutch Republic at the end of the sixteenth century.[65] Nor was Tone a committed separatist from his earliest days, as his biographers rightly note. That said, there was a separatist tone to his writings, a willingness to consider the separatist option, and ultimately a desire to embrace separatism that marked Tone out as the first Irish separatist.

Tone later claimed that in one of his earlier pamphlets, *Spanish War!* (1790), he 'advanced the question of separatism with scarcely any reserve'; in fact, overtly separatist sentiments were well concealed in this tract: his demand for a national flag, navy and army could have been accommodated within the existing Anglo-Irish relationship.[66] On the other hand, such appendages were the usual ones for fully sovereign states and it is clear that Tone was, in effect, attempting to move the issue of national independence onto the agenda of Irish politics. He moved very cautiously. In his pamphlet, *An Argument on Behalf of the Catholics of Ireland* (1791), he started to answer those who claimed that 'Ireland is unable to exist as an independent state' – but then apparently thought better of it:

There is no one position, moral, physical or political that I hear with such extreme exacerbation of mind as this which denies to my country the possibility of independent existence. It is not, however, my plan here to examine that question. I trust that whenever the necessity arises as at some time it infallibly must, it will be found that we are as competent to our own government, regulation and defence as any state in Europe. Till the emergency does occur it will but exasperate and inflame the minds of men to investigate and demonstrate the infinite resources and provocations to independence which every hour brings forth in Ireland. I shall therefore content myself with protesting on behalf of my country against the position as an infamous falsehood insulting to her pride and derogatory to her honour and I little doubt if occasion should arise but that I shall be able to prove it so.[67]

Some months earlier, in his letter to Thomas Russell, which subsequently gained notoriety when it fell into the hands of the authorities, Tone admitted that as 'for separation...I give it to you and your friends as my most decided opinion that such an event would be the regeneration to this country', but at the same time he confessed that 'that opinion is for the present too hardy'.[68] Tone undoubtedly harboured separatist thoughts from an early date, but while he was prepared to contemplate the hitherto unthinkable, he still remained a reluctant separatist and his advocacy of it – if the word is not too strong – was confined to private letters and conversations. Perhaps it was fortunate for Tone's later reputation that Lord Clare was not so discreet; using Tone's incautious letter to Russell as his evidence, Clare denounced the United Irishmen as out-and-out separatists. Tone was forced to defend himself and in July 1793 he penned his reply to the editor of the *Freeman's Journal*. In this letter, Tone made it clear that he was not, at least not yet, an advocate for separation. On the contrary, he claimed, if the connection were one of 'perfect equality, equal law, equal commerce, equal liberty [and] equal justice', then such a link would be 'highly beneficial to both' countries; but so long as the 'gross corruption in the legislature' continued, so long as there was a 'sacrifice of [Ireland's] interests to England', then the separatist option – 'a question of weighty and serious import indeed' – would make advances. 'I for one do not wish to break that connection', he added, 'provided it can be, as I am sure it can, preserved consistently with the honour, the interests and the happiness of Ireland. If I were, on the other hand, satisfied that it could not be so preserved, I would hold it a sacred duty to endeavour by all possible means to break it'.[69] Tone was surely being disingenuous here: he must have known that reform would never be achieved in Ireland, that 'the honour, the interests and the happiness of Ireland' would attract scant attention during the war; that after 1793, perhaps even before, the only alternative, as Clare never ceased to pronounce, was union or separation, not union or reform. Reform to Clare and increasingly to British ministers, was merely another word for separation.[70]

It was Tone's realisation that such was the case, that the republicanism which he sought could be achieved only through breaking the link, that drove him along the road to separation. Other republicans, William Drennan for example, resisted this logic, and sought through their involvement in education and civic improvement to bring about that classical republicanism which alone would 'save the nation'.[71] Drennan and others shied away from separatism because they feared that the numerical superiority of Irish Catholics and indeed the very nature of Irish Catholicism might in fact prevent the realisation of republican ideals if Ireland were separated from England. Tone, however, had been an activist on behalf of the Catholics and was convinced that the perceived repellent aspects of Irish Catholicism would wither in a republican environment. So far as the Pope's power was concerned 'every liberal extension of property or franchise to Catholics will tend to diminish it. Persecution will keep alive the foolish bigotry and superstition of every sect...Persecution bound the Irish papist to his priest and the priest to the Pope: the bond of union is drawn tighter by oppression: relaxation will undo it'.[72] The example of French Catholics in overthrowing despotism and achieving liberty was further evidence that Catholics had that vital *capaces libertatis* which republicans had long doubted. However, so long as the connection with England remained, Tone believed that his republican ideals could not be achieved. Moreover, as unionist sentiment spread in the 1790s it was evident that the connection might in fact become ever closer, and hence more corrupt. Tone therefore welcomed the international crisis provoked by the French Revolution for it offered that 'emergency' (Tone) or *occasione* (Machiavelli) which republicans everywhere had long seen as necessary to the fulfilment of their plans. The separatist and republican moment had arrived and Tone prepared to act.

2

POLITICAL CLUBS AND SOCIABILITY
IN REVOLUTIONARY FRANCE: 1790–4

Claude Mazauric

Sociability and revolutionary political culture

In the flood of studies, colloquia and publications that was produced by the bicentenary of the French Revolution,[1] one of the
most important recurrent themes has been the 'political culture'
that was either created during the Revolution, or manifested by it.
I will define political culture for the purposes of this paper as the
collection of symbols and representational forms, the rationales
and types of collective or individual practices, which are mobilised
to realise the objectives of power within a given society.[2] Such a
definition enables us to eliminate from consideration events
which were so unusual or exceptional as to leave no lasting traces,
or cultural or mental manifestations which are not related to the
acquisition of power. Thus, not everything is directly related to
politics, although anything can contribute to a political event.[3]

With this in mind, we can say that the revolution in France
allowed the French people, subjects of one of the oldest and most
stable monarchies of *ancien régime* Europe, to pass from a society
of orders, dominated by an absolutist state hallowed by the theory
of divine right, to a civil society founded on the recognition of the
rights of the citizen. This new civil society emerged hand in hand
with the creation of a new type of state, whose legitimacy came
not from the past, but from the will of the sovereign nation itself,
expressed through elections or direct action. This was a decisive
change. It may not have constituted a total break with the past, as
de Tocqueville clearly noted during the nineteenth century, but it
was sufficiently radical in relation to the conservatism of the years
1776–88 to be perceived as, and called, a *revolution*.[4] We know
also that this revolution was intended to be universalist, both in its
language and in its central ideological aims ('Men are born and

remain free and equal in rights', in the words of the Declaration of the Rights of Man in 1789). This in turn caused violent opposition from those, beginning with Burke, who were worried by the implications of talk of universal rights, and who tried to play down its vast importance and Promethean significance by attempting to reduce the whole event to something both ordinary and specifically French.[5] The rapid and chaotic sequence of events which began in 1789, followed by the war in 1792 and the ensuing violence, did indeed help to obscure the significance of the universalist message of the Revolution. Nevertheless its profound ideological impact, along with its revival by events, arguments and historiographical disputes ever since, have combined to make the French Revolution the decisive moment – or at least the most obvious moment – of the general process of transition towards the political culture of modernity.

For proof of the general acceptance of this in our own day, one has only to turn to the introduction of Furet and Ozouf to their *Critical Dictionary of the French Revolution*: 'at stake between 1787 and 1800 was not the substance of society, but its principles and government'.[6] How did this happen, in what ways and with what results? These are the historical questions which remain high on the agenda of current debate.[7]

Proceeding at a hectic and often breathless pace, revolutionary change in France – for both its participants and its onlookers – was carried out within the framework of collective rules and interactive practices which took the form of specific and immediate structures of sociability, and recent research has considerably clarified these practices. The very use of the term 'structures of sociability' as a tool of ethno-sociological analysis for historical events presupposes some agreement as to its value and validity in this context. In using the term 'sociability', I do not intend to refer to a supposedly 'natural' tendency innate in man himself, argued in leading works of political philosophy from Aristotle to Pufendorf.[8] Instead, my use of the term is essentially pragmatic, based on the use made of it by contemporary historians such as Maurice Agulhon and ethno-historians in general. They use it to describe forms and institutional processes through which the socialisation of individuals or groups, and the acculturation of the young in historical societies, takes place.[9] However, I also intend to give a supplementary dimension to these structures by analysing their political function in the revolutionary period. I shall therefore also consider them as possible underlying elements of what I have referred to above as revolutionary political culture.

As far as the French Revolution goes, this use of the term 'sociability' is valid enough. Sociability became politicised as a way of implementing the general will, through the ideas of Jean-Jacques Rousseau and the practice of the French Revolution. Let us recall that Rousseau believed that 'self-love' – the source of unsociability and self-centredness – clashed with the other 'natural feeling' of pity, what he called 'an innate repugnance of seeing a fellow being suffer'. The sense of pity, 'reducing in each individual the operation of self-love, helps the mutual conservation of the entire species'.[10] Rousseau saw all the other social virtues flowing from this contradiction between self-love and pity, and taken together they seemed to him to be the only form of sociability possible: one which 'tightens the links of society through personal interest'. This kind of sociability therefore had nothing to do with *natural* sociability, but was inherent in the creation of the social contract, itself the basis of human and political society. In his well-known *Profession of Faith of the Savoyard Vicar*, Rousseau does seem to imply a natural tendency of men towards sociability, but as Robert Derathé has shown, this was only potential; its realisation required the development of social man, of his experience and his knowledge.[11] In other words, it entailed the entirety of processes through which his socialisation was realised.[12] From this perspective, 'structures of sociability' can be viewed as part of a slow historical evolution, marked by periods of immobility and then of the kind of sudden change that Kant, himself a good disciple of Rousseau, believed that he saw in the French Revolution. In Rousseau, however, the natural tendency towards sociability could bring about a total dependence of the individual in relation to another individual or group. That is why the realisation of the contract, and respect for the reciprocal duties required for the preservation of the rights of the individual and the durability of the community, presupposed the inclusion of the natural tendency of man towards conscience and the will to preserve one's rights. In other words, it required civic virtue.[13] In this sense, we can say that with the French Revolution, which in this respect was very Rousseauist, sociability – along with its structures, organisation and manifestations – became an appeal for citizens to practise virtue, as well as an explicit condition of social man's regeneration. This lies at the very heart of the development of the Revolution from 1789 onwards, and its mission until 1800.[14]

From this, it follows that if sociability is democratic – in the sense that all men potentially have it within themselves – then its structures, its organisation and its practical development are questions of organisation and action. For the creation of the structures of sociability, as several contemporary historians have convincingly shown, requires as its prerequisite the transition from the individual to the collective to be accompanied by loyalty to a common cause, co-operation in a shared project, and the setting up of a communal way of doing things. As such, each structure of sociability has certain characteristics, which are common to them all. In the first place, they all have the ambivalence which derives from the fact that the structure is both a way of integration into a wider society – but also sometimes one of exclusion – and the means of creating something different, or even of total transformation. Secondly, each structure is dependent on the time and place in which it operates, for a structure of sociability is always an *historical* structure of sociability. Finally, its internal workings are always split between the particular wish that it expresses and the external pressures which affect the rules of the group and the practices that grow up from interaction between the structure itself and its surrounding environment.[15]

It is from this double perspective – that of the novelty of the questions posed in 1789, and the underlying structures of sociability – that we will look at the political clubs that emerged in the Revolution. For the Revolution marked a decisive point in the transformation of sociability into a crucial tool for change in the political and social order.

The originality of Jacobinism as a political movement
The creation of clubs that were specifically political coincides with the beginnings of the Revolution. On 10 November 1788 it was reported that a 'constitutional club' was meeting in Paris at the home of Adrien Duport, to prepare submissions to be made to the King and to suggest reforms.[16] Among the participants were Condorcet, Dupont de Nemours, La Fayette, Talleyrand, Mirabeau, Destutt de Tracy, Noailles, D'Aiguillon, and many others – all of whom were to be among the initial leaders of the political activity

that was just beginning. The members of this 'Society of Thirty' – wealthy bourgeois, aristocratic nobles linked to the magistrates of the Parlements and other sovereign courts, economists and writers associated with Diderot's *Encyclopedia* – constituted an élite which had no intention of widening its ranks. On the contrary, it was intent on reserving for itself a monopoly of political influence over a monarchy which was close to collapse. The only force that the Society of Thirty intended to use was the force of a newly emerging 'public opinion', which they referred to, but without trying to organise or encourage it in any meaningful way. Their aim was to manipulate this opinion in the classic tradition of Orléanist politics. Their model of sociability was explicitly that of the English-style club, or the *sociétés de pensée* (debating clubs) which had existed under the *ancien régime*, now to be infused with a political aim and pursuing the double objective of promoting a spirit of reform on the one hand, and defusing the risks of political or social subversion that might come from below on the other.[17]

Until the summer of 1791 and the great debates which rocked the Constituent Assembly and public opinion over the role of political clubs and their compatibility with the free expression of the sovereign body, many clubs sprang up, which were organised on the model of élite sociability pioneered by the Society of Thirty.[18] Such, for example, was the *Société des amis des noirs* which had existed before the revolution, but came back to life briefly when it broke out. Or the short-lived *Société de 1789*, founded by the Abbé Sieyès in 1790, partly to counteract the influence of the Breton club – by then the Jacobin club – but which was little more than an academic salon bringing together a handful of great leaders for politico-constitutional dinners. Another was the *Société des amis de la constitution monarchique*, where monarchists who supported an English-style constitution met along with French-style moderate constitutionalists.

The Cordeliers club, created in April 1790 and soon called the *Société des amis des droits de l'homme et du citoyen*, was different. Although its democratic radicalism was enough to cause several Parisian 'fraternal societies' to rally quickly round it and later to draw fellow radicals from elsewhere in France, the Cordeliers club never really became the centre of an influential network of political societies on a nation-wide scale. Apart from the federation of fraternal societies set up in Paris in 1791, and the support given to the club by the sections and the *Enragés* in 1793, the Cordelier movement never managed to put together a structure, even when attempts were made in October and November 1793 to establish central committees for the popular societies of Paris.[19] Its various leaders – Danton, Marat, Hébert and others – were never quite clear as to what they wanted. As far as they were concerned, their authority was entirely based on their having a willing audience among the inhabitants of their own area, namely the Section of the *Théâtre français* on the left bank of the Seine, and they then hoped that this influence would spread wider afield until it influenced public opinion, the various administrative bodies and Jacobin clubs, through the impact of their own reputations and through the publication of their speeches in the press.

Founded on 21 February 1790 and active from 13 October 1790 onwards, the *Cercle Social* was another early club. It attracted crowds to the Palais Royal for its weekly meetings, which were essentially lectures on social and political philosophy. But if the organisers of the Circle, who met as a 'Directory', were careful to make sure that the contents of these lectures were published in the press, they never wanted to build a stable or well-organised structure of sociability tailored to the administrative and political structures of revolutionary France.[20] The same was true of clubs set up in several cities and towns throughout France during the early months of 1790, many of which were politicised revivals of old *sociétés de pensée*, Masonic lodges, reading clubs, and literary circles where the local élites met.[21]

Existing on both the right and the left of the political spectrum, in Paris and the provinces, these political societies all had a narrow social base, with little desire or interest in providing themselves with the means of transcending the sociological or geographical limits of their make-up. The rather uncertain nature of their political role and their tendency to sway under the influence of different leaders made them more like politico-academic temples, or classical electoral meetings, designed to influence an ill-defined and vague public opinion.[22] None of them, with the possible exception of the Cordeliers in July 1791 and in the autumn of 1793, or of the Feuillants in the summer of 1791 (and the Feuillants even then were echoing the style of the Jacobin club they had just left) really showed any sign of the kind of concerns regularly evident in the Jacobin club. These were, firstly, the desire to meet as a group containing both elected deputies and ordinary members, in order to discuss in advance the decisions due to be taken by the legislature; and, secondly, the determination to organise a tightly knit network capable of uniting practical policies with a concerted effort to ensure the triumph of a political orientation, and not just an isolated decision. It is this double aim which from the autumn of 1789, and especially from the spring of 1790, gave novelty and specific character to the Paris Jacobin club and the Jacobin movement.

The Jacobin club that met in the rue Saint-Honoré in Paris and grew out of the club of Breton deputies which had first met at Versailles on 30 April 1789, began life as an extra-parliamentary body, but it was always closely linked to the existence of a national legislature. Its members were deputies and well-known journalists and publicists, whose sole objectives were to prepare the way for the debates of the National Assembly by discussing issues in advance. But once its members had adopted a position on any topic, the deputies among them had the duty of defending and supporting that position, and this gave the club a formidable political influence. However, despite its thousand or so members, the club protected itself against having too democratic a membership by imposing a high subscription rate. If it had remained bound by its statutes and by its narrow social base, it would never have evolved and would only have become a kind of enlarged *Société des trente*, active and well organised, but little more than a manifestation of traditional Parisian élite sociability, adapting to new forms of the representative-style politics at a time of extreme political tension. Jacobinism's uniqueness lay in its orientation towards parliamentary action and the influence that its huge network of clubs gave it over elected political and administrative bodies throughout the country. An organisation which both responded to and mobilised its members, this complex structure was designed to show the support of a well-informed and decisive political opinion towards the propositions formulated by the Paris club – this 'boulevard' of liberty – and by its spokesmen in the parliamentary assemblies. Beyond the crises and somersaults of daily political life, this double characteristic was as evident when Barnave or Laclos were the influential figures in the club (1790–1), as when Brissot and Pétion (1791–2), or Robespierre and Billaud-Varenne (1793–4) were its undisputed leaders. The only differences were that by the time of the Terror the network of clubs had become more numerous and disciplined, and because the role of popular societies had been conceptualised and legally defined as a part of the structure of revolutionary government in the decree of 14 *frimaire*, the Paris club was in a position to exercise a decisive influence.[23]

Two important crises made the Jacobin movement into an integral part of the Revolution. The first occurred between 18 July and 12 October 1791: from the time when Robespierre issued his first circular calling on affiliated societies to reject the division in the club caused by the secession of the Feuillants to the decision to admit the general public to club meetings. The second was in the autumn of 1793, when the consolidation of the revolutionary government and the success of its policies came to depend on its ability to harness the power of the clubs and transform them into a structure for controlling the whole political life of the republic at a time of war.

This integration of the club network into the Revolution took place in a series of stages, about which historians are in general agreement.[24] I will not reopen the debate on the timing of the development of Jacobinism, but merely recall its major steps. Firstly, four years of expansion as a type of political sociability existing on a national level with geographical variations, but with the Paris club playing a central role and its political crises affecting the rhythm and development of provincial affiliates (276 in December 1790, 543 in March 1791, 833 at the end of June 1791; then after a period of decline and stagnation, 798 in October 1793 after the federalist crisis). After those four years, there was one year of ideological and institutional domination which saw a Jacobin hegemony over revolutionary France. Then, finally, a long sequel after the political catastrophe of Year III (1794–5), when 'Jacobinism' became the ideology of a minority and a legacy to be handed on to a small core of republicans in the following generation – left-wing opponents of the Directory, Consulate and Empire, or the radicals and revolutionary democrats of the nineteenth century.[25]

The real question, however, is whether it is possible or even legitimate to use the concept of 'party' to define the Jacobin movement during its period of importance between September

1793 and 9 *thermidor*. In other words, was the kind of sociability shown by the Jacobin movement the same as that of a modern political party? To reply to this question, we need to know something about the network of popular societies as it existed during its peak in Year II.

The network of popular societies and Jacobinism

The research of Boutier and Boutry is now complete, and we are waiting for the definitive results to be published as a volume in the series entitled *Atlas de la Révolution française*.[26] In the spring of Year II (1794) almost 5,500 French communes (5,332 according to the figures published by Boutier and Boutry in 1989) had a popular society – 13 per cent of the total. All departmental capitals (usually towns of 15,000 plus), 98 per cent of the district capitals, and 59 per cent of the canton capitals (usually semi-rural *bourgs*) had one. For the rest, there were few rural societies, except in certain departments in inland Provence or in the rural manufacturing areas of the north-west such as the Seine-Inférieure and the Pas-de-Calais, which had a large number. Whereas on 31 December 1790 only 10 departments had a political club affiliated to the Paris Jacobins in their principal town, by June 1791 only the Lozère and the Hautes-Alpes lacked one, ample proof of the dynamism of the urban club network in its initial stages. And thanks to the sophistication of Boutier and Boutry's research, we can analyse the situation three years later even more closely.

The rate of creation of new societies reveals 'regional profiles' (the term used by Boutier and Boutry) in the dynamic of the political sociability inherent in the phenomenon of popular societies. Less than 6 per cent of clubs were established before 1791; 15 per cent date from 1791, and 18.1 per cent from the period between January 1792 and October 1793, which was a particularly important period marked by tense political struggles. However, 65.1 per cent of clubs were founded in Year II (1793–4). The map drawn up by Boutier and Boutry reveals both continuity and change in the geographical spread of clubs. The strongest initial areas were in the Midi, at first in Aquitaine and then in 1792 in Provence and the southern Alps; here the traditions of urban sociability, rooted in the towns and semi-rural bourgs analysed so carefully by Agulhon, strongly autonomous local communities dominated by their wealthier inhabitants, facilitated the creation of an early political sociability which built on previous structures.[27]

In 1793 and 1794 this model changed radically. The dynamic of growth moved towards manufacturing areas, and to areas of large-scale farming in the north-west and the western edges of the *Massif Central*. Two 'recalcitrant' zones (essentially areas where few clubs existed outside urban areas) appear in the west and the east of France, the very areas which showed the most resistance to the Revolution. In the thirty-two departments of the Midi two sub-zones can be seen: a western and peripheral Midi where clubs were founded later and more rarely than on average; and an *Occitania* further to the east which had more clubs and was dominated by larger ones; these had a strong spirit of autonomy and were a dominant influence over whole groups of neighbouring rural societies. A third of the communities in Provence and in the Drôme had a *société populaire*. In the Gard, the Hérault, and as far as the Tarn and Tarn-et-Garonne, the figure was between a third and a fifth, while in the other departments of the Midi it was always less than fifty clubs per department. In northern France, and particularly in the north-west, most clubs were set up at the time of the failure of the 'federalist' rebellion in the summer of 1793. Here a type of political sociability emerged which was based on the existence of clubs at the level of the bourg or of a collection of associated village communities, linked in turn to clubs in neighbouring towns (Rouen, Le Havre, Yvetot, Bernay, etc. in the case of Upper Normandy, which has been studied by Danielle Pingué).[28] They in turn were affiliated to the Paris Jacobins. There was also a thriving network of clubs in Artois,[29] and in the Sarthe.[30]

Parallel to the emergence of this network, which expanded at different speeds in different areas, we can also see a growth – but again an uneven one – in the activity of all societies. Boutier and Boutry rightly emphasise that the activity of clubs varied according to factors such as the impact made on them by representatives sent from Paris, the rapidity and quality of the news that they gained from the press, and the dynamism of local leaders. According to them, 'even in Year II, clubs did not respond to the Revolution in uniform fashion'.[31]

The network of popular clubs grew so rapidly because of the generalisation of common practices of sociability: affiliation and correspondence, the reception and speeches of missionaries from other clubs, and the receipt of circulars. All this is well known, but it should be noted that the result was the implantation during Year II of what can best be called a multipolar spider's web of clubs, tightly knit in some places, looser in others, all radiating out from a Parisian 'centre'. Yet despite this 'centre', there was always a lively tendency for direct links to grow between clubs in different departments, a tendency which offset the influence of the mother club in Paris.[32]

Given the importance of the club network, one might be tempted to conclude that its homogeneity was the result of identical political attitudes. But nothing could be further from the truth. Until the political crisis which saw the guillotining of Hébert and Danton in *ventôse* and *germinal* of Year II, many societies in various departments supported different policies, and the sectional societies did so too. This is why Robespierre and the Committee of Public Safety decided to move quickly to control the club movement and to limit its influence in the spring of 1794, once *hébertistes* and *dantonistes* had been eliminated. Even after this attempt at centralised control, and despite the way in which speeches in clubs from then on appeared to reflect the conformist line laid down in Paris and transmitted throughout the country by the press or circulars,[33] strong differences of opinion, of sensibility, and of support for government policies can be seen. This was because the clubs were never political robots controlled from Paris, as Michelet believed, or as Augustin Cochin – who used the pejorative term 'machine' to describe their organisation and workings – affirmed.[34] Research has now increasingly revealed that the only way to understand the creation of such a vast movement of political association is through the analysis of its structures in terms of structures of sociability.

Let us therefore isolate the overall characteristics which allow us to look at the popular societies in terms of sociability. Firstly, not everyone could join. The very young, and women, were excluded because they were not citizens in the *political* sense of the term. However, anyone could attend debates, either in a special part of the meeting place, or in some cases sitting alongside full members. In practice, and often in theory, the only way of gaining membership was to be sponsored by an existing club member. From the autumn of 1793 the incidence of periodical purges became widespread, designed to separate the wheat (authentic members) from the chaff (careerists, moderates or troublemakers). In Paris as in the departments, some societies – or alternatively certain leaders claiming access to a superior form of truth – arrogated the right to 'regenerate' clubs which were moribund, conservative or dying on their feet, by the use of purges or by founding the society again from scratch. So there were always effective mechanisms for controlling entry to popular societies, and this enables us to differentiate them from administrative bodies or the wider social group in their community from which membership was drawn.

In sociological terms, the composition of popular societies was never identical to that of local society, although this is an essential characteristic of all forms of sociability. There were almost no workers, even in manufacturing towns and rural areas; few active peasants, even in rural bourgs, and very few of such peasants were day labourers. If some liberal nobility remained members up to the end, despite the legal disabilities supposedly imposed on them, they were few in number and lacked real influence. The trading and merchant middle class, artisans and shopkeepers, manufacturers, administrators, lawyers and writers, artists, actors, soldiers, and constitutional priests (until the autumn of 1793) make up the categories most frequently found in clubs, and from whose ranks the leadership and the political missionaries were most frequently taken. From existing data we can say that, at their height, the clubs attracted 2–4 per cent of the total population, or a total of between 500,000 and 1,000,000 members. This corresponds to one adult in ten, but in areas where the middle-class categories cited above were well represented, the proportion is nearer to one in four or one in five. So the clubs represent a model of sociability which was both bourgeois and petit bourgeois, and which contributed to the politicisation of the middling classes in French society. This is of importance for our understanding of the formation of mentalities in modern France.[35]

The internal workings of the clubs was often copied from the Parisian model, or from that of a neighbouring club. They included parts of the rules of previous *sociétés de pensée*, of Masonic lodges, of confraternities of penitents, and of reading clubs. Many members, especially in the early stages, brought to the organisational methods of their clubs habits and methods that they had previously acquired elsewhere. This is sufficiently well known for us not to dwell on it any further.[36] Yet the purely secular nature of

the rules, the regulations for the election of officials, the recruitment of members, the organisation of debates, the management
of money and collective practices, the definition of objectives and
outside contacts, shows a wish, common to both Paris and the
very smallest provincial clubs, to make themselves independent of
political power and local society, in a way which is common to all
forms of sociability. After *thermidor* it was precisely this wish for
separation which fomented anti-Jacobin feeling and led directly to
their isolation and destruction. From being structures of integration into a revolutionary and republican France, they became
meeting places for the excluded once the processes of 'de-Jacobin-
isation' and 'de-sansculottisation' got under way in Year III.[37]

We must however stress the elements of this revolutionary
sociability which distinguish it from pre-existing sociability. Firstly, its very existence and purpose, as was recognised after September 1791, was political, something that would have been inconceivable under the *ancien régime*.[38] Its function, as Robespierre
constantly insisted, was to be publicly active, militant in its cause,
and openly proselytising.[39] Because of this, it tended to take over
political activity which originated outside its control, and mould it
into the shape of its own dominant opinion. In Year II, after the
decree of 14 *frimaire*, its monopoly position meant that meetings
of citizens, of administrations, of districts, communes and watch
committees, were all brought together in the same power structure, under the control of socially well-defined categories. Hence
the claim that this kind of organisation represents the first *modern*
form of the totalitarian state, put forward by Hannah Arendt.[40]
This would be a fair enough remark if the clubs had a definite
class content, if they had been rigorously structured into a national hierarchy, and if their members were strictly organised. But this
was not the case. It is a mistake to take at face value the high-
flown rhetoric in which clubs proclaimed their submission to
political authority as a proof of their patriotism. And it should be
noted that members of Jacobin clubs were never the majority in
any legislature of the period, and not even among the members of
the Mountain who were themselves in a minority in the Convention during 1793–4.

However, there is no doubt that the mother society in Paris
had a crucial influence, an influence successfully relayed to the
more important departmental societies below it. Several charac-

teristics prove this. Firstly, in the rue Saint-Honoré, member deputies and Parisian militants worked together to plan legislative debates, and were well aware of the importance of so doing: affiliated societies received news of the views that had been adopted in Paris through circulars and press articles (notably in the Paris club's newspaper, the *Journal de la Montagne*), and they were simultaneously called upon to show their support. The proof of Paris's special role as the centre of activity is provided by the fact that Robespierre went to the Jacobins on the evening of 8 *thermidor* – the eve of his fall – to read his famous speech denouncing his colleagues, which had already received a lukewarm response from the Convention. Would he have gone there if the club had not played a central role in the formation of political opinion, not just in Paris but in the whole of the republic?

How could it have been otherwise? Until June 1791, then from June 1793 onwards, most of the leaders of the Paris club were deputies, even though deputies were never a majority of the membership as a whole.[41] Out of 1,500 members in 1793, Tacheva's analysis has identified 856. They include 177 members of the Convention, of whom only 117 were members of the Mountain; this is less than half the 294 deputies analysed by Brunel as *montagnards*.[42] Perhaps some of the other *montagnards* had links with the club in their own department, but that does not undermine the striking fact that they had no links with the Paris club. It is nevertheless the case that Paris Jacobinism during Year II, the time when it exerted an important influence on the political life of the whole republic, mobilised a political élite formed over the four initial years of the Revolution, which was national in character. Despite periodic purges, expulsions and affiliations, the club never changed: its essential core, its prestige, its ability to influence its 'brothers and friends' in affiliated societies, gave it the power to exercise a Parisian *hegemony* over the network of popular societies, while they in turn took part in the creation of a *Jacobin* hegemony over revolutionary France.

A party or not?

In his well-known *Prison Diaries*, Antonio Gramsci examined Jacobinism and saw it as the extreme form of 'revolution in action'.[43] His interest was prompted by a wish to analyse more closely the 'economico-corporate' weaknesses of Italian history prior to the Risorgimento. In contrast to the Italian experience, and drawing on the work of Albert Mathiez, he saw Jacobinism as the incarnation of a 'party' capable of uniting town and country-side in a class 'alliance' against the parasitic sectors of society left over from the old social structures. By exercising a total control (which he defined as a moral, ideological and cultural domination of new values, and the exercise of political control), the Jacobin Party embodied the emergence of a radical 'national and popular' will, without which the development of a bourgeois state would have been impossible. This neo-Marxist analysis, which puts together in a particularly coherent way the previous ideas of Marx (when he wrote on the 'heroic illusion' of the main personalities of the revolution),[44] Kautsky, Lenin[45] and Trotsky, acted as a stimulus to historians of his age, and even to authors who in the tradition of Michelet, Cochin or Taine were horrified by the Jacobin 'model'.[46] Also a Gramscian, but in a rather reductionist way, Albert Soboul referred to the network of popular societies as a 'party machine'.[47] In several publications I have also gone so far as to use the term 'party' to describe the Jacobin movement during the Terror, believing that I could discern in it the existence of a political proto-party, on the lines of those that subsequently developed in the nineteenth century.[48]

However, let us look at the facts. For the last two centuries, a national political party in a representative régime – and not necessarily a democratic one – can be identified by the holding of regular party congresses, which elect the ruling body of the party for the interim periods. Such a party, whose function is to take up a position in the 'political space' of society, usually creates the means of controlling its members or spokespersons through establishing a minimal 'party discipline', infringement of which can result in exclusion, punishment, etc. Contemporary parties usually distinguish between elected deputies (who hold a mandate from the electorate thanks to the support of the party) and the party leadership (where deputies can well be in a majority, but as party members rather than deputies).[49] In addition all contemporary parties, even those with the loosest and most relaxed rules, operate some kind of system whereby the centre is subject to control from the periphery, and the summit from the base. In their functions, political parties 'combine' – in the words of the constitution of the French Fifth Republic – to express the public opinion of the nation: they are a condition of the integration of citizens into the political world, and a guarantee of the stability of state institutions.

At no stage in the Revolution did the Jacobin movement fulfil any of the above conditions: there was overlap between the parliamentary group and the Jacobin leadership; there was a refusal to hold any kind of national 'congress' or meetings between local clubs (something expressly forbidden in October 1793), and national leaders who were never elected because there was no integrated hierarchy distinguishing the top from the bottom. But above all, I would point to the repeated refusal of all the revolutionaries of 1789 and 1793 to accept the establishment of parties. In their view, political parties would hinder rather than help the expression of the national will. All of them followed Rousseau, and although from 1791 onwards an exception was made for independent political clubs, it was because of their voluntary nature, and because their role was to educate, inform and improve the political culture of citizens and administrators by public activity. Even the decree of 14 *frimaire* gave the clubs only these limited functions.[50]

So we can reasonably conclude that a 'network of popular societies' is not the same thing as a 'Jacobin party'. The confusion arises from retrogressive projection of the idea of party (in the form of a 'republican' or 'working-class' party) onto the structures of political sociability of the Revolution – revered by many since because of their effectiveness and the Revolution's importance. In doing this, historians and theoreticians of the left, along with supporters of revolutionary movements of our own times, have taken over – but distorted – the very term that anti-Jacobin historians had initially produced, in using words such as 'machine' or 'boa-constrictor'[51] to describe the creation of the network of popular societies. This kind of terminological distortion is regrettably common in historical debate.

However, Jacobinism existed, even if the inventor of the term, the Abbé Barruel, used it in the hope of exorcising it for ever.[52] As a means of carrying out a radical political programme, as a means of forming and generalising a type of broad and public sociability adapted to the period which covers the collapse of the *ancien régime* and the democratic reconstruction of political life, and also as a means of producing an ideology and a code of values which legitimised its action in the eyes of history, Jacobinism was a movement which responded to the needs of its time. The fact that it produced at the same time some negative values (bureaucracy, conformism, pointless violence, iniquities and tyrannical actions directed against individuals, etc.) must be considered in the overall context of its activities, and the balance sheet considered fairly, in the light of the objectives that it pursued and achieved: the creation of a republican political culture amongst a great many French people, their acceptance of a representative régime (the legislative centralism or 'légicentrisme' criticised by Jacques Guilhaumou), the political and military triumph of the ideas of the French Revolution, the integration into the newly created nation of the millions of commoners previously excluded from any sort of political control over their lives – in short, those things which we call political progress.

Therefore, although I believe it in the end necessary and legitimate for the sake of historical accuracy not to resort to the use of the word 'party' to define Jacobinism in the French Revolution, I would not like, in renouncing use of the word, to be accused of underestimating the great significance, coherence and efficiency of what it represented in this very special period of revolution.

3

PRESBYTERIAN RADICALISM

Pieter Tesch

The events of those fatal days in early June 1798 in Down, Antrim and Derry may not have been quite as spectacular and on such a scale as the events in Wexford, but their consequences were probably as traumatic locally as those in south Leinster. However, the events and personalities of the Ulster rebellion remain obscure. Compared with the attention that has been paid in the last two hundred years to the priests in Wexford, very little is known about the role of the rebel Presbyterian clergymen of east Ulster.[1] The Presbyterian minister of Greyabbey on the Ards peninsula, Rev. James Porter, was hanged in front of his meeting-house for alleged involvement in the rebellion. Two 'probationers' or 'licentiates' were also hanged in the aftermath of the rebellion on the Ards peninsula, the 'backyard' of the Londonderry family, Archibald Warwick in Kircubbin, and Robert Gowdy in Dunover. In south Derry the Tipperary Militia burnt down the Presbyterian meeting-house in Maghera where the Rev. John Glendy, a prominent radical in the 1780s and 1790s, had ministered; he had gone 'on the run' following the defeat of the rebels at Antrim.[2]

The involvement in the United Irish movement of substantial numbers of middle- and lower-class Presbyterians, in virtually all parts of Ulster, urban and rural, represents the transformation of different strands of Presbyterian radicalism in response to fundamental changes in the province's economy and society. The Presbyterian ingredient was the driving force within the United movement in Ulster, and combined the different elements into one more or less cohesive radical movement with a specific programme.[3] The transformation in Presbyterian radicalism after the rebellion is often used to explain the change among Ulster Presbyterians in their political and theological outlook from Whig, liberal and republican into Tory, conservative and unionist.

Although this concept in itself has been severely challenged, it is not the subject of this essay; rather an attempt is made here to explain how diverse elements of Presbyterian radicalism coalesced during the eighteenth century, becoming in the 1790s a radical political and social movement which eventually attempted revolution.

The diverse elements of Ulster Presbyterian radicalism are theological and political; for many in the eighteenth century, theology and political ideology were not yet completely divorced. That divorce was the result of the Enlightenment and of the fledgling 'democratic revolution' at the end of the century, and mediated by the structural changes in Ulster's economy and society in the same period. These diverse elements reflect the peculiar position of Presbyterians in Irish society in general and in Ulster in particular, and reflect how the Presbyterians reacted to social changes during the eighteenth century which profoundly affected their position.

In eighteenth-century political terms the Ulster Presbyterians considered themselves as the full-blooded supporters of the Glorious Revolution or 'True Whigs'. Their view was not shared by the Anglican establishment in Ireland, and in the 1690s the scene was set for a lasting conflict within Irish Protestantism between the ruling Anglicans and the Protestant Dissenters, of which by far the largest group were the Presbyterians concentrated in Ulster. It is revealing that the Administration, with their supporters among the Established Church and the landed aristocracy, successfully restricted emigration from Scotland during the harvest failures of the 1690s to the nine counties of Ulster, where Scottish Presbyterians already formed the majority of Protestants since the plantations.[4]

The 1704 Test Act forced Presbyterians to leave the corporations of Derry and Belfast; this caused a revival of the pamphlet war between the Anglicans and the Presbyterians which had begun with George Walker's and John Mackenzie's rival accounts of the siege of Derry. In 1709 Dr William Tisdall, vicar of Belfast and friend of Swift, in *A Sample of True Blue Presbyterian Loyalty*, attacked an address 'from the Dissenting ministers in the North of Ireland' to Queen Anne in which they protested that they had always been loyal to the crown. Dr Tisdall in 1712 continued the attack in his pamphlet *The Conduct of the Dissenters*, which criti-

cised both the behaviour of Ulster Presbyterians after the
Restoration and the political advances they had made in the after-
math of the Revolution, which were indeed then being reversed.
In the following year came two replies, *A Sample of Jet-Black
Prelatic Calumny* by Rev. John McBride, and the very substantial
*Historical Essay upon the Loyalty of Presbyterians in Great Britain and
Ireland* by James Kirkpatrick, later a member of the Belfast Society
and a leading writer for the Non-Subscribers.[5]

These works of McBride and Kirkpatrick were the first reflections by Ulster Presbyterians on the events of the seventeenth
century in general and on the Glorious Revolution in particular.
The crucial question for them was to explain how loyalty to the
king could be reconciled with opposition, even embracing armed
opposition, to his laws and church. Both pamphlets argued for
limited monarchy, and for the right of opposition if the king tran-
gressed the limits of his authority. Although both were vague in
regard to defining the limits of royal authority, they disputed Tisdall's accusation that the Presbyterian church claimed authority
over civil magistrates. They defended the right of dissent, not as
grounded in any divine right inherent in the Presbyterian clergy's
status as leaders of a correctly governed church, but based on individual conscience. In Kirkpatrick's words, 'if we once believe that
their consciences truly dictated to them the points wherein they
differed from the Established Church, they could not (without
manifest contempt of the authority of God) forbear to put their
principles in practice'. In itself this did not confer the right to
overthrow the established order, but it could be invoked if there
was excessive repression of dissent, arbitrary government, or the
pursuit of policies strengthening popery. In summary, Kirkpatrick's argument was that Presbyterianism encouraged individual self-reliance in opposition to arbitrary authority in both
church and state: 'the ecclesiastical constitution of the presbytery
does provide such effectual remedies against the usurpation and
ambition of the clergy, and lays such foundations for the liberty of
the individual in church matters, that it naturally creates in the
people an aversion from all tyranny and oppression in the state
also'.[6]

After 1714 the pamphlet war subsided almost completely, only
to resurface in 1787 when Richard Woodward, Bishop of Cloyne,
published *The Present State of the Church of Ireland, containing a*

Description of its Precarious Situation and the Consequent Danger to the Public. Woodward's alarmist pamphlet was written in reaction to the Munster Rightboys who had demanded that tithes should be abolished, or at least abated. The bishop's ostensible purpose was to prove to the 'gentlemen of landed property in this kingdom' that the Established Church was essentially incorporated with the state, and was 'in imminent danger of subversion'. The pamphlet was clearly more than a narrow defence of the tithe system, and Woodward linked the survival of the Established Church to the survival of the state and of the social order for which it stood.[7] Woodward's pamphlet was answered by two Presbyterian ministers who had recently been prominent in the Volunteer and reform movements in Ulster, Samuel Barber, minister at Rathfriland, County Down, and Dr William Campbell, minister at Armagh city; they were the unofficial leaders of the Synod of Ulster during the 1780s. In Barber's *Remarks on a Pamphlet entitled 'The Present State of the Church of Ireland'*, he asserted that Christ was himself crucified for attempting to overthrow a religious establishment, and that if Luther, Calvin, Cranmer and Knox had submitted to ecclesiastical establishments, there would have been no Reformation. Barber added mischievously that it was wrong for the Established Church to deprive her 'elder Roman sister', from whom she had obtained her own orders, of her inheritance.[8]

Barber's pamphlet drew a response from two Anglican clergymen, Dr Robert Burrowes, a Fellow of TCD, and Rev. Edward Ryan. In his turn Barber issued a rejoinder, and Dr William Campbell issued another reply to Woodward's attack, titled *A Vindication of the Principles and Character of the Presbyterians in Ireland*. Dr Campbell compared the position and role of the High Church party with that of the Presbyterians, accusing the former of being at least crypto-Jacobites. As a non-subscriber, he protested that under the constitution the clergy had too much political power, and he made it clear that he would equally object to such power ever being exercised by Presbyterian ministers.[9]

Between the 1720s and 1780s the position of Ulster Presbyterians had been transformed socially, economically, politically and ideologically. With the Hanoverian succession the High Church partisans had been weakened, and the persecution of Presbyterians was replaced by practical toleration. The Presbyterian church was allowed to develop freely, but Presbyterians failed to regain political influence because clauses in the Test Act, despite endless lobbying, were not repealed; Presbyterians remained barred from the municipal corporations. In Ulster they were still in too weak a socio-economic position to use the franchise in parliamentary elections to challenge the Anglican establishment. Against this background we can see the beginning of Presbyterian emigration to America – a steady trickle in the 1710s, a substantial stream in the later 1760s.[10]

Toleration allowed Presbyterians to diversify into a variety of occupations and positions, rather than (as once seemed possible) forcing them into a closed and united front against the hostile world of the Anglican establishment. Nevertheless, like English Dissenters, Ulster Presbyterians remained excluded from participation in the politics of the state in which they lived. Brooke has argued that Presbyterians in the north-east compensated by developing a regional identity and a more vigorous and cohesive social structure than within the wider state of which they were part.[11] The Synod of Ulster, the main Presbyterian body in Ireland, assumed the status of a quasi-national church, representing a regional society that was self-sufficient and distinct from the political society governed by Dublin and London. Internally the Synod of Ulster certainly had the appearance of a national church, incorporating within itself a spectrum of theological and political views, surrounded by liberal and fundamentalist dissenting fringes, the Non-Subscribing Presbytery on the former, and the Seceders and Convenanters representing the latter.

Ulster Presbyterians specialised in polemical theology, focusing on the degree to which a true church could recognise and co-operate with, or accept the assistance of, a state which supported a prelatical establishment. From the beginning, their literature addressed the overlap between religion and politics, the relations between church and state. Both liberals and fundamentalists took a position as to how relations with the government should be conducted; attitudes varied from qualified support to outright opposition. In the theological fragmentation of Ulster Presbyterianism, with the development of its various fringe elements, the close theological and ideological ties with Scotland are easily discernible. The first to break away were the liberals, those Presbyterians who accepted scripture as the supreme authority and rejected subscrip-

tion to man-made confessions like the Westminster Confession of
Faith. These Non-Subscribers were centred on a debating club,
the Belfast Society.[12]

The first subscription dispute in the Synod of Ulster began
after the publication in 1719 of a sermon by a prominent member
of the Belfast Society, John Abernethy, minister at Antrim, which
was entitled *Religious Obedience Founded on Personal Persuasion*. The
main body in the Synod, which held scripture as the supreme
authority but also required subscription to the Westminster Confession as a subordinate standard, rejected Abernethy's argument;
they were soon called 'Old Light' believers, while the non-subscribers were labelled 'New Light'.

The dispute was partially resolved when the Non-Subscribers
were assigned to a separate body, the Presbytery of Antrim, and
expelled in 1726 from 'judicial communion' with the Synod of
Ulster. In practice, relations between the Synod and the Presbytery of Antrim remained cordial, and the New Light wing
within the Synod gained strength during the eighteenth century.
Quite a number of the Presbyterian ministers who played a
prominent role in liberal and radical politics in the 1780s and
1790s belonged to the New Light wing of the Synod, but there
were numerous exceptions.

The strength and persistence of New Light theology in the
Synod of Ulster is not a little due to the influence of the Scottish
universities, especially Glasgow, where the majority of the Ulster
ministers were educated and trained. This brought them into contact with the wider world of the Enlightenment, through the
Scottish version of it. Of fundamental influence was the son of an
Ulster Presbyterian minister, Francis Hutcheson, who held the
chair of Moral Philosophy in Glasgow. Hutcheson taught that
political and social questions were ultimately moral questions, and
that therefore one had the responsibility to establish a just political order which would provide for the 'greatest good of the greatest number'. In his *Short Introduction to Moral Philosophy*, Hutcheson instilled a powerful lesson in the hearts and minds of his
Ulster students for the ministry:

When the common rights of the community are trampled upon...then as the governor is plainly perfidious to his trust, he has forfeited all the power committed. In
every sort of government the people have the right of defending themselves
against the abuse of power.

At the other end of the spectrum, on the fundamentalist fringes, the preoccupation with church-state relations was equally strongly influenced by the Scottish element. After the 1712 Patronage Act a number of Presbyterian ministers and elders seceded from the Church of Scotland because they disagreed with the church's acceptance of the Act. The Seceders strove to secure the renewal of the Solemn League and Covenant of 1638 and 1640, and they regarded themselves as a 'true' church whose doctrines did not distinguish between the religious and the political. Although patronage did not exist in Ulster, the Secession appealed to those Presbyterians who disliked the broad tolerance of the Synod of Ulster. To a greater extent than the Synod of Ulster, Irish Seceders were alienated from the Established Church because it was a prelatical church. The overthrow of prelacy (episcopacy) was for them a religious duty, and they had a necessarily hostile attitude towards a government that supported it. Before the Seceders were well established in Ulster, their parent body split in Scotland over the purely Scottish issue of the burgess oath – into 'Burghers', who held that the oath (requiring jurors to 'profess the true religion presently professed within the realm and authorised by the laws thereof') was lawful, and 'Anti-Burghers', who held that the oath was unlawful.[13]

This was not an issue in Ireland, but the closeness of links with Scotland ensured that Secession Presbyterianism was introduced into Ulster in its divided manifestation. An Anti-Burgher Presbytery was erected in 1750 and a Synod in 1788. A Burgher Presbytery was erected in 1751 and a Synod in 1779. The two Seceder wings argued bitterly, while each attacked the Synod of Ulster and the government. Until 1784 Seceders were excluded from the subsidy towards ministerial salaries given by the crown, but when in that year the Regium Donum to the Synod of Ulster was increased, Lord Hillsborough (who feared the liberal politics of the Synod of Ulster) managed to have the Seceders also included in the subsidy, a clear manoeuvre to divide the Presbyterians in County Down, where they threatened his political interests.[14] In the aftermath of the rebellion, only two Burgher ministers were implicated, Rev. James Harper of Rasharkin, and Rev. Thomas Smith, but the Castle was informed on several occasions of the seditious inclinations of the Seceder laity. The well-known United Irish activist, James Hope, the Templepatrick weaver, was

brought up in the Anti-Burgher church of Lyle Hill. He later
wrote that after the Regium Donum had been extended in 1784,
the minister explained the prophecies of the downfall of Turk and
Anti-Christ solely as the destruction of the Pope and popery
whereas before that, he had included the 'purging of the blood
that lay unpurged on the throne of Britain'.[15]

The involvement of Seceder ministers in the United Irish
movement and the rebellion was indeed relatively small, compared with the involvement of ministers belonging to the smallest
and most radical of the fundamentalist churches on the Presbyterian fringe, the Covenanters or Reformed Presbyterians. The
Reformed Presbyterians had refused to recognise the Revolution
settlement of 1688–9 because it entailed the establishment of
prelatical churches in Ireland and England, and was thereby a
denial of the Covenant. The first Reformed Presbytery in Ireland
was formed in 1763, but it collapsed in 1779 due to emigration.
The second Reformed Presbytery was formed in 1792, declaring
from the beginning its principled refusal to recognise the legitimacy of the (non-covenanted) secular government of the day; it
consisted of no less than three ministers (Rev. William Gibson,
Rev. James Orr and Rev. William Stavely), and two probationers
(John Black and Samuel Brown Wyle).[16]

Ulster politics at the grass-roots level was deeply affected by
this backdrop of radical and polemical theology. The role of the
minister was pivotal in the formation of both religious and political
opinion; even in the late eighteenth century east Ulster was still
basically a rural society, despite the impact of linen. A few notable
exceptions apart, there was not a Presbyterian gentry. With their
total exclusion from the legal profession and their virtual exclusion
from political life, there was no real Presbyterian middle class outside Belfast. This vacuum at the local level was filled by the Presbyterian minister and to a lesser extent by the medical doctor.
Through the minister, local society was linked to the world
beyond the parish and through him new ideas filtered through.[17]
However, literacy levels were highest among Presbyterians; ability
to read the Bible was regarded as essential for all adults.

Presbyterian radicalism and its transformation during the eighteenth century was rooted in its ideology, but it also reflected the
peculiar Presbyterian position in Ulster's economy and society.
During the eighteenth century the economy developed strikingly,

with Ulster becoming Ireland's most advanced province in rural industry, commerce and agriculture.[18] This was not achieved without the consequential break-up of traditional society, and unrest was expressed in various forms. The Ulster emigration to North America, mainly by Presbyterians, has been much commented on by Irish and American historians, trying to explain its causes and development. In the mix of the 'push' and 'pull' factors, socio-economic reasons played at least as significant a part as 'ideological' reasons. Emigration, however, is often regarded by social historians of 'traditional' societies as an expression of dissatisfaction and structural tension.[19]

In the second half of the century rural discontent in Ulster also found expression in outbursts of agrarian rebellion. In the 1760s and 1770s Ulster was hit by two such movements, both of which consisted mainly of Presbyterian cottiers, weavers, and tenant-farmers, the Hearts of Oak (1763) and the Hearts of Steel (1769--73). The first movement lasted only one summer; it was a spontaneous outburst, originating in mid-Armagh and east Tyrone, and it spread like a bush fire to six counties in mid- and south Ulster forming a crescent west of the Bann from Derry to Monaghan. Dickson has suggested that the Oakboy movement was more public and self-confident than the contemporaneous agrarian societies in Munster, and that it was primarily a tax revolt.[20] The Oakboy grievances, however, included the whole list of agrarian grievances, but especially tithes and other church duties levied by the Anglican clergy, the county and parish cess, and the compulsory six days per annum labour on roads. Rectors and gentry, whose enthusiasm for spending on roads and bridges had pushed up the local rates, were visited in mass demonstrations and forced to promise not to increase tithes and cess, nor to enforce the road-labour requirements.

Very little physical force was used by the Oakboys, yet the authorities reacted with swifter and sharper repression than in Munster; in a series of bloody encounters with the army, led by local magistrates many of whom had originally fled, a dozen or more Oakboys were 'militarily executed'. In the subsequent trials, however, the authorities found it impossible to secure convictions as the mainly Presbyterian 'middling orders', who sat on the petty juries, refused to convict the alleged Oakboys, often their neighbours and co-religionists, on charges of treason.[21]

Before the decade had passed a new agrarian rebellion, that of the Steelboys, broke out in 1769, originating on the huge Donegall and Upton estates in south Antrim. By 1772 the movement had spread across a swathe of countryside, mainly east of the Bann from Derry to Armagh (where the earlier name of Oakboys reappeared). Uniquely for an Irish agrarian rebellion, tenant-farmers played a prominent role in the original formation of the movement, aiming their actions directly against landlords, their agents, intermediate gentry, and land-speculating Belfast merchants. The most daring exploit of the Steelboys in the early phase of the movement was the rescue from Belfast jail of one of their leaders. A number of Belfast's leading citizens who later played a prominent role in the Volunteer and Reform movements, such as Dr Haliday and Waddell Cunningham, were directly threatened.[22]

The Dublin authorities did not intervene initially, and the Steelboys began to spread slowly but steadily, mainly into County Down, so that by early 1772 they threatened the established order and the rule of law from Derry to Armagh. As it spread, its range of grievances extended from agitation against large-scale releasing operations and high rents to embrace the older grievances of cess, tithes, etc. Army reinforcements were sent in, followed by large-scale house searches and mass arrests, causing a panic throughout north-east Ulster. But again juries refused to co-operate, and emergency legislation was rushed through parliament. The Trials Act, however, did not deliver the required results. Many left Ulster; overseas emigration in the period between 1769 and 1774, on the eve of the American Revolution, soared to probably around 40,000 *in toto* for those years.[23]

In 1774 the government introduced a further piece of repressive legislation to prevent Presbyterians from using their voting power to frustrate the imposition of cess in the parish vestries. According to Dr William Campbell, a New Light minister from Armagh, the Vestry Act originated in 'the motherland of superstition and bigotry, the County of Armagh'.[24] The act led to further unrest and hostility among Presbyterians, but in a departure from the previous Oakboy and Steelboy movements, this resentment was now channelled into political action. Petitions were organised and, with the 1776 general elections looming, Presbyterians threatened to run independent candidates. In County Derry the American-born and Princeton-educated Presbyterian minister of

Ballykelly, Rev. Benjamin McDowell, was prominent in the campaign against the Vestry Act and in support of running an independent candidate. In the end, one of the sitting MPs, Thomas Conolly, successfully proposed the repeal of the Vestry Act in the spring session of parliament in 1776. The independent candidate withdrew in County Derry, but in neighbouring County Antrim, an independent candidate, James Wilson, was elected, the first in a long series for that constituency until 1797.[25]

The American Revolution, the anti-Vestry Act agitation, and the 1776 general election acted together as a watershed in Ulster Presbyterian politics. In his manuscript history, Dr Campbell noted that

the Presbyterians of Ulster condemned this war as unjust, cruel, and detestable. They beheld it with anguish and with horror, as the most wanton, unprovoked despotism. Their friends and relations abounded in the different provinces of America, and they heard with pride that they composed the flower of Washington's army, being carried on by a native love of liberty, to encounter every danger for the safety of their adopted country.[26]

Before this episode the involvement of Presbyterian ministers in popular movements had been very shadowy, but from the mid-1770s ministers of different 'Lights' began openly to take an active role in public life. They embraced the Volunteer movement, acting as chaplains and publishing Volunteer sermons, and they subsequently threw themselves into the parliamentary reform movement in Ulster. It was in this period that four Presbyterian ministers rose to prominence who were subsequently to make their mark on radical politics, and would eventually be implicated in 1798, the Old Light ministers Sinclare Kelburn (Belfast) and John Glendy (Maghera, Co. Derry), and two County Down New Light ministers, William Steel Dickson (Glastry and later Portaferry on the Ards peninsula), and Samuel Barber (Rathfriland).

The authorities in Ulster viewed with alarm the spontaneous rise of Volunteer companies during the American war, making comparisons with earlier agrarian movements. On 14 March 1779 Lord Abercorn's agent, James Hamilton, wrote from Strabane to his master how 'your Lordship, years before the Oakboys, apprehended that there would be a rising in this country; I really think that very little would stir them up now, there are many just now in desperate circumstances.'[27] On 5 December he confided that the Volunteers are certainly driving at something more than defending us from invaders; I am sure that a free trade would not content the first stirrers up of it... The two companies of this town declared they would not serve under anyone who lived in England...I saw a letter lately...from a young lady at Lurgan, in which she said that there had been a letter intercepted in a post office near that, from one dissenting minister to another, saying as if they would be soon ready to rise...[28]

The local Volunteers were still the object of Hamilton's suspicions in May 1780: 'the first cause given for their associating (to oppose invaders) is now even spoken of now, but [it is] openly declared to have the laws reformed to what they think their right...'. However, in December Hamilton was writing that the violence of the neighbouring Volunteers was 'I hope abated'.[29]

The government responded to Presbyterian militancy with a number of concessions: in 1780 the clauses in the Test Act against Protestant dissenters were abolished. Further concessions followed in 1782 with the first recognition of Presbyterian marriages, and a specific concession to Seceders allowed them to swear with uplifted hands instead of kissing the Bible. In the 1783 general elections John O'Neill and Hercules Rowley were returned as independent MPs for County Antrim, while Sharman and Todd Jones were returned for the borough of Lisburn. But in County Down the Ulster Presbyterian activists suffered a defeat when their candidate, Robert Stewart sr, later Lord Londonderry, was unsuccessful in spite of the best efforts of Barber and Steel Dickson. The Seceders, who regarded Stewart with suspicion because of his connection with a Non-Subscribing congregation, had supported Lord Kirwarlin, son of the Earl of Hillsborough.

In the Synod of Ulster Dr Robert Black, then a New Light minister in Dromore, was a close associate of the Stewart family; like them he was initially a liberal and a reformer, but in the 1790s he strongly opposed the influence of radicals and United Irishmen in the Synod of Ulster, in close co-operation with Robert Stewart jr (later Lord Castlereagh). Black was involved in negotiations with the government regarding the establishment of a Presbyterian college for the training of ministers, and for an increase of the Regium Donum. His efforts were partially successful, although he was so disappointed with an increase of only £1,000 in the latter in 1784 that he nearly refused to accept it. It was understood that Lord Hillsborough had had a proposed increase to the Synod of Ulster reduced, and had instead secured a £500 grant to the

Seceders, who up until then had condemned the Synod of Ulster for accepting a royal subsidy.[30]

In spite of these concessions the politically active Ulster Presbyterians continued to press for parliamentary reform and, more hesitantly, for Catholic emancipation. The Duke of Portland, writing to Thomas Pelham on 27 October 1783, referred to the 'soi-disant National Congress' and its declaration in favour of Catholics, designed to win over the 'inferior orders' of Protestants; he noted at the same time that the Presbyterians wanted to have an increase in the Regium Donum. Portland therefore recommended that men like Mr Dawson, the unsuccessful candidate for County Armagh, and Dr Campbell, should be privately contacted, to tell them 'not to provoke the government. In that case justice could be done to that respectable body of loyal subjects.' In 1784, however, some in government complained that concessions to Presbyterians had not had the desired result. Hillsborough complained to Lord Northington on 11 February that 'the Presbyterian parsons are fomenting a turbulent spirit. There never was a worse piece of policy than the rewarding of those incendiaries, for it is impossible to gain them.' He further complained that Newry and Carrickfergus were as bad as Belfast, to which the government had finally sent troops. Later that year on 10 June, Edward Cooke wrote that Pitt had now decided that parliamentary reform was not feasible in Ireland, but it should not cause any further problems, as pressure for reform was subsiding, the South was quiet and the North not as bad, although 'the Presbyterians are nearly mad for parliamentary reform'.[31]

By the mid-1780s the reformers had lost the initiative and the conservatives had regained lost ground. Indicative of this trend was the pamphlet war initiated by Dr Woodward. Campbell's pamphlet against Woodward was his last public activity on behalf of Presbyterianism and liberal politics. In 1789 Campbell withdrew from the Synod of Ulster after it had met in Dungannon and elected Robert Black as agent for the Regium Donum in his place. Campbell left Ulster and went to live with the Bagwell family in Clonmel, with whom he had connections. But by that time reformers and radicals had again taken the initiative – as a result of a domestic political crisis (the Regency question), foreign developments (the French Revolution), and a general election in the making (that of 1790). These election battles were much con-

tested in Ulster, especially in County Down: through robust campaigning by, amongst others, Steel Dickson and Barber, Robert
Stewart jr was elected on the Whig, independent ticket. In the
same year Samuel Barber was elected Moderator of the General
Synod. At the end of his term on 29 June 1791 he preached a
sermon based on Revelation, xviii: 20: 'Rejoice over her, thou
Heaven, and ye holy apostles and prophets for God hath avenged
you on her.' In his sermon Barber strongly endorsed the French
Revolution:

that nation [France] renowned in arts and arms will now be the refuge and asylum
of the brave and good in every nation. Seated in the midst of Europe like a lily on
a hill to shed Light, Liberty and Humanity all around. Happy Country! where the
rights of man are sacred, no Bastille to imprison the body, nor religious establishment to shackle the soul. Every citizen free as the thoughts of man.

In the sermon Barber denounced the fourth-century Council
of Nicea because 'about 300 bishops arrogated to themselves the
government of the church and decreed what they thought to call
Christ, to which we all must submit under the pain of the most
severe punishment in this world and an exclusion from the Kingdom of God hereafter', adding tellingly that 'here commences the
famed alliance between Church and State and the opinions of the
reigning Emperor became those of the Church'.[32] In Barber's eyes
the Council of Nicea initiated the reign of the Anti-Christ, and
the French Revolution was the omen of its ultimate fall. Although
a radical in politics, a prominent member of the New Light wing
of the Synod of Ulster and consequently latitudinarian, or liberal,
in his theology, Barber's millenarian views in relation to contemporary events were also shared by many Old Light ministers.
    After the founding of the first society of United Irishmen in
Belfast in October 1791, Steel Dickson took the test in Belfast in
December. Other ministers followed, although records are difficult to establish. Dickson had been present at the great Volunteer
gathering in Belfast on 14 July to celebrate the Fall of the Bastille,
where a resolution in favour of Catholic emancipation was passed.
Other ministers present then included Sinclare Kelburn and
Thomas Ledlie Birch, the 'Old Light' minister at Saintfield who
later emigrated to America after being acquitted of involvement
in the rebellion.
    In 1792 the Ulster United Irishmen began publication of the
twice-weekly *Northern Star*, edited by the prominent Belfast mer-

chant and radical Samuel Neilson, son of a minister and a ruling elder in Kelburn's church. The *Northern Star* played a crucial propaganda role in the organisation of the Ulster Reform Convention, which was eventually held on 15–16 February 1793 in the Dungannon Presbyterian Church. Its minister, William Stitt, was then Moderator of the Synod of Ulster. Steel Dickson, Kelburn and Glendy played an important part in the proceedings.[33] The Reform Convention was attended by 117 delegates representing Counties Down, Antrim, Derry, Donegal, Tyrone, and Dartry Barony in Monaghan, in a way reflecting the strength of Presbyterian Ulster. Its resolutions were quite moderate, and it was not as impressive as the Dungannon Volunteer and Reform Conventions of the early 1780s. It stood in the shadow of the greater Catholic Convention at Dublin held the previous December. Yet it had the same mobilising effect on Ulster Presbyterians as the agitation and organisation of the Back Lane Convention had on Irish Catholics.[34]

The *Northern Star* reported on all the preparatory meetings, held in almost every Presbyterian district in the province. As a result of these meetings the United Irish organisation was able to diffuse into precisely these districts in subsequent years. Reporting on a meeting held at Taughboyne, County Donegal on 15 January 1793, the Rev. Thomas Pemberton, the Church of Ireland rector, wrote to the Marquis of Abercorn concerning the widespread 'fermentation' among the country people:

my parishioners are chiefly Presbyterians, and with that class of men the levelling and republican principle more particularly prevails. The Roman Catholics are perfectly quiet, both in my parish, and as I am informed, in the whole neighbourhood. I cannot find that there was a single papist at the Taughboyne meeting [to elect delegates to be sent to the convention at Dungannon]: they were all Presbyterians and Seceders.[35]

In June 1793 Steel Dickson was elected Moderator of the General Synod at Lurgan; Neilson was also present as an elder with Sinclare Kilburn. Ledlie Birch, who had come second in the ballot for the moderatorship, was asked to preach. His sermon was not unlike that of Barber two years before in its very millenarian tone:

we must think that the final overthrow of the Beast, or opposing power, is almost at the door; and especially we may observe in a certain contest the seeming accomplishment of the Battle of Armageddon, in which the Beast and his adherents are to be cut off, as a prelude to the peaceful reign of a 1000 years.

In the same year Steel Dickson published a compilation of three sermons, one from the early eighties and two that were more recent, one having been composed in 1792 and the other after the Dungannon Convention; these appeared under the title *Scripture Politics*, and were said to be as influential in Ulster as the works of Paine.[36]

By 1793 the different strands of Presbyterian radicalism in Ulster, theological, ideological, political and agrarian, had been fused into one more or less cohesive radical movement. This movement, as expressed in the United Irishmen, possibly did not represent the majority of Presbyterians in Ulster, especially when moderate liberals like Dr William Bruce, Dr Robert Black, Dr Halliday, Henry Joy, Robert Stewart and Lord Castlereagh, to name but a few, disassociated themselves, or even became ardent government supporters. But it certainly represented a substantial and determined minority, who eventually took the ultimate consequence of their stand. It was also a 'rainbow coalition' against the establishment in church and state, bringing together diverse interests and aspirations, millenarianism and secularism, advanced radicals and agrarian rebels; and despite severe government repression, especially in 1797, the movement held together and, as Curtin argues below, they 'turned out' in impressively large numbers in 1798.

4

WILLIAM DRENNAN AND THE DISSENTING TRADITION

Ian McBride

As a politician, poet and educationalist with a career that spanned
forty years, William Drennan has many claims on the attention of
the Irish historian, but it is as a founding member of the United
Irishmen that he is chiefly remembered. Although the exact
sequence of events leading up to the societies' launch remains
obscure, Drennan dated the origin of the United Irishmen to the
plan that he had submitted to the Belfast Volunteers in June 1791,
which called for the formation of an Irish Brotherhood.[1] Echoing
his earlier attempts to revive the 'ghost of volunteering', he had
proposed

a benevolent conspiracy – a plot for the people – no *Whig* Club – no party title –
the Brotherhood its name – the Rights of Men and Greatest Happiness of the
Greatest Number its end – its general end real independence to Ireland, and
republicanism its particular purpose.[2]

The actual form taken by the societies owed more to Tone's
Argument on Behalf of the Catholics (1791) than to the 'Brotherhood' paper; nevertheless both societies adopted Drennan's test,
he was elected president of the Dublin branch, and he was the
author of many of their productions.
    It was one of these, the 'Address to the Volunteers', which
occasioned the trials of Hamilton Rowan and the proprietors of
the *Northern Star*, supplied the pretext for the clampdown on Volunteering and the banning of conventions, and eventually led to
the arrest of Drennan himself in 1794. In a speech intended for
delivery at his trial, Drennan sketched an outline of his life
designed to demonstrate the consistency and sincerity of his political actions since his enrolment as a Volunteer. His political principles, he declared, were grounded in the fundamental rule of
Protestant dissent that every man has a right to judge for himself

in matters of religion. It was this independence of mind, he believed, which made Dissenters the natural guardians of the British
constitution. He boasted:

I am the son of an honest man; a minister of that gospel which breathes peace and
goodwill among men; a Protestant dissenting minister in the town of Belfast;
who[se] spirit I am accustomed to look up, in every trying situation, as my media-
tor and intercessor with Heaven. He was the friend and associate of good, I may
say, great men; of Abernethy, of Bruce, of Duchal, and of Hutcheson...[3]

In Drennan's invocation of a dissenting radical heritage one
can detect his anxiety to disassociate himself from 'French principles'. While the United Irish test was a translation of 'liberty,
equality and fraternity' into the Irish context, Drennan repeatedly
attributed his radicalism to his father and, in particular, to his
early classical upbringing. When a government agent made a bid
for Drennan's services he answered,

that I had early formed my principles in politics and that my father to his last hour
had desired me never to forsake them, and here, on recollecting that best of men,
and thinking that I saw his meek and venerable form and face bending over me
with a placid and approving smile, I burst into tears and remained for some time
much affected.[4]

The passage is typical of the religiosity which Drennan
brought to political questions and of an almost mystical awareness
of his intellectual genealogy. Beyond his father hovered a host of
ancestral ghosts. In one bizarre scheme for a monument to the
benefactors of mankind in 1813, he suggested that busts of Marcus Brutus, Cato the younger, Tacitus, Newton, Milton, Algernon Sydney, Locke, Luther and Franklin might be placed around
a model printing press inscribed with the words, 'great emancipa-
tor of mankind'.[5]

Fellow worshippers at such a pantheon might have included
many of the 'commonwealthmen' or 'True Whigs' of the eighteenth century. Caroline Robbins, in her pioneering study of the
subject, briefly mentioned Drennan amongst the Irish upholders
of this tradition which stretched back through the English Commonwealth of the previous century to the republics of the ancient
world.[6] However, the language of civic humanism, and of its radical political incarnation, classical republicanism, has only limited
application as a framework for the study of political thought in
late eighteenth-century Ireland.[7] It represents only one strand of a
rich and eclectic radical legacy that was undergoing rapid trans-

formation. Furthermore, classical republicanism came to Drennan, and to other Irish Presbyterians, via two routes – the moral philosophy of the Scottish Enlightenment, and the political ideas of Protestant dissent – and it acquired a distinctive colour along the way. Its Irish manifestation begins with the first generation of Non-Subscribing or 'New Light' Presbyterians.

The Scottish Enlightenment and Irish Presbyterianism

Little is known of Drennan's father, the Rev. Thomas Drennan.[8] Following the usual theological training at Glasgow University, he moved to Dublin in the early 1720s to assist Francis Hutcheson in the management of a dissenting academy. Hutcheson was already attracting international notice on the basis of several philosophical treatises, and in 1729 he was elected to the chair of Moral Philosophy at his old college. The academy was wound up, and Thomas Drennan returned to the North, where he was soon invited to minister to the congregation of First Belfast as a colleague of the Rev. Samuel Haliday.

The impact of Hutcheson's teaching at Glasgow between 1730 and 1746 was to earn him a reputation as the 'father of the Scottish Enlightenment' – which the recent historiographical upheaval in that subject has only served to enhance. But Ulstermen John Abernethy and James Duchal also found an audience outside Ireland for their controversial and devotional writings. Both began their careers with the Presbyterian congregation in Antrim, and ended up in the Wood Street meeting-house in Dublin. Abernethy was particularly admired for his pamphlets attacking the Test Act, and his later sermons were regarded as establishing new standards of taste. The circle of friends was completed by William Bruce, the Dublin bookseller and publisher who specialised in dissenting sermons and philosophical works. For the rest of his life Thomas Drennan, though a lazy correspondent, kept in touch with Hutcheson and his Dublin friends, and many of their letters were carefully preserved by his family.

Throughout the eighteenth century, the vast majority of dissenting ministers received their education at Glasgow and Edinburgh, the former leading by four to one. An analysis of the matriculation albums of Glasgow reveals that 16 per cent of those who signed the register between 1690 and 1820 identified themselves as *Scotohiberni*, and when we turn to the graduation records

the proportion rises to a third. The peak of this influx coincides
with the zenith of Scottish learning; the number of Irish graduates
rose from 24 per cent in the 1750s to 46 per cent in the 1760s,
and to 47 per cent in the 1770s, but began to decline thereafter.
Accessible and affordable, Glasgow kept its edge over the Scottish
capital, but with the rising reputation of Edinburgh's medical
school a third of the medical students there were Ulstermen by
the late eighteenth century.[9] Together these ministers and physi-
cians carried the distinctive ethos of the Scottish universities into
Ulster, where they dominated cultural and social life. The network of kinship which bound together dissenting ministers gave
this social nexus even greater cohesion. Thomas Drennan and
Francis Hutcheson were related by marriage, and William Bruce
was Hutcheson's first cousin. The Bruce family provided recruits
for the ministry for six generations, one a close friend and confi-
dant of William Drennan in his youth.[10] The New Light intelli-
gentsia, then, formed a closely knit community, a distinct social
layer through which political ideas were articulated and dissemi-
nated.

New Light Presbyterianism

The campaign against compulsory subscription to the Westminster Confession of Faith had its origin in the Belfast Society, an
association of clergymen, theological students and laymen which
met under the direction of John Abernethy. At a time when the
Trinitarian controversy was emerging in England and Scotland
the orthodoxy of these young men inevitably came under suspicion, and the views of the members were nicknamed the New
Light. The objections of several of these ministers to the Westminster Confession provoked an increasingly hysterical response
at the annual meetings of the Synod of Ulster. The subscription
controversy was finally resolved in 1726 by the segregation of the
Belfast Society ministers in the independent Presbytery of
Antrim.

The first salvo in the attack on subscription was Abernethy's
sermon *Religious Obedience founded on Rational Persuasion* (Belfast,
1719). In this and subsequent works, Abernethy opened up Irish
Presbyterianism to the latitudinarian currents sweeping through
Calvinist churches everywhere. The Belfast Society maintained
that human knowledge of the creator was necessarily limited; con-

sequently an infinite diversity of opinions on theological questions was inescapable. Human imperfection therefore demanded the exercise of charity and forbearance. Abernethy and his colleagues eschewed the kind of controversy – concerned with scriptural minutiae and doctrinal niceties – which they felt had disfigured the Reformed churches in the past. Rather they stressed the fundamentals subscribed to by all Protestants, which could be deduced from the scriptures by any rational being.[11]

The tenets and attitudes shared by the New Lights can be quickly summarised. The doctrines of original sin, reprobation and election were superseded by a belief in the fundamental goodness and perfectibility of man; an emphasis on morality and virtuous conduct replaced rigid adherence to doctrine; man's sociability and his duties to the community were accentuated, as well as his devotion to God. The Christian religion as preached by Abernethy was no longer to be enforced by the punishments and rewards of the next life, but was justified according to its practical benefits and utility, its role in the gradual civilization and refinement of human society.[12]

At the centre of the argument against subscription lay the right of private judgment – the exemption of matters of conscience from human jurisdiction. The moral autonomy of the individual was central to the New Light understanding of the relationship between God and man: salvation lay not in conformity to articles of faith, but in the scrutiny of the scriptures and in rational persuasion, that is, 'assent formed upon evidence and attentive reasoning'.[13] To constrain freedom of enquiry was to restrict the religious liberty so essential to human fulfilment, and this applied not only to the Westminster Confession, but to the Sacramental Test. In the 1730s Abernethy and William Bruce led a campaign against the Test Act, basing their arguments not on the conventional historical grounds of Presbyterian behaviour during the Williamite wars but on the natural right of worshipping God according to the dictates of one's own conscience.[14] The New Light understanding of religious liberty, moulded during the subscription controversy, gave rise to a powerful critique of all creeds and confessions which ultimately challenged the alliance of church and state. As the theological bonds of Presbyterianism came to be progressively loosened, dissenting ministers increasingly derived their character and cohesion from a passionate commitment to civil and religious liberty.

As the New Light gradually spread throughout the Synod of Ulster, the self-perception of Irish Presbyterians was transformed. Dissent from the Established Church was no longer justified on doctrinal grounds, but because it was obvious that 'where conscience is to be the sole guide, authority can have no place; that no man can have authority over any other; and that no man can invest another with authority over himself...'[15] The antithesis of civil and religious liberty was to be found in 'popery', the system of spiritual enslavement traditionally associated with Rome, which was being redefined in a more abstract way to denote the spirit of persecution which had corrupted all organised religion. Thus, for Abernethy, Roman Catholicism was to be opposed not because of its errors, but because it denied moral self-determination which was seen as pivotal to Christianity.

When it comes to specifics, the Non-Subscribers are extremely difficult to pin down. The original New Light ministers protested their orthodoxy, and argued that their differences were confined to trivial points; yet when challenged on doctrinal questions, they resorted to evasion and obscurantism. Once separated from the Synod of Ulster, the non-subscribers felt less need to placate popular suspicions concerning their views, and increasingly they preached on the human pursuit of virtue while paying lip-service to Christian revelation. After Abernethy's death, Duchal discovered some 'pretty amazing' passages in his diary, but in keeping with New Light discretion, these remained secret.[16]

There can be no doubt that later non-subscribers slid further along the slippery slope to full-blown Unitarianism. The doctrine of the Trinity was the main casualty of the increasing elevation of scientific reasoning. Christ's role in the redemption of humankind became marginalised as the son of God was demoted to the status of a human teacher of a pure system of morality. William Drennan greeted the progress of Paine's atheism with cheerful indifference: 'Trust like a papist', he advised his sister, 'for, if you doubt like a dissenter, the same restless faculty that rejects the Athanasian creed...will begin to nibble at the Incarnation, the Miraculous Conception, etc., and thus Priestly lifts the hatch for Paine to enter.'[17]

If the annual sermons preached before the assembled ministers and elders of the Synod can be taken as representative, the late eighteenth century saw a renewed confidence in the progressive unfolding of religious understanding which could reach apocalyptic dimensions. In 1774 the outgoing Moderator, William Campbell, looked forward to a new reformation, an age of enlightenment when the dark clouds of popery and superstition would be dispelled.[18] In 1791 Samuel Barber, Presbyterian minister of Rathfriland and founder of a United Irish society there, interpreted events in France in the light of biblical prophecies which foretold the downfall of Anti-Christ. Heartened by the news of French Catholics throwing off the shackles of civil and religious thraldom, he prepared his hearers for the collapse of all religious establishments.[19] Religious imagery was easily transposed to the political system, where centuries of superstition had apparently clouded the pure principles of the British constitution. Drennan always claimed to be a dissenter in two ways, protesting against the abuses which had polluted the constitution as well as the errors which had perverted Christianity:

The same sanctified veil of mystery has been thrown over civil and religious matters; and the same timidity in questioning the supposed perfection of this complex sort of being, called King, Lords and Commons, has bound down its votaries into a sort of political bondage unworthy of free-men, and men of free-thought. The alliance of Church and State has preserved and sanctified the abuses of both...[20]

The influence of Hutcheson

The theoretical underpinnings of New Light teaching were in large measure supplied by Francis Hutcheson's moral philosophy.[21] That quintessentially Scottish discipline encompassed not only ethical theory, but politics, economics and, inevitably, theology. Through his work at Glasgow, Hutcheson hoped 'to promote the more moderate and charitable sentiments in religious matter in this country, where there yet remains too much warmth and animosity about matters of no great consequence to real religion'. The tributes of both students and admirers like Alexander Carlyle and Dugald Stewart testify to his success.[22] Originally conceived as a refutation of the self-interested accounts of human behaviour associated with Hobbes and Mandeville, Hutcheson's philosophy described a benign deity presiding over a morally regulated world in which humans naturally tended to behave in ways conducive to their mutual benefit. The empirical evidence for this theory rested on the 'moral sense', a natural faculty which approves benevolent conduct in ourselves and others.

Scholars of Hutcheson's philosophy have noticed a disjunction between his Dublin writings and his Glasgow textbooks.[23] On his arrival in Scotland, Hutcheson followed his predecessor in teaching the natural law theories of Grotius and Pufendorf, and his later works included long discussions on natural rights and contract theory. Yet the jurisprudential tradition always remained secondary to his preoccupation with civic morality, and there are signs that he incorporated these themes into his 'system' only with considerable difficulty. In a remarkable chapter on 'extraordinary rights', he makes it clear that natural law may be overridden in the interests of the public good; in the last resort, all other considerations are subordinated to the welfare of the citizens. The greatest happiness of the greatest number, the famous formula invented by Hutcheson, provided the moral framework within which all relationships operate, whether parent and child, governor and governed, or, significantly, mother country and colony.[24] Political institutions must therefore be designed to facilitate virtuous conduct, to enable the citizen to realise his moral potential. These doctrines made greater room for popular sovereignty than the vague and diffuse court/country debate. Hutcheson's espousal of the right of resistance was the most radical of the Scottish Enlightenment.[25] One student recalled how, in the middle of the '45 rebellion, his teacher had attacked those commentators who evaded the implications of the Glorious Revolution, an event which Hutcheson interpreted as 'the unanimous voice of a free and independent people – throwing off the oppressive yoke – and dethroning a tyrant who had forfeited his right to reign over them'.[26]

Hutcheson's moral and political philosophy was authentically classical and republican in inspiration, and differed markedly from the Dutch jurisprudence taught by his predecessors. His writing forms a vital link in the process whereby conceptions of civic virtue, filtered through the writings of Harrington and his followers, were integrated into the mainstream of British political thought.[27] In Dublin he had won the admiration and assistance of Robert Molesworth, the original commonwealthman, who provided the crucial connection with Shaftesbury and other disciples of Harrington. While Hutcheson was enjoying Molesworth's patronage, the latter had befriended a society of Glasgow students (which included many Irishmen) and assiduously recommended to them the classics of the 'real Whig' canon: Harrington, Machiavelli, his own works and those of Shaftesbury.[28]

The enduring popularity of Harrington and his disciples derived from their adaptation of classical conceptions of citizenship to accommodate the freeholders of Hanoverian England. Reconciled to the limited monarchy of the ancient constitution, republican thought was channelled into the safer ideology of balanced government and the independence of the House of Commons. Its exponents demanded the subordination of private interest to the common good, and the increased participation of citizens in public affairs, most typically through the formation of a citizen militia. Early United Irish propaganda was to echo this old opposition rhetoric in calling for fresh injections of public spirit to halt the degeneration of the body politic. Drennan believed that

were it not for the spirit of republicanism which exists among…[the dissenters], the constitution must be destroyed, for even though this spirit be contrary to the form of the constitution it serves to keep up the proper balance against all the other selfish principles that in King Lords and Commons counteract *public* good.[29]

While the current interest in civic languages of political discourse shows no sign of abating, it remains extremely difficult to gauge the impact of such ideas. Classical republicanism in the eighteenth century survived in a rhetorical and ritualised form, and must be traced through lists of toasts, and through the use by propagandists like Drennan of pen-names such as 'Brutus' and 'Sidney'.[30] Such images conditioned the ways in which political events were perceived and, after the American Revolution, the more radical elements of republican theory would be reactivated.

The Hutcheson legacy

Historians who search for references to Hutcheson in the pamphlet literature of the eighteenth century will be disappointed, yet his influence on political thought can be mapped, particularly in the context of the American colonies.[31] To trace the transmission of Hutchesonian ideas in his native country, one must begin with his circle of friends. During the 1720s Hutcheson and some others had formed a club in which papers were read on philosophical subjects; naturally the members were keen to follow his philosophical development.[32] The publications of his Glasgow period were sent to William Bruce in Dublin, who then passed them around his Irish friends for criticisms and observations.[33] In addition to the maintenance of a regular correspondence, Hutcheson often had an excuse to visit his Irish friends – he had inherited

Irish property which required his presence – and in 1744, when
he refused offers of the Edinburgh chair of Moral Philosophy on
grounds of ill-health, he remarked: 'Indeed my only views, in my
castle building, are returning to Ireland some few years hence...to
spend the dregs of life among a numerous set of old comrades and
kinsmen'.[34] After Hutcheson's early death, appropriately during a
visit to Dublin, these comrades and kinsmen ensured that his
memory was cherished by Irish Presbyterians. In 1755, when *A
System of Moral Philosophy*, the posthumous synthesis of Hutcheson's work, was being prepared, it was natural that the Glasgow
publisher should seek Bruce's help in tidying up the manuscript.
The advance subscriptions of Irish Presbyterian ministers were
collected by Bruce with the help of Dr Haliday – who had
received his early education from Thomas Drennan, before studying under Hutcheson at Glasgow.[35]

   The activities of William Bruce provide a useful corrective to
the received picture of an Irish Presbyterianism preoccupied with
theological squabbles until shaken up by the American and
French Revolutions. We have already noted him as Abernethy's
partner in the 1730s campaign for the repeal of the Test Act. In
the early 1750s, a string of pamphlets written in defence of the
Irish linen industry and the privileges of the Irish parliament
established his credentials as a prominent patriot.[36] His memory
was revered by the Patriot Clubs of Armagh and Antrim later in
the decade. A satirical attack on the 'True Commonwealth's Men'
of the latter club pictures them drinking toasts to Marcus Brutus,
Cato and William Bruce.[37]

   Shortly after the *System* finally appeared, Bruce died and was
buried in the same grave as Hutcheson. He was instantly accorded
a sort of cult status. A lengthy Ciceronian tribute to the two
cousins was composed, to be inscribed on a proposed monument.[38] In Dr Haliday's first foray into the clumsy but patriotic
verse which entertained a generation of Belfast Whigs, Hutcheson and Bruce were likened to Cicero and Brutus.[39] A more elo-
quent pen described Bruce as a master of 'that part of ethics, that
important part, which relates to the natural rights of mankind; to
the foundations of civil government; to the just measures of
authority and submission; to civil and religious liberty, and the
unalienable rights of conscience'.[40]

   Another of the ubiquitous Bruces, William's nephew James,

travelled in France and Geneva as the tutor of Robert Stewart, later Lord Londonderry and father of Castlereagh. While supervising Stewart's studies in Geneva, he wrote to his uncle complaining of the moral and political philosophy courses there. The Genevans, he found, were 'equally ready to embrace the doctrines of Hobbes as those of Mr Hutcheson', and considering that some of the English gentlemen there would later acquire positions of influence, he introduced them to Hutcheson's works in order to 'excite some spirit of liberty and enquiry among them...'[41] Archibald Maclaine, who became a probationer of the Presbytery of Armagh in the same year as Hutcheson, but later ministered in the English church at The Hague, persuaded a French ecclesiastic there to translate Hutcheson's *Compend* into his native language.[42]

James Bruce and Archibald Maclaine represented a new generation of Irish dissenters schooled in Hutchesonian notions of virtue. The Irish intake at Glasgow tended as a group to matriculate into the moral philosophy class. Hutcheson in particular attracted many students from Ireland – indeed this was one reason for his appointment – and he often looked after their material as well as spiritual welfare.[43] His eloquence and personal charm inspired unusual devotion among his students. In the year of William Drennan's trial, two old college friends, the English dissenter Samuel Kenrick and the Scottish Presbyterian James Wodrow, wondered how Hutcheson would have reacted to the events of the 1790s. Appalled by the Scottish treason trials, Kenrick lamented the persecution of 'the descendants of his [i.e. Hutcheson's] disciples'. He wrote, 'I feel a glow overspreading my heart at the very name of Hutcheson – from whose lips, like those of old Nestor you will know, persuasion flowed sweeter than honey – when it recalls to my mind his last farewell, warm effusions poured forth in defence of British liberty in the critical years of 1745 etc.'.[44] Wodrow later recalled that 'by his lectures on government, he revived the spirit of Whigism in this part of the kingdom, and infused them into the minds of his scholars so deeply, that scarcely one of them deserted them afterwards'.[45]

Hutcheson's residual republicanism was watered down by his successors in the chair of Moral Philosophy, Adam Smith and Thomas Reid. Republican themes later resurfaced in John Millar's lectures on civil law, which had a profound influence on the future United Irishman William Steel Dickson, but on the whole the

Scottish moderates drifted towards a conservative defence of the British constitution.[46] Nevertheless, the emphasis on the inculcation of civic virtue became rooted in Scottish moral philosophy, and it is here that the real Hutchesonian legacy is to be found.[47] It is not unlikely that William Drennan's own interest in Hutcheson would have been stimulated by his college friendship with Dugald Stewart, later Professor of Moral Philosophy at Edinburgh.[48] The same ethos prevailed at the dissenting academies established at Strabane and Belfast in the 1780s.[49] Some idea of the syllabus they pursued can perhaps be inferred from the minutes of the Presbytery of Antrim, which trained its own students in the late eighteenth century. Candidates for the ministry were examined on a predictable Scottish diet of Hume, Reid and Blair, but Hutcheson's *Compend* and Abernethy's *Attributes* were prescribed texts.[50]

Conclusion

To locate Drennan's politics in the environment sketched above is not to belittle the achievement of Paine and later radicals whose popular impact has been well documented. Concepts of democracy and popular sovereignty were brought into sharper definition by the debate on the French Revolution, while large chunks of mainstream Whiggery were hastily discarded. A full account of Drennan's intellectual formation would require some discussion of the impact of the American Revolution and the development of demands for fuller political representation in the 1780s.[51] Nevertheless, Drennan's resort to the hallowed names of the first Non-Subscribers was much more than a rhetorical flourish. The new radicalism of the revolutionary decade ran in channels already worn smooth by the ideological currents of an indigenous dissenting tradition. Older frames of reference lingered on: Drennan's brotherhood paper coupled 'the rights of men' with 'the greatest happiness of the greatest number'.[52] In the addresses and resolutions of the United Irishmen, notions of moral responsibility and the self-government of the citizen recur which derived not from Paine but from Rational Dissent, and which are crucial to understanding Presbyterian attitudes to Catholic emancipation.

After the collapse of the Reform campaigns of the 1780s, the challenge of recasting this language to accommodate the Catholics of Ireland became unavoidable. 'It is a churlish soil', wrote Drennan of the Catholic mind, 'but it is the soil of Ireland

and must be cultivated, or we must emigrate.'[53] The French Revolution, with its message that a Catholic country was capable of exercising civil and religious liberty, combined with debates within the Dublin Catholic Committee, seemed to herald a new era of liberty.[54] Defending the first meeting of the United Irishmen to a sceptical friend, Drennan wrote:

if the Protestants are much more enlightened in regard to civil and religious liberty they will by this mental intercourse most rapidly give light to the more opaque body...ignorance will become knowledge, bigotry liberality, and civil freedom must necessarily terminate in the pure principles of Protestantism.[55]

It is in the context of this enterprise – the Presbyterian cultivation of the Catholic mind – that Drennan's contribution to the United Irishmen can best be assessed.

5

THE BELFAST MIDDLE CLASSES IN THE LATE EIGHTEENTH CENTURY

W. H. Crawford

The town of Belfast was only beginning to be regarded as the regional capital of north-east Ulster in the 1780s and 1790s. It had of course been recognised for more than a century as one of the more important Irish ports, but it was still a relatively small town with a hinterland limited to south Antrim and north Down. Constituted as a corporate town in 1613, it was long dominated by its ground landlord. It had not yet become the commercial centre of the Ulster linen industry; even in the 1780s the whole-sale market in Dublin attracted as much white linen as the Belfast and Newry markets put together, while the markets for brown or unbleached linens in several other Ulster towns did more business than that of Belfast.[1] Nor was it the capital of Protestant dissent, as none of the several Presbyterian groups accorded its ministers or meetings particular primacy. It was not yet a leader in education.

The tide of history was nevertheless running in Belfast's favour. It was to be one of a number of provincial towns in Britain and Ireland soon to be transformed by the urban and industrial revolutions.[2] By 1800 Belfast was emerging as the regional capital because its resources and its potential matched the demands of a changing economy. As opportunities presented themselves the progressive elements in Belfast seized them. Economic success boosted their self-esteem and class consciousness, so the majority of them supported first the demands for parliamentary reform and later republicanism until 1798, when a trial of strength with the government forced them to revise their position.

According to a 1791 census Belfast had just over 18,000 inhabitants, about one-tenth of Dublin's population. Although it was reckoned to be the third port in Ireland after Dublin and Cork,

Belfast may have been smaller in size than Waterford, Limerick and Drogheda. Yet its population had more than doubled over the previous thirty years. It was, indeed, experiencing something of a renaissance. In the early 1750s the town had fallen into a ruinous state with many dilapidated buildings; this was because the majority of urban leases had expired and it was feared that the town would lose 'both its trade and inhabitants if it is not speedily supported by proper tenures'.[3] It was only in the late 1760s that the sole ground landlord, the absentee fifth Earl of Donegall, granted a plethora of new leases across his vast estate. The town of Belfast took on a fresh and attractive aspect because clauses in the leases specified the size and height of buildings as well as the use of brick for construction; the new buildings presented a uniform and modern appearance.[4] This was enhanced by the construction of several public buildings, notably an assembly room in 1769, a poor house and a parish church in 1774, a new Presbyterian church in 1783, a theatre in 1784, and the White Linen Hall in 1785. None of these was remarkable for its size or pretensions to architectural elegance.[5] While he never became a resident of the town, the fifth Earl (later created first Marquis) led these developments and was responsible also for the completion of the Lagan canal linking Belfast with Lough Neagh.

It was important for the reputation of Belfast at that time that the Marquis himself had taken these initiatives. He was represented in the town by his agent, who exacted the respect and deference due to his master. The conservative elements in the town rallied around the estate interest, and Belfast Corporation was controlled by the Donegall family, who nominated the sovereign (or mayor) and approved all bye-laws.[6] They also nominated all the burgesses, many of whom were non-resident. Their sole function was to maintain Donegall's prerogative to nominate two representatives to the Dublin parliament; in the 1783 election, for instance, only five burgesses voted. A leading Belfast physician expressed the sentiments of the townspeople about the Corporation: 'We like not [that] this paltry oligarchy, the Corporation, should take the lead, and the more respectable people of Belfast follow as their trainbearers.'[7] As the Corporation had no property or other income of its own to pay any officials, they were appointed by a manor court presided over by Donegall's nominee as seneschal. At one time a substitute body, known as a 'corporation grand jury', had been selected from among the townspeople to handle everyday matters, but this body had fallen into abeyance. In its absence the sovereign was required to carry out not only legal duties but also supervision of the markets; he had to organise town meetings, either on request or on his own initative, to take the opinion of its citizens. The parish vestry was used to collect rates for lighting, paving and watching the town but on occasion the legality of these rates was challenged. The inadequacy of the system of local government was fully revealed in the 1790s, and in 1800 a special act of the Irish parliament nominated twelve commissioners and made arrangements for their successors:[8] they were required to be resident householders, possessing real estate of at least one hundred pounds clear yearly value or two thousand pounds personal estate.

Although the act made provision for an 'heir apparent of a peer or lord of parliament' becoming a commissioner, the original nominees were all middle-class. This is not surprising since Belfast was neither a parliamentary, administrative nor legal centre; nor did it support a cathedral; and it boasted few attractions for the aristocracy. Their absence left the middle classes to cope with the problems generated by an expanding town, as well as to exploit the opportunities created by its commercial development. The plural form 'middle classes' describes the contemporary situation more accurately than the singular, as various groups displayed little cohesion in Belfast as late as the 1770s.[9] There were very few town-gentry but substantial numbers of leisured folk of independent means. Clergy, medical men, and schoolmasters of repute were held in high esteem and formed the core of an influential group of professionals. More numerous than all of these groups were the merchants and shopkeepers. Compared with Dublin, however, even the merchant class was small. When Chambers of Commerce were founded in both Dublin and Belfast in 1783, Dublin could boast 293 subscribers while Belfast had 59. Of the latter, less than half were engaged in international trade. But the reputation of this minority was formidable and their connections far-reaching. Among the most prominent were Waddell Cunningham and Thomas Greg whose firm Greg, Cunningham & Co. had in the 1760s been reckoned one of the largest shipowners in New York. Among others who had been successful in the Americas before returning to Belfast were Valentine Jones in

Barbados and Hugh Montgomery in Virginia. International trade was more profitable, if riskier, than the coastal trades. These men co-operated to build a strong mercantile community that was capable of providing a range of maritime services such as the discounting of bills of exchange and the organising and insuring of ships and cargoes. Some merchants were wholesalers of wine, timber, tea or flax seed, others developed the processing of tobacco, sugar, salt, flour, mustard and beer. Some invested in ropeworks, cordage and sail-cloth manufactories, others in ironfoundries. The linen industry needed merchants to import potash and oil of vitriol for bleaching, while the recently established cotton industry required brokers to handle its raw material. It was the merchants who raised the money to bring in skilled managers for the new glassworks, pottery and textile printing concerns.[10] Belfast's prior commercial success was responsible for the marked development of its industrial base after 1780, and it was shortly to secure the bulk of the linen export trade by providing the services required by country bleachers.

In the early 1770s there had been little evidence of the powerful community spirit that developed over the decade 1775 to 1785. The catalyst was the American war. Ironically the prospect of hostilities had led more than 240 'merchants, traders, and other principal inhabitants of the town of Belfast' to petition the king in 1775 in favour of peace.[11] In the spring of 1778, when the Dublin government reckoned that it could not afford the cost of calling out the militia, Belfast formed its first company of Volunteers. At first this move was regarded as an expedient until the government could organise the militia.[12] When this did not occur, Volunteering quickly became respectable and in 1779 the government reluctantly authorised county governors to issue militia arms to Volunteer companies;[13] in October 1779 parliament passed a vote of thanks 'for their spirited exertions in defence of the country'. Soon afterwards the Volunteers began to voice political demands. When Free Trade was granted in December 1779, they demanded legislative independence. The success of the Dungannon Convention of February 1782 served only to increase the enthusiasm of the Volunteers for political agitation.[14] It is significant, therefore, that the Corporation of Belfast, which included Henry Joy, refused to hold a public meeting of 'the burgesses, the gentlemen, the clergy, freeholders, and principal inhabitants' to discuss the

Dungannon resolutions.[15] Not everyone was carried away on the tide.

One of the most important characteristics of the Volunteer movement in Belfast, as elsewhere, was the readiness of men to lay out their own money for uniforms and equipment and to give up their time for drills, parades and reviews. This trait was reflected in Belfast in the revival of freemasonry which occurred soon after the arrival in town of a flamboyant excise officer and impresario named Amyas Griffith. Prior to his arrival, only 104 members had been registered in the three Belfast lodges, one of which was dormant. In January 1781 Griffith and two friends revived Lodge 257 and renamed it the Orange Lodge.[16] It was an immediate success and by April 1783 provoked the following hyperbole: 'the procession was conducted by the Orange Lodge, so confessedly acknowledged the first in Europe, being composed of 150 gentlemen, among whom are noblemen and commoners of the very first distinction'.[17]

The successes of the Volunteers and the freemasons were eclipsed in importance, however, by the events that led to the construction of the White Linen Hall in Belfast. Although this episode has been overlooked in national histories, it was cardinal in the development of Belfast. What started out as a battle of wills between the northern linen-drapers and the Linen Board in Dublin escalated into a controversy between Belfast and Newry as to the most suitable location for an Ulster White Linen Hall, and thence into Belfast's assertion of its claims to be capital of the North.[18] The origins may be traced to the American war since it was Spain's entry into that war in June 1779 that greatly reduced imports of barilla ash for bleaching. Experiments using lime as a substitute brought complaints from England about spoiled cloth, and therefore the Linen Board secured the passage through parliament of a new act that made the bleachers liable for faults and required them to deposit considerable sums of money as bonds from which fines could be deducted by the Linen Board without appeal. The northerners were so angry that they mobilised against the act. An anonymous letter-writer stressed the mood when he wrote about the prospect of a meeting called for Dungannon early in August 1782:

I believe said meeting will be of more consequence to Ireland than the famous Dungannon meeting in February last, as on the result of this meeting depends the linen trade and also the peace and harmony of this province who to a man are averse to said act and resolutely determined not to comply with it let the consequence be what it may.[19]

The Board withdrew the scheme in the face of this angry protest.

The success of the northern linen-drapers followed hard on the heels of the decision by the Belfast Volunteers to call another convention to consider what the British parliament had conceded by legislative independence. Just as the Volunteers went further to demand that the British government should renounce all right to legislate for Ireland (conceded in April 1783), so the linen-drapers argued that they had secured no more than 'a temporary suspension of some parts of a late act of parliament, which were deemed injurious to the linen trade and incompatible with the freedom and safety of those concerned in it...' They organised another meeting for Armagh on 2 December 1782, and summoned delegates 'from the general body of linen merchants' to consider courses of action and 'look up to parliament for that complete security, which, in a country governed by laws, parliament alone is competent to give'.[20]

A divisive issue was raised by the Newry merchants when they claimed that their landlord, Mr Needham, was prepared to support the construction of a White Linen Hall in Newry, both by granting a good site for the building and by giving a subscription.[21] They must have been amazed at the speed of Belfast's reaction, for within a month a subscription list to build a White Linen Hall in Belfast had attracted at least 150 subscribers, who pledged more than £17,000.[22] The subsequent controversy as to the proper location for the Ulster White Linen Hall was conducted through the newspapers, and it sheds much light on contemporary views about the linen industry, as well as about Belfast's standing in the province.

Like many towns in Ulster both Belfast and Newry already had brown linen markets where drapers purchased webs of cloth from rural weavers (there was a statutory obligation that all linen be sold in public markets).[23] Since 1728 the Linen Board had operated a White Linen Hall in Dublin where northern drapers marketed their finished cloth. Usually Dublin factors or middlemen with capital bought the cloths and held them for sale to buyers in England. Over the years, however, many English wholesalers established direct links with the northern drapers and cut out the middlemen. By 1782 many Ulster drapers believed that they could afford to build and administer their own White Linen Hall. This they knew would require considerable capital to provide ready cash for the markets by discounting or purchasing the bills of exchange in which the merchants were paid from England. Both the Belfast and Newry merchants well understood the value of securing a White Linen Hall, but in this controversy the Belfast men revealed much more confidence in their ability to fund the construction of the linen hall and to finance the trade. Newry based its claim on its central position for marketing the coarse and middle-priced linens from south Ulster and on its well-placed harbour for sailings to Liverpool and Chester. Belfast, however, argued that its bleachgreens were already finishing much of the coarser linens as well as the fine linens of the Lagan valley, and that Belfast Lough provided the safest harbour on the east coast of Ireland.[24] At the Armagh meeting on 2 December 1782, Newry merchants secured the support of most of the linen-drapers from mid-Ulster, especially those who resented Belfast's claims to primacy in the trade. Seeing that they would lose the vote, the Belfast delegates withdrew from the meeting and refused to recognise its decision.[25] Soon both towns were constructing White Linen Halls, and each came into operation in 1784. In May 1785 nine major Belfast houses set up the Belfast Discount Office and within a decade several other financial institutions boosted its commercial life.[26] Two groups of merchants also established shipping companies specifically for the linen trade.

The whole scale of the enterprise caught the public's imagination and an editorial in the *Belfast News-Letter* of 28 June 1785 applauded its success:

From the very large and complete assortment of linens at this market, and the attendance of so many of the principal English and Scottish buyers, we understand that both buyers and sellers agree in declaring that they now look upon our White Linen Market as certainly established...Our quays at present and during the last week furnished a very agreeable spectacle; the ships for London, Chester, Liverpool, Whitehaven, Workington and Glasgow ranged in a line and gaily dressed with colours and streamers flying, taking in their cargoes of white linens sold in our Hall. The quays covered with the packs and boxes have a most pleasant appearance, heightened by the fine weather. Much praise is due to the Committee for conducting the ships in the linen trade, for having good vessels ready for the places above-mentioned: and the gentlemen concerned in the Discount Office must feel themselves highly gratified in the reflection that they have been able (notwithstanding the unexpected magnitude of the sales) to discount all the paper that has been offered, and thereby enable the drapers to lay in fresh assortments in the Brown Markets.

To the Presbyterian mind these scenes must have seemed as visions of the new Jerusalem. Their enemies had been dumb-founded while their own exertions had been mightily rewarded.

The confidence of the merchants at this time is reflected in their decision in 1783 to set up a Chamber of Commerce. The initiative however did not come from Belfast: it followed the examples of first Glasgow (in January) and Dublin (in March), and it may have had difficulty in reaching its professed target of fifty members. At first the council of the Chamber was very active under Waddell Cunningham as Chairman, meeting once a week. It organised petitions to parliament for placing a lighthouse on the South Rock off the Ards coast, and for the improvement of Belfast harbour. Both were successful and the outcome of the second was an act creating in 1785 'the Corporation for Preserv-ing and Improving the Port and Harbour of Belfast', led by Wad-dell Cunningham, manned by the chief merchants, and known to posterity as the 'Ballast Board'. This body had the river surveyed, and it then organised pilotage and navigation aids and an ongoing programme of dredging and wharf-construction (it was this which attracted William Ritchie from Scotland to set up a ship-building yard and a graving dock). Subsequently the Chamber proved to be effective in mobilising discussion and then action on specific issues such as the Lagan Navigation, although it found it always difficult to maintain a satisfactory level of everyday commitment by the members. The Chamber, however, reflected the success enjoyed by the merchants in the previous decade. They succeeded in gaining a new control over their future and they were in excel-lent shape for coping with the great expansion of trade that the nineteenth century would bring.[27]

The Belfast merchants were also actively involved in politics through their membership of the Volunteers. By 1783 the local Volunteer leaders had concentrated their attention on reform of the Dublin parliament, declaring that 'from an equal representa-tion, chosen by the free uninfluenced voice of the people and by frequent elections...every blessing must result'.[28] For the 1783 election they tried to force their candidate for Belfast on Lord Donegall but were rebuffed. In retaliation Waddell Cunningham stood for Carrickfergus in 1784 against the influence of Donegall and was returned to parliament, only to be unseated on the grounds that his Belfast supporters had used undue influence on his behalf. That failure added to the repulse of the National Convention in Dublin by the House of Commons in the autumn of 1783, the rejection of a subsequent parliamentary reform bill, and the anti-climax of the 1784 congress in Dublin.[29] Yet, although the Volunteers' campaign collapsed, the political economy of Ulster had been radically changed. The new middle classes had gained enough confidence to articulate their needs and they had learned the niceties of political procedure.

Agitation for parliamentary reform was revived after 1789 by the outbreak of the French Revolution which attracted great attention in Belfast. There it was publicly viewed as a French attempt to duplicate the Glorious Revolution of a century before: Belfast enjoyed the spectacle of what appeared to be the middle class in France destroying aristocratic and clerical privilege. The call for parliamentary reform was revived in March 1790 by the Belfast First Volunteer Company and echoed two days later by a well-attended meeting of the principal inhabitants, emphasising their distaste for government corruption.[30] The less radical elements tried to counter. A contemporary has suggested that it was 'from a just and probably well-founded dread of the increase of democratic principles in the town of Belfast' that Lord Charlemont proposed the institution of a Whig (or constitutional) Club on the lines of a similar club in Dublin. The Northern Whig Club, which held its first meeting in March, secured its membership from the landed gentry in the Belfast region and some of the more eminent Belfast merchants.[31] On 14 July 1791 they celebrated the second anniversary of the Fall of the Bastille in conjunction with the Volunteers. A resolution that day to admit Catholics to the rights of citizenship had been withdrawn for fear of causing division, but it was subsequently received and adopted by the First Belfast Volunteer Company.[32] It was probably in opposition to the limited aims of the Northern Whig Club that the Society of United Irishmen was constituted in Belfast in October 1791. Whereas its object was to procure 'a complete reform in the legislature, founded on a communion of rights, and a union of power, among Irishmen of every religious persuasion', conservatives like Henry Joy suspected that it aimed for 'the entire separation of this country from England, and the erection of a democratical commonwealth in its place'.[33] To advocate the aims of the Society of United Irishmen the *Northern Star* newspaper was launched in January 1792. Later that month a large town meeting agreed to the following petition to parliament, but only after the sections in italics were expunged:

We therefore pray, that the legislature may be pleased to repeal, *from time to time, and as speedily as the circumstances of the whole kingdom will permit,* all penal and restrictive statutes at present in existence against the Roman Catholics of Ireland; and that they may thus be restored to the rank and consequence of citizens, *in every particular.*[34]

This brought the whole issue of Catholic emancipation into the limelight. As none of the radicals objected in principle to an extension of the franchise, the main point of contention was whether it should be 'immediate' or 'progressive'. Those who favoured the gradual approach argued that they needed evidence confirming that the Catholic clergy and laity were committed to civil and religious liberty. Although the 'immediates' easily carried the vote in a well-attended town meeting, the 'graduals' were able to muster more than 250 names.[35] This was the controversy that Wolfe Tone had found when he visited Belfast in the previous autumn and about which he had argued with the Presbyterian minister and headmaster of the Belfast Academy, Dr William Bruce. In essence Bruce was wary of the influence of the Catholic church, could not bring himself to trust the Catholic majority in power, and feared the likelihood of a challenge to property.[36]

After the outbreak of war with France in February 1793 the Dublin government took a stronger line with the radicals in Belfast. They were well aware that they were dealing with a considerable number of able and successful businessmen intent on fundamental political change and gaining support throughout the kingdom. To foil them the government had to restore the nerve of the aristocracy and the conservatives, and to seize the initiative. Through the unpaid magistracy and the court system, they tried to procure information against the United Irishmen, but it was always found very difficult to secure credible witnesses or to get juries to convict. An Indemnity Act was passed early in 1796 to protect magistrates who had acted over-zealously, and later an Insurrection Act, directed against unlawful oath-taking, enabled the Lord Lieutenant to proclaim a county or part of it as being in a state of disturbance. By April 1797 the only county that had been fully proclaimed was Down; substantial parts of five other Ulster counties were also picked out.[37] In October 1796 Habeas Corpus had been partially suspended and within a year more than 500 arrests had been made. At the same time parliament, under great pressure from the gentry, authorised the creation of a yeomanry on English lines, to assist the army and act as an armed constabulary. To ensure its loyalty, officers and sergeants were appointed by the government, which enforced military regulations. By June 1798 there were 40,000 yeomen, a third of them mounted. In Belfast the conservatives had managed only with great difficulty to raise a cavalry corps and later an infantry corps in 1796.[38] In September of that year the army sealed off Belfast and arrested the leading United Irishmen. This was done again late in April 1797 and thirty more prisoners were sent to Dublin. At the end of May the presses of the *Northern Star* newspaper were wrecked by the Monaghan militia so that it was never able to resume publication:[39] this deprived the radicals of their major propaganda weapon. The army meanwhile concentrated on disarming the province and weakening its military potential by shows of force wherever it was opposed. Belfast, however, appears to have remained quiet, controlled by a system of written passes and military patrols.[40]

When the insurrection came in June 1798 there was a considerable turn-out, first in south Antrim and then in north Down, so that substantial military forces were required to suppress them. Notable also, however, were the defections, including many of the leading lights in the United Irishmen. There was indeed a hard core of Belfast radicals and Presbyterian clergy, but they seem to have been carried along by great masses of country people who differed little in their politics from the Oakboys and Steelboys. With the benefit of hindsight a contemporary gave this assessment of those who supported the United Irishmen in 1797:

The high respectability of the greater number of those who attended these meetings, and their attachment to the principles of the constitution, rendered them above even suspicion of their being engaged in revolutionary schemes. Yet, from their liberal use of the phraseology of the disaffected, it would seem that they had either, for a time, been deceived by their specious language, or feared to deviate from it, though for years previous, it had been notorious that if ever for a moment reform had been contemplated, it had long since ripened into rebellion... An intimate friend of the writer, who, from the formation of a united society in his neighbourhood, to their last meeting, held office in their civil and military organisation, assures him that he never even heard Roman Catholic emancipation or parliamentary reform mentioned in their meetings; their object, at all times, being a separation from Great Britain, and the establishment of a republic as in France...It is nevertheless certain, that for some time previous, many of the higher classes had become seriously alarmed at the progress of the United Irishmen – and though comparatively few of these had, as yet, joined their ranks, a sudden fear had spread over the country, that, as in France, from law breakers they might become law makers. Hence they deemed it expedient to seem friendly disposed, or at least passive, as the pistol or dagger had denounced the danger of an active opposition.[41]

These observations suggest a proposition that the development of a middle class in Belfast, very conscious of its achievements in the previous two decades, had driven a large and permanent wedge between the townspeople, and the farmers and weavers in the surrounding countryside. After 1800, for example, the townspeople would not have condoned an invasion such as had been achieved by the Steelboys just before Christmas 1770, which culminated in the destruction of Waddell Cunningham's house and the liberation by force of prisoners from the town jail.[42] Belfast responded to the American Revolution by founding the Volunteers and many identified with the ideals of the French Revolution by inaugurating the United Irishmen. Their political awakening was a consequence of the great advances in communications occurring throughout the Atlantic world. They soon became aware, however, that the excitement they had generated in the rural areas was translating their high-flown political idealism into the more practical language of popular, traditional demands. When the government forces suppressed the risings in Antrim and Down in June '98, the Belfast middle classes were free to secure their own revolution in local government and regional leadership.

6

PARLIAMENTARY REFORM IN IRISH POLITICS: 1760–90

James Kelly

Parliamentary reform had been an important issue in Irish politics for several decades before the United Irishmen were established to secure it in 1791. The convergence of a number of factors in the mid-eighteenth century encouraged the middle-class interests, which provided reform with its main activists, to embrace a political programme aimed at making government more responsive to their needs. One of the most significant factors was increased literacy, but the improvement in the kingdom's economic fortunes and the decline in sectarian animosity had an equally liberating impact.

The new mood of self-assuredness to which these developments gave rise was first revealed during the Lucas affair. But it was the stimulus given to popular politics by the Money Bill dispute of 1753 that prompted the Protestant middle class to cast off the deferential role they had long accepted, and to develop a programme that reflected their aspirations to participate more fully in the political process. This was a development of seminal significance. In the early eighteenth century when calls for parliamentary reform were made, they had emanated from within the aristocratic élite which dominated Irish representation, and they were prompted by the need to correct deficiencies in existing electoral arrangements rather than by a wish to broaden the representative base. In 1727, for instance, Marmaduke Coghill, one of the main parliamentary managers of the day, called for legislation to eradicate electoral 'bribery and corruption' for this precise reason. Indeed, freeholders were quite content with this, Archbishop King observed, as they were predisposed to vote as their landlords directed, provided the candidates they voted for were 'unexceptionable p[er]sons of known good affection to his Majesties service'.[1] Thirty years later, freeholders in urban areas, where the process of popular politicisation had taken firmest root, were less prepared to play so self-effacing a role. The campaign they initiated in the 1760s grew in ambition and scope over several decades until it reached its eighteenth-century peak in the shape of the United Irish plans for parliamentary reform in the 1790s.

The main political grievance of those who defined themselves as 'independent freeholders' in the 1760s was the absence of a provision for calling regular general elections. George II reigned for thirty-three years (1727–60), and the fact that there was but one general election between his accession and demise prompted calls in the election that followed his death for reforms to ensure that this did not happen again. Mercantile and citizens groups in Dublin felt most strongly about this, and they urged 'a law for limiting the continuance of parliaments in Ireland to seven years, as in Great Britain' because, they maintained, 'perpetual parliaments' were inimical to the true principles of liberty. They endeavoured to win parliamentary support by calling on freeholders not to vote 'for any person...who shall not first publicly declare that he will faithfully use his utmost endeavours to procure such like salutary law'.[2] Their campaign was not without impact. A number of successful candidates did agree to support a septennial bill, and they raised the matter repeatedly in the Irish parliament in the 1760s. Moreover, their cause was given a fillip in 1763 with the foundation by Charles Lucas of the *Freeman's Journal*. This news-sheet repeatedly and insistently urged the advantages of limiting the duration of parliaments, the need to restrict Dublin Castle's capacity to use the pension list to forge a working majority in the House of Commons, and the necessity of eradicating 'close' boroughs in order to make the representative system more responsive to the needs of the population.[3]

Dublin was the main centre of reformist activity in the 1760s. Guided by Lucas, who represented the city between 1761 and 1771, weighty Protestant middle-class interests like the Guild of Merchants and the Corporation of Stationers embraced the reformist message.[4] In view of this, it is more than a little ironic that the ratification of an Octennial Act in 1768 owed more to the exigencies of high politics than to the efforts of reformers, but they could take satisfaction from the fact that it was they who had kept the issue before the public throughout the 1760s. Moreover, their core support continued to grow: the publicity afforded John

Wilkes's electoral struggles against aristocratic interests in Middlesex, the unease concerning the British government's efforts to bring the American colonists to heel, and the controversial efforts of Lord Townshend to bring 'government back' to Dublin Castle, all contributed to a public perception that current political structures were unresponsive and unrepresentative. Wilkes's impact on middle-class Irish Protestants can be gauged by their willingness to name children after him, and they readily concluded, echoing the American colonists and the British parliamentary opposition, that the real object of government policy in the late 1760s was not administrative efficiency, but despotism. As a consequence the cause of parliamentary reform continued to attract support among the Protestant and, less visibly, among the Presbyterian middle classes, despite their failure to make an impression in the 1768 general election. Even the death of the inspirational Lucas in November 1771 failed to break the momentum.[5]

Lucas's successor as leader of the Dublin and, by extension, the Irish advocates of reform was Sir Edward Newenham, the Dublin-based MP for Enniscorthy. He was ably supported by an *ad hoc* grouping of young radicals – of whom Napper Tandy and John Binns were the best known. Throughout the early and mid-1770s, they endeavoured to perpetuate Lucas's reform message by cultivating his memory and by convening regular public meetings to pressurise MPs to follow the lead of their freeholders on popular issues.[6] The reformers' priority in the early 1770s was therefore to reform political practice rather than political structures. Most MPs were strongly resistant to the idea of acting as their constituents determined, but this did not deter Newenham or Tandy. They and their supporters believed that 'the people, in a political sense, must ever be considered as our sovereign Lord, or king over all' and, because the Irish parliament was corrupt, 'the voice of the people' alone could 'save the constitution'. The Protestant population of Dublin shared this point of view, and they approved a resolution proposed by Tandy at a public meeting of 'freemen and freeholders' held in November 1773 that sternly reprobated electoral entertainment, which the reformers deemed a symbol of political corruption. At the same time, political debates hosted by the Society of Free Citizens, in which Tandy was a leading light, popularised the language and issues of parliamentary reform.[7]

Encouraged by the success of their efforts, by the level of public interest in the 'association' movement in Britain, and by the imminent general election, bodies of 'independent free-holders' formed 'societies' and 'associations' in 1774–5 in what was the most sustained initiative so far to persuade parliamentary candidates to respond to their constituents' instructions. By mid-1774, elaborate oaths committing MPs to support a popular political programme had been circulated. The Grand Jury of County Dublin brought the 1773 resolution of the freemen and freeholders of the city against electoral 'entertainment' to national prominence by ratifying a series of resolutions against 'entertainment', the transport of electors to the polls, and the employment of excessive 'agents, lawyers and clerks'. The *Hibernian Journal* and the Society of Free Citizens promulgated the arguments of reform to a receptive audience.[8] Aristocratic figures like Thomas Conolly and Sir Allen Johnston resolutely opposed these efforts to alter political practice, but when they tested public opinion on the issue at a meeting of freeholders convened at Kilmainham on 9 January 1775, they were utterly vanquished.[9]

The activities of the Dublin reformers encouraged others. In County Westmeath, for instance, 'independent freeholders' publicly refused to support their sitting MPs unless they took a 'test' similar to that approved at Kilmainham. In County Antrim, Presbyterian interests were so disenchanted by the action of their MP, John O'Neill, in sponsoring a bill which included a clause prohibiting them from voting in vestries, that they founded an 'association' to advance and fund the candidature of Captain James Wilson, who promised to be more responsive to their political needs.[10]

In simple electoral terms, the reformers' campaign registered only modest success in the 1776 election. According to the *Hibernian Journal*, a mere thirty-seven of the 300 MPs elected could swear that they were returned without resorting to 'bribery'. Despite this, the reformers took satisfaction from the triumphs of James Wilson in County Antrim, Sir Edward Newenham in County Dublin, and Travers Hartley and Sir Samuel Bradstreet in Dublin city.[11] But when compared with the fifty peers and sundry commoners who now controlled 234 of the 300 seats in the Commons and who were overwhelmingly hostile to change, the reformers were a small and not very influential rump. Given this situation, their leaders quickly concluded that the goal of a 'free

parliament' was unattainable in the short term, and so they subordinated advocacy of this issue in the late 1770s to support for the
causes of free trade and legislative independence.

These were by no means lost years, however. The participation
of middle-class Protestants and Presbyterians in the campaigns
for free trade and legislative independence and, above all, their
membership of the Volunteers strengthened their resolve to eradicate political 'corruption, avarice and venality'. It also educated
the middle classes in the principles of political agitation, and they
endeavoured to implement what they had learnt when the cause
of parliamentary reform became a truly national issue for the first
time in the early 1780s.[12]

Parliamentary reform in the 1780s

The first clear signs that the proponents of parliamentary reform
believed the moment opportune to reanimate their campaign
came in the winter of 1781–2 during a trough in the agitation for
legislative independence. Activated by the apprehension that parliament might continue to obstruct their demands, the Patriot
press prepared the ground by debating the merits of electoral
reform, while numerous Volunteer corps approved resolutions
similar to that ratified by the First Ulster Regiment at Armagh in
December 1781, which averred that 'the most effectual methods
must be pursued to root corruption and court influence from the
legislative body'.[13] The Dungannon Convention in February 1782
and the concession of legislative independence a few months later
boosted the Volunteers' commitment to their cause, although the
country was preoccupied with 'renunciation' for most of the
summer and winter of 1782–3. The enthusiasm with which
dozens of Volunteer corps supported the resolution agreed by
delegates of 304 corps at Dungannon on 21 June 1782 in favour
of 'the more equal representation of the people' indicated that
this was fast emerging as the most important issue of the day for
the middle-class rank and file membership of the Volunteers.[14]

The ardour displayed by various Volunteer corps for the cause
of parliamentary reform in 1781–2 was primarily prompted by the
eagerness of the Protestant and Presbyterian middle classes to
gain fuller access to the political process. It also drew impetus
from the conviction, articulated most cogently by Richard Lovell
Edgeworth, Francis Dobbs, John Jebb and William Drennan, that

if the reform of Anglo-Irish constitutional and commercial relations was not followed by 'internal' parliamentary reform, the
'venal' Irish parliament would

by degrees yield everything but the name of freedom; and the slow but certain
influence of corruption may in after years, reduce you to the same subjection,
which you have so nobly shaken off by the well-timed exertion of national courage,
and unexampled prudence.[15]

This argument was taken up and popularised by journalists and
pamphleteers in the spring and summer of 1783, who insistently
emphasised the threat posed to the 'constitution of 1782' by the
'servile tools of venal prostitution in the senate'.[16] Few if any
reformers had a clear idea as to the precise reforms they sought.
They maintained that their object was not to innovate but to
restore the constitution to its original purity by removing corrupting excrescences that had evolved since the Irish aristocracy began
to monopolise representation. In practice, however, the language
of reform used in 1783, much of it borrowed from the 'Association' movement in Britain, was manifestly more radical than that
used in the early 1770s. The reformers were less interested now in
persuading MPs to follow the instructions of their constituents,
and more eager for a fundamental reform of the representative
system. Most envisaged some reduction in the number of corporation boroughs, an increase in the number of MPs returned for
populous county and urban constituencies, the broadening of the
franchise, and triennial or even annual parliaments.

There was little enthusiasm among established political interests for such suggestions. The fact that parliament was not in session makes it difficult to assess the strength of political opinion,
but the negative reaction of MPs to Sir Edward Newenham's
move for leave to introduce a bill for a more equal representation
in mid-1782 indicated that a campaign for parliamentary reform
would not originate from within the Commons. The Volunteers
of Munster hinted briefly that they would assume the mantle, but
the blandness of their resolutions at Cork on 1 March suggests
that a majority did not possess the necessary vision.[17] In fact, it was
not the Volunteers of Munster or Leinster, but those of Ulster
that initiated and directed the most sustained reform campaign yet
seen in Ireland.

Middle-class Presbyterians were awakened out of the political
torpor in which they had languished for much of the century by

their involvement with the Volunteers. The repeal of the Sacramental Test in 1780 and the resolutions of the Dungannon Convention in February 1782 encouraged them to believe that a new, more inclusive political era was within reach. Their enthusiasm for parliamentary reform was demonstrated on many occasions at Volunteer reviews in 1782 and early 1783. It was a meeting of delegates of 45 Volunteer corps at Lisburn on 1 July 1783 that signalled the full commencement of a campaign for reform; this meeting appointed a Committee of Correspondence with responsibility for 'collecting the best authorities and information on the subject of parliamentary reform', for presentation at 'a general meeting of the Volunteer delegates of Ulster', scheduled to take place at Dungannon on 8 September.[18]

Guided by William Sharman of Moira Castle and Henry Joy of Belfast, the Committee of Correspondence applied to the most eminent liberal and radical politicians in Britain and Ireland for advice on a range of policy matters. The responses of the Irish figures consulted were short and unsatisfactory. Both Henry Grattan and Lord Charlemont professed themselves well-inclined, but they were distinctly uneasy at the suggestion that the Ulster Volunteers should prepare a specific plan of reform; they believed that this was parliament's exclusive prerogative. 'The measure alone should be recommended without specifying any mode whatsoever,' Charlemont advised. Henry Flood was less cautious, but he too failed to provide the Committee with the detailed information it desired. Indeed, only the English parliamentary reformers directly answered the Committee's queries. They were by no means united on an appropriate programme of reform for Ireland, but they did suggest that the duration of parliaments should be limited to one or three years; that some corrective action, including the abolition of 'small and decayed boroughs', should be taken to create more equal constituencies; and that there should be a 'prudent' extension of the franchise lest a more radical proposal 'transfer[red]...to Catholics an influence in election...dangerous to the state'.[19]

While the Committee collected evidence to draft a set of resolutions for the upcoming Dungannon Convention, scores of local Volunteer reviews and election meetings won over large sections of the population to the cause of parliamentary reform. The question of electoral candidates taking a 'test' to obey the instructions

of their constituents was made an issue in considerably more constituencies in the 1783 general election than in 1776, and some
freeholders manifested their convictions on the subject by voting
for popular candidates in defiance of their landlords' wishes. The
electoral successes of the reformers in 1783 were few in number,
but victories in County Kerry, Lisburn, Cork city and county and
a number of other constituencies were encouraging.[20] In the light
of this, it is not surprising that the delegates of 272 Ulster Volunteer corps which assembled in Dungannon in September had no
hesitation in approving a radical programme. They were clearly
impressed by the advice received from England, because they
approved resolutions in favour of annual parliaments, abolition of
decayed and depopulated boroughs and the redistribution of their
seats to 'counties, cities and great towns', compensation of the
owners of abolished boroughs, a secret ballot, reduction in the
duration of elections, and disfranchisement of those who abused
the electoral system. They also sought extension of the franchise
to all Protestant males who possessed a forty-shilling freehold,
who owned property worth £20 or more, or who paid rent of £5
or more per annum. It was also suggested that the franchise
should be extended to Catholics on the same terms. When it
emerged that there were sharp differences of opinion on this issue,
it was deemed preferable to leave this matter for the adjudication
of the Grand National Convention, which was scheduled to meet
in Dublin in November to determine on a plan of reform for submission to parliament. Even without a provision for Catholic
enfranchise-ment, this was a radical programme. If implemented,
it would fundamentally alter the Irish representative system; the
reformers were encouraged to believe that success was likely by
the ease with which the Dungannon resolutions were ratified at
provincial meetings of Volunteer delegates in Munster, Connacht
and Leinster.[21]

As delegates gathered in Dublin in early November for the
Grand National Convention, perspicacious observers were acutely
aware of the problems they had yet to overcome if they were to
achieve reform, and that the most likely cause of difficulty was
'the rock of religion and indulgence to Catholics', as William
Drennan put it. On paper, at least, the Convention was a most
impressive gathering, with no fewer than 59 MPs and six peers
among the assembled delegates. But to their dismay, the Conven-

tion had barely commenced its deliberations when it was thrown
into turmoil by George Ogle's communication of a letter, pur-
portedly by Lord Kenmare, denying that Catholics sought the
vote. It subsequently emerged that the 'letter' was a forgery, but
Ogle's intervention effectively ensured that the Convention did
not afford the issue of Catholic enfranchisement a full and open
debate, while the efforts of figures loyal to Dublin Castle to 'per-
plex...proceedings and [to] create confusion' threatened to undermine the Convention in the public mind. But for Henry Flood,
who brought a measure of organisational and political realism to
proceedings, it is likely that Dublin Castle would have achieved its
object of 'bringing the meeting into contempt'. Instead, Flood
successfully negotiated approval of a moderate plan of reform.[22]
The most significant policy consequences of this were rejection of
the resolutions approved at Dungannon for annual parliaments
and a secret ballot, and the modification of several of the other
resolutions agreed in September. It was decided, for instance, to
make the controversial issue of borough reform more palatable by
proposing that 'decayed' boroughs could best be eradicated by a
combination of measures rather than by abolition. These included
geographical enlargement, the grading of the minimum number
of voters in boroughs according to density of Protestant population, and the restriction of the franchise to Protestant freeholders
worth forty shillings and to leaseholders worth £5 in the decayed
boroughs. Penalties against electoral corruption were also relaxed,
as was the ban on pension-holders sitting in parliament. By contrast, the decision to reduce elections to one day actually represented a strengthening of the resolutions sanctioned at Dungannon.[23]

The dilution of the Dungannon resolutions emphasised the
anxiety of the principals in the Convention to secure approval for
a plan that stood a realistic chance of winning parliamentary
approval. Despite this, moderates like Lord Charlemont and
James Stewart, MP for County Tyrone, were still uneasy. They
believed that the correct step procedurally was for the Convention's plan to be referred to county meetings and for the people to
petition parliament in support of it, but a majority of delegates
were determined that the resolutions should be presented to parliament immediately. This was the course adopted. But despite a
number of vigorous contributions in support of the measure in

the House of Commons on 29 November, there was a strong majority against reform. The reason many MPs gave for opposing the measure was that it was 'inconsistent' with the principles of liberty for the House of Commons 'to receive propositions at the point of a bayonet'. In truth, most were simply opposed to any modification of the political system. The bill was soundly defeated; with it, the Ulster Presbyterian initiative to make the Irish parliament more inclusive of the whole Protestant population came to a sudden, inglorious conclusion.[24]

The failure of reform 1783–1785

The decisive rejection by the Irish parliament of the Grand National Convention's reform bill in November 1783 tipped the scales within the reform movement in favour of the moderates, who believed that the correct and most likely means to reform the legislature was from within. Their strategy was to demonstrate the high level of popular support for reform by presenting petitions. Although their campaign won widespread support (twenty-two counties and eleven urban areas petitioned the House of Commons) in the winter and spring of 1783–4, they had no more success than the Grand National Convention. When they presented a reform bill in parliament in March, it was defeated by an equally decisive margin.[25]

The rejection of two reform bills within such a short space of time was a pivotal moment in eighteenth-century Irish politics. It signalled unequivocally that the Protestant aristocratic élite which dominated both houses of the Irish parliament was not prepared to share power with the middle classes, though they had recently profited from and welcomed their support on the issues of free trade and legislative independence. This response was particularly ill-received by radical middle-class interests in Dublin, who had kept a low public profile during 1783 and early 1784 in anticipation that the Irish parliament would respond favourably to the clear evidence that the people desired reform. The failure of the Volunteer campaign in 1783 disappointed them, but when the House of Commons chose, in the spring of 1784, to respond to the moderates' campaign in a like manner, and to refuse to approve a modest measure of protecting duties designed to relieve the hard-pressed population, their patience snapped. Led by Napper Tandy, John Binns and William Arnold, Dublin once

again moved to the forefront of Irish radicalism and reclaimed the
reform initiative which it had ceded to Ulster in the early 1780s.[26]

Napper Tandy's attempt to activate a campaign for radical parliamentary reform in the summer of 1784 took place against a
backdrop of acute civil disorder, as the Dublin populace attempted to enforce a non-importation agreement against foreign tex-
tiles. With the help of the leading Dublin and Ulster radicals,
Tandy secured approval for a series of resolutions asserting the
people's right 'to correct abuses in the representation whenever
such abuses shall have so increased as to deprive them of their
constitutional share in their own government' at a public meeting
of citizens of Dublin on 7 June. Resolutions specifically singled
out the need for more frequent elections and for more equal constituencies, and in an unambiguous affirmation of radicalism the
meeting approved a resolution professing their desire 'to extend
the right of suffrage to our Roman Catholic brethren' consonant
with the preservation of a Protestant constitution.[27] Their goals
established, the immediate priority of Tandy and his colleagues
was to identify a way forward. They did not have the support of
the Volunteer network available to the Ulster reformers in 1783;
therefore a subcommittee, established at the Dublin meeting to
oversee their campaign, called on the freeholders of every county
and the major urban areas to elect five delegates to a national
reform congress that would meet in Dublin on 23 October.[28]

Tandy and his colleagues were giving a hostage to fortune by
recommending extension of the franchise to Catholics. As
William Todd Jones explained, the radicals did so in the belief
that this would ensure them Catholic support, and that it would
create an unstoppable reform momentum. They did not reckon
on the scale of resistance, despite the fact that there was virtual
unanimity in radical circles that the franchise could not be ceded
to Catholics worth less than £50 per annum and that the Protestant constitution must be preserved. Yet the simple mention of
the subject cost them the support of many moderates whose
goodwill was vital to their success. The most costly defection was
that of Lord Charlemont. The 'Volunteer Earl' was totally
opposed to the enfranchisement of Catholics, and he used his
enormous influence to excite a strong public mood of opposition
throughout Ulster by opposing pro-Catholic resolutions at every
Volunteer review that he attended. Charlemont's actions exposed

the deeply held suspicions of Catholicism harboured by most Presbyterians and effectively destroyed any chance the radicals had of building a strong support base in Ulster.[29]

Elsewhere things did not proceed any more favourably. Harassed by the Castle's propaganda machine, the reformers' attempts to convene meetings of freeholders to elect delegates were resisted in every quarter. Encouraged by the Castle, aristocratic interests persuaded a total of twenty-three county sheriffs to decline the Dublin committee's request to convene freeholder meetings. Resistance was not so intense in urban areas, and although determined freeholders in a number of counties and towns successfully circumvented the powerful aristocratic alliances forged to resist delegate elections, they were unable to recreate the momentum of 1783. Indeed, Tandy and his allies were forced to take such extraordinary measures to overcome the legal obstacles put in their path in Dublin city that the moral, if not the actual, victory went to the Castle.[30]

This inability during the summer of 1784 to excite a sufficient level of public support for their programme ensured that the reform Congress was, in the words of Lord Earlsfort, 'a poor repetition' of the Grand National Convention. Only forty of the 95 delegates turned up, and while these included such notables as Henry Flood, William Sharman and Sir Edward Newenham, the Assembly of Delegates (as the Congress was renamed) did not possess moral authority to develop a plan of reform. A number of bland resolutions were approved, but there was no disguising the fact that the reform campaign of the Dublin radicals had wilted.[31] Unwilling to admit defeat, delegates approved a resolution calling on the 'counties of cities and great towns' that had not appointed delegates to do so before their next meeting, scheduled for 20 January.[32] In some respects, this was the triumph of optimism over common sense. But once the incubus of Catholic enfranchisement was removed, leading Ulster reformers re-entered the movement; encouraged by William Drennan's spirited *Letters of an Irish Helot*, some of the energy and enthusiasm so palpably absent in 1784 was rekindled.[33] At least ten counties and four urban areas convened to choose delegates in the winter of 1784–5 in defiance of threats of prosecution, and this ensured a fuller attendance at the January meeting of the Assembly of Delegates. However, the Assembly was still unable to provide the cause of reform with the direction

it so badly needed as the delegates failed to reconcile the conflicting aspirations of radicals like Hamilton Rowan, who urged a
secret ballot and the disfranchisement of rotten boroughs, and
moderates like Henry Flood, who wished the Assembly to endorse
the Grand National Convention's plan. It was agreed that they
should reconvene on 20 April, but by then it was too late; reform
in 1785 was a political irrelevance. Its decline was underlined by
the failure of Henry Flood's 1785 reform bill to excite more than
a flutter of excitement. William Drennan compared it rather aptly
'to a balloon left in the clouds...now precipitating from...auda-
cious height into vast vacuity'.[34]

Conclusion

The failure of so many reform initiatives between 1783 and 1785
was due primarily to the determined opposition of established
interests in Ireland. They were ably supported by the Irish administration at Dublin Castle and the British government in London
during most of this period; these guardians of the Anglo-Irish
nexus feared that any attempt to make the 'corrupt' Irish parliament more representative would endanger the Anglo-Irish connection. Even when the Prime Minister took a contrary view, as
William Pitt did in the autumn of 1784 when he advocated 'a
sober and rational' measure of reform for Protestants only (otherwise, he maintained, 'we may keep the parliament and lose the
people'), the resistance he met with in Dublin obliged him to give
way.[35] Most Irish officials, and the aristocratic interests that gave
them such resounding majorities in the House of Commons in
1784, identified reform with 'democracy', and 'democracy' with
'despotism', and they could not be persuaded to see it otherwise.
But the failure of reform in the 1780s cannot be explained solely
by reference to its opponents.[36] The reformers contributed to
their own downfall by allowing their differences on Catholic
enfranchisement to weaken their momentum. It is difficult to see
how they could have reconciled the widely divergent positions
taken on this question, given the deep historical suspicions of
Catholicism that informed the outlook of most Protestants and
Presbyterians, but as long as they remained divided on it, their
opponents could rest content that their 'ascendancy' was safe.

   That said, the failure of reform in 1783–5 was just another in
the long series of reversals experienced by the proponents of par-

liamentary reform in the late eighteenth century. The conservative revival of the mid-1780s gave reformers little opportunity to press their case during the remainder of the decade; yet it was during these years that William Drennan developed the ideas which made his contribution to the foundation of the United Irishmen so seminal.[37] This continuity is further illustrated by the fact that at least thirty of the members of the first Dublin United Irish society were involved in the reform or protectionist movements in 1784. Several of these – Wolfe Tone (who was on the Trinity College reform committee), Hamilton Rowan, Napper Tandy and Drennan – were key members of the society, while a number of others – Richard McCormick and John Keogh – were already playing a leading role in the Catholic Committee. The radicals of the 1790s certainly believed that they were continuing a struggle that was already several decades old. The *Northern Star*, for example, reprinted the Duke of Richmond's 1783 *Letter to Colonel Sharman* in 1794; the previous year the Volunteers of Belfast had linked their current activities with those of 1779 and 1783.[38] In view of this, and of the existence of a persistent reformist tradition in eighteenth-century Irish politics, the place of the United Irishmen in, and the debt they owed to, this tradition deserves more attention than it is usually afforded.

7

THE POLITICS OF DUBLIN CORPORATION: 1760–92

Jacqueline Hill

We are inclined to think of the setting up of the United Irishmen
as introducing a marked and immediate discontinuity into Irish
politics. On the crucial question of the extension of political rights
to Catholics the 1780s had seen some false starts, and after 1784
the decade was spent in largely inconsequential political skirmish-
ing on different issues. However, following the French Revolution, and the coming together of radicals both in Belfast and
Dublin to pursue parliamentary reform and political rights for
Catholics, the picture changed: 'Irish radicals', it has been
claimed, 'profoundly and fervently believed in religious liberty,'[1]
and as the Catholic question came onto the political and parliamentary agenda during 1792, the forces of radicalism and reaction
became increasingly polarised over this issue, with the slogan
'Protestant Ascendancy' serving as the touchstone. If an illustra-
tion of the new polarisation were needed, then Dublin Corporation appears to fit the bill perfectly. Even as the parliamentary
session opened in January 1792 (amid reports that Catholics were
meeting to press for further relief, and that such a measure would
be proposed), the Corporation, at its quarterly meeting on 20 January, agreed on a pre-emptive address to the king, urging him 'to
preserve the Protestant ascendancy inviolate'. A follow-up address
was adopted, directed at the city's MPs (Henry Grattan and Lord
Henry Fitzgerald), entreating them to use 'all your influence and
great abilities' to oppose any changes tending to 'subvert the
Protestant Ascendancy in our happy Constitution'.[2]

It is noteworthy that neither of these addresses provoked much
in the way of opposition within the Corporation itself. The lower
house, the 'city commons' on which sat representatives of the
twenty-five guilds,[3] had a reputation for radicalism and active support for Patriot causes, but on this occasion, when the address to

the king reached the lower house (it had originated with the board of aldermen) the response was muted. A motion that consideration of the address be postponed did go to a division, but it was lost by twenty-one votes to seventy-six. No challenge was offered to the address that was to be sent to the city MPs. Such an indifferent showing by the radicals did not go unnoticed in the opposition press.[4] Criticism centred on the absence from the meeting of the leading radical in the lower house, the man who had helped establish the Society of United Irishmen in the capital two months earlier, James Napper Tandy. Tandy's son James, together with other United Irishmen including Patrick Ewing (who like both Tandys represented the Merchants' guild) and George Binns,[5] ironmonger and member of the Smiths' guild, took part in the debate on the first address, but it was felt that the absence of Tandy senior had detracted from the opposition performance. Tandy was driven to issue a statement that he had been confined to bed by illness on the day in question, and that in any case his views on the Catholic question were well known.[6]

The passing of these addresses was also noted further afield. They provoked Edmund Burke, whose son Richard was then acting as agent for the Irish Catholics, to a damning criticism of the appeal to 'Protestant Ascendancy', a term which he believed, if not absolutely new, was now being pressed into service in a new and wholly reactionary spirit.[7] Worse was to follow. Later in the year the Corporation issued its *Letter to the Protestants of Ireland* calling on Protestants throughout the kingdom to rally behind 'Protestant Ascendancy', and clarifying that this meant, in the Corporation's view, the maintenance of a Protestant political establishment from top to bottom. In the meantime, a leading promoter of the January addresses, the silk merchant William Cope, had been overwhelmingly endorsed by the lower house in the Easter ballot for sheriffs to serve for the ensuing year.[8] Could any clearer indication be needed to show that the Corporation, lower house as well as aldermanic board, had lined up on the side of reaction?

Further examination of the ballot for sheriffs reveals some apparent inconsistencies. Ever since the Dublin City Corporation Act of 1760 (33 Geo. II, c.8) had removed the sole power of selecting the two sheriffs from the Lord Mayor and aldermanic board, the city commons had been entitled to participate in the selection process by nominating eight of its members for the office, out of which the aldermen then selected two. Sheriffs had many important duties, including overseeing the city courts and prisons, selecting juries, conducting parliamentary elections and chairing meetings of the city commons. Moreover, by virtue of selection for the office they became eligible for election as aldermen and ultimately as Lord Mayor. The office was therefore a key one, and (since nomination was by ballot) it commonly bore the hallmarks of a popularity contest. Those eligible for nomination were the 96 guild representatives; those taking part in the ballot included, besides the 96 themselves, the 'sheriffs peers', numbering at this time about three dozen, comprising those who had served the office of sheriff or had paid the fine (200 guineas) to avoid doing so.

It has already been noted that one of the eight nominees on this occasion was William Cope, who had introduced the motion to address the city MPs back in January. In March, following the rejection of a Catholic petition by the House of Commons, it was Cope who proposed the appointment of a city commons' committee to thank the MPs for their action, a move which attracted unfavourable comment from the radical press (the *Morning Post* deplored 'the biggoted [*sic*] Junto in the Common Council, appositely denominated the *Indigo Squad*').[9] Notwithstanding such criticism, Cope received a massive 104 votes (119 members were present, though the total number of votes cast [843] suggests that perhaps as few as 106 took part in the ballot).[10] But other even more notorious 'ascendancy' activists, such as John Giffard (of the Apothecaries' guild), George Sall (of the Smiths' guild), and the merchant Robert Powell, fared less well. Sall and Giffard received forty-nine and forty-eight votes respectively, well below those in the top eight. Powell received just three votes. These three men had all featured in a *Morning Post* blacklist of those who should on no account be nominated.[11] On the other hand, the top eight included four men warmly endorsed by the *Post*, including two United Irishmen: Napper Tandy (71 votes) and Patrick Ewing (62 votes).

That men with political views so apparently at odds as Cope and Tandy should both have been among the eight nominees could conceivably be explained by the presence in the city commons of both 'ascendancy' and radical factions; but in view of the voting system in which each member voted for eight nominees, it is impossible to avoid the conclusion that a substantial number (at least 56 and possibly many more) must have voted for *both* Cope and Tandy. It is the purpose of this paper to offer some suggestions as to how such a result may be explained. It will be argued that, notwithstanding the foundation of the United Irishmen, the prominence given to the Catholic question in the winter of 1791–2, and Burke's portentous reflections on the significance of the appeal to 'Protestant Ascendancy', civic politicians in Dublin, and even the radical press, were still very much engaged in fighting old battles.

Dublin Corporation politics before 1792

Dublin Corporation's politics in the eighteenth century was indelibly marked by the Glorious Revolution and its Williamite consequences in Ireland. One of the results of the revolution throughout the British dominions was to confirm and copperfasten Protestant control at central and local levels. A second result was to highlight the importance of corporate bodies as checks on the arbitrary power of the monarchy. This was originally a Whiggish doctrine, drawing on a mixed blend of corporate values, notions of the 'ancient constitution', and the neo-Harringtonian republican tradition with its ideas of constitutional 'balance' between the one, the few, and the many (or monarchy, aristocracy, and democracy, as it was often understood in the later 1600s and 1700s).[12] However, the integrity and independence of corporations was such a useful rallying cry against the court or against local oligarchies that it soon became a standard refrain for opposition groups of all kinds, even including Tories. In a political world that took inequality and hierarchy for granted, the doctrine was of value to certain relatively marginal groups precisely because it could legitimise opposition to oligarchy, without necessarily raising the dreaded spectre of 'mob rule' or 'levelling' tendencies.[13]

It was particularly this strand of political thinking on which Charles Lucas and James La Touche were able to draw in their campaigns for the reform of Dublin Corporation, beginning in the 1740s and bearing fruit, after mixed fortunes, in the 1760 Dublin City Corporation Act. Lucas had contended, with a certain amount of plausibility, that the oligarchical power enjoyed by the aldermen in Dublin Corporation was, at least in part, a legacy of Stuart misrule.[14] Since the introduction of the 'New Rules' for regulating Irish corporations in 1672, the Lord Mayor and twenty-four aldermen had enjoyed exclusive rights (subject to approval by the Irish Privy Council) in the selection of the Lord Mayor and sheriffs, as well as in the choosing of new recruits to their own body. They even selected the guild representatives on the city commons, from double returns supplied by the guilds. For Lucas, this represented 'a manifest tendency to a kind of *Aristocracy*, or rather, an *Oligarchy*, which is unnatural to and inconsistent with the Constitution of this *City*'.[15] The fact that he and La Touche were able to point to ancient charters, extending corporate rights not merely to the aldermen, but to 'the commons and citizens' (i.e. burgage-holders and property-owners rather than the population at large) impressed the commons and the city electorate (the 3–4,000 Protestant freemen of the guilds), if not the aldermen or the Administration. Although the campaign failed in the short term, the need for reform, in one of the most rapidly growing large cities in Europe, was inescapable, and the 1760 Act took some modest steps towards breaking down the aldermanic monopoly of civic privilege.

Even before this measure was passed, the city commons had been showing signs of greater assertiveness, manifested in such developments as keeping a separate journal, and improving their committee system. The Act naturally boosted its members' self-esteem by giving them a share in the selection of the Lord Mayor, sheriffs and aldermen, while the guilds gained the right of selecting their own representatives. In any case, for several decades their members had been accustomed to hear that independent corporations were the bastion of constitutional liberties, and with Charles Lucas as one of the city MPs from 1761 to 1771, it is not surprising to find that the guilds and the commons adopted a higher political profile, venturing to pass many resolutions of an opposition or 'Patriot' tendency on the main political issues of the day, such as support for shorter parliaments, free trade and Irish legislative independence.[16]

This more active political role produced its own problems. In particular, the commons developed the classic opposition preoccupation with the need to safeguard its own independence. During the 1760s and 1770s the number of jobs and the level of salaries in Corporation employment were increasing, but the commons took steps to deter freemen from seeking to represent their guilds on the Corporation as a stepping-stone to civic office. According to contemporary wisdom, derived from the neo-Harringtonian republican tradition, only those who enjoyed independent means were likely to possess the necessary 'virtue' to uphold the common good; constitutional freedom would be at risk if those who ought to be its guardians were themselves dependent placemen. The *Standing Rules and Orders of the Commons of the Common-Council of the City of Dublin* (1772) lists a number of resolutions which reflect this concern. Two examples may illustrate the point: anyone chosen by their guild as a representative on the commons 'who holds any place of employment, (to which a salary is annexed) or is a pensioner in, or under the Corporation of this city, he shall vacate the said employment, or lose said pension' (article xx); 'that from and after the 24th December, 1771, no member of the commons be elected to any place of profit or emolument in this city, or employed in any of the city-works' (article xxiii).[17] And there is some evidence to suggest that these rules were at least partly enforced.[18]

During the 1780s a new anxiety emerged. The Dublin Police Act of 1786 (26 Geo. III, c.24) created a number of salaried posts – divisional justices, police commissioners – in the gift of government, intended to be filled by members of the aldermanic board.[19] The Act was unpopular on many grounds; it was an opposition axiom that a paid, uniformed and armed police force under the control of the state was a grave threat to civil liberties; the new police, who replaced the old locally-controlled watch, were claimed to be officious and ineffective in their duties, and to cost the citizen dear by way of extra taxation. But above all, for the city commons the new arrangements raised the danger that the aldermen, and through them the Corporation as a whole, would succumb to the lure of government patronage and thereby irredeemably compromise the Corporation's role as a constitutional watchdog.

As the city commons' fears on this score began to crystallise, the selection of aldermen came in for close scrutiny. Since 1785 sheriffs' peers (i.e. those eligible for election to the aldermanic board) had been asked by the commons to sign a pledge not to accept any government place or pension if they were elected aldermen. In 1786 it emerged that signing this pledge had not deterred Alderman Richard Moncrieffe from accepting the post of divisional justice. Summoned before the city commons to explain his conduct, Moncrieffe asserted that he saw no incompatibility between his pledge and the office he now held, and indicated that he had no intention of resigning it (nor did he do so). Despite this setback, sheriffs' peers continued to give a verbal pledge to maintain their independence should they be elected to the aldermanic board.[20]

During the next two years, the campaign to repeal the Act, backed by parliamentary as well as civic opposition forces, gained strength from the manifest inadequacies of the new system. The police failed to prevent large-scale rioting on two occasions in 1787, and an attempt to suppress May Day disturbances in 1789 ended ignominiously with the police having to be rescued by the army.[21] Even the aldermen began to display doubts, especially those in contention for the mayoralty (which usually but not invariably went by seniority). Since the approval of the city commons was needed to endorse the choice of the alderman for Lord Mayor, it was a matter of prudence on the part of candidates for the office to distance themselves from the new police system. In May 1789 John Exshaw, the most senior member of the board, resigned his post as divisional justice before the quarterly meeting at which he was, as expected, chosen as Lord Mayor for the ensuing year. At Michaelmas, his inauguration as Lord Mayor inspired the city commons to commit themselves to keeping up the campaign against the Act, pledging themselves (with only one dissentient voice) not to vote for any person 'to be chief magistrate of, or representative in parliament for this city, who holds place or employment in an establishment so universally odious to the public in general'. The aldermanic board, however, negatived this resolution, as well as a similar one passed by the commons at its quarterly meeting in January 1790.[22]

It could hardly therefore have come as a surprise when, at the Easter quarterly meeting in April 1790, the city commons refused to approve Alderman William James (next in line according to seniority) as Lord Mayor elect, for he was a police commissioner. An epic battle ensued, which lasted for almost four months.[23] During that period the commons rejected all the names submitted to them by the aldermen, defied the Privy Council (which ruled in favour of James), took the extraordinary step of holding a meeting without being summoned by the Lord Mayor, and chose the most junior of the aldermen, Henry Howison, to be Lord Mayor elect, claiming that, since the board had failed to send down a name acceptable to them, it was their duty, under the 1760 Act, to proceed to an election. A general election took place in May; since the parliamentary opposition had thrown its weight behind the commons, eulogising corporate freedom as the key to constitutional liberty, the two opposition candidates, Henry Grattan and Lord Henry Fitzgerald, were triumphantly returned, receiving twice as many votes as the aldermanic candidates. When the Privy Council stuck to its decision in favour of Alderman James, the commons threatened to withhold his salary as Lord Mayor and to retake the Mansion House into the Corporation's possession. At last, in August, James gave up the struggle. He resigned as Lord Mayor elect, and his colleagues bowed to the inevitable and sent down Howison's name to the commons for their approval, which was duly given by 97 votes to six. Thus the danger that 'the first local Corporation in the Kingdom [would come] under the control and direction of the minister' (as the guild of Merchants put it), or that Dublin would become 'an Aldermanic borough' (as the Smiths' guild feared) was averted, for the time being at least, and the commons and guilds returned to the attack on the police system itself, an attack which continued until the Act was repealed in 1795.[24]

One other point is worth making in connection with this struggle by the city commons to defend the principle of independence. Corporation records show that those members most forward in the campaign were rewarded with high votes in the annual shrieval elections. More than anyone else, that meant James Napper Tandy. Between 1785 and 1791 Tandy was regularly among the eight nominees for sheriff; he was never out of the top three, and on three occasions he headed the poll. Patrick Ewing, also closely connected with the campaign, fared almost equally well; over the same period he was invariably among the eight nominees, and usually in the top three.[25] For obvious reasons, neither of them was actually chosen for the shrieval office by the aldermen. By contrast, the few who were active in the aldermanic interest (notably John Giffard) did not figure among the nominees chosen by the commons.

If these events, illustrating the city commons' and guilds' exertions in the Patriot cause at this period, have not received the attention they deserve,[26] the reason may well be that for all the softening of attitudes that had taken place since the early 1700s, a sectarian dimension persisted in civic thought. Back in 1770, when the Bishop of Derry, Frederick Hervey, was about to renew his campaign to find a formula for an oath that would allow Catholics to testify their allegiance and thereby obtain some relief from the penal laws, both houses of the Corporation joined in a resolution to grant him honorary freedom of the city for, among other things, 'his attention to the church and making of converts'.[27] (It is only fair to add that the Bishop's own motives for the campaign were somewhat ambiguous.)[28] Soon afterwards, the Corporation began to signal its approval of converts by granting freedom of the city to applicants from a gentry or professional background who had 'renounced the errors of the church of Rome and embraced the Protestant religion' (again, the approval of both houses was necessary for such freedoms to be granted).[29]

Protestant claims to regulate Catholic trade had been completely abandoned by the late 1770s, and when the penal laws relating to ownership of land, education and freedom of worship were relaxed in 1778 and 1782, both houses of the Corporation retrospectively approved these steps, but they firmly indicated that political rights were quite another matter.[30] This was a direct snub to Tandy, who in the course of preparations for the reform congress of 1784 had tentatively raised the question of Catholic political rights, but had been forced to abandon it for lack of support. He was present at the quarterly meeting which adopted the address opposing such rights, but made no move to oppose it.[31] Nor is there evidence in surviving guild records to suggest that he had any support on this issue from the guilds; after 1784, the question dropped out of sight, not to be revived until 1792.

Yet the Corporation frequently stressed its commitment to 'civil and religious liberty', and this does, on the face of it, suggest hypocrisy. The problem arises because this phrase is interpreted according to modern, rather than contemporary, assumptions. During the eighteenth century it was still widely acknowledged in Protestant countries that the two main barriers to constitutional and religious freedom were arbitrary monarchy and 'priestcraft' – meaning the usurpation by a clerical caste of functions properly exercised by the laity and the civil power. Only an Erastian religious settlement in which the church was prepared to recognise its proper subordination to the state could offer the prospect of the full civil and religious liberty that was one of the fundamental rights of man.[32] It was further generally acknowledged, by many thinkers of the Enlightenment from John Locke onwards, that the established churches of England, Ireland and the other British dominions fulfilled this crucial condition.

The position of the Catholic church was much more ambiguous. The Papacy had historic claims to temporal as well as spiritual power over Christian princes and their subjects; although these claims had not been acted upon since the wars of religion, the Vatican was reluctant to abandon them. There were sections within the international Catholic church, such as the French Gallicans, who took the view that the church should properly come under the supervision of the state. And the Papacy itself suffered setbacks in the second half of the eighteenth century, being forced in 1773 to dissolve the Jesuits who had been strong contenders for Papal claims. But the matter was still contentious. That was why, even as late as the 1770s, the task of devising an oath which Irish Catholics might take to testify their allegiance to a Protestant king was fraught with difficulty; also, why several Irish Catholic bishops disapproved of the oath, and why the Vatican, though it did not actually condemn the oath that came into operation in 1774, did not commend it either.[33] This created serious difficulties for lay Irish Catholics who naturally wanted the abolition of the entire penal code. Many were individually prepared to adopt a 'Gallican' view of church/state relations, but obviously they could not speak for the head of their church. Some of them began to toy with what was still, before the nineteenth century, a comparatively rare and unorthodox position, even for reformers: the doctrine that was to become one of the hallmarks of nineteenth-century liberalism, the separation of religion and politics, of church and state.[34] This brought them closer to that section among the Protestant dissenters in Ireland who were influenced by United States developments in the 1780s, and especially the new constitution of 1789, which involved the separation of church and state. By 1792 all this had made only a limited impact on Dublin Protestants, almost nine-tenths of whom were members of the established Church of Ireland.[35]

The significance of Corporation politics

Returning to the events of early 1792, with the benefit of hind-sight, we know that the appeal to 'Protestant Ascendancy' (though not new) indicated that the political establishment, led by Dublin Castle, intended to make a strong stand against the British government's bid to capture Irish Catholics for the cause of counter-revolution by granting them political rights.[36] We also know that this stand had some success in 1792, and that 'Protestant Ascendancy' went on to become one of the great divisive slogans of the revolutionary era. It is doubtful, however, whether matters appeared so clearly to most members of the Dublin city commons, or even to the opposition press. As already noted, their response to the Corporation's 'ascendancy' addresses was muted. That was because Protestant Ascendancy (or 'Protestant control') described a condition that most of them took for granted. The real political battleground lay elsewhere; on the issue of the new police, and of corporate independence.

The *Hibernian Journal*, for instance, gave a good deal of space to the arguments of the radicals against the addresses, but only became really animated in reporting an amendment to the royal address proposed by Patrick Ewing.[37] Ewing suggested that since an address to the king was a relatively rare event, members should seize the opportunity to urge his majesty to abolish 'that odious, expensive, ineffectual and corrupt system, the police establishment'. The *Journal* waxed lyrical over this proposal but, after reporting an extended debate, the paper regretted to inform its readers that Ewing had been prevailed upon to withdraw the amendment, 'and thus fell one of the best concerted measures ever suggested for obtaining relief from this obnoxious and insupportable system'. As the Easter quarterly meeting approached, the *Morning Post* urged the city commons to stand firm against the police system, and suggested that raising the cry of 'Protestant Ascendancy' was nothing but a diversionary tactic to increase '*police influence*'. The paper warned that 'the police party in the commons hug themselves in secret exultation at the imagined downfall of Mr Tandy's popularity — and the hope of regaining their corrupt influence in the common council'.[38] In the *Hibernian Journal*, 'An Old Free Citizen' commended a panel of nominees for sheriff, on the grounds that they had the correct views on the police system:

England is free, Ireland is only nominally so. Why? The people here are not united, not unanimous. Let us then think and act like men. Let the citizens of Dublin give an example. Let the extermination of the Police be their first object. Let not the officers of that body share the city honours, and let the inhabitants, session after session, petition Parliament against an institution, founded in corruption, and continued for the sake of patronage...[39]

According to this correspondent, five of the guilds had instructed their representatives to vote against any candidate for Lord Mayor who either held, or had held, a police post. Furthermore, when those members of the city commons in the 'Independent' interest held a meeting to conduct a straw poll ahead of the Easter assembly,[40] the result accurately predicted the results of the ballot itself: the eight nominees for sheriff in 1792 contained no member who had been active in support of the police. Two aldermen with police posts were rejected for Lord Mayor in favour of Alderman Smith, who had no police connection.[41]

There remains the case of William Cope. Granted that the eyes of the city radicals and the opposition press were fixed on the issue of the police rather than on 'Protestant Ascendancy' (and Cope had no record as a police supporter), nevertheless, from the outset, members of the commons had been urged not to endorse the 'ascendancy' appeal. Cope had been very prominent in promoting that appeal, and indeed was later to claim that he had done so at the prompting of John Lees, the head of the Irish Post Office, thus confirming contemporary suspicions of Castle/Corporation collusion.[42] But his role evidently did him no harm when it came to the ballot. On the contrary, he received a massive endorsement.

Once again, the explanation for Cope's success must be sought in contemporary preoccupations. Cope had never attracted the personal abuse directed at other ascendancy activists such as John Giffard, thought to be dependent on Castle patronage for his livelihood, or George Sall, the buttonmaker whose talk of 'Protestant Deesendancy' and 'Harry Stocracy' was held up to ridicule.[43] Nor did he figure on blacklists of those who should not be nominated for sheriff. There were various reasons for this. He was a wealthy merchant, importing supplies for the silk and cotton industries; like Tandy, he was a founder member of the Chamber of Commerce, set up to promote the interests of merchants (of all religious persuasions), a member of the Ouzel Galley Society, and of the Dublin Society.[44] In all these respects, he was the sort of man the radicals wished to see elected to responsible civic posts: possessed of independent means, he would be above the temptations of patronage and 'corruption', and accordingly able to fulfil his proper constitutional role. Most importantly, he was not identified with the police. And on this occasion he was prepared to offer more. Direct evidence is lacking,[45] but it seems likely that both he and the tobacconist Lundy Foot (who received an equally overwhelming endorsement in the ballot at Easter 1792, and who had no record as an activist of any kind) had made the commons an offer they could not refuse. If nominated, and subsequently chosen to serve as sheriff by the aldermen, they would decline the office and pay the fine of two hundred guineas, which by custom went to the Corporation's favourite charity, the King's Hospital or Blue Coat school, recently rebuilt and badly in need of funds.[46] The commons would have lost nothing, since they would simply proceed to another ballot; and that, in the end, is what happened. A subsequent ballot for nominees (in May) produced a list which was even more satisfactory to the reformers: it contained neither police nor 'ascendancy' activists, and three United Irishmen.[47] The old political battles were still to the fore.

In conclusion, it is apparent that the ideological legacy meant that it was always going to be difficult to reconcile Dublin Protestants to the idea of Catholics as equals in the political nation. In early April 1792 the *Morning Post* reported a dreadful fight that had taken place in a public house near Dame Court between two 'chairmen' (carriers of sedan chairs) over religion, which had apparently broken out when one (an ex-servant of the Church of Ireland Archbishop of Dublin) announced that popery was a religion for knaves and fools.[48] Nevertheless, Dublin Protestants in general were relatively confident and secure; they still represented up to 40 per cent of Dublin's huge population, and still dominated the world of commerce as well as the professions. And there were signs that the old exclusive attitudes were changing; a few days earlier the same paper had welcomed a decision by the Protestants of St Catherine's parish to donate £60 alike to the Protestant and Catholic lower clergy of the parish.[49] Given time, perhaps, further adjustments would have taken place. But in 1792, time was not on the side of gradual adjustments. The pressure of international events was setting a new polarised political agenda:

for or against the French Revolution, for or against the government, for or against the extension of political rights to Catholics.

8

BURKE AND IRELAND

R. B. McDowell

Edmund Burke spent the first twenty years of his life in Ireland and was bound to be significantly influenced by his Irish background: his home in Dublin, a large city with many facets; his Quaker school in County Kildare; his years in Trinity College, a very efficient educational institution; and his visits to his mother's Catholic relations in Munster, affectionate kinsmen, living in rural surroundings which delighted him and where Irish was widely spoken – had Burke this in mind when he wrote that 'most ignorant and barbarous nations have frequently excelled in similitudes, comparisons, metaphors and allegories',[1] figures of speech which he himself used very effectively. It was in Munster that he must have been struck by the plight of his Catholic relations, country gentlemen deprived of the privileges which went with their status, and begun to feel that abhorrence of oppression which later he wrote 'is interwoven in my very nature'.[2] But when considering Burke's Irish background it is important to keep in mind that many of its components were English – even if English with a difference. The Irish world in which he grew up had numerous ties with Great Britain and was proud to share the British cultural heritage – religious, political and social. The Church of Ireland, 'our Anglo-Irish Church',[3] conformed closely to the Church of England, the Irish constitution was modelled on the British, Dublin bookshops were crammed with British books and magazines and Trinity, where the classics occupied much of the undergraduate's time, revered Newton and Locke.

In any event, from 1750, when he left to keep his terms in the Middle Temple, Burke was based in England. When a sensitive man changes his geographical and social environment, it is always tempting to look for tensions in his inner life – what is sometimes called his struggle for identity. But Burke shows no obvious signs of strain. Coming from an anglicised background he fitted easily enough into English life. The London publishers were encouraging. His Sabine farm was in Buckinghamshire. When he entered the House of Commons, he found himself in an assembly in which there were many Scotsmen, Welshmen, Irishmen and provincial Englishmen, and if his brogue was noticeable, much more so were his spectacles. With the great landed magnates who formed the core of his party his relations were very happy. He respected their rank, public spirit and broad acres. They admired his great gifts and very gracefully subsidised him. Burke naturally was aware that he might be involved in a conflict of interests between Ireland, 'the place of his nativity', and Great Britain, which had taken him into her bosom and raised him from nothing to a seat in the national council.[4] In such a situation his course was clear, either to resign his seat (a very unlikely step) or to consider British interests as paramount. But Burke trusted the problem would not arise. Great Britain and Ireland were both parts of the same mighty empire, 'extended under Providence by our virtues and fortunes' and inspired by British liberty.[5] Any measure which benefited Ireland would ultimately serve England and Burke wrote near the end of his life: 'I cannot conceive how a man can be a genuine Englishman without being at the same time an Irishman...[and] I think the same sentiments ought to be reciprocal on the part of Ireland.'[6]

Though Burke regarded Ireland 'as the country to which I am bound by my earliest instincts',[7] by 1772 he had, he wrote, lost interest in Irish politics; 'the whole chart of the country begins to wear out in my memory'. Shortly after he declared he had 'lost the true practical notion of the country'.[8] Admittedly forty years after he had left Ireland Burke asserted: 'I think that for a resident in England I know the country I was born in.'[9] But reliance on memory (that defective, highly selective instrument) has its dangers, and in his later years Burke may have had in some respects a better balanced picture of America or India than of Ireland.

As a very active member of the House of Commons and an Irishman he naturally delivered his opinions on those Irish issues which arose at Westminster – opinions which were sometimes out of alignment with prevalent trends in Ireland. A generous imperialist and early free trader, he hoped in the 1760s that Ireland might be 'hooked' into the imperial commercial system,[10] and he

was anxious to remove gradually the restraints on Irish trade. In
1777 he was prominent amongst the group of MPs who pressed
for trade concessions to Ireland, and in letters addressed to his
apprehensive Bristol constituents he enunciated what was to
become a truism in liberal circles, that *laissez-faire* was enlightened and benevolent self-interest. In May 1779 he was pressing
for the formation of 'a well considered plan' for regeneration of
Anglo-Irish commercial relations, adding that he did not think
'the roots of the Irish discontent to be struck very deep'.[11] He
soon received a severe shock – the Irish agitation for 'Free Trade'
developed on menacing lines and before the close of the year,
North, acting with uncharacteristic speed, introduced a programme of sweeping concessions. This threw Burke and his
fellow Whigs off balance. They could not oppose and were reluctant to commend. Burke, in his own words, 'sat sullen and
silent'.[12] This reserved approbation aroused resentment in Ireland
and Burke tried to disarm his critics by his *Letter to Thomas Burgh*,
a brilliant exposition of how policy could evolve as the result of
conflicting pressures. The episode left him with the impression
that 'in my countrymen there is a jealousy, a soreness, and readiness to take offence, as if they were the most helpless and impo-
tent of mankind, and yet…a boisterousness in their resentment, as
if they had been puffed up with the highest prosperity and
power'.[13] Six years later Burke, as an imperial free trader, might
have been expected to have approved of Pitt's Commercial
Propositions, but the Whig opposition was smarting under a
humiliating defeat at the polls and Burke contented himself and
his party by vigorously criticising details in Pitt's plan.

Turning to Anglo-Irish constitutional relations, in the 1760s
and 1770s Burke seems to have been quite satisfied with the status
quo. In 1775 he declared that with Ireland, 'a great and flourishing kingdom' possessing 'a separate but not independent legislature', everything was 'sweetly and harmoniously disposed for the
conservation of English dominion and the communication of
English liberties'.[14] He dismissed Lucas, one of the first 'patriots',
as a mountebank,[15] and he condemned two innovatory proposals –
George Grenville's scheme of imperial defence which would have
increased Ireland's tax burden, and the Absentee tax of 1773
which he believed would weaken the links, economic, social and
political, between Great Britain and Ireland. In Ireland opposition

to the tax emphasised that it might prove the prelude to a general land tax. On occasion he approached Irish issues from a Westminster standpoint. The prorogation of 1772 illustrated the increasing influence of the executive which the Rockingham Whigs were struggling to diminish; the use of the Volunteers (which Burke pointed out were an illegal force) demonstrated the ineptitude of North's administration. In 1775 he proposed that the Irish parliament might intervene to redress the balance at Westminster by refusing to assist Great Britain in the opening stages of the American war and 'interpose a friendly mediation'. But the Irish parliament, displaying 'a grandeur of meanness', refused to act as 'the guardian angel of the whole empire', the role assigned to it by Providence and Burke.[16] Two years later, in 1777, Burke made a second unsuccessful attempt, through Charles James Fox who was touring Ireland, to enlist influential Irish politicians in the anti-war camp.

In July 1781 he thankfully pronounced 'the Irish sea of tempestuous memory to be smooth as a mill pond',[17] so he must have been unpleasantly surprised when in April 1782, just after he took office, the new ministry was confronted with a determined demand for Irish legislative independence. In debate he argued that before anything was granted 'there should be a reciprocal compact between the two countries'[18] – the policy at first supported by Fox – and when the Declaratory Act was repealed, he hoped that Ireland would take the initiative in proposing that there should be a negotiated 'clear and solid settlement', between Great Britain and Ireland.[19] However, from the summer of 1782 he accepted Irish parliamentary independence, hoping that 'mutual affection will do more for mutual help and mutual advantage between the two kingdoms than any ties of artificial connection'. But he deplored a policy which took Ireland 'out of the constitutional protection of the empire'.[20] Even in writing to Grattan he referred to 'the great but perilous blessings of liberty and independence'; he assumed the Lord Lieutenant would be appointed by the British cabinet and he did not cease to assert that since 'the closest connection between Great Britain and Ireland, is essential to the well being...of the two kingdoms...I humbly conceive that the whole of the superior, and what I should call *imperial* politics should have its residence here...and that Ireland...ought politically to look up to Great Britain in all matters of peace and war, in all those points to be guided by her, and in a word with her to live and die'.[21] Moreover he was insistent that Great Britain was not to blame for all of Ireland's ills. They originated in Ireland and the worst fault British statesmen could be accused of in relation to Ireland was that they wished to 'hear of it and of its concerns as little as possible'.[22] Burke's lack of enthusiasm for Irish legislative independence was intensified from the beginning of the 1790s by his dislike of the ultra-Protestants whom he thought controlled the Irish administration. But it also reflected his metropolitan attitude, the outlook of a man who lived in London and was very proud of his Westminster seat.

Burke was profoundly concerned with one Irish domestic issue, a question with wide implications – Catholic/state relations. Not only did he deeply sympathise with his Catholic kinsmen but the penal laws ran counter to his conception of society, his religious feelings and his sense of justice, nourished by his study of the law (civil and common) which he saw as the embodiment of wisdom and experience. For Burke, society was a complex organism, composed of individuals, orders, corporations, professions, 'a partnership of all science, all art, of every virtue and perfection', held together by beliefs, laws, conventions, 'imperceptible habits',[23] laudable customs, principles and prejudices, instituted by 'the awful author of our being',[24] the 'Captain of our Salvation',[25] for the guidance, restraint and happiness of mankind. A vital, unifying, correcting force in society was religion – the established church in England, the Catholic church in France, Brahminism in India[26] – each contributing to making 'a people happy and a government flourishing'.[27] Burke's recognition of the social value of a variety of religious experiences accorded with his own theological position. As a young man he had read the principal theological writings 'on all sides', published during the previous two centuries and, 'confused and confounded',[28] had remained a loyal Anglican 'by choice, taste and education', strongly attached to the Church of England, a church which 'harmonises with our civil constitution and with the frame and fashion of our society'.[29] But though by preference a Protestant and an Anglican, he was convinced that all Christian bodies professed the same hope and that each Christian denomination had some merits – indeed he even had a certain respect for 'the Synagogue, the Mosque and the Pagoda'.[30] Concerned for 'Christianity at large',[31] Burke was acutely aware of the strong and dangerous currents in contemporary thought which were weakening the hold of orthodox Christianity on European intellectual life. His first published work was an attempt to discredit Bolingbroke's deism and he was anxious that Christians should unite in defence of their faith against a philosophy which, in 'this unenlightened age',[32] renders 'odious or contemptible that class of virtues which restrain the appetite'.[33] The penal laws accentuated divisions among Christians and weakened three great social ligaments – religion, the family and property. By penalising the Catholic clergy they brought religion into contempt. They attacked the authority of the father over his children and the husband over his wife, and by interfering with the descent and purchase of property and by forbidding Catholic investment in real property, they threatened private property, the great guarantee of individual liberty and 'the first origin, the continued bond and the ultimate end' of society.[34]

From the outset of his political career, Burke was a fervent supporter of Catholic relief and since he was not a Catholic his advocacy was distinguished by the passionate, and at times uncritical enthusiasm of an outsider who has committed himself to a cause or a people. He began his long struggle on behalf of the Irish Catholics when he returned to Ireland in 1761 as private secretary to the Under-Secretary in an administration which was favourably disposed to the Catholics, who themselves were making tentative efforts to obtain relief. Burke drafted a petition for the Catholic Committee and prepared a devastating analysis of the penal laws, either for publication or to act as an *aide-mémoire*. Then he underwent a traumatic experience. He was shocked by the reaction of the authorities and the Protestant gentry to the Whiteboy disturbances in Munster. Burke accepted 'the punishment of low people for the offences usual amongst low people',[35] but he was deeply disquieted by the harassing of Catholic landed gentlemen, large farmers, professional men and opulent merchants who were threatened by 'forged conspiracies, and judicial murders'.[36] His interpretation of the disturbances may have been distorted – he overstressed the sectarian aspect, underrated the importance of economic factors, and exaggerated the severity of the measures taken to restore order – but the episode made a profound impression on him and coloured his views on the attitude of the Protestant ruling world to the Irish Catholics. Nevertheless, in spite of

what Burke termed 'the force of powerful and inveterate prejudice',[37] the Catholic Relief Acts in 1778 and 1782 removed many
of the disabilities and restored 'to civil society so many hundred
thousands of human creatures', leaving them free to enjoy the
fruits of 'their industry, skill and good economy'.[38]

When at the beginning of the 1790s the Irish Catholics began
to ask for a fresh instalment of relief, the French Revolution had
changed the political landscape and Burke was now the renowned
champion of the traditional European order against the 'mingled
scene of crime, of vice, of disorder, of folly, of madness'.[39] To
Burke, who once said that 'opinions influence the passions and the
passions govern man',[40] the Revolution was a doctrinal struggle
which would decide the shaping and shape of European society.
To resist the revolutionary contagion it was necessary to rally in
defence of the established order and civilisation all men of sound
principle. The Irish Catholics, whether 'the old gentlemen who
still retain their religion and estates' or 'the new race of Catholics
who have risen by their industry and their good fortune to considerable opulence',[41] were clearly, from their 'religious principles,
church polity and habitual discipline',[42] natural conservatives. So
in Burke's opinion it was urgently necessary to scale down the disabilities and settle 'all descriptions of people [in Ireland] upon the
bottom of one protecting and constitutional system' so that they
could make head against 'the common enemy of the human
race'.[43] The Catholics themselves started a vigorous agitation for
relief in 1791 and from then on Ireland became for Burke a major
preoccupation. He published a pamphlet advocating Catholic
relief, and at least 95 of his surviving letters written between 1792
and 1797 deal in whole or in part with 'the melancholy subject of
Ireland'.[44] In these letters powerful argument, wise apophthegms,
flashes of perception are blended with outbreaks of vehement
indignation, black humour and that excessive overstatement
which both provides a release for the emotions and enables a
polemicist to drive home his point. Written at a time of crisis they
reflect both Burke's mature political judgment and his spontaneous, often exasperated, reactions to the course of events.

Because he believed that circumstances, not abstract theory,
dictated what political privileges should be granted to dissenters,
Burke considered that disabilities should be abolished 'leisurely,
by degrees', and 'portion by portion' in 'a progressive way' which

might conciliate the predominant party – the 'pacification of Ireland', he wrote, 'is my great object and whether this is obtained by a little more or a little less on the one side or the other is of little importance'. In 1792 he strongly supported Catholic enfranchisement and from 1795 he contended that Catholics should be admitted to parliament. But he stressed that for the foreseeable future, given the existing electoral structure, which he did not wish to change, Protestant parliamentary predominance would continue. Presumably Catholic property, especially landed property, would in time exert its legitimate influence, but this would be a very gradual process. Burke once remarked, 'a great part of my idea of reform is to operate gradually'. After all, if the Catholics constituted 'the great mass of the people', the members of the Established Church held 'most of the ultimate and superior property of the kingdom' and formed 'the leading part of the nation'. It perhaps should be added that Burke did not expect the Irish Catholic clergy to have much political influence. By training and discipline they were admirably fitted for the pastoral care of their largely poor and uneducated flock. But the administration of the sacraments – to a great extent a matter of routine – did not confer coercive power, and 'if the Catholic clergy should be so unwise as to meddle in political matters...they would lose the little consideration they possess'.[45] Burke probably derived his views on the place of the Catholic clergy in Irish society from his Munster relations, Catholic gentlemen who respected the clergy but felt they should be chary about moving out of their own special sphere.

Convinced that his conciliatory policy was morally right and politically expedient, Burke was angered by the reluctance of a large and influential section of Irish Protestant opinion to grant further relief. This opposition is understandable. After the Relief Acts of 1778 and 1782, any significant concessions to the Catholics would involve power-sharing; and Irish Protestants who had read the *Reflections on the Revolution in France* – there had been eight Dublin editions and the author had received an honorary degree from Trinity – must have been well aware of the danger that concessions might set in motion a progression of events which would lead quickly to institutional and social disintegration. Quarrels amongst allies can be remarkably acerbic and Burke was intensely exasperated by the failure of Irish Protestant conserva-

tives to perceive the difference between reform and innovation
and by their obstinate refusal to accept that the preservation of
the existing order depended on a flexible response to pressure. As
he put it, 'I would have the door opened, and not broken open.'[46]
He vented his anger on the Irish administration and its supporters, 'the Castle Ascendancy', 'the jobbing ascendancy', 'insane
tyrants', who 'considered the outlawry of the great mass of the
people as an unalienable maxim' of government, and who by their
'innumerable corruptions, frauds, oppressions and follies' were
promoting Jacobinism by encouraging people to think that the
interests of the few and the many were incompatible.[47] Burke was
a master of the grotesque and his picture of the men in power in
Ireland, officials and politicians, who in fact combined public
spirit, a measure of self-interest and a strong hankering after a
familiar political pattern, is remarkably black. Moreover when he
refers, as he frequently does, to how the Catholic community was
oppressed he seems to forget how he had rebuked those who
spoke of France under the old régime 'as if they were talking of
Persia bleeding under the ferocious sword of Taehmas Kouli
Khan'.[48] And it should be added that in a more relaxed moment in
1794, he described Irish politicians as 'cheerful, companionable
and hospitable'.[49]

During 1792 he was so committed to the Catholic cause and so
irritated by the attitude of the Irish conservatives that anomalous-
ly he praised the addresses issued by the Dublin Society of United
Irishmen as 'rational, manly and proper' – except in respect to the
British connection.[50] He approved of Todd Jones's *Letter*,
although he wished some things had been left out;[51] he was
delighted to hear from his son, Richard, whose knowledge of Ireland was recently acquired and highly biased, that the northern
dissenters were not disaffected to the constitution and were content to let the established church 'stand as an institution of state';
and after the Catholic petition was rejected by the House of
Commons in February, he declared that 'only a strange man, a
strange Christian and a strange Englishman would not rather see
Ireland, a free, flourishing, happy, *Catholic* country though not
one Protestant existed in it, than an enslaved, beggared, insulted,
degraded Catholic country as it is'.[52] This was a rhetorical expression of momentary frustration. A year later Burke was very
pleased with the Catholic Relief Act of 1793 which, by enfranchis-

ing the Catholics, 'restored three million citizens to their king and
country', and he was confident that if means were taken to 'abate
the spirit of jobbery in the principal people...that mutinous spirit
which is the very constitution of the lower part of our compatriots' would be defeated.[53] All was going well and it seemed would
go better when in 1794 Fitzwilliam, Burke's friend and pupil, was
designated Lord Lieutenant.

The Fitzwilliam débâcle came at a time when Burke was subjected to incessant stress and strain. He had lost his only son and
his health was bad. Shortly after Fitzwilliam's return from Ireland,
the Hastings impeachment ended with the accused acquitted on
all charges; the grand coalition against France began to fall to
pieces; and worst of all, the British government towards the close
of 1795 publicly announced that it was willing to negotiate with
France. 'To whatever part of the compass I turn my eyes,' Burke
wrote, 'I see nothing but difficulty and disaster.'[54] Ireland was certainly included in his range of vision and added greatly to his
depression. From the end of 1795, it was clear that Ireland, 'not
the least critical part of the empire',[55] might become the target of a
French expeditionary force. In Ireland there were the United
Irishmen who 'without any regard to religion club all kinds of discontent together' and it was impossible, Burke wrote, 'not to be
frightened at the regularity, the order and the combined movement of which so many persons, low and illiterate in appearance,
are capable'.[56] More painful was the danger that the Catholics
might be 'Jacobinised'.[57] In May 1795 he noticed the tone of a
great Dublin Catholic meeting was 'wholly Jacobinical'. He was
afraid that the Catholic leadership might be inclined 'to melt their
cause into the general mass of uncertain discontent' and to join a
national movement.[58] By 1796 he had an idealistic programme for
the Irish Catholics. He already hoped that the Catholic church in
Ireland, unendowed and without the trappings of an establishment, would exhibit 'the image of a primitive Christian church'.
Now he wanted the whole Catholic community to display a fusion
of political quietism and Puritanism. They should show a greater
'indifference to political objects', keeping their distance from
those who would snub them, 'their proud Lords' and the seditious
who would use and then victimise them. They should cultivate
self-reliance and 'change as much as possible those expensive
modes of living and that dissipation to which our countrymen in

general are so much addicted'. 'If I had youth and strength', he
wrote, 'I would myself go over to Ireland to work on that plan.'[59]

Burke was alarmed and disgusted that in a period of intense
danger, power and responsibility should remain in the hands of
the Irish administration, 'the little blackguardly clique', that 'low
order of things', 'a very minute part of that small faction', which
though totally ignorant of 'the art of governing' had managed to
persuade the British government that the only hold England had
on Ireland was to keep them in power.[60] By 1796 'that knot of low
jobbers' was relying on military force to maintain order, 'subject-
ing the lives and liberties of the whole nation to Luttrell'.[61] Burke
believed that disorder must be punished and he did not object to
'the use of the military arm in its proper place and order' (he even
granted that there might be in its use 'lapses', 'which will happen
to human infirmity at all times and in the exercise of all power').[62]
But he was quick to denounce the oppression of 'the poor people'
and to insist that the upholders of order must act in accordance
with the law – if the law was too weak it could be amended but if
it were disregarded the people would be taught to despise it, and
if parliament failed to keep a close watch over the exercise of
power, the representative system, which Burke revered, would be
brought into contempt.[63]

By the close of 1796 Burke was forced to accept that the disor-
ders in Ireland were a war between 'property and no property,
between the high and the low, the rich and the poor'. It was a situation in which the government must side with property and use
all its resources to maintain order.[64] It was also a situation in
which Burke knew where he stood. Though he viewed all human
hardship with compassion he had no doubt that a striking degree
of economic inequality was inevitable and ultimately benefited
society – this was starkly set out in the *Fragment on Scarcity* composed in 1795. Nor did he suggest that the Irish agrarian system
was markedly ill-adjusted. Years earlier in 1748 when he was
about twenty, he had depicted in a short essay the poverty of the
Irish peasantry and outlined a programme to be pursued by a
public-spirited landlord – reducing rents, careful selection of tenants, improvement clauses in leases and encouragement of manu-
factures (domestic industry) – all of which would both benefit the
tenantry and increase the value of the estate.[65] But Burke's interest
in Irish agrarian reform soon faded; he was away from Ireland and

concerned with greater and more immediate issues, and in later years the one defect in the Irish agrarian system he referred to was the denominational imbalance – most landlords Protestant, the great majority of the tenantry Catholic.[66]

Burke had been for thirty years a practising politician for whom a major problem was a challenge demanding a bold solution. But he had to admit that when he contemplated the Irish situation in 1797, he was baffled – 'as to my suggesting anything I am at my wits end'.[67] Hesitantly, he thought that the admission of Catholics to parliament might go a long way towards quieting the country – by removing a stigma and demonstrating that the state was not hostile 'to those who compose infinitely the larger part of the people'.[68] This involved a change of men in Ireland and that obviously could occur only if there was a change of administration in England. Burke was continuously criticising Pitt's cabinet, 'cowardly, sneaking statesmen', but the only alternative – a broad-bottomed coalition could be dismissed as wishful thinking – was the opposition, 'French Jacobins...paying their court to sedition at home and to a ferocious despotism abroad'.[69] Therefore he could scarcely wish or work for the removal of Pitt. Then even if the Irish junta was dismissed, how was it to be replaced?

Fitzwilliam's friends in Ireland were going the full length of Jacobinism. Admittedly they had been irritated beyond bearing by the junta, but whoever was to blame the public suffered, because the Irish Whigs were now engaged in pulling up the landmarks of private property and attacking the connection. Moreover they had pledged themselves to parliamentary reform and if this was enacted in Ireland it would be hard to resist reform 'on this side of the water', a 'preliminary step to our ruin'. On his deathbed in the summer of 1797 Burke dwelt on Grattan's address to the citizens of Dublin which had just been printed. Admiring some of the stylistic touches, he deplored 'the bad politics, of beginning, continuing, ending with what is called parliamentary reform'.[70]

Up till now I have been engaged in what some may think was a humdrum task, trying to determine the pattern of Burke's opinions and feelings on Ireland – to some extent from the scattered and impulsive 'mental eructations' (to use his own term). Now may I turn for a moment to speculation. Twenty years after his death the general situation was from Burke's point of view much less depressing than it had appeared in 1797. The allied armies had reached Paris; Louis XVIII was on the throne of his ancestors, the old régime in Europe had shown remarkable resilience and conservatism was being rejuvenated by romanticism. But what about Ireland? One venerable Irish institution, parliament, had vanished. In Burke's opinion a union between Great Britain and Ireland was 'a bold experimental remedy, justified, perhaps called for, in some nearly desperate crisis of the whole empire'. Given this general principle, would Burke, in spite of his innate conservatism, have felt compelled at the close of the eighteenth century to support Pitt's radical remedy for Irish discontents? Burke would certainly have been perturbed by developments in Irish Catholicism in the early nineteenth century. The agitation for emancipation was becoming associated with democracy and, to advance a little, attacks on tithes and the endowments of the establishment were to threaten property rights. Then the Catholic church, confidently and boldly emphasising its doctrinal inheritance, was aggressively engaged in vigorous controversy with the other denominations in Ireland (who did not fail to retort in kind). Burke, highly critical of democracy, concerned to defend property rights and broad in his churchmanship and his theological sympathies, would have been distressed by these developments.

9

JOHN FITZGIBBON, EARL OF CLARE

Ann C. Kavanaugh

John FitzGibbon, the Earl of Clare, loomed large in the thoughts of leading United Irishmen. Wolfe Tone made frequent allusions, sometimes ironic, more often bitter, to 'my friend, FitzGibbon' in his journals.[1] The Sheares brothers wrote a savage broadside calling for his assassination.[2] Madden, the nineteenth-century historian of the United Irishmen, portrayed him as the English government's demon-in-chief, ruthless and cruel in his public measures, vicious in his private life.[3] FitzGibbon was equally apocalyptic in his loathing of the United Irishmen; he employed all his considerable powers of rhetorical terror against them, portraying them as atheists, Jacobins, and cynical corrupters of the credulous, ignorant Irish lower orders. Nor did he shrink from personal denunciations of individual United Irishmen. Tone could barely write coherently about the public denunciation which FitzGibbon inflicted on him in 1793.[4] Sentencing Simon Butler for defaming the House of Lords in that same year, FitzGibbon gave him a dressing down so insulting and demeaning that Butler tried, unsuccessfully, to challenge his judge to a duel.[5] FitzGibbon's private comments were even more bloodcurdling. In letters to his lifelong *cher ami*, Lord Auckland, he gloated over Lord Edward Fitzgerald's imminent 'exit from the scaffold', and he could see no reason why Tone should not make a similar exit, even though he was already on his deathbed.[6]

FitzGibbon, however, often showed great kindness to individual United Irishmen and their families. He acted as a financial and legal counsellor to Hamilton Rowan's wife while her husband was in exile.[7] According to Barrington, he attempted, albeit unsuccessfully, to save Henry Sheares from death, though he insisted that 'John Sheares cannot be spared'.[8] If he anticipated Lord Edward Fitzgerald's demise, he arranged a final meeting between Lord

Edward and his aunt, Lady Louisa Conolly, and wept as he witnessed it.[9] Nonetheless, many of his acts of grace well suited his
ultimate purpose, which was to discredit and destroy the United
Irishmen. In the summer of 1798, alone of all the members of the
Irish government, he pressed for acceptance of the proposal made
by the United Irish state prisoners: clemency and exile in return
for testimony about their activities.[10] If the prisoners' testimony
was blatantly self-serving, so was FitzGibbon's use of it. Through
selective quotations and wilful distortion, he asserted once again
his fixed premises about the original evil of the United Irishmen
and all their works.[11]

FitzGibbon's relentless and sometimes vindictive opposition to
the United Irishmen did not originate in thoughtful or well-rea-
soned philosophical differences. Although possessing a keen and
penetrating intelligence, he was no intellectual. On the contrary,
he was a hardened, cunning, highly effective practical politician.
FitzGibbon's family origins and his reaction to (or more accurately against) them shaped his attitude towards the United Irishmen.

Ironically, FitzGibbon's family came from the social background that provided so many recruits to the United Irishmen,
the Catholic professional and large farming classes. His many
political enemies, United Irish and those otherwise disposed, frequently claimed that FitzGibbon's ancestors were little better
than *spailpíní*.[12] Perhaps in reaction, one of FitzGibbon's cousins
later made grand, and probably illusory, claims of a vast estate lost
through mischance.[13] The reality appears to have been neither
wronged gentility nor melodramatic penury, but middling respectability. His earliest known ancestor was a medical doctor; his
grandfather, possibly a middleman or gentleman farmer, married
into a well-to-do family with extensive holdings in Cork and Limerick, and there was enough money to send his father to France
where he briefly studied medicine.[14] John FitzGibbon the elder
soon abandoned this profession for the more lucrative one of law,
enrolling in the Middle Temple in 1728.[15] He was called to the
bar in 1731; in the same year he made the obligatory recantation
of his ancestral religion and enrolled as a convert.[16]

Later commentators made much of the contrast between the
virtuous patriotic father and the corrupt, power-mad son. Ferrar's
History of Limerick, published in 1787, portrayed the father as an
honest Roman, honourable, benevolent and disinterested:

He died...deservedly regretted as an able lawyer, a humane landlord, and an honest man, who preferred the shade of retirement to the sunshine of a court.[17]

The son, then enjoying the sunshine of the lively Rutland vicere-gal court, did not merit so much as a passing mention: Ferrar evidently did not think him worthy of comparison with his father. In his memoirs of his own father, Henry Grattan, jun., played on the same noble Roman theme:

Mr. John FitzGibbons [*sic*]...was father to the earl of Clare, but a very different character, plain, straightforward and unostentatious. He lived retired and much respected...[mistrusting] parade and grandeur, except for the true grandeur of simplicity.[18]

Edmund Burke in old age proudly claimed him as a relation, and praised him as a 'good Irishman'. He also portrayed old FitzGibbon as a man tragically torn between sympathy for his 'blood', i.e. the Irish Catholics, and ambition for his family.[19]

Other sources reveal a somewhat less edifying side to old FitzGibbon. In Lord Kenmare's manuscripts, he appears as a cunning, rather unscrupulous figure, well versed in the complexities of the penal laws, and ably using his knowledge to enrich himself.[20] In effect the penal laws made old FitzGibbon; fees from such cases constituted the bulk of his massive legal earnings. It is true that William Gerard Hamilton accused him of crypto-Catholic sentiments; Hamilton had apparently won favour with FitzGibbon, 'who is a Papist', by abusing King William.[21] It is also true that Burke came to admire and respect old FitzGibbon, not only for his admirable character as an Irish patriot, but for his able defence of Burke's Catholic kinsman, James Nagle, when he was accused of complicity in the original Whiteboy agitation.[22] It would have been perfectly logical for old FitzGibbon, a former Limerick Catholic, to have had no great love for King William. Lingering family feeling, as well as skill and the prospect of a fee, undoubtedly made him an able advocate for Nagle. He had, moreover, the capable support of impeccably Protestant colleagues, such as Scott and Yelverton.[23] But occasional displays of atavistic Jacobitism and of family loyalty by no means detract from his fundamental religious opportunism. According to James Roche, a family friend and an invaluable gossip, old FitzGibbon 'refused all religious assistance on his deathbed'.[24] In short, he appears to have lapsed into religious indifference or outright atheism. Unbur-

dened by any inconvenient belief, he could exploit the penal laws
to the great advantage of himself and of his new-made Protestant
family.

His Irish patriotism also was an uncertain quantity. He entered
the new parliament of 1761 as a member for Newcastle in County
Dublin, and seems at first to have inclined towards government.
William Gerard Hamilton, then acting as personal secretary to
Lord Halifax, expressed some satisfaction at an obscure service
performed by FitzGibbon.[25] He does not seem to have received a
suitably satisfactory return for his services, in the form of money
or patronage. By 1763, he defected to the opposition benches,
where he made thunderous speeches against the 'servile and corrupt', and where he conveniently forgot his own connivance in
Hamilton's quest for Irish office and lucre.[26] Although there were
fitful proposals to elevate FitzGibbon to the bench, nothing ever
came of them; in the 1770s he was still crying in the opposition
wilderness.[27] During Harcourt's administration, he refused to vote
in favour of a resolution supporting the 'unjust' war against the
Americans.[28] Old FitzGibbon was always ready to turn again,
given encouragement. His most fundamental loyalties lay with
himself, his family and their interests. His application for a bish-
opric for his son-in-law, William Beresford, evoked this dry comment from Lord Harcourt's chief secretary: 'generally in opposition, yet will ask great favours at the most critical time'.[29]

This apparently amoral man's schemes for advancement centred on his youngest son and namesake. In him, old FitzGibbon
instilled his vast store of legal knowledge and skill. Tone
described young FitzGibbon as 'a compendium of Coke upon
Lyttleton' as taught by 'his papa'.[30] To judge by his own public
pronouncements, FitzGibbon adored his father. He referred to
his 'esteemed and honoured father' several times in his will, and
spoke with particular affection of 'the attachment' which 'my
most worthy and respected father manifested in every stage of his
life to his children'.[31] All this dutifulness and affection sounds
rather suspicious. Given the father's consuming ambition, it is difficult to believe that he was not, in fact, demanding and domi-
neering. In the end, it is impossible to know whether young
FitzGibbon was the pride or the pawn of his father. In the terms
that mattered to old FitzGibbon, their relationship was a clear
and resounding success. In spite of Barrington's claims that the

younger FitzGibbon 'at first attended but little to the duties of his profession', a fee book unearthed at an auction sale in the nineteenth century suggests instead a diligent lawyer with a growing and lucrative practice.[32] He not only adopted his father's profession but he imbibed all of his father's ambition. If anything, the younger FitzGibbon was the more determined and more singleminded in his quest for power.

FitzGibbon also possessed his father's sharp intelligence. This trait, allied to his extensive experience on the Munster circuit, gave him an exceptionally keen insight into the realities of Irish society, and an equally keen insight into the best means of manœuvring through its treacherous currents. He also seems to have learned from his father's mistakes. Old FitzGibbon had veered from government to opposition, with the result that no one trusted him and, even worse, no one gave him office. The younger FitzGibbon mapped out a clear, consistent strategy for advancement, which he followed to the end of his life.

An absolute rejection of his Catholic antecedents and a fierce identification with the Protestant interest lay at the heart of his strategy for advancement. FitzGibbon later made the claim that reason and sincere theological conviction lay at the heart of his abhorrence of Roman Catholicism.[33] This claim is dubious. Given his worldly, sensual nature, FitzGibbon's religious vision was probably limited: God was a celestial Lord Lieutenant and Jesus was his Chief Secretary. FitzGibbon rejected the powerlessness and degradation attached to Catholicism in eighteenth-century Ireland. The Whiteboy *grande peur* which had gripped Protestant Munster during his young manhood undoubtedly strengthened his impulse to move as far from his Catholic origins as he could.

FitzGibbon later claimed his 'esteemed and worthy father's' sanction for this act of renunciation. He informed Sir Lawrence Parsons that his father had frequently warned him of the innate evil of Irish Roman Catholics:

My father was a popish recusant. He became a Protestant and was called to the bar, but he continued to live on terms of familiarity with his Roman Catholic relations and early friends and he knew the Catholics well. He has repeatedly told me that if ever they have the opportunity, they would overturn the Established Church and resume the Protestant estates.[34]

While his father may indeed have said something like this, the spirit of these remarks was different from similar ones made by the son. The elder FitzGibbon was probably making a straightforward observation, with the chill-minded realism that seems to have been his dominant characteristic. The younger constantly raised the spectre of the 'old inhabitants' brooding with 'sullen indignation' over their wrongs to justify the Protestant oligarchy and to rally its frequently lax members.[35]

In spite of his best efforts, the younger FitzGibbon remained an outsider in the Protestant ruling class which he dedicated himself to upholding. The obscurity of his family, their legendary lowliness and his father's education in France haunted and embarrassed him throughout his career. The Catholic origins of the FitzGibbons inspired numerous colourful myths. It was frequently claimed that old FitzGibbon had been 'tonsured at St Omers' and, perhaps in consequence, the younger FitzGibbon was sometimes mocked as 'FitzJesuit' or 'FitzFriar'.[36] In response, FitzGibbon expressed contempt for those he served. He reserved his severest comment for such Protestant patriots as Flood, Grattan and Charlemont. He took every opportunity of reminding them that in spite of their lofty pretensions to nationhood, they were mere descendants of freebooters, dependent on English power to protect their ill-gotten gains.[37]

More than injured feelings accounted for these appeals to the might of England. He also came to recognise that the true fulcrum of power lay with the English government and not with the arrogant, quarrelsome Irish Protestant élite. This insight came at a particularly opportune time. FitzGibbon's political career began at a time when the English government was attempting to reassert control after the overthrow of the 'undertakers'. They were on the lookout for bright, hungry young men to fill the ranks of the new government party. In the earliest stages of his career, FitzGibbon of necessity identified himself as an Irish patriot. In the late 1770s, when FitzGibbon entered parliament, that party was in its truculent ascendant. But once the opportunity (and the promise) of office offered itself, FitzGibbon coolly shed his patriotic proclivities, and embraced the English government's interests. To his credit, he served the English interest steadfastly, and with fervour. As Westmorland recognized, defending and promoting the English interest was his true religion: 'he has no god but English government'.[38] Indeed, FitzGibbon found deep emotional satisfaction in his religion of imperialism. It offered the grace of power and office, and the exquisite pleasure of domination, not only over Irish Catholics, but over the Irish Protestants who despised him.

It would be easy to dismiss FitzGibbon as a particularly unattractive careerist. But, however squalid his master motives, he did have admirable, indeed likeable, qualities. While FitzGibbon was not an especially cultivated man, his letters, speeches, and legal opinions show no mean literary talent. His prose is terse, clear and often striking: in particular, his chancery opinion in the case of *Redingon v. Redington* is a *tour de force* of social and psychological insight, and a letter recounting the dowager Duchess of Leinster's marital history is a racy, if cruel, comedy of manners.[39] In his private life, he demonstrated patient kindness to his scatter-brained, sometimes adulterous, wife and to his often lazy and feckless FitzGibbon relations.[40] His correspondence is full of acts of generosity and thoughtfulness: ordering Limerick gloves for English friends, praising an estate agent for a job well done, pleading for a stay of execution for the son of his shepherd (FitzGibbon had no illusions about the son: 'I have strong grounds to believe that he is very criminal', but he pitied the father, 'a very honest man').[41] His acts of grace to various United Irishmen have already received mention. If he fought hard and unscrupulously for power and place, he did try, however fitfully, to act with responsibility once he obtained them. Even his worst enemies acknowledged his integrity and ability as a judge.[42] Finally, he took his role as an improving landlord very seriously. To appeal once again to the evidence of his letters, they reveal fairness to his tenants and a clear grasp of agriculture.[43]

FitzGibbon's social grudges sometimes tainted his good qualities as judge and as landlord. In his court, he overacted the role of avenging champion of the poor and oppressed, and in parliament, he indulged in many tedious lectures on the irresponsibility and neglect of his fellow landlords.[44] In some respects his displays of paternalistic virtue were a form of showing off, on a par with his gaudy carriage and epicurean dinner parties. They were meant to demonstrate that John FitzGibbon, the son of a former scholar at the Irish College, had a finer sense of aristocratic responsibility than those with more established pedigrees. In the light of the historiographical drubbing FitzGibbon has suffered for more than two hundred years, it would be unfair to over-emphasize his moral vanity or to deny his genuine impulses of compassion and honour.

Above all, FitzGibbon, in spite of his insecurities and prejudices, had an essentially sound grasp of Irish society and politics.
His constant harping on the menacing Catholic masses, 'brooding
in sullen indignation' on their historical wrongs, was far more
than the ranting of a social and sectarian renegade. The Protestant élite did indeed depend for their political survival on a strong
English presence and on a sectarian monopoly. Equally sound was
his claim that wholesale enfranchisement of Catholics, reform, or
grandiose claims of nationhood carried grave risks, given the
paucity of Protestant numbers and the raw memories of conquest
and dispossession. The bloodshed of the 1790s certainly proved
FitzGibbon's point about the hatreds still lingering in Ireland,
while the decline of Protestant political influence following the
final grant of Catholic emancipation bore out another frequently
made prediction. No doubt on an abstract moral level, his political views were cynical and repugnant. He uncritically accepted a
power structure that many Irish, Catholics and Protestants,
abhorred. But his experience as an outsider of Catholic descent
unquestionably gave him a clarity of mind possessed by few of his
contemporaries.

His perceptions, as well as his self-interest, made him a relentless opponent of early manifestations of Irish patriotism in the
guise of reforming Volunteers and Whigs. This same combination of perception and personal interest inevitably made him a
fierce antagonist of the United Irishmen. They embraced every
element he most hated in Irish society and in Irish political life:
feckless, irresponsible Anglicans with impractical schemes for
reform, pushy, disaffected Catholics, and 'restless, republican'
Presbyterians. (FitzGibbon's loathing for this last group is frequently underestimated.)[45] Their manifesto, calling for the union
of all Irishmen, regardless of religion, a reformed, non-sectarian
parliament, and radical autonomy from England, threatened the
very foundation of his power and violated every political and historical instinct in his being. Inevitably, he drew on his great store
of cunning and ruthlessness not only to banish or hang the United
Irishmen, but to defame their dangerously seductive political programme.

His exchange with MacNeven during the Secret Committee
examinations of 1798 is particularly enlightening. At one point,
MacNeven, himself a Catholic, tried to explain the opposition of

the United Irishmen to all church establishments. He would, he declared, 'no more consent to the [establishment of Roman Catholicism]...than I would to the establishment of Mahometism'.[46] In writing up his report, FitzGibbon wilfully took this to mean that MacNeven was bent on destroying, not *religious establishments* but *religion itself*, Catholic as well as Protestant.[47] MacNeven, in fact, was a dutiful Catholic, whose elaborate requiem mass was the wonder of New York city.[48] FitzGibbon succeeded in portraying MacNeven as a bloodthirsty infidel, and himself, for one brief amazing moment, as a defender of the Catholic religion.

The most singular irony about FitzGibbon is that he could have made a very capable and dedicated United Irishman under other circumstances. Arguably, had he been born ten or twenty years later, the intoxicating new philosophy of liberty, equality and fraternity might have influenced him more than his father's crabbed opportunism. Moreover, his advance to high office was never assured. Many members of the English government, particularly Pitt, had little love for FitzGibbon, probably because he was so nakedly ambitious. He received his two greatest offices, attorney-general and lord chancellor, mainly in default of other suitable candidates, English or Irish.[49] What would FitzGibbon have done had his beloved English persistently frustrated his desire for power and office? This speculation is not entirely idle. Towards the end of his life, FitzGibbon, finding his powers considerably curtailed after the Act of Union, became disillusioned with the English. In a letter to Auckland, he declared that he 'should look forward to new scenes of misery and confusion [i.e. rebellion] here...with very little feeling'.[50] While in part this was florid self-pity, the letter suggests that had his ambitions been disappointed earlier, FitzGibbon might well have considered radicalism and revolution as a means to power. The detested 'Black Jack' of later nationalist legend might well have taken his place in the pantheon of United Irish heroes.

10

ARCHBISHOP TROY, THE CATHOLIC CHURCH AND IRISH RADICALISM: 1791–3

Dáire Keogh

In looking at the reaction of the church to radicalism in the 1790s it has been traditional to divide the decade in two halves, taking the failed Fitzwilliam viceroyalty of 1795 as the dividing line. In many respects this neat division makes sense and provides an adequate framework upon which to hang an analysis of the decade. With Fitzwilliam's recall, hopes for emancipation were dashed and constitutional politics offered little prospect for the removal of remaining Catholic disabilities. Against this background, radicalism was transformed, moving from reform towards an underground revolutionary position. Ironically, however, the failure of the Catholic relief bill of 1795 and the arrival of Lord Camden guaranteed the success of the bishops' scheme for a national seminary for Ireland. With the Royal College firmly established, the hierarchy appeared satisfied and vacated the political arena, adopting instead a mantle of steady loyalism. However, this choice of 1795 as a turning-point simplifies the complexity of the decade and blurs any proper understanding of the period. In many respects the markers had already been laid down with Hobart's Relief Act and the subsequent Convention Act of 1793. From that point onwards the Catholic position became increasingly polarised, and in many cases the pastors were left with the unenviable options of following their flocks or being left isolated.

The Catholic church's reaction to the radicalism of the 1790s has conventionally been examined in the light of the 1798 rebellion: this has created a distorted image of reality since the involvement of so many priests in the events of that year has led to an over-estimation of the influence of the clergy. The religious factor in 1798 was the element which attracted most attention from contemporary commentators in their efforts to explain the events of that year. Yet until very recently, modern writers have ignored this factor and sought explanations elsewhere. And with the exception of some regional studies,[1] a standard interpretation of clerical involvement remains which preserves many of the stereotypes of previous centuries. Likewise, modern studies of Irish links with France in the revolutionary period have failed to place clerical reaction to radicalism in Ireland within a European context and in consequence Ireland has been examined in isolation from the continental crisis facing the Catholic church in the 1790s.[2]

For Tone and the reformers, the French Revolution represented the morning star of liberty for Ireland, but for the great majority of the Catholic clergy it was the incarnation of all that was anathema to Christianity. Few groups in Irish society possessed the same continental connections as the clergy, and their first-hand experience of the Revolution was unrivalled. Its progress and the spread of the French principles alarmed them greatly. The church had been one of the earliest victims of the Revolution; all ecclesiastical property had been seized, and the regulars disbanded; the 1790 Civil Constitution of the clergy effectively brought papal jurisdiction in France to an end.[3] The experiences of the Irish priests in France and the accounts they carried certainly contributed to anti-revolutionary feeling in Ireland. Such experiences, however, did not necessarily determine the future behaviour of these priests and many of them later became involved in the United Irishmen. Valentine Derry records meeting James Coigley shortly after the latter's return to Ireland in 1789. Coigley, who later would be tried and executed as a United Irish emissary to France, gave Derry 'a most satisfactory account of the causes and progress of the Revolution'. At that stage the priest was certainly no friend to the Revolution, having narrowly escaped being lanternised in Paris and choosing to return and 'die in any manner' in Ireland rather than swear against his conscience.[4] Fr Mogue Kearns had actually been hanged from a lamp-post in Paris, and Michael Murphy had escaped a similar fate in Bordeaux. Nevertheless, Leonard McNally commented in the wake of the 1798 rebellion that the priests and country schoolmasters were the principal agitators of 'French politics' and that amongst the priests it was those expelled from France and the fugitive students that had been the most active.[5]

The fate of the church in France aroused great sympathy among the Irish hierarchy and they took every step necessary to stem the growth of what Thomas Hussey described as 'the French disease'.[6] Through an extensive network of continental contacts and agents the bishops were continually informed about the plight of the church in Europe where it seemed that every day the Revolution made greater inroads into religion. Above all the hierarchy sought to prevent a similar occurrence in Ireland; in this context the transformed Catholic Committee presented an ominous spectre.

The revolutionary ideals of Liberty, Equality and Fraternity possessed enormous appeal for the Catholic community which, despite the minor Relief Acts of 1778 and 1782, was still greatly frustrated by the application of the penal laws.[7] Catholic interests had long been represented by the Catholic Committee, but within this body tensions were apparent in the 1780s as a confident new middle class began to challenge the old aristocratic leadership. In the past the Committee had been content with deferential appeals to the King for some measure of relief, but conscious of their greater social and economic standing, the Committee became increasingly active as an effective pressure group in Dublin politics during the 1780s. French revolutionary influence accelerated this transformation and in December 1791 Lord Kenmare and the aristocratic old guard withdrew from the Committee, leaving the leadership to John Keogh, Thomas Braughall and other advanced radicals. Under the influence of French ideology, this renewed leadership demanded redress for Catholic grievances as a right, rather than as a reward to be sought with deference.[8]

The growing alliance between Catholics and radical Presbyterians also alarmed the hierarchy and they shared the Castle's anxiety about the dreadful progeny of such an unnatural union. Cardinal Antonelli had been informed of events in Ireland by Fr Charles O'Conor of Belanagare, and the Prefect instructed the bishops of Ireland to take appropriate evasive measures to halt any junction with the Presbyterians.[9] Antonelli wrongly assumed that the hierarchy had it in their power to call their flock back from the edge, but by the end of 1791 the pace of change in Ireland had already accelerated beyond their control.

Archbishop John Troy had quickly responded to the growing crisis; anxious to rescue the Catholic body from any imputation of disloyalty, he wrote to Hobart, the Chief Secretary, and argued that if Catholics were given a share in the franchise they would fall under the influence of their natural leaders, the clergy, gentry and merchants. These leaders would in turn become more resistant to radical ideas; with their own position secured, the influence of the United Irishmen, the Catholic Society and other radical groups would be weakened. Troy, however, unlike Burke, would never have accepted an alliance with the Presbyterians, even if it was to defeat them at a later stage. In fact Troy outlined for Hobart the dangers of the dissenting influence on the Catholics, and spoke of episcopal appointments of parish priests being rejected in some country places along French lines, under the 'encouragement and connivance of Protestant gentlemen'.[10]

The decision of the Kenmarites to present an independent address of loyalty to the Lord Lieutenant in December 1791 created a deep rupture within the Catholic body; Kenmare was formally expelled from the Committee which condemned the 'insidious and servile address calculated to divide the Catholics of Ireland and eventually defeat their application for relief'.[11] The lines were now drawn for the ensuing conflict between the aristocratic Kenmarites and the advanced Dublin leadership. The Catholic community was polarised in its loyalty as both sides sought support for their stance. Troy attempted to rally the hierarchy to his and Kenmare's side. Just before Christmas 1791 he wrote to Bishop Moylan of Cork explaining his reasons for signing the address, declaring it absolutely necessary that he step forward in a decided manner, at a time when Catholic loyalty was under question and in the face 'of the most extravagant levelling principles'. Though confident the storm would soon cease, he was determined to stand firm, otherwise the clergy would 'become obnoxious and be reputed the authors of sedition'. Troy requested that Moylan would relay his sentiments to the remaining Munster bishops.[12]

Troy was certain of a favourable response from Bishop Teahan of Kerry, given Kenmare's influence, and the Catholics of Kerry promptly published a loyal address.[13] But Troy's own suffragans in Leinster had less success in winning popular support. Bishop Delaney's address in Carlow received only forty-two signatures, while Bishop Lanigan could muster a mere sixty-three names in Kilkenny. The Bishop of Wexford, James Caulfield, was especially opposed to hardline Catholic politics and it is not difficult to imagine his chagrin on receiving only eleven signatures from a

congregation of over two hundred in Wexford town; this followed
a challenge to the address from Edward Hay and James Edward
Devereux, whom the bishop regarded as a 'young hot headed lib-
ertine'.[14] The paltry Wexford address was never presented and the
only other bishop to sign a petition was Thomas Costelloe of
Clonfert.[15] The Ulster bishops retained their composure and
remained aloof throughout the crisis. Patrick Plunkett of Meath,
however, criticised Troy's decision to side with the aristocratic
faction and believed some compromise should have been reached.
Besides, the divisions in Catholic ranks had resulted in 'no small
amusement of a host of foes'. Had some compromise or adjourn-
ment taken place Plunkett, who had spent twenty years in France
and led the Gallican party in the Irish hierarchy, believed that 'we
should be more respectable at the moment'.[16]

Troy had obviously hoped for a unanimous response from the
hierarchy, but in this his judgment was faulty. Secession illustrated the deep divisions within the Catholic body and highlighted
the hierarchy's delicate hold on the loyalty of their flock. A resolution of the General Committee of the Catholic body on 15 January 1792 criticised the seceders for their attempt to 'form divisions and to disseminate discord' amongst Catholics. More
ominously for the hierarchy, the seceders were castigated for
attempting to 'seduce the Roman Catholic clergy from the laity,
and to set them at variance, converting the ministers of the
Gospel into instruments of oppression'. All of this, the seceders
were warned, tended to break the purest source of confidence and
endangered 'the very being of religion in the minds of the
people'.[17] The implication was simple; either the clergy joined
with the people, or the people would go it alone.

This lesson was not lost on the radicals who throughout 1792
and 1793 exploited episcopal weakness for all its worth. In January
1792 Sir Hercules Langrishe introduced a bill in the House of
Commons which granted limited relief for Catholics.[18] The bill
stopped far short of total Catholic demands, but sufficient concessions were made to turn the parliamentary debate into an anti-
Catholic tirade. There was particular resentment amongst the
Catholic Committee at the insults hurled in their direction and
attempts made by the ultras to blacken their body. The Committee members were portrayed by Sir Boyle Roche as 'shop keepers
and shop lifters', Duigenan referred to them as 'men of low and

mean parentage', while the loyal prints repudiated the right of this 'small popish faction to speak for the Catholics'.[19]

The Committee responded to these accusations in parliament with publication of a formal 'Declaration' of the civil and religious principles of the Catholics which sought to demonstrate that these principles were in no way incompatible with the duties of citizens or 'repugnant to liberty, whether political, civil or religious'.[20] The Declaration attempted to clear many of the age-old suspicions surrounding Catholicism and it renounced such notions as the Pope's deposing power, his infallibility, his civil authority outside the Papal States, and the acceptability of breaking faith with heretics. It also renounced all interest in forfeited estates and declared that, were the Catholics restored to the franchise, they would not use that privilege 'to disturb and weaken the establishment of the Protestant religion or Protestant government in the kingdom'.[21]

The Committee decided to muster the assistance of the Catholic clergy to secure maximum support for the Declaration throughout the country. Troy for once rallied to their assistance, and the Dublin chapter promptly signed the Declaration.[22] Troy was acting independently of the hierarchy and his eager response, despite obvious reservations on certain aspects of the Declaration, reflected a desire to bring his isolation from the Committee to an end. No doubt he was also aware of criticism that the bishops appeared more concerned with government approval than with the sufferings of their people.[23] The committee's success in obtaining so many signatures to the Declaration was largely due to their effective marshalling of the clergy through the country. Smyth has described the opposition of the parish priest of Duleek, County Louth to the Declaration as 'far from typical', but there is little doubt that the clergy were in many cases intimidated into supporting the venture against their own better judgment.[24] Bishop Caulfield complained to Troy of the 'violent and sullen mood' of the people of Wexford, and their 'plan to give the clergy nothing if they do not come into their measures'. This threat was confirmed by John Keogh who confided to Thomas Hussey that 'the people seem well inclined to give them [the non-co-operating clergy] the French cure'.[25]

A similar ambiguity surrounds the clergy's support of the Convention. Certainly Troy had not convinced the Committee of his commitment to their policy, and he was still regarded with suspi-

cion by the leadership. In March 1792 he was seen leaving the
Castle, and Randall McDonnell later called on him to ascertain
the nature of his conversation with Major Hobart. Caulfield was
aware that Troy would be called on to account for his actions and
tipped him off, warning the archbishop that 'if you do not acquit
yourself with candour, you should be laid aside'. Under this kind
of pressure Troy was left with no choice but to declare his intentions 'beyond any possibility of doubt', and he wrote to all the
bishops of Ireland requesting their assistance in forwarding the
planned Convention.[26] Further indications of such pressure being
brought upon the bishops is reflected in reports reaching London
that Keogh had interrupted a meeting of the Munster bishops at
Thurles and threatened them with a revival of the Whiteboy tactics of withholding dues, unless they lent their support to the
Committee. The tenor of Keogh's letter to Thomas Bray in the
following month, however, gave no hint of tension between himself and the prelates.[27]

The Committee had scored a major coup in winning the support of the Catholic clergy for their planned Convention, and the
huge response to the Declaration and the election of delegates
finally scotched the shopkeeper jibe. Nevertheless images of
chapel meetings assembled on the instructions of the Committee
did little to calm episcopal anxieties and also served to fuel loyalist
fears. The ever-sharp Sir Richard Musgrave described the clergy
as 'never failing to inspire their flocks with admiration of the
Gallic nation and with the most inveterate hatred towards the
English', pointing for example to the activities of James Coigley
amongst the Defenders and afterwards amongst the United Irishmen. Nevertheless, popular support for the Committee had
placed the clergy in an impossible situation. Edmund Burke's
advice to Bishop Francis Moylan summed up their dilemma; he
advised minimal involvement in the Committee business, at the
same time urging the hierarchy to avoid any suggestion of opposition to the aspirations of the Catholic laity.[28]

For the most part the hierarchy tried to walk this tightrope,
and the surviving correspondence reflects their deep-felt tensions
and discomfort. There was a growing fear that their discreet
approach had failed to stem the spread of Jacobinism. The excommunication in September 1792 of Robert McEvoy, a priest of the
Dublin diocese, reflects this anxiety in the mind of Troy, particu-

larly as McEvoy (dismissed for taking a wife) justified his actions by appealing to the decrees of the French National Assembly. Troy immediately saw parallels between the Catholic Convention and the National Assembly, and his pastoral announcing the excommunication condemned the Assembly decrees concerning religion, characterising them as universally tending to 'establish the dominion of a selfish intolerant philosophy'.[29] The Bishop of Killala, Dominic Bellew, also became alarmed at the potential of the Committee, and suggested that the hierarchy be given greater authority within the body. 'Damned kind', was Tone's response, while a furious Keogh condemned the bishops as 'old men used to bend to power, mistaking all attempts at liberty as in some way connected with the murderers of France'. Still, memories of the Kenmare split were too recent in episcopal minds to allow for any rash behaviour and in general the bishops favoured a united stance with the Committee.[30]

In this spirit Troy and Moylan attended the Convention in Dublin in December 1792, having initially been opposed to taking any part in the proceedings. Now, apprehensive lest their motives for staying away could be misrepresented, they wished to avoid further tension.[31] Troy's apprehensions were quickly removed by the great applause that welcomed the two prelates to Tailors' Hall and the bishops were placed on each side of the chairman at the opening session. The two returned to the convention on 8 December when the petition, already approved and signed by the delegates, was read aloud. Significantly, the petition was presented to the bishops as a *fait accompli* and was in effect merely read for their information, with no implication that their approval was sought on its content. Nevertheless Moylan and Troy signed the petition on behalf of the prelates and clergy of Ireland. Further reflecting the movement in his position, Troy regarded the petition as 'perfectly unexceptionable', and delivered a rousing speech to the assembly in which he proclaimed the determination of the clergy to rise or fall with the people.[32]

The hierarchy were now tainted in conservative eyes by their association with the Committee and their participation in the 'Back Lane Parliament'. Indeed the whole Convention was represented as a papist assembly which only the active co-operation of the clergy had made possible. The influential role of United Irish members within the Committee also disturbed Protestant sensitivities, while Troy's promise to rise or fall with the Committee seemed to place him inextricably at its head.[33]

In the marathon Commons debate which followed the introduction of Hobart's relief bill, the anti-Catholic rhetoric that had characterised the 1792 session was revived with even greater ferocity. Alarmed at this development the bishops sought once wished to emphasise their loyalty publicly. In particular they attempted to distance themselves from any suggestion that they had been winking at the activities of the Defenders, a topical issue given the House of Lords enquiry into Defenderism. Conscious that further relief might be endangered by such accusations, the four metropolitans issued a pastoral in January 1793 in which they denounced the actions of 'seditious and misguided wretches of every religious denomination'. The bishops stressed the connection between obedience and additional relief, and urged their flock to avoid 'idle assemblies' and any appearance of riot.[34]

Troy developed these themes with customary zeal in his *Pastoral Instructions in the Duties of Christian Citizens* in which he addressed the arguments raised by Foster, Fitzgibbon and the ultras. In the pastoral the bishop endeavoured to counter the black propaganda levelled at the church; it aimed to end once and for all any question of Catholic disloyalty to king and constitution, or of a Catholic predilection for arbitrary government. Catholics were by nature loyal and dutiful subjects, he argued; the church had always taught obedience to constituted authority, whether the government be aristocratic or democratic. In response to suggestions that Catholics were unfit to enjoy the benefits of a free constitution, the pastoral pointed to modern republics which had been established by Catholics themselves.

Once again Troy's independent stance brought a barrage of criticism from a variety of sources. Instead of the intended conciliatory effect, the pastoral was greeted with anger in both houses of parliament. In the Commons, Patrick Duigenan was particularly critical and described it as 'a political tract, containing arguments not a little hostile to the established constitution in church and state', while in the upper house Bishop Charles Agar and Lord Clare took exception to Troy's reference to the Catholics as 'an enslaved people'.[35] It appeared as if Troy was advocating republican government and the very reference to 'citizens' in the title was taken to confirm this opinion.[36] Within the Catholic

Committee itself the pastoral was greeted with no small degree of resentment. Anthony Thompson, the Committee member for Thurles, lamented that it was deficient in political sensitivity and had provided ammunition to their enemies by resurrecting 'controversial material long confined to the dormitory'.[37] In the pastoral's second edition, Troy clarified much of the ambiguity and singled out the British constitution for specific approval.[38] Nevertheless the ultras remained unconvinced of Troy's loyal sentiments, and the commotion which the pastoral had raised in the Commons left Hobart with no choice but to attach a new oath to his relief bill, as he believed it 'essential to the security of the Protestant establishment that such tenets should be clearly disavowed'.[39] This development can hardly have been welcomed by Troy, who must now have questioned the wisdom of publishing the pastoral in the first place. His intention of rescuing the Catholics from any suggestion of disloyalty had completely backfired and he was now placed in the compromising position of having to accept an oath based on the Committee's Declaration. Given the opposition of the Irish hierarchy to the 'Protestation' of the English Catholic Committee there can be little doubt of their anger at being forced to accept what was in effect an Irish equivalent. Troy's credibility in the eyes of the Holy See also suffered and Valentine Bodkin, agent of the Archbishop of Cashel, later reported how he had lost 'much of his credit and vogue' by failing to refer the oath to Rome for approval.[40]

The joy which accompanied the 1793 Relief Act soon evaporated as Catholics considered what had still been withheld. The concessions were indeed significant, but partial relief failed to satisfy the demands of many activists for total emancipation; to them possession of a share in the franchise without the right to sit in parliament made no sense whatever. Tone aptly described their anger when he declared that if the Catholics deserved what had been granted, they also deserved what had been withheld.[41] Added to this was Catholic resentment at the hostile speeches which had marked the bill's passage through parliament.

The combination of these factors led to a growing polarisation of the Catholic community: as the Committee dissolved itself, many of the radicals naturally drifted towards the United Irishmen. Disaffection became widespread in the wake of the 1793 session and Edmund Burke complained to Grattan of the 'mutinous

spirit' which he believed had become the very constitution of the
lower part of his compatriots. This growing support for republicanism was also commented on by Musgrave who noted that the
general horror at the barbarities of the French republicans began
to abate in the minds of the Catholics from that time on. This
observation is borne out by Troy's decision to postpone his
intended service following Louis XVI's execution. Indeed Troy
wondered if it would be wise to hold it at all, considering the
scandalous objections made to it by 'our own people' in Dublin.
Yet Troy came under increasing pressure from Rome to call his
people back to a sense of duty. [42]

By the summer of 1793, however, Catholic agitation had taken
on a life of its own and the clergy were in no position to exercise
control over the course of events. The previous two years had
brought the country to an unprecedented level of politicisation
and few Catholics can have avoided being caught up in the political frenzy. The clergy had played an important role in this development in that the Catholic Committee had harnessed their
organisational resources and used them to carry through their
political programme. The role of the parish meetings throughout
1792 had given the illusion of a powerful church, one capable of
exerting real influence over its members. This power however was
illusory, and the fleeting and erratic efforts of Troy in particular
reflect the delicate nature of the bond between priest and people.
In reality the priests could at most only motivate a willing flock,
and the threats made to various bishops by John Keogh, James
Edward Devereux and the more radical Committee members
reflect the new-found confidence of the laity in manipulating the
real fears of the clergy. The Kenmare secession illustrated for
Troy the limitations of clerical influence, and his confused reaction to the events of 1792 and 1793 represent an attempt to
respond to this changing relationship. While Troy and the Irish
bishops reluctantly identified this new balance of power, both the
Roman and Castle authorities failed to acknowledge that a shift
had taken place. Despite information to the contrary, the Dublin
authorities continued to presume throughout the 1790s that the
hierarchy were in a position to regulate at will the behaviour of
their people.

11

PAINE AND IRELAND

David Dickson

On 5 June 1792 'Thomas Paine, author of the Rights of Man' was proposed for honorary membership of the Dublin Society of United Irishmen by Randal McAllister and James Moore. There had been support in the Society for such a gesture for several months, but the rules excluded honorary membership as a category. It required a proposal to rescind the rule in question before the compliment to Paine could be considered. There was an undercurrent of opposition to the Society making such a clear-cut identification with Paine's outspoken political radicalism; what seems to have been a compromise proposal was brought forward in May – that both Paine and Priestley should be so honoured. The Painite enthusiasts stifled this, and the proposal for Paine alone was finally carried on 8 June by 36 votes to 6.[1]

McAllister the proposer was a Protestant bookseller/publisher, then trading in Grafton Street; in the previous spring he had been the publisher of the first cheap Dublin edition of *The Rights of Man*, Part I.[2] In this he was acting as agent for the 'Whigs of the Capital', an association of radical guild politicians led by James Napper Tandy which had gone on to form the most important bloc of founder members of the Dublin United Irish Society. At the end of 1792 McAllister took control over the city newspaper closest to the Society.

James Moore of College Green, Paine's seconder and a leading Catholic bookseller/publisher, was at this time producing the first (and only) Irish edition of the *Encyclopaedia Britannica*, but he was also one of the many booksellers involved in the first major Dublin edition of *The Rights of Man* I in March 1791, and was involved in Paine reprints later in the decade. He also produced the sole Irish edition of a major if more demanding radical text, William Godwin's *Enquirer* in 1797.[3]

The commercial rewards of the Burke/Paine controversy for the Dublin book trade were far from negligible. But Paine's honorary membership was more than a smart move by radical booksellers to maintain the interest of the market: the Castle's United Irish mole, Thomas Collins, inferred that the Society vote on Paine would 'show in a great measure how we stand to *act* on other occasions'.[4] In the summer of 1792, some United Irishmen, both in Dublin and Belfast, were evidently unnerved by Paine's undiluted republicanism and his attack on the 'fraud and imposition' of monarchy; yet, at least until his September flight to France, it was difficult from within the movement to criticise Citizen Paine openly. He had already achieved enormous symbolic significance for Irish radicals.

Prior to 1792 Paine had paid almost no attention to Ireland. His American employer and first printer of *Common Sense* in 1776 had learnt his book-making skills in Dublin,[5] but neither then nor in the 1780s had the Irish implications of American independence or of British reformism caught Paine's interest. His reading did admittedly include Thomas Leland's *History of Ireland* (1773) – he cited it as an authority on Jacobite brass money in his *Dissertations on Government* in 1786;[6] in the following year he made his first direct comment on Irish politics in *Prospects on the Rubicon*, written probably in Paris:

England and Ireland are not on the best terms. The suspicion that England governs Ireland for the purpose of keeping her low to prevent her becoming her rival in trade and manufacture, will always operate to hold Ireland in a state of sentimental hostility with England.[7]

This was a fairly conventional and unengaged American perspective. And there is no suggestion of any deepening of interest in things Irish between 1787 and 1791, despite his being based mainly in England once again and befriending several leading expatriate Irishmen.[8]

What changed this was not any shift in Paine's spectrum of political concerns or interests, but the very specific reaction in Ireland to the appearance of *The Rights of Man* I in the course of 1791. The great assault on Burke's *Reflections* was an extraordinary commercial and political success throughout the English-speaking world, but notably so in Ireland. Paine himself was aware of this: commenting on the sales of *The Rights of Man* I in November 1791, only eight months after the publication of the first edition, he informed a friend that in England 'almost sixteen thousand has gone off – and in Ireland above forty thousand'.[9] Paine may have been inclined to talk up the sales of his works (in 1802 he was to claim that in aggregate nearly half a million copies of *The Rights of Man* had been sold in Britain and Ireland),[10] but what is striking in this context is that Paine believed that Irish sales were so far ahead of English ones before Part II had appeared. There is no explanation in Paine's writings or correspondence to account for the scale of early Irish sales. Paine had clearly not engineered it himself. The extraordinary reception of *The Rights of Man* in Ireland made Paine an enthusiastic if not very well-informed advocate of Irish radical causes, notably in France during his ten-year residence there.

Paine almost certainly never visited Ireland. There were rumours, even in Dublin Castle, of a visit to Belfast in September 1791, and some evidence that he intended to accept an invitation to participate in the Bastille Day celebrations there in 1792, in the wake of his recognition by the Dublin United Irishmen.[11] But at that point the imminent threat of arrest in England, as the government began its crack-down on seditious publications, made France a far more attractive destination than Ireland for the footloose Paine.

The Rights of Man, *Part I*

Burke's entirely hostile reading of events in France had disturbed and embarrassed Whig/radical opinion in Ireland in the autumn of 1790. Reformers of all colours had taken early comfort from the Revolution, and a number of 'popular' victories in the 1790 general election had built up Irish reformers' expectations. Such a devastating critique from among the ranks of Whiggery was profoundly unsettling. Paine's response several months later was seized upon not least as a means of restoring morale among the advanced reformers.

Within days of its London publication, a 2s. 2d. edition of *The Rights of Man* I was printed in Dublin and offered for sale by John Rice of College Green who presented Paine as 'the Luther of political reformation', and stated that with his edition 'the Irish nation are now presented with an uncastrated copy of Rights of Man', unlike the supposedly censored first London printing.[12] No copy of Rice's edition is recorded, indicating a small print run. A larger printing meanwhile was organised, bearing the imprint of 36 Dublin booksellers. Whether this was an authorised edition is not clear; it was certainly not a 'pirate' one, produced merely to capture covert British sales.

It has frequently been claimed that there were in all some thirteen Irish editions of *The Rights of Man* I. In all likelihood there were only seven in 1791, the last of which admittedly called itself, following a London revision, the *thirteenth* edition. There were it seems six printings or editions in Dublin, one in Derry – produced 'at the desire of a society of gentlemen' – and, remarkably, none in Belfast, despite Tone's famous observation in October 1791 that 'Paine's book' had become 'the Koran' of the town.[13]

The first three Irish editions, comprising it was said a total print run of 10,000, were exhausted before the end of May,[14] a situation all the more striking since three Dublin newspapers, the *Morning Post, Hibernian Journal* and *Dublin Weekly Journal*, and one Belfast paper, the *Belfast Newsletter*, had printed series of lengthy extracts of *The Rights of Man* I. The *Newsletter* had indeed been rather selective, but the successful *Hibernian Journal* serialised it *in toto* between 8 April and 3 June 1791. The serialising of pamphlet essays was standard practice in the late eighteenth-century press; extracts from Paine's *Common Sense* had been published in the *Freeman's Journal* in 1776, and Burke's *Reflections* had recently been given the same treatment in Dublin papers. However, the level of newspaper exposure of *The Rights of Man* I was unprecedented.

The most important ingredient in the pamphlet's Irish success was the decision of the Whigs of the Capital to raise subscriptions for a fund to underwrite a large-scale subsidised printing. Most but not all of the thirteen-man committee set up in early April for this purpose were close allies and political partners of Napper Tandy; they included the great ironfounder of Church Street, Henry Jackson, who was to name his country residence Fort Paine.[15] McAllister was one of two bookseller/printers on the committee, and first supplies of the sixpenny edition were available from him within weeks. The eventual print run of the cheap edition (presumably in two tranches) was reported to have been 20,000;[16] if Paine's estimate of Irish sales as of November 1791 was of the right order of magnitude, then the cheap edition accounted for about half of total sales that year. The Dublin radicals who had created a cheap version so quickly remained energetically committed to its distribution in the months following. Even as early as June 1791 an Irish reply to Paine attacked the 'republicans' and Presbyterians who were then distributing 'six-penny pacquets of sedition' to what the author claimed were a semi-literate population.[17]

In England during 1791 there were also several cheap printings of *The Rights of Man* I, but nothing on the scale of the Dublin initiative. Possibly drawing on this Irish precedent, Paine was contemplating in November 1791 a huge low-cost print run of 100,000 of the two parts in Britain, but it was not until May 1792 and the London Corresponding Society's edition that a cheap British equivalent was produced.[18] It was this and similar tightly set versions of Paine's gospel which have conventionally been regarded as the first to have had political consequences and to have been widely read in English artisanal and labouring households. But it was the earlier subsidised distribution of *The Rights of Man* I in Ireland that was decisive in strengthening the morale of Irish radicals and widening their urban and literate support before the launching of the United Irish movement. In the words of Under-Secretary Cooke in November 1791, 'Paine's doctrines have too much effect on the middling classes.'[19]

The Bastille Day reviews in Belfast and Dublin held in the previous July were a barometer of Paine's reputation. At the flamboyant Volunteer display in Belfast, Paine was only one among twelve absent heroes toasted (and the portraits on their marching banners were restricted to Franklin and Mirabeau),[20] but at the Dublin demonstration organised by the Tandy party, Paine's great work was invoked to stir the faint-hearted: 'a lantern decorated with a transparency heralding "the rights of man" was the standard' for the evening procession of city Volunteer corps making their way to St Stephen's Green under Tandy's command. According to a predictably jaundiced report in Giffard's *Dublin Journal,* 'whenever the magic lantern appeared the inhabitants were obliged to illuminate their windows, on pain of instant demolition, by the rabble that followed in its train'. Houses which refused to acknowledge the Painite lantern were stoned, he claimed, so that before the evening was over the army was called out. On the Green a cannon and two field-pieces were discharged.[21] It was one of the crowning moments of Tandy's political career.

The effect of *The Rights of Man* I on Irish politics was therefore unprecedented: announcing the arrival of Part II in February 1792 a Belfast bookseller claimed that *The Rights of Man* had been 'read perhaps more universally than any pamphlet during the present century'.[22] Martha McTier's comment to her brother William Drennan on reading it caught the essence:

I never liked kings and Paine has said of them what I always suspected, truth seems to dart from him in such plain and pregnant terms, that he, or *she* who runs may read...[23]

Yet as other contributors in this volume demonstrate, the seeds of Irish radicalism in the 1790s were several in kind, and were not suddenly scattered abroad in 1791. Paine's assertion of popular sovereignty and universal rights was only novel in its plain and unqualified definition. The revival of radical interpretations of contract theory among English parliamentary reformers during the American war had resonated in the writings and speeches of the advanced patriots and reformers in Ireland at that time. Even in the polemic of the Munster Rightboys, 'American' political language had found occasional echoes: a published resolution, purporting to come from a meeting of 'Munster peasantry' in 1786, asserted that 'by the common rights of mankind, the aggrieved are warranted to seek redress...[24] But Paine's vigorous rejection of prescriptive rights, of the tyranny of history and of the false rights of past generations to bind the present day had great force in Ireland as in Britain because of the racy directness of his unadorned writing and the memorable freshness of his imagery. No such subversive text had ever circulated so widely in Ireland.

The Rights of Man therefore helped to prepare the ground which the United Irishmen were to till. This would not have happened without the Whigs of the Capital who so assiduously fanned the demand for Paine during 1791 and managed to supply it. The virtue of *The Rights of Man* I for the Tandyites was that it helped them consolidate their position *vis-à-vis* the parliamentary Whigs in leading and moulding Irish 'popular' politics. The successful launching of the United Irish societies at the end of the year was at least in part a vindication of this policy. It was appropriate that the radical newspaper launched by the Carey brothers in Dublin on 10 November 1791, the day after the founding of the Dublin United Irish Society, should have as its main title

Rights of Irishmen.[25] The most tantalising link between Paine and the launch of the United Irish societies was Tone's *Argument on Behalf of the Catholics* which had appeared in August 1791. The intimate, chaste style of Tone's prose and the uncomplicated logic of the argument suggest a literary debt to Paine; its commercial success in the autumn of '91 (about 6,000 copies were sold in six months) was a measure of its political role in softening Presbyterian doubts as to Catholic ambitions.[26]

The Rights of Man, *Part II*

The Rights of Man II was published in London on 9 February 1792 and three days later Patrick Byrne produced an Irish edition.[27] Rival cheap sixpenny editions were published during April in Dublin and Belfast; booksellers offered it together with 'the French constitution and catechism', or the United Irish-sponsored *Digest of the Popery Laws* by Simon Butler. Part II however was much more selectively excerpted by the newspapers; even the new *Northern Star* published sections of it rather cautiously.[28] The more cogent and schematic attack on the illegitimacy of the British constitution, Paine's insistence on a non-monarchical republic, and the innovative social radicalism of Chapter 5 were strong wine; plans for progressive taxation, state pensions, a dole for the poor and universal education were unashamedly justified; and its explicit assertion that an hereditary monarchy was by its nature illegal took Paine and his supporters far beyond the outer limits of Whiggery. 'Liberty and equality' were now intertwined more closely with Paine's name than with events in Paris. But, as in Britain, Paine's concept of equality of rights, of representation and of security, was probably misread by most, and too often interpreted as an equality of wealth and income as well.[29]

The printing history of *The Rights of Man* II in Ireland is obscured by plans unfulfilled and ambiguous claims put forward in an atmosphere of increasing repression.[30] There were evidently fewer distinct editions of Part II, but novel ideas for the diffusion of the two parts were emerging. In May 1792 United Irishmen in Coleraine were reported to be preparing an Irish translation; nothing came of this (although shortly afterwards abridged translations were produced in Welsh and Scots Gaelic).[31] In January 1793 the Society in Dublin were planning a fund to underwrite a short penny-edition.[32] 'The most inconceivable industry', ob-

served the *Hibernian Magazine* that month, had been exerted 'to
obtrude this book on the minds of the public'.[33] By now United
Irishmen, north and south, were using the resources of the movement to publish and rework combinations of extracts and slogans
from Paine as a means of projecting their programme. Thus when
the Dublin Society sanctioned a large print run of John Keogh's
polemical essay advocating a speedy coalition of Catholics and
Presbyterians in September 1792, it was signed 'Common
Sense'.[34] Drennan, always anxious to cut Paine's intellectual significance down to size, privately complained of such policies:
'Tandy likes rather too much to publish.'[35] The diffusion of the
thoughts of Citizen Paine was to take many forms, but as a
process it continued to be refined up until 1798.

Late in 1792 the now completed text of *The Rights of Man* was
supplemented by Paine's last work composed in England, his even
more outspoken *Letter Addressed to the Addressers*, 'the best short
statement of his republicanism'.[36] There was a particular piquancy
in its rejection of the possibility of an internal reform of the
British parliament and its advocacy of a national convention of
democrats to draft a new constitution: for as Moore, Byrne and
eight other Dublin booksellers were publishing an Irish edition of
the *Letter*, the countrywide organisation of the Catholic Committee's representative national convention was underway. For the
Dublin radicals it must have been an agreeable coincidence.

By the end of 1792 the cult of Paine as martyr in the cause of
liberty and equality was taking shape. It was not of course specific
to Ireland and was a direct consequence of the counter-attack
from above. His September flight to France and his December
trial *in absentia* were covered extensively in the Irish press (and ten
booksellers produced a Dublin edition of the trial transcript).[37]
The campaign of vilification against Paine in Britain in the winter
of 1792/3, including the ritual burnings of his effigy, was echoed
in Castle statements and in the conservative Dublin press, notably
in Giffard's *Dublin Journal*, which systematically ridiculed the
arguments in *The Rights of Man* II.[38] A more intellectual attack
came from Thomas Elrington, a Fellow of TCD, who sought to
demonstrate the spurious Lockean ancestry of Painite ideas to the
college students, many of whom had been highly receptive to
Paine.[39] Their task was made easier by the repudiation of Paine by
moderate Whigs: the Earl of Charlemont, who in October 1792

was complaining of 'Paine's monstrosities'; Sir Laurence Parsons, who penned a fairly subtle critique of Painite principles in 1793; and the publishers of the *Belfast Newsletter*, who now gave much space to hostile assessments of Painite democracy.[40]

The crack-down on printers and booksellers associated with Paine was intensified after his trial in England, and in Ireland a string of indictments was issued against radical printers: 'the Attorney General...has by that means made the printers of Dublin pretty quiet', it was prematurely reported in January 1793.[41] That month the twelve proprietors of the *Northern Star* were indicted, and the United Irish owner of the *Hibernian Journal* was briefly held in jail on the order of the Commons; two months later McAllister was sent to prison by similar means, which apparently precipitated his bankruptcy. The other United Irish newspaperman in Dublin, Peter Cooney, was gagged by the Attorney-General the following September. Of the leading printers associated with Paine in Dublin, only the canny Byrne, his Catholic and radical sympathies notwithstanding, escaped being legally silenced.[42] Another early victim of the counter-offensive was Tandy himself: faced with charges of distributing the *Common Sense* pamphlet in Louth and, more seriously, of taking a Defender oath, he fled abroad.[43]

In a curious way both conservatives and radicals tended to highlight the role of Paine's writings in the increasingly polarised politics of 1793. On the one hand the upsurge in Defenderism and rural conflict was blamed by Castle papers on the new insubordination and 'resistance to the laws, originating in the confused notions of Mr Paine's villainous pamphlets, so industriously dispersed throughout the country last summer by...the United Irishmen', a theme which was echoed in the Lords' Secret Committee of that year.[44] George Knox, a level-headed observer of developments in Ulster, characterised the process in medical terms: 'the North is certainly completely inoculated by Paine who persuades every man to think himself a legislator and to throw off all respect for his superiors'.[45] But for the stronger radicals, mythologizing Paine also had its advantages at a time when public invocation of his name was legally hazardous. Two instances in the latter part of 1793 suggest the totemic quality of Paine's image and of the Rights-of-Man slogan. In August a series of public meetings were held on the steps of the Royal Exchange in Dublin where men 'not altogether of the lowest class' met 'to discuss politics after their own way'; the leading figure, Richard Dry, was reported to have been waving *The Rights of Man* when arrested. Another report claimed that a dispute between loyalists and radicals had broken out at the Exchange, and Dry had 'elevated a picture of Paine on his head' to rally the 'mobility'.[46] Three months later, a United Irish dinner in a city tavern included several toasts and incidents not reported in the press:

Tom Paine's health was drunk with the greatest fervancy [*sic*] and enthusiasm, the Volunteers of Ireland and speedy resurrection of them, a speedy and general revolution throughout Europe...When Paine's health was given his picture was introduc'd and received a general embrace. Several French songs were sung by Mr Sheares...[47]

This enormous veneration of Paine in Irish radical circles registered with the man himself, particularly after he became domiciled in France. As Thompson has recently shown, Paine's links with the Irish radicals in Paris in the winter of 1792/3 were intimate and enthusiastic; he was at the famous dinner in White's Hotel in November 1792 where Lord Edward Fitzgerald discarded his title and John Sheares proposed the main address of support for the French government. Fitzgerald gave a fulsome report of Paine's qualities as a host, and their friendship won Paine over to the idea of French military intervention in Ireland, a scheme which he put to Lebrun, the Foreign Minister, in December 1792. Oswald's secret mission to Ireland on behalf of the French government in 1793 was a direct consequence of Paine's representations. It seems to have had the unfortunate effect of giving United Irish leaders a dangerously over-sanguine impression of French commitment to Ireland.[48]

The Age of Reason *and beyond*
Paine's political influence in France sharply diminished in the early months of the war with the eclipse of the Girondins. Shortly before his detention he completed Part I of *The Age of Reason*, a racy if highly eclectic attack on institutional Christianity, designed to counter what Paine considered the destructive implications of revolutionary atheism. This was published during his long imprisonment. For many of his admirers – in Britain, America and Ireland – his new tack was at best politically embarrassing, at worst it put into question his very integrity. His deistical views divided

middle-class Irish radicals at what was already a time of great difficulty.[49]

Editions of *The Age of Reason*, Part I were published in Cork, Dublin and Belfast in 1794 and 1795, and they stirred up a striking range of radical responses – none quite so blunt as Tone's private comment that it was 'damned trash'.[50] In Cork the Presbyterian Rev. Thomas Hincks published a rebuttal to counter the local support for Paine's religious views expressed in Denis Driscol's *Cork Gazette*, the only Irish newspaper endorsing his views at that point.[51] Two politically radical east Ulster Presbyterian ministers also wrote in defence of revealed religion against Paine, and were published in Belfast.[52] Thomas Russell was involved in a short pamphlet against Paine's deism, also published there,[53] and another of Tone's close friends and an early United Irishman, Whitley Stokes FTCD, wrote a didactic critique of *The Age of Reason* which he said was then (March 1795) circulating among Trinity students.[54] In the same month the Rev. William Jackson, the radical English Anglican languishing in Dublin's Newgate on charges of high treason, felt compelled to write against Paine, completing his moving apologia only weeks before his suicide.[55] Father William Gahan of John's Lane seems to have been the first Catholic priest to write an attack on Paine (published in 1798); no rebel priest, he nevertheless echoed some of Jackson's phrases in his criticism of Paine, 'this great champion of Liberty and Equality...vain enough even to turn creed maker'. Yet even he admitted the potency of Paine's pamphlet:

[Paine] seems to possess the power of conveying what he says in plainer and more striking language than the generality of other witnesses. His style is insidious and insinuating...[56]

These rebuttals from radicals, priests and ministers are the best evidence that even in his more eccentric and ill-judged endeavours the power of Paine's pen in Ireland was formidable. Some leading radicals, notably the Munster circle of Driscol, the Sheares and the O'Connors, welcomed Paine's deism, and others saw political value in its anti-clericalism; it could help cement cross-denominational political alliances and trust. William Putnam McCabe, one of the most committed and energetic Belfast United Irishmen, was reported to have circulated *The Age of Reason* 'among one hundred workmen [in Belfast] answering their several objections

to any part of it'.[57] In Dublin, Henry Hutton, one of Tandy's publication committee in 1791 and a former city sheriff, was characterised in an anti-radical handbill to have been formerly

a religious quack, who used to exalt himself on beer barrells to deal out divinity;
but has laterally [*sic*] become the distributer of Tom Paine's aethistical [sic] pamphlets.[58]

At one of the Defender trials in February 1796, a Dublin tailor
gave evidence as to the staple reading matters at the Philanthropic
Society, the largest artisanal political club in the city in 1794/5,
with between 100 and 140 members: 'Paine's Age of Reason was
the object of our studies.'[59]

Thus despite the hostile reception of Paine's religious broadside among Irish radicals and the fact that only one newspaper
supported him fully in 1794/5, his scorning of the religious traditions that divided Irishmen made his religious radicalism opera-
tionally useful, and such was his status that *The Age of Reason* was
widely circulated. Mary McCracken recalled for Madden her
memories of its divisive impact even during 1798: United men in
the camp at Ballynahinch had thrown 'a great number of this
work ... into the houses' nearby:

a great number of pious Covenanters left the camp in consequence of the irreligious expressions and profanation of the Sabbath day, saying it could not have the
blessing of God, and I was shocked in Kilmainham to find them endeavouring to
keep up each other's spirits by making a jest of death...[60]

Despite such controversies, the essay did not weaken the continuing circulation, albeit often in abstracted form, of Paine's other
writings. Indeed Driscol was apparently more successful in the
Cork region during 1795 than ever before; Leonard McNally's
colourful reports to the Castle from the Cork assizes that year
may exaggerate but are still credible. He emphasised

the avidity with which Paine's principles of society and religion have spread their
influence. His works are in everyone's hands and in everyone's mouth. Large editions have been printed off by O'Driscol...and sent over the country; they have
got into the schools and are the constant subjects of conversations with the
youth.[61]

Commenting the same week on the restless 'working artisans' of
Dublin, Francis Higgins picked out those 'something above the
common babble, who by reading newspapers, Paine's politics of
Liberty and Equality' were becoming truly desperate.[62] John

Stockdale, Dublin printer and United Irishman, produced a composite volume of Paine's works, apparently early in 1796; indicted shortly afterwards for seeking 'to destroy and overturn the lawful government...and to excite sedition and rebellion', he was reported to have 'a great many volumes...for sale at his dwelling in Abbey Street...and in the outhouses to the said dwelling'.[63]

Paine's last major pamphlet of this period, *Agrarian Justice*, developed his earlier ideas on poverty and its political implications; where formerly he had seen poverty as primarily a consequence of taxation, he now recognised that it was a structural result of civilisation. He elaborated the case for a land tax and state intervention in welfare provision.[64] The essay was reprinted by Driscol in 1797, and was serialised in Arthur O'Connor's *Press* towards the end of that year. It is difficult to determine how far the social radicalism of sections of *The Rights of Man* II and of *Agrarian Justice* influenced the very small number of socially radical essays appearing in the later 1790s in Ireland. In these, demands for the redistribution of income were always directed against landed not commercial wealth, yet occasionally there were echoes of the welfare proposals in Chapter 5 of *The Rights of Man* II.[65]

The process of disseminating elements of Paine continued during the United Irish drive for rural popular support between 1796 and 1798. This was evident in the pages of the *Press*: with a circulation peaking at around 6,000 early in 1798 it was even more successful than the *Northern Star* in building up a radical readership, a remarkable achievement given the climate of overt repression.[66] The publishers of both the *Star* and the *Press* became involved with gathering and publishing collections of political ballads: *Paddy's Resource*...first appeared in Belfast in 1795, and with major amendments and additions was reissued in Dublin three years later as *Paddy's Resource; or the Harp of Erin Attuned to Freedom*. The prominence among these political ballads of references to 'Paine' and 'Rights of Man' is striking; 'God Save the Rights of Man' and possibly other ballads may have had American derivation, but most came from the pens of United Irish leaders in Belfast and Dublin. 'God Save the Rights of Man' was an immediately popular air, those which sought more didactically to elaborate Painite ideas probably less so. It is noticeable that there was a blunter, more violent tone to the 'Painite' ballads introduced in the Dublin edition of 1798:

Should tyrants e'er your Rights invade,
Crush at a blow the serpent brood;
Upon his neck indignant tread,
And sound your Freedom in their blood.[67]

But such ballads were not it seems translated into Irish, so that the penetration of the simplest Painite phrases must have been defined regionally: Ulster (and counties adjacent), most of Leinster and the towns of the south. But one tantalising hint of linguistic osmosis is suggested by (of all things) the reported passwords of the United Irish Society established in Philadelphia in 1797: '*codramaght*' (= *cothroime* [equality]?), and '*saoirseaught*' (= *saoirse* [liberty]?).[68] It would be revealing to discover the currency of these terms within the spoken language of the 1790s.

One of the beneficiaries of General Humbert's August 1798 landing in Mayo was a local millwright, liberated from Castlebar jail where he had been incarcerated a year previously for handing out *The Rights of Man* in Westport.[69] Reporting closely on the fate of that expedition was the Paris paper *Le Bien Informé*.[70] Its fascination with the Irish rebellion and the United Irishmen arose from the fact that Paine lived with the paper's editor and wrote extensively on matters Irish for it. Paine's renewed interest in Ireland seems to have been stirred by the arrival in Paris from America of Napper Tandy in June 1797. Tandy finally had the opportunity to befriend the man whose writings he had done so much to promote. The two men, of similar age and social habits, became close companions; Paine's frequent patronage of the 'Irish Coffee House' in Paris and his attendance at the St Patrick's Day dinner in 1798 were linked to this friendship (and presumably also to their mutual love of heavy drinking). The Tandy/Paine axis split the Irish *émigrés*, and Tone had nothing but contempt for Tandy's pretensions.[71] The extensive coverage of Irish news throughout 1798, as Le Biez illustrates below, was strongly coloured by Paine's support for Tandy's hopes and plans. After Tandy's abortive return to Ireland as a French general and his final capture, Paine privately but ingeniously lobbied for his release.[72] And in what was his only specific piece on Ireland in print, Paine published an article in *Le Citoyen français* in September 1801 advocating the liberation of Ireland by means of an invasion from the United States.[73] When Tandy was finally released and deported from Wicklow to Bordeaux in March 1802, it was assumed that Paine would provide support for him.[74] In fact Paine made his long-delayed return to the United States the following September, and a rather pathetic figure he cut there in his final years. Yet it was Irish friends, old and new, the *émigré* United Irishmen – including Thomas Addis Emmet, whom he made his executor – who befriended him to the bitter end.[75]

A final assessment of the impact of Paine on Irish political culture remains elusive. The immense short-term popularity of his writing with its humour and word-plays, its graphic metaphor and memorable phrases, cannot but have influenced all radical writing in Ireland in the 1790s. The main texts did 'transform the resentment of grievances into a sense of systematic oppression', helping for instance to politicise popular antipathy towards wartime excise taxes.[76] But insofar as the spread of Painite ideas coincided with the frenetic efforts of the Catholic Committee to organise a democratic mandate for their policy, it is not self-evident that they needed Tom Paine to win massive endorsement. In Britain rights, universal or otherwise, became the central concern of most radical writing, whereas in Ireland the 'rights of man' were being transmuted into the rights of Irishmen.

In the longer run radical contract theory and indeed natural rights philosophy as a whole were doctrines soon to be set aside in prevailing political discourse; Bentham's damning epitaph stood for many: 'natural rights is simple nonsense; natural and imprescriptible rights, rhetorical nonsense, nonsense upon stilts'.[77] Paine had no ideological framework to offer the craftworker or the agricultural labourer struggling to assert collective rights in the following century; it was left to others to elaborate the rights of labour. Yet in the bitter politics of O'Connellite Ireland, the language of rights survived: 'rights' were juxtaposed with 'wrongs', allowing Paine to be reintroduced into a bizarre gallery of folk heroes in contemporary balladry.[78]

The most profound consequence of the Painite 'flood' may possibly have in the reaction to it: the wave of radical pamphlets, broadsides, newspapers and songsheets gave government and conservative forces in Ireland, as in Britain, a profound shock and prompted them to organise with dramatic urgency the mass distribution of alternative literature. The scale of the re-publicising activities of the Irish Association for Discountenancing Vice (founded in 1792) is remarkable: it claimed to have circulated 120,000 copies of Hannah More's 'cheap repository' tracts in 1796 alone, challenging both the political literature of the moment and the underworld of suspect chap-book literature.[79] Simple government propaganda pamphlets, such as Arthur Young's *French Fraternity*, 13,000 copies of which were produced in 1798, were flowing from the Dublin printing presses on a novel scale.[80] The accelerating output of Catholic devotional literature was a complementary reaction. Popular education and the control of its content was moving to the top of the political agenda.[81]

12

SCOTTISH RADICALISM AND THE UNITED IRISHMEN

John Brims

As early as June 1791, when a paper was being circulated in Dublin outlining plans for a secret society dedicated to parliamentary reform, Catholic emancipation and greater Irish independence from London, it was proposed that part of the business of such a society should be to enter into 'communication with similar societies abroad, as the Jacobin Club in Paris, the Revolution Society in England, [and] the Committee for Reform in Scotland'.[1] While the United Irishmen were primarily concerned with the liberation and reform of their country they were, as McDowell has put it, 'inspired…with a sense of being participants in a great European drive against tyranny and anachronistic privilege'.[2] They did not, as yet, look abroad for military assistance in their struggle to reduce the corrupting influence of English government in Ireland, but they did seek moral support and intellectual stimulus from like-minded organisations in other countries in a common struggle of peoples across the world for liberty. 'Let the nations go abreast,' the Dublin radicals proclaimed, 'let the interchange of sentiment among mankind concerning the rights of man be as immediate as possible.'[3]

Almost ten months after the first Society of United Irishmen had been formed in Belfast in October 1791, a Scottish group consisting of Foxite Whig gentlemen, middle-class burgh reformers, and radical artisans met together in Edinburgh's prestigious Fortune's Tavern on 26 July 1792 to form themselves into 'a permanent society under the appellation of the Associated Friends of the People'.[4] The new organisation declared that their objectives were 'to attempt by all constitutional means, the attainment, first, of an equal representation of the people, and, second, of a more limited duration of parliamentary delegation'.[5]

There was nothing here of the high-flown rhetoric of interna-

tional radicalism. No appeal was made for fraternal solidarity with
the peoples of France, Poland or Ireland, neither was there any
allusion to the international nature of the great political drama
into which they were seeking to draw the Scottish nation. The
Scots reformers of summer 1792 couched their demands in the
pedestrian, prosaic language of Whig constitutionalism and limited their political horizons to the problems of Great Britain. This
political insularity did not, however, reflect the real sentiments
either of the sort of men from whom the Association drew its support, or of the nation at large. For example, James Thomson Cal-
lender, a member of the Canongate No. 1 Society of the Friends
of the People and a vigorous pamphleteer in the cause of reform,
had some months earlier berated Britain's *ancien régime* for pursuing an imperialist foreign policy founded on 'the principles...of a
robber';[6] only a few days after the Fortune's Tavern meeting a
subscription was opened in Perth 'for assisting the people of
Poland to defend their country and liberties'.[7] The Fortune's
Tavern resolutions reveal not an insularity of mind nor a meanness of spirit, but rather a calculated decision to distance the
infant reform movement in Scotland from the principles of international radicalism, especially those of the French Revolution.
The leaders of the new Association sought to assure the public
that their movement owed nothing to the natural-rights theories
associated with France but aimed only to restore the ancient
British constitution to its original purity.

This attempt to differentiate the Scottish reform movement
from apparently similar ones in other countries was designed to
win the confidence of the landed classes and the urban bourgeoisie, who had grievances of their own and who might therefore
be persuaded to support a constitutional reform movement
uncontaminated by dangerous radical heresies. It was not unrea-
sonable for the founding fathers of the Association to think that
they could win over country gentlemen who had complained so
loudly about 'aristocratic domination' of county politics and the
urban businessmen who for a decade had been trying to slay the
hydra-headed corruption which supposedly was gnawing at the
vitals of their communities.[8] Indeed, in the summer of 1792 it
appears that some country gentlemen had indicated a willingness
to join a Scottish association modelled on that of the London
Society of the Friends of the People; and some leaders of the

burgh reform movement had not only expressed support for a Scottish organisation dedicated to achieving parliamentary reform, but had also been actively involved in setting up the Association.[9] No sooner, however, had the inaugural meeting been arranged than some of the intended participants began to have second thoughts. Doubting whether the leadership could control the plebeian mass membership it sought to attract, and fearing that the Association would soon abandon its moderation and adopt radical, even revolutionary, policies, they withdrew their support, leaving the leadership dangerously isolated from the traditional political nation.

Deprived of the support of a majority of the landed gentry and a majority of the urban middle class, and denied the organisational experience and political weight which the country and burgh reformers could lend, the Scottish Association of the Friends of the People made only limited progress during the summer and early autumn of 1792. Footholds were established in the major urban centres of Dundee, Edinburgh, Glasgow and Perth by the end of September,[10] but the Association had as yet failed to secure a presence in the smaller towns and villages of Scotland. It was certainly an important enough body in its own right to attract the attention of government ministers and their spies, the press, and the politically aware public. However, much of that initial attention was focused on its potential rather than its actual strength. But the last quarter of 1792 saw the movement expand rapidly both in membership and in organisation throughout lowland Scotland. By the end of the year, there was hardly a town south of Aberdeen without its own Society of the Friends of the People; in Ayrshire, to take one example, societies had been formed in Galston, Newmilns, Kilmaurs, Kilwinning, Kilmarnock, Fenwick and Saltcoats; in Fife, the movement had established a presence in Dunfermline, Pathhead of Kirkcaldy, Auchterderran, Leslie, Anstruther and Auchtermuchty.[11] The strength of the movement, however, cannot be estimated solely by the growing number of active societies or even by its expanding membership. Some reformers never bothered to establish a formal organisation or to advertise their activities, being content instead to meet informally in each other's houses.

Their conservative opponents were disturbed not so much by the thousands who actually joined the Friends of the People but rather by the more general ground swell of popular support for radical reform. At Rothesay, the Marquis of Bute observed that 'even in this sequestered spot...liberty and the rights of man are inscribed upon every door of the cotton mill at Rothesay [and that] the general conversation of the work people tend that way'.[12] The thousands of artisans and workmen who flocked to the banner of reform in the last few weeks of 1792 were not attracted by the sort of moderate constitutional reform envisaged by the Foxite leadership of the Friends of the People. Their political Bible was Tom Paine's *Rights of Man* rather than William Blackstone's *Commentaries on the Laws of England*, while their inspiration was drawn less from the Whig constitutionalism of eighteenth-century Britain than from the contemporary democratic revolution in France. After Dumouriez's thrilling victories at Valmy and Jemappes over the supposedly invincible 'armies of despotism', the Revolution was now apparently secured within France and poised to sweep across Europe. The Friends of the People chose to ignore the sensational events on the Continent and refused to join their English and Irish colleagues in sending congratulatory addresses to the French National Convention, but their attempt to distance themselves from international radicalism was doomed to failure. The Dundee crowd which erected a tree of liberty to celebrate Dumouriez's entry into Brussels demonstrated their commitment to radical change at home by decorating the tree with a banner bearing the motto 'Liberty & Equality, No sinecures'.[13] In vain did the Dundee Society of the Friends of Liberty publish resolutions condemning 'riotous and disorderly meetings',[14] and the claim that the growing momentum behind the Scottish campaign for radical political change was unconnected with events on the Continent was beginning to look threadbare.

When the Scottish Association of the Friends of the People assembled at their first convention on 11 December 1792, they were faced with a serious dilemma: should they hold fast to the alliance with the London Friends of the People, continue to distance themselves from Jacobinism both at home and abroad, and concentrate their energies on organising respectful petitions in favour of parliamentary reform? Or should they reject the moderate, reformist strategy of their founders, proclaim their adherence to the cause of the rights of man, and devote themselves to organising a mass movement openly committed to the sort of radical programme which was clearly capable of attracting substantial support within the artisan community?

The debate on the movement's future strategy was centred on the resolutions brought forward by John Morthland, a Whig party activist and former Advocate Deputy in the Fox-North administration, and on an address from the Dublin Society of United Irishmen presented by Thomas Muir, a young, ambitious and radical advocate who had done much to organise the Association in the Glasgow area. Morthland's resolutions were intended to reaffirm the Association's commitment to constitutional methods and objectives in the face of both growing popular support for radical Painite policies and a loyalist offensive which sought to portray the reformers as Jacobin revolutionaries. The resolutions were cleverly drafted, being phrased so as to maximise support for a policy that was apparently moderate and undoubtedly constitutional, and to isolate the republican Painite delegates. After some debate, the convention resolved to declare its abhorrence of 'public discord' and 'an equal division of property', and its willingness to assist in repressing 'riot and tumult'; it was agreed that 'great abuses have arisen...from a neglect of the genuine principles of the Constitution', and that the removal of those abuses necessitated 'an equal representation of the people in parliament' and 'frequent' elections.[15] The only heated debate occasioned by Morthland's resolutions revolved around the proposal to commit the Association to 'maintain the established Constitution of Great Britain...consisting of...King, Lords and Commons'.[16] This unequivocal statement of support for the tripartite Whig constitution was opposed by a number of delegates, with several arguing that the phrase 'King, Lords and Commons' be dropped,[17] one subtle soul suggesting that the convention resolve to 'acknowledge' rather than 'maintain' the constitution.[18] In the event, the overtly republican delegates were outvoted by a large majority. The outcome of the debate, however, may have turned on tactical considerations rather than fundamental principles. Some of the reformers who were themselves attracted to republicanism believed that the country was not yet prepared to adopt a republican constitution,[19] and argued that there was no political profit to be gained from embracing an unpopular policy which would only strengthen the hands of both the government and the newly established loyalist associations.

The convention's behaviour was determined in part by the need to avoid giving the increasingly alarmed authorities any excuse to crack down on the Association's activities, and in part by the belief that new support could be obtained *en masse* only if the movement could reassure prospective recruits of its moderation. Thus Morthland's studiously moderate resolutions were accepted, and the published minutes of the convention were doctored to make it appear that they had been passed without opposition.[20] The convention also agreed to send its delegates to sign the loyalist Goldsmith's Hall Association's declaration,[21] and forced Thomas Muir to withdraw the address he had presented from the Dublin Society of United Irishmen.[22]

The rejection of the Irish Address (as it was called) was decided only after a series of heated debates which split the convention. There was much in the address that was attractive to the delegates. It appealed to the principle of international solidarity, and there was little objection to the principle of close links between reform movements in two nations within one empire.[23] Most Scots reformers, indeed, would have agreed with the assertion in the United Irishmen's address that 'our cause is your cause' and that 'our rights and wrongs are the same'. The problem, the majority of delegates believed, lay in the intemperate and dangerously nationalistic language of the address. It congratulated the Scots for attempting to determine their own future, recording the Dublin Society's joy that 'you do not consider yourselves as merged & melted down into another country, but that in this great national question you are still Scotland – the land where Buchanan wrote, and Fletcher spoke, and Wallace fought'. While most of the delegates would doubtless have been pleased by the United Irishmen's recognition of Scotland's national identity within the British state and the national nature of the Scottish Association's campaign, many would have been deeply concerned by references to Buchanan, the great sixteenth-century Scottish 'republican' ideologist, to Fletcher, the republican arch-opponent of the parliamentary union of 1707, and to Wallace, the popular hero of Scotland's war against imperialist England in the 1290s. That concern, however, turned to alarm when the delegates read that Scotland was 'willing' reform 'with the unity and energy of an embodied nation', and that 'it is not the constitution but the people which ought to be inviolable'.[24] The tone of the address contrasted starkly with the mood of the convention which had just resolved to maintain the established constitution and was clearly anxious to distance itself from anything which even hinted at revolutionary intentions; the Scots reformers had consistently declared that their objective was to reform the British constitution, and they had no ambitions to renegotiate, far less to dissolve the parliamentary union with England. And while the associators hoped to put together 'a general association of the whole people' of Scotland, the delegates were well aware that much still needed to be done before their ambition was realised. They did not claim to represent the Scottish nation, 'embodied' or otherwise.

Rejection of the Irish Address must have come as a shock to the Dublin United Irishmen who had been assured by Thomas Muir prior to the convention that the Scots highly approved of their 'principles and pursuits' and would offer 'the most strenuous support and co-operation'.[25] Muir, indeed, may well have encouraged the Dublin Society to send their address. He had established a close political friendship with Archibald Hamilton Rowan earlier in the year and, in the period immediately preceding the convention meeting, their correspondence had become more frequent.[26] The content of this correspondence is not known, but it is very likely that they discussed the desirability of forging links between their two organisations to increase pressure on their respective parliaments to grant reform. The similarities between Muir's strategy and those of the United Irish leadership are striking. While William Drennan was urging the Ulster reformers to hold a provincial convention which, having ascertained and 'embodied' public opinion, would remain sitting until reform had been granted,[27] Muir was delivering a speech in Edinburgh arguing that only a national convention could focus and strengthen public opinion and, by applying concerted pressure, force parliament to accede to the convention's demands.[28] It is also possible that Muir influenced the content and tone of the Dublin Society's address. The violently Anglophobic and nationalistic content of Muir's memoranda to the French Directory in 1797 and 1798 is well known, but the young advocate may have been attracted to nationalist ideas even at this early stage of his career. During the meeting of the first convention, Muir answered the claim of an English *émigré* delegate that 'Scotland and England are but one people' by arguing that Scotland was a quite separate country with a distinctive legal system;[29]

on another occasion, he repeatedly assured the convention that the ancient Scottish constitution was as free and democratic as that of Anglo-Saxon England.[30] Given that the published resolutions, declarations and addresses of the Scottish associators were hardly suggestive of a commitment to republicanism, it may be that the United Irishmen's nationalist interpretation of Scottish history and the Scottish parliamentary reform movement was reinforced by the letters they had received from Thomas Muir.

In rejecting the Irish Address, the Scottish Association rejected both an alliance with the United Irishmen and the republican nationalism to which the Irish appealed. If a 'revolutionary moment' had existed at the end of 1792, the Scottish Association had let it pass. The convention had in effect decided that the quasi-millenarian optimism and political enthusiasm of the Scottish *menu peuple* were to be discouraged. The energies of the people were to be channelled into, firstly, defending the Association's constitutionalist credentials from loyalist propaganda attacks and, secondly, a petitioning campaign in support of Charles Grey's expected motion in favour of parliamentary reform.[31] The events of the first four months of 1793 did not suggest that the convention had backed any winners. The loyal declarations of individual societies and of the convention itself failed to reassure the nervous Scottish bourgeoisie and landed classes while, psychologically, these gestures placed the movement on the defensive and destroyed the popular optimism that had fuelled the movement's growth during the previous year. Thus when it came to organising petitions in support of Grey's motion, the Association found it impossible to mobilise public opinion and even, in some cases, to rouse the societies of the Friends of the People into distributing the petition for subscription.[32] In the event, the campaign faltered and became something of a fiasco, with only twenty-one petitions being forwarded to London for presentation to the House of Commons.[33] The associators had failed to place parliament under any pressure to concede their demands. On 7 May, Grey's motion for a committee of enquiry into the state of representation was defeated by the crushing margin of 282 to 41.[34]

In the wake of this disaster, the reformers' morale plummeted. Attendance at meetings declined, membership subscriptions remained unpaid, and some societies suspended their activities altogether.[35] The need to review the movement's strategy was clear. The initiative came from Thomas Hardy, the Scots-born secretary of the London Corresponding Society, who wrote to the Edinburgh Association of the Friends of the People urging that their societies should 'unite...not only with each other, but with every other society throughout the nation' and suggesting that 'the firmest measures' be adopted.[36] Hardy's overture was well received by the leadership of the Scottish Association; by the end of the summer of 1793, a new strategy had been agreed. The vacillating leadership of the London Society of the Friends of the People would be rejected along with the studiously moderate policies it had advocated, and the Scottish Association would unite with the popular English radical societies to form 'a union of counsels and union of wills' which would 'compel an attention to their just and reasonable demands'.[37] There would be no more deferential supplications to parliament. A united, resolute British reform movement would demand democratic reform. The stage had been set for the meeting of the 'British Convention' and for confrontation with government.

During the summer of 1793 an address from the four Societies of United Irishmen of Belfast had arrived in Edinburgh. This address, drawn up in February but delayed by communications difficulties, was accompanied by a letter dated 1 May 1793 from William Mitchell, the Belfast secretary, informing the Scots that 'the province of Ulster is able...to protect itself against those who are nick-named its Protectors' (i.e. the army), and asking 'whether the Societies of the Friends of the People and Parliamentary Reform are as numerous and spirited as some months ago'.[38] The first notice taken of these letters in Scotland was at the meeting of the third national convention of the Scottish Association, which assembled in Edinburgh on 29 October 1793. The tardy despatch of invitations to the English societies prevented the timely arrival of delegates from south of the border, but the convention proceeded to its business and prepared the ground for a future British Convention. The delegates unanimously agreed to declare for universal manhood suffrage and annual parliaments, voted for a democratic propaganda offensive, and resolved 'unanimously' to express their 'ardent desire to cultivate a more close union with England'.[39] Curiously, however, there was no decision to support such a union with the United Irishmen, and, so far as is known, the convention failed even to reply to the Belfast address. This failure to respond to a friendly address, which advised the Scots of the progress of the reform movement in Ireland, expressed the Belfast societies' pleasure at the political awakening of Scotland, and urged the Scottish association to persevere in the 'arduous' struggle, appears at first sight baffling. The same political logic which persuaded the Scots to embrace those English radical societies they had formerly kept at arm's length, would also have encouraged them, it might be thought, to co-operate closely with the United Irishmen. It seems likely in fact that the delegates were as alarmed by the nationalistic tone of the second Irish address as their predecessors had been by that of the Dublin society.[40] The Belfast societies' declaration that the Irish had long been astonished that 'Scotland should have so long forgotten her degraded state as a nation, slept over her political insignificance, [and] silently acquiesced in the mockery of a popular representation among the Senators of another nation'[41] would have won few admirers among delegates determined to create a new democratic British state and in so doing cement the constitutional ties between Scotland and England.

The Scottish reformers, however, were not indifferent to developments in Ireland nor to the progress of the reform movement there. The introduction of the Irish Convention bill in July 1793 and its rapid progress through the Irish parliament were watched with great interest and increasing alarm by the Scottish associators. Archibald Hamilton Rowan echoed the opinions of his Scottish counterparts when he declared, in a letter to Norman Macleod, the radical Foxite MP for Inverness-shire, 'that the destruction or establishment of the rights of mankind in one nation conduces a similar consequence in its neighbouring state'.[42] The Scots (and English) democrats were convinced that George III's government was rehearsing in Ireland those repressive measures it intended to introduce shortly into Britain.

Delegates assembled again in Edinburgh on 19 November 1793 in what became the British Convention; they met in an atmosphere of crisis precipitated, they believed, by a government intent upon destroying British liberties and plunging the country into tyranny. The despotic intentions of government were proved, they argued, not only by the passage of a Convention Act designed to prevent the effective representation of popular grievances, but also by the use of the Scottish courts to criminalise all attempts to mobilise and organise public opinion in support of parliamentary reform. In such an atmosphere, sinister rumours of government plans to land German mercenary troops secretly in Britain were readily believed. The mood of the Scottish Association of the Friends of the People was well caught by its secretary, William Skirving, who wrote to the Laurieston Society on 16 October 1793 arguing that 'if we do not at this time strenuously maintain our rights we may be...made slaves'.[43] Convinced that only the adoption of the 'firmest measures' would save the country from a rapidly approaching despotism, the delegates tried to intimidate the enemies of liberty. On 23 November they unanimously agreed to unite the reform movements of Scotland and England and to restyle their assembly 'the British Convention of the Delegates of the People Associated to obtain Universal Suffrage and Annual Parliaments'.[44] Despite this name, the delegates did not intend to set themselves up as an alternative and more legitimate representative assembly than parliament, but meant only to affirm Anglo-Scottish radical solidarity in the struggle for democratic reform. Two days later, having considered 'the oppressed state of their brethren in Ireland, and the unconstitutional Act of the last session of their Parliament, called the Convention Act',[45] the convention resolved to extend radical solidarity across the Irish Sea. Henceforth, it was agreed, 'all or any of the patriotic members of the Society of United Irishmen shall be admitted to speak and vote in this convention'.[46] No sooner had this motion been passed and 'guaranteed' by the 'solemn joining of hands', than Alexander Callander moved that the introduction into parliament of a Convention Bill 'as passed in Ireland, for preventing the people from meeting according to their just rights by the Revolution' should be regarded as a signal to the societies to choose delegates 'to meet in convention to assert their rights'.[47] After considerable debate, during which there was much loose and wild talk about 'the duty of resistance by force of arms',[48] an amended and extended motion was passed stipulating the grounds upon which a convention of emergency would be activated to meet in 'permanent' session to defend liberty and the cause of reform 'until compelled to desist by superior force'.[49]

While there can be no doubt of the democrats' determination to resist the tyranny they saw approaching so rapidly, they were in no position to implement the threatened insurrection. The Association in Scotland had neither weapons nor a military organisation. Moreover, they had made no attempt to suborn the armed forces, and there was little or no evidence to suggest that the army would prove anything other than loyal to the government in any confrontation with the radicals. Like much else at the British Convention, the talk of resistance and appeal to arms were mere empty posturing. It provided the authorities with the opportunity they had been looking for to disperse the convention, arrest its leaders, and bring them to trial for sedition. Following its dispersal, the associators were stigmatised as revolutionaries and criminalised as seditious. Attempts to defend themselves against these charges both in the High Court of Justiciary and in print failed, and the reform movement simply collapsed under the weight of repression and hostile public opinion. Many societies disbanded their organisation, while others saw their attendances fall dramatically as frightened and disheartened reformers fled the political battlefield.[50]

By the spring of 1794, the cause of parliamentary reform in Scotland had no apparent future, and Scottish democrats were faced with a stark choice. They could either wait indefinitely in prudent silence for circumstances to change, or they could transform themselves into a revolutionary organisation dedicated to the violent overthrow of the old régime. Some radicals, led by Robert Watt, a former government spy, turned immediately to insurrectionary conspiracy. The 'Pike Plot' was still in its embryonic stages in May 1794 when the chance discovery of pike-heads led to the conspiracy being detected and its leaders arrested; the plotters' organisation was rudimentary, their funding limited, and their planning sketchy. The plan was to seize the leading figures of the government in Scotland and the judiciary, to capture Edinburgh Castle, and to establish a provisional government in the hope that this putsch would paralyse government in 'North Britain' and act as a signal to like-minded radicals in England and Ireland to mount their own coups.[51] So far as is known, however, there was no attempt to establish the contacts which would have facilitated the co-ordination of the insurrection throughout the three kingdoms.

The public execution of Robert Watt for high treason on 15 October 1794 served to remind his would-be imitators of the dreadful price paid by failed revolutionaries, and for a year and a half Scottish radicalism remained politically dormant. Only an organisational structure which would offer them a measure of security against informers and a plan of insurrection which promised them the prospect of success could revive it. Both were offered by the United Irishmen, who began to re-establish contacts with the Scots in the spring of 1796. Wolfe Tone recorded in his diary on 9 April 1796 that Captain Aherne had been in Scotland recently and that 'there is some scheme going on there'.[52] Tone had no interest in Scotland, believing that it was a diversion from the task of liberating Ireland, but other leading United Irishmen, particularly in Ulster, held a different opinion.

In July 1796 Joseph Cuthbert and Thomas Potts of one of the Belfast United Irish societies returned from Scotland in 'high spirits', reporting that they had taken 'the new Irish Constitution for the inspection and approbation of the Scots', and that 'the Scotch were willing and ready to act with the Friends of Liberty in Ireland'.[53] A more sober assessment of the progress of the infant Society of United Scotsmen was offered around the same period by another Belfast United Irishman, John Simpson, who reported that 'the Scotch were not possessed of sufficient energy; but their [*sic*] was decent fellowes among them, and they were coming on surprisingly'.[54] These early contacts between the Ulster United Irishmen and the Scots radicals were subsequently strengthened. Delegates from the north of Ireland travelled frequently to Scotland to pass on information about the progress of the United Irishmen, report on negotiations in Paris between their agents and the French Directory, gather intelligence on the United Scotsmen, and assist in expanding the radical organisation of the United in Scotland. Some of these delegates attended meetings of the national committee and were afforded access to the most confidential information. One such delegate was Dr Thomson of Ballynish, who informed a baronial committee at Saintfield, County Down, on 21 October 1797 that the 'Scotch Constitution...is word for word the same as the Irish' apart from the substitution of 'North Britains' for 'Irishmen', and that he had attended two meetings of the United Scotsmen's national committee on 10 May and 10 September, when it was reported that the number of 'United Britains' had increased from 2871 to 9653.[55]

The Scottish authorities were aware of the contacts between

the Ulster United Irishmen and the Scots radicals, and they made strenuous efforts to restrict them. Excise officers were instructed to keep a close watch on vessels arriving from Ireland, apprehend 'suspicious' persons, and return those with whom they were not satisfied.[56] There were serious doubts about the legality of such measures, but they were imperiously swept aside by Robert Dundas, the government's chief law officer in Scotland, who ordered their implementation. It is doubtful, however, whether the apparatus of the late eighteenth-century British state was capable of preventing political intercourse between Ireland and Scotland and, in truth, Dundas's orders did nothing to halt either the intercourse or the massive emigration of radical Irishmen from Ulster to Scotland following the imposition of martial law in the province in 1797. Many of these *émigrés* joined or established their own societies of United Scotsmen, and the Scottish authorities quickly came to regard the United Scotsmen as little more than an overseas branch of the United Irishmen. There was clear evidence of Irish involvement in the United Scotsmen, particularly in Ayrshire, and the Scots radicals in describing the expansion of their organisation referred to the 'planting of Irish potatoes',[57] but the growth of the United Scotsmen in areas such as Fife, Angus and Perthshire where Irish immigration was very limited suggests strongly that the movement remained essentially indigenous in character.

While the military crackdown in Ulster provided recruits for the United Scotsmen from among the *émigré* Irish community, the growth of the society was largely fuelled by popular discontent arising from the Scottish Militia Act of 1797. Widely viewed as an unconstitutional and sinister measure which sought to conscript the sons of the 'lower orders' while allowing the offspring of the wealthy the option of purchasing exemptions, the Militia Act was violently opposed in many parts of the country.[58] The resultant disturbances, which saw the destruction of lists of those liable to serve in the militia, the intimidation of those responsible for drawing up and revising the lists, and the coercion of landed proprietors into signing bonds promising to refuse to implement the act, were well organised but spontaneous. If, as has been suggested, the United Scotsmen sought to exploit the opposition to the Militia Act in order to precipitate an insurrection,[59] it is more than passing strange that there were no anti-militia disturbances in the organisation's heartlands in Glasgow and Paisley. Insofar as the United Scotsmen were involved in organising opposition to the Act in parts of Fife and Perthshire,[60] their objectives appear to have been limited to demonstrating to the common people the weakness of the old régime in the face of organised resistance, thereby improving the society's standing within the community and facilitating its further expansion. The United Scotsmen were not intent on promoting a premature Scottish rising but rather on preparing the ground for an insurrection which would accompany the landing of a French army in either Britain or Ireland.

The United Scotsmen sought consistently to co-ordinate their plans with their colleagues in Ireland and England, and with the Directory in Paris. To this end, delegates moved between Scotland, Belfast, Manchester, London and Paris exchanging intelligence and plans. The important decisions, however, were made in Paris – where the United Scotsmen had limited influence, compared with the powerful Irish lobby in the city led by the formidably persuasive Tone. Even Muir's arrival in Paris in December 1797 did little to alter the balance of power within the *émigré* community there. Seizing the opportunity afforded by Napper Tandy's proposal to organise an Irish rising without the assistance of a French invasion force, Muir earned Tone's lasting hatred by lobbying the French government for an army of liberation to be dispatched to a supposedly staunchly republican Scotland, whose people would rejoice at the chance to break the chains of English misrule.[61] Although Muir's memoranda were calculated to exploit internal Irish policy disagreements and to appeal to French perceptions of modern Scottish history, they had in fact no impact on French decision-making. Ireland rather than Scotland continued to hold French attention as an invasion target. When the Irish rose, however, they did so with only the most limited support from France, and with none whatsoever from either Scotland or England. The promised force of between 100,000 and 200,000 Scottish insurgents never materialised.[62] Indeed, there is no evidence of any attempt by the United Scotsmen to organise even the most limited form of insurrectionary action in support of their Irish allies. Whether the United Scotsmen were unwilling to commit their organisation to armed struggle during the summer of 1798, or were simply incapable of doing so, is still unclear. Given the circumstances, however, the United Scotsmen's leader-

ship could have been under few illusions about the likely consequences of local insurrection. Its objective would have been
merely diversionary and, with respect to Scotland at least, the outcome would almost certainly have been total and bloody defeat.
Nevertheless, although there were good practical reasons for not
rising in rebellion, the United Scotsmen had broken their promise
to the United Irishmen and had abandoned their allies in their
moment of greatest need.

13

FREEMASONRY AND THE UNITED IRISHMEN

Jim Smyth

For conspiracy theorists the 1790s were a golden age. Stunned by the French Revolution and its European impact, anxious conservatives sought to explain these events in terms of a deliberate, deep-laid design. Most famously the Royalist (and, ironically, Jesuit) émigré, the Abbé Barruel, claimed in his influential multi-volume *Memoirs of Jacobinism* (1797) to have uncovered a vast international Masonic-illuminati plot to destroy the Christian religion and to overthrow the established order. In the same year John Robison reiterated these charges in *Proofs of a Conspiracy against all the Religions and Governments of Europe, carried on in the Secret Meetings of Freemasons, Illuminati and Reading Societies*, although he explicitly exempted British Masons from stricture. Nor did conservatives have a monopoly of such theories. During the 1770s both the American colonists and the Rockingham Whigs traced the source of the British government's coercive policies to a 'ministerial plot' against liberty. In 1791 the Irish radical William Drennan drew a distinction between 'benevolent conspiracies' based on republican virtue and conceived in the interests of 'the people', and those 'malignant conspiracies which courts and classes have formed'. [1]

Like earlier providential explanations of political change, these conspiracy theories were straightforward, easy to grasp and, to the eighteenth-century mind, believable. Modern historians are less credulous, preferring more complex and impersonal 'models' of causation. [2] Yet if conspiracy theories usually reveal more about the psychology of their advocates and their audiences than they do about conspiracies, it does not follow that they are, therefore, always baseless. In the course of the 1790s certain Italian Masonic lodges behaved much as Barruel would have expected. He would not have been surprised, either, by those Welsh lodges 'patronised by unitarians of Jacobin and Paineite sympathies',[3] nor by the activities of some of their fellow Masons in Ulster during the same period.

Irish historians have long been aware of a connection between Freemasonry and radical and popular politics in the late eighteenth century. A Masonic dimension has been identified in Volunteering, in Defenderism, in the United Irish movement and in the early Orange Order. But this phenomenon has not generated the attention that it deserves. Since craft rules stipulate that members leave their political opinions at the lodge door, Masonic historians have hurried over what they consider as the regrettable and aberrant political entanglements of the 1780s and 1790s in rather indecent haste. Less predictably, the anti-Masonic historiography is equally slim. The first (and only) Barruel-style account of the 1790s did not appear until 1937, with the publication of Leo McCabe's hysterical, clericalist polemic, *Wolfe Tone and the United Irishmen: For or Against Christ?* Ireland's premier conspiracy theorist at the time, Sir Richard Musgrave, had almost nothing to say on the subject of masonry.[4] Barruel's English translator, Robert Clifford, compared United Irish structures with those of the illuminati, and remarked that the executed Defender captain, Lawrence O'Connor, was a Freemason, but conspicuously avoided implicating Irish Masons as a body in any revolutionary conspiracy.[5] The apolitical and socially respectable reputation of the Irish craft may not have survived the 1790s entirely unscathed,[6] but neither did it, in the view of contemporaries like Musgrave and Clifford, conform to the sinister, irreligious, European pattern.

In practice Irish Freemasons were a politically heterogeneous group. The officers of the Grand Lodge were recruited, as in England, from the upper ranks, albeit the Whiggish upper ranks, of the social élite, and they remained impeccably loyal throughout the crisis. In Munster, critics denounced the craft as 'aristocratic'.[7] The relationship between Masonry and the first Orange lodges – and the term lodge was not merely coincidental – has already been noted.[8] Masonry was sensitive to local conditions and was therefore most radical, and later most disaffected, where radicalism and disaffection were strongest: in mid- and east Ulster and in Dublin. For all its diversity, however, the Masonic ethos was nonetheless attuned to the radical cause.

What strikes outsiders about Freemasonry most forcefully is its cult of secrecy, its arcane symbolism and ritual, and its bogus 'traditions'. These have purpose and function, and United Irishmen, Defenders and Orangemen all borrowed freely from Masonic terminology and practice. Drennan suggested the Masonic model for the future United Irish organisation, which he at that stage called the 'Brotherhood', and recommended secrecy and ceremonial to give the new society popular allure and internal cohesion.[9] The esoteric style of Defender catechisms, passwords and hand-signs bears an unmistakable Masonic imprint. John Magennis, the Defender leader in County Down, adopted the title 'Grand Master'.[10] Clearly the language and imagery of Freemasonry was ready to hand. Indeed, at one level, Freemasonry and the popular political movements answered the same social and recreational needs.

Mercifully, the debate about the origins and antiquity of the craft need not detain us. What is of interest to the non-Masonic historian is the manner in which, in the early eighteenth century, non-operative or 'speculative' lodges – that is, lodges composed of men who were not actually stonemasons – first evolved as private clubs, usually convened in taverns, where men could socialise outside older (often contracting or moribund) corporate and confessional structures. Freemasonry thus met the perennial human impulse to associate, which church or guild no longer fully satisfied. Its success, like that of another great eighteenth-century institution, the coffee house, was symptomatic of a changing, modernising, some would say secularising, society.

In England, where the first Grand Lodge was established in 1717, freemasonry also represented a reaction against the political and religious strife of the seventeenth century. The discussion of politics was expressly forbidden. The craft subscribed to a 'Supreme Being', the 'Grand Architect of the Universe', a deity equally acceptable – or objectionable – to Catholic, Protestant and dissenter; its secular credo promoted charity and public benevolence. Moreover, the central allegorical conceit of the Masonic system, the master-builders and the construction of King Solomon's Temple, has been read as a metaphor for the making of an ideal society.[11] And in theory the craft itself anticipated that higher moral order: all Masons were equals and brothers. Although Scottish and Irish Masonry had their own origin myths, it is fair to view the English experience as the exemplar, and its appeal to contemporaries of all creeds and classes is not in doubt. The tolerant, latitudinarian and 'progressive' ethos of the institution travelled well in the Europe and North America of the Enlightenment. Indeed, depending on the perspective which is adopted, the spread of Masonry may appear as a source, as a medium or transmitter of, or as an institutional response to the new intellectual climate.

The Irish Grand Lodge was founded during the 1720s. In spite of papal bulls excommunicating Freemasons in 1731, 1758 and 1786, the official history of the Grand Lodge maintains that the majority of members in the eighteenth century were Catholic. In the 1790s these included the prominent Catholic Committee activists, Theobald McKenna, W.J. MacNeven and, at the very end of the decade, Daniel O'Connell.[12] Socially, membership stretched from the titled nobility down through the merchant and professional élites to lodges of a 'low order'.[13] Interestingly, the so-called 'ancients' in England were initially formed by Irish artisans working in London, who had been excluded from the lodges precisely because of their lowly social status.[14] Unofficial, or 'hedge', masonry, and 'thumping matches' (fights) between Freemasons and Defenders, and Freemasons and Orangemen,[15] provides further evidence of how the craft straddled the different worlds of élite and popular culture.

Whatever the reasons for its popularity, and it should be remembered that the craft indulged the tastes for the mysterious, the secret and the occult as well as those for fraternity, conviviality and benevolence, Freemasonry continued to grow. In Ireland it entered a phase of rapid expansion in the early 1780s. A book of Masonic lore republished in Belfast in 1783 noted that 'lodges which have long lain dormant and neglected, are now forming and reconstituting with redoubled ardour, indeed 'tis now not only honourable but fashionable to be a free mason'.[16] This revival appears to have been stimulated by the other fashion which animated Irish public life in this period: Volunteering. Entire lodges enrolled as Volunteer companies.[17] By 1804 there were 104 lodges in County Antrim, 92 in Tyrone and another 151 in Armagh, Derry and Down.[18]

Sheer numbers and fashion alone help account for the influence of Freemasonry on the popular political movements of the 1790s. Equally important, certainly for the United Irishmen, was

Masonic 'ideology', which was non-sectarian, rationalistic and 'enlightened'. Thus many of the Freemasons and Volunteers of the 1780s became the United Irishmen of the following decade.[19] The ideological affinity between the craft and radicalism emerges vividly in the declaration issued by the County Tyrone Freemasons at Dungannon in 1793:

We view with pleasure the rapid progress of liberty in France, supported by reason and philosophy, and founded on the grand principles of our institution; whilst we glory in the reflection that our illustrious brother Washington and the masons of America were the saviours of their country and the first founders of the Temple of Liberty – are we to see Irish masons made the tools of corruption? We are no advocates of passive obedience and non-resistance, fealty to our sovereign does not require us to support corruption.

Elsewhere the address, a veritable conspectus of advanced Whiggery, condemns the penal laws, the game laws, unjust taxation and the abuse of parliamentary patronage. It defends the freedom of the press and demands 'an adequate representation of all our fellow citizens' in the House of Commons.[20] The radical *Cork Gazette* staked out the ideological common ground more succinctly: 'Liberty and Equality', it affirmed, 'have ever been the proud motto of all good free masons.'[21]

The Tyrone meeting which issued this declaration adroitly side-stepped the ban on politics by dissolving itself and reconvening as an 'assembly of masonic citizens'. They were nonetheless reprimanded by the Grand Lodge, and by their loyalist colleagues in County Armagh.[22] The meeting was, in fact, a classic example of what in the 1930s would become known as the 'popular front' strategy, organised in this instance by the United Irishmen, Dr James Reynolds and William Richardson. Numerous other lodges from mid- and east Ulster met in late 1792 and early 1793 to offer public support to the United Irish-led campaign for parliamentary reform.[23] The other main 'front' organisation was the Volunteer movement. During 1792 Volunteer companies began, in Wolfe Tone's phrase, to 'spring up like mushrooms',[24] many – though not all – dedicated to reform. Again the revival was welcomed by radical Freemasonry. As one address put it, 'let every lodge in the land become a company of citizen soldiers...let every Volunteer company become a lodge of masons'.[25]

The career of James Reynolds, the president of the Tyrone meeting and probably the author of its declaration, epitomises eighteenth-century Freemasonry at its most politically subversive. As a Volunteer and reformer in the 1780s, he was one of the first to seek an accommodation with the Catholics. The fact that another prominent pro-Catholic Volunteer, William Todd Jones, was also a Mason, is not, it has been suggested, accidental. Both these men, in other words, took the non-sectarian principle of their craft seriously.[26] In the 1790s Reynolds was active once more in the agitation for parliamentary reform. Summoned before a secret committee of the House of Lords in 1793, he went to prison for refusing to testify. After his release Reynolds served as chairman of the Dublin Society of United Irishmen on a number of occasions before emigrating to the United States in 1794. In Philadelphia he was a leading member of the shadowy Society of United Irishmen in America, which was internationalist in the Jacobin (and Masonic) style, and which, as the local *Federalist* paper pointed out, used Masonic idioms in its oaths and tests. Initiates were sworn to secrecy in the name not of God but of the Supreme Being. In 1801 Reynolds, an ardent Jeffersonian, composed a radical Utopia, on the strength of which he has been described as America's first Utopian socialist. 'Lithconia', as he called it, was a priestless as well as a classless society, and Reynolds thereby pushed the deist, rationalist and fraternal elements in Masonic thought to their outer limits. This intriguing political fantasy first appeared in the pages of *The Temple of Reason*, a Jeffersonian and deist newspaper, edited by another Irish exile, Denis O'Driscol. Reynolds was by no means a typical Mason, but Freemasonry did help shape his political and intellectual milieu.[27]

After the eclipse of the reform movement in 1793 Masonry continued to play an important role in radical politics. The logic of the revolutionary strategy and republican objective which the United Irishmen now adopted demanded the creation of a mass-based clandestine organisation. This task entailed the creation of a secret centralised military structure, and the superimposition of that structure onto pre-existing networks of Defender lodges and Painite artisan clubs. Belfast and later Dublin acted as the organising centres, despatching emissaries – recruiting sergeants, couriers and propagandists rolled into one – to the countryside. At the precise moment, the spring of 1795, when the United Irishmen embarked on this missionary programme, a number of key agents,

Henry Joy McCracken, Samuel Kennedy and Bartholomew Teeling, joined Masonic lodges. That most peripatetic of all emissaries, William Putnam McCabe, was also a Mason. The purpose of this systematic infiltration is obvious. Membership of the craft gave United Irish agents access to another ready-made lodge network, and enabled them to call upon their Masonic brothers' hospitality as they travelled around the country.[28]

Some lodges, useful because they provided a pretext for meeting legally, became United Irish 'fronts'. By 1796 government intelligence indicated that every United Irishman in Belfast was also a Freemason, and suspects were subsequently arrested during military swoops on lodge meetings. An entire lodge was taken into custody after a raid on a Newry tavern in 1798.[29] A similar, though less uniform, pattern is discernible in Dublin. There, revolutionary cells met under the guise of Masonic lodges, including one attended by 'Watty' Cox, editor of the intemperate *Union Star*. In November 1798, several Dublin lodges were suspended by the Grand Lodge pending enquiries into the activities of their members before and during the rebellion.[30] Not surprisingly, the Tyrone Masons were likewise suspected of disaffection. William Richardson, Reynolds's collaborator in 1793 and the local agent for the United Irish newspaper, the *Northern Star*, appears to have directed the United Irish underground movement in mid-Ulster through Masonic channels. General Knox proposed a ban on Masonic gatherings and predicted that after the troubles had subsided 'it will be found much treason is kept alive thro' every county in the north thro' the medium of Free Mason lodges'.[31] It was reports of this kind which prompted the chief secretary, Thomas Pelham, to write to the Grand Master, Lord Donoughmore, in 1797, requesting him to check those who sought to turn the craft 'into a political engine'.[32]

It has been argued that Europe in the age of revolutions cannot be properly understood apart from its 'Masonic milieu'.[33] Certainly in the Irish case, but particularly in Ulster, the importance of Freemasonry in the political and social life of the period is beyond dispute. Commenting on divisions in the craft aroused by the reform agitation in 1792, Drennan's sister, Martha McTier, observed, 'The freemasons appear splitting and if they die, change, or reform, what but Christianity will remain unshaken?'[34] Three years later, Lord Abercorn described Freemasonry as the 'rock of the north', and warned that 'if real care is not taken, the country will split upon it'.[35] Such perceptions no doubt explain why Dublin Castle was so keen to prevent a United Irish take-over. Unlike modern historians, the authorities could not afford to treat conspiracy theories lightly.

Appendix

The following abbreviations have been used: 'Personnel', listed in R.B. McDowell, 'The Personnel of the Dublin Society of United Irishmen, 1791–4', *Irish Historical Studies*, II (1940–1), pp.12–53; Mem. Reg., Members Register, 1st series, The Grand Lodge of the Free and Accepted Masons of Ireland, Dublin.

Borland, Archibald: Cappagh, County Tyrone. Arrested 26 April, 1798 and charged with high treason. Borland's petition to the government of 25 December, 1798, was 'supported by the Freemason lodge, 350' (Nat. Archives, State Prisoners' Petitions, carton 19).

Boyle, James: Coagh, County Tyrone. Reputedly master of a local lodge. In 1798 he attended Glasgow University, where he had allegedly 'went with a collected purse for the purpose of making United Scotsmen' (Andrew Newton to Dublin Castle, 9 February 1798 [Reb. Papers., 620/35/130]).

Caldwell, Dr James: Magherafelt, County Derry. Testified before the Lords Secret Committee in 1793.

Campbell, Alexander: Aughnacloy, County Tyrone. Secretary to Lodge 599, which, in General Knox's opinion, was 'composed of the greatest rascals in the North' (Knox to Cooke, 7 May 1798 [Reb. Papers, 620/37/3]).

Cooney, Peter: Dublin. Editor of the *Morning Post*. According to the informer Francis Higgins, Cooney although not himself a United Irishman was a member of the same Masonic Lodge as the prominent Dublin republican Matthew Dowling (B. Inglis, *The Freedom of the Press in Ireland, 1784–1841* [London 1954], pp.86–8; information of Higgins, 20 January 1797 [Reb. Papers, 620/18/14]).

Cox, Walter 'Watty': Dublin. Editor of the *Union Star* (Inglis, *Freedom*, pp.89–9; information of Higgins, 29 November 1797 [Reb. Papers, 620/36/226]; Mem. Reg., Lodge 324).

Dowling, Matthew: Dublin. ('Personnel'; information of Higgins, 20 January 1797 [Reb. Papers, 620/18/14]).

Gelling, David; Dublin ('Personnel'; Mem. Reg., Lodge 2).

Haslett, Henry; Belfast. Founder member of the first society of United Irishmen (L. Dermot, *Ahiman Rezon* [Belfast 1783], p.xxii; Mem. Reg., Lodge 257).

Hawesworth, Amory; Dublin ('Personnel'; Mem. Reg., Lodge 190).

Jones, William Todd; Lisburn, County Antrim. MP for Lisburn, 1783–90 ('Personnel'; *Ahiman Rezon, p xxi* ; Mem. Reg., Lodge 257).

Kennedy, Samuel; Belfast. Printer of the *Northern Star* (Mem. Reg., Lodge 762).

McAllister, Randal; Dublin. Proprietor of the *Rights of Irishmen*; *National Evening Star* ('Personnel'; Inglis, *Freedom of the Press*, pp.65–6; Mem. Reg., Lodge 190).

McCabe, Thomas; Belfast. Founder member of the first Society of United Irishmen. Father of William Putnam (Mem. Reg., Lodge 684).

McCabe, William Putnam; Belfast. United Irish organiser (Information of John Bird, alia 'Smith', Nat. Archives, Frazer MSS lA.40.111a/20 & 35).

McCleary, William: Belfast. Founder member of first Belfast Society of United Irishmen (*Ahiman Rezon*, p.xxii).

McCracken, Henry Joy; Belfast. United Irish Leader. Commander at the battle of Antrim: executed 1798 (Mem. Reg., Lodge 783).

McKenna, Dr Theolbald: Dublin. Member of the Catholic Committee ('Personnel'; Mem. Reg., Lodge 190).

MacNeven, Dr William James: Dublin. Member of the Catholic Committee and of the United Irish executive. State prisoner; banished, 1798 ('Personnel'; Mem. Reg., Lodge 792).

Munro, Henry: Lisburn, County Antrim. United Irish commander at Ballynahinch, 1798; executed (TCD, Madden Papers MS.317, Mem. Reg., Lodge 193).

O'Connor, Lawrence: County Kildare. Executed Defender Captain (*Morning Post*, 8 September, 1795; R. Clifford, *Application of Barurel's Memoirs of Jacobinism to the Secret Societies of Ireland and Great Britain*, p.25).

Orr, William: County Antrim. Executed 1797. Elevated to instant martyrdom by his United Irish colleagues and given a 'Masonic funeral' (P. Robinson, 'Hanging Ropes and Buried Secrets', in *Ulster Folklife*, xxxii [1986], pp.4–15).

Reilly, James: Dublin ('Personnel'; Mem. Reg., Lodge 141).

Reynolds, Dr James: Cookstown, County Tyrone ('Personnel'; Crossle and Lepper, *History of the Grand Lodge*, I, p.297; Lodge 768; see notes 26 & 27).

Richardson, William: Moy, County Tyrone. In General Knox's view 'a dangerous fellow' (Knox to Cooke, 6 June, 1798. [Reb. Papers, 620/38/61]).

Riddal, James: Dublin ('Personnal'; Mem. Reg., Lodge 141).

Rowan, Archibald Hamilton: Dublin ('Personnel'; W. Geoghahan, *The History and Antiquities of the First Volunteer Lodge of Ireland* [Dublin, 1912], p.16.

Sparks, Richard: Dublin ('Personnel'; Mem. Reg., Lodge 620).

Stockdale, John: Dublin. Printer of the United Irish newspaper*The Press*. According to the informer, Leonard McNally ('JW'), Stockdale was a member of the same lodge as Matthew Dowling ('Personnel'; Reb. Papers 620/36/227).

Tandy, George: Lisburn, County Antrim. The brother of James Napper Tandy (Mem. Reg., Lodge 193).

Teeling, Bartholomew: Lisburn, County Antrim. Participated in General Humbert's Irish expedition, 1798; executed (Mem. Reg., Lodge 193).

Tennant, William: Belfast. Founder member of the first Belfast Society of United Irishmen (*Ahiman Rezon*, p.xxii).

Wilkinson, James Tandy: Dublin ('Personnel'; Mem. Reg., Lodge 190).

14

THE INTERNAL POLITICS OF THE UNITED IRISHMEN

Louis M. Cullen

The evolution of the politics of the United Irishmen has been obscured by an over-emphasis on the loss of momentum in radical politics in 1793–4. This view has been generally supported in turn by allusions to the alleged conservatism of the Catholics. Propertied Catholics, it is argued, concentrated on enjoyment of their new political rights after 1793; in consequence, a novel divide emerged between them and other Catholics, who felt betrayed; only the Fitzwilliam episode resurrected radicalism. On this thesis, the recovery of radicalism, lacking wellsprings of its own, was merely reactive to events; in the case of the Catholics it was a response to their being denied final emancipation, not an underlying political interest, which brought them into an unqualified radical alliance in mid-decade. It has also been maintained in this context that the Defenders were a separate organisation, originally driven by agrarian, sectarian or even millennial motivations. An integral part of this scenario has been the presentation of the United Irish movement as divided into quite distinct bodies, the so-called first and second societies. The only notable exception to this amorphous interpretation is the article by Nancy Curtin which emphasised, against the drift of other writing, very considerable continuity between the first and second societies.[1]

A class conflict did not exist or emerge among politically active Catholics in 1793–4. They got remarkably few posts as justices of the peace, few appeared on grand juries and, with a handful of exceptions, propertied Catholics were kept out of militia officerships. Moreover, the militia raised wider questions, such as the compulsory attendance at Established Church service by the men. If anything, Catholics drew closer together in 1794. The sole support for the 'divide' thesis comes from John Foster, hardly a representative authority on this subject, who had long and bitterly opposed the Defenders in Louth.[2] Eager to detach propertied Catholics from radicalism, and prepared as a realist to go a long way to attain that end, he had secured several officerships for Catholics in the Louth militia. The hope that Catholics could be detached amounted to no more than wishful thinking by a handful of contemporaries.[3] Fingall was quite keen in 1795 to emphasise to Fitzwilliam, from whom he expected much, the usefulness of gentry such as himself,[4] but he had become utterly marginalised in political terms. The equally subservient and irrelevant Kenmare peddled similar views.[5]

County Louth was the scene of intense and ongoing political struggle. This emerged in the early 1780s over the issue of admitting Catholics to the Volunteers; the town of Drogheda did not accept Foster's county leadership on this issue. Hence, the Defenders, originating in precisely the same issue in Armagh, had an appeal in Louth: the movement spread to Louth as early as 1789. The attack, on Foster's instructions, on a County Louth popular assembly in 1792, and the hardline resolution of the County Louth grand jury condemning the Catholic Convention, were part of the political response to this new situation:[6] both events in turn provided scope for counter-propaganda. Tone, returning with Neilson to the North in August 1792, stayed at the house of James Bird in Drogheda 'amongst a parcel of girls all the evening'; Tandy distributed the highly politicised tract *Common Sense*, with its distinctive northern message, in Louth in the same autumn. The arrest of three Drogheda members of the Catholic Convention (including Bird) in 1794, and the murder charge against John Fay, secretary of a meeting of County Meath Catholics in October 1792 which had repudiated the anti-Catholic resolutions, were simply further rounds in the political war. The largest regional network of political resistance to Catholic claims in Ireland was centred on Downshire and Annesley in County Down, Foster in both Louth and Meath, and Gosford as leader of a more diffuse faction in Armagh.

Ulster emerges in Catholic national politics for the first time in the 1780s, a trend coinciding with the shift of anti-Catholic politics from its County Cork leadership and reflecting the relative political incapacity of the second Lord Shannon, to a new Downshire-Foster axis. In Ulster, and especially its south-east fringe, the only broad nucleus of comfortable Catholics was to be found on the Monaghan-Louth border around Carrickmacross and Dundalk, and in south Down. In and close to the towns of Newry and Rathfriland, there survived almost uniquely for Ulster a handful of Catholics with gentry pretensions, and a numerous but modestly circumstanced Catholic middle class. In the case of south Armagh and Carrickmacross, Catholic Committee and revolutionary politics both revolved around a handful of individuals, the Carolans in particular, persistently radical and maintaining contact with the Teelings and with Dundalk.[7] James Coigley (or Quigley), Bernard Coyle, Valentine Derry, the Teelings and John Magennis supplemented this axis, communicating with the radical figures of Russell, Neilson, and McCracken in Belfast, and Alexander Lowry and several Presbyterian ministers in Down.

A central feature was the systematic if largely silent exploitation of the discontents and expectations of this Catholic milieu by Belfast and Dublin radicals in and after 1792. By December of that year, Drennan was convinced that 'Neilson is somehow in partnership with the Catholics here, and has, perhaps, made some others (W. Sinclair, for instance), of the same mind'.[8] Russell travelled widely in the North in 1793 and 1794, as did Coigley.[9] As early as November 1793 Mrs McTier noted of Thomas Russell that 'his dress betrays poverty, and he associates with men everyway below himself, on some of whom, I fear, he mostly lives...'[10] In February 1795 Drennan declared that 'I have always judged [Russell]...an agent of the Catholics or of Tone, their chief agent, instructed to reside in Belfast, to report what is going on, and to influence, as desired'.[11] Coigley and Russell superintended the creation of radical popular organisation beyond Belfast in the Catholic hinterland of Newry, in more distant parts of Antrim and, more unevenly, in less promising territory in Derry, Tyrone and Fermanagh. By 1795 Bernard Coyle and James Coigley, in close collaboration with the Belfast radicals, were the central figures in Armagh. John Magennis was the main figure in Down, with a close rapport with Alexander Lowry, the key United Irishman of west and south Down. As County Antrim had a liberal political representation which supported reform and emancipation and the Teeling family had a uniquely high profile for a Catholic family in Ulster, the county was less in need of wholetime radical action than its neighbours. In the 1790 election, with an assured radical outcome in Antrim, Luke Teeling transferred his efforts to Down.[12] The transfer of the attentions of his younger and very radical son, Charles, in the mid-1790s to neighbouring Armagh and Down, repeated this pattern. The south Ulster-north Leinster region was in fact remarkably close-knit. Charles Teeling's mother was a Taafe from Smarmore Castle in Louth; Maginnis was his brother-in-law. Coigley himself moved to Dundalk apparently in or after 1795 where his relative Valentine Derry was reputedly leader of the Louth Defenders. Bartholomew Teeling likewise moved residence for political reasons to Dundalk. Behind all these figures and the Belfast focus for their activities was the peripatetic Russell.

Catholics and the Dublin United Irishmen

The evidence about Catholics in the early United Irishmen comes in the main from bigotedly anti-Catholic individuals: Leonard McNally, Thomas Collins and William Drennan. Collins, the informer in the United Irishmen, even feared that if Catholic demands were met, 'the day is not far of [*sic*] when *high mass* with all its mummery will be performed in Christ Church'. Not only was McNally, on the evidence of Collins's reports, the most vociferous anti-Catholic member of the Dublin committee, but he wished to force differences with the Catholics out into the open. Thus on 28 December 1792, when there was, according to Collins, 'a very great distrust entertained by the Protestants against the papists', it was McNally, alleging of the Catholic members that 'there had been a very great backwardness in a certain description of our members', who sought a 'call' of the society in a fortnight's time to 'judge of the disposition of the members in general'. This was an attempt to claw back the ground lost narrowly in the preceding week when the Catholics had their way on a controversial issue. On 4 January, when Emmet proposed a committee to plan for full political representation, McNally wanted to make a distinction between Catholics and others. When McNally's demand duly came up as an agenda item on 11 January, there was 'a very full meeting particularly of papists nearly 160 members in all', and the roll call was postponed.[13] This was the largest turnout of members at any meeting except that of 21 December 1792. Significantly, Catholic members and those like Emmet sympathetic to them disliked McNally, whose own letters to the Castle later in the decade reveal his hatred of Catholics and his strong religiosity; he regarded the Catholic United Irishmen as deists.

In the case of Drennan, the only one of these three worthies who was not a spy, dislike of Catholics was obsessive, and often based on petty or superficial motives; he regarded them 'as cunning, uncandid, close, plotting and circumventing'. As far back as the mid-1780s he had seen Newry as stirring with 'pigs and papists'.[14] His interest in accommodation with Catholics was based on fear (as was his sister's) and on the revealing calculation that the Catholic spirit, which he disliked, was 'the soil of Ireland and must be cultivated or we must emigrate'.[15] So pathological was his dislike that it transferred itself into a distrust of Protestants close to the Catholics, whom he regarded as their tools. It is significant that Drennan was the main backer of the anti-Catholic McNally, and that McNally himself recorded the anti-Catholic views of Drennan and his sense of the ingratitude of the Catholics.[16] Among the United Irishmen, Simon Butler was stated to be anti-Catholic by such a connoisseur of prejudice as Drennan himself.[17]

Offsetting sources to these prejudiced witnesses are lacking. In particular there are no Tone diaries for 1793, 1794 and 1795. Moreover, the only concrete support for an apolitical role by Tone in these years are statements, thirty-five years later, by Tone's son;[18] they are ambiguous, and capable of carrying quite a different significance to that attached to them. Tone lost no time in seeing William Jackson in 1794; according to Rowan it was only for family reasons that he declined a suggestion that he should go to France. He also showed no hurry to leave the country after his undertaking in May 1794, not departing until public references to him in the Jackson trial in April 1795 and in the debate on the Catholic bill in May combined to make his position untenable. In the interval, in December 1794, he had assumed the prominent position of agent to the Dublin committee of Catholics; the contrast in the committee's tone in 1794 compared with 1792 was more political than religious.

A further distorting element is the fact that Catholic political behaviour has largely been seen through the framework presented by MacNeven in 1807 in his *Pieces of Irish History*, and by T.A. Emmet in his *Towards the History of Ireland*, which appeared in the same volume. MacNeven, however, had played no prominent political role until the end of 1794; as a member in 1797–8 of a faction within the United Irishmen, his views as well as his politics were in essence those of Emmet. Emmet claimed that the Defenders in 1794 'were also as yet unconnected with any persons of information or an higher order'. He represented Tandy's contacts with the Defenders as a personal initiative, and implied that they had non-political origins, acquiring non-sectarian aims only as they spread.[19] He then proceeded to draw a picture of an entirely new society of United Irishmen emerging in 1795 and of novel links subsequently developing with the Defenders. He stressed that Tone in 1795 was uninvolved, and was *approached* by the committee of Antrim as he was about to go to America.[20]

The two strands of the Dublin United Irishmen

The United Irishmen were divided from the outset. There were those who saw the Society as a highly political body eager to identify issues on which to wage a public and high-profile campaign against government, and others who wanted to create a broader alliance, organised in depth. Those who favoured an open campaign were Butler, Drennan, Rowan and Emmet. The first three dominated office, monopolising the post of president in 1792; each was elected on one occasion to the presidency during 1793. The first break in this pattern was in May 1793 when Henry Sheares was elected president.[21] Prominent though he was, Emmet stood outside this group, handicapped by his late admission to the Society (he became a member only in December 1792). He was the only one of the prominent early United Irishmen group who remained a member of the reorganised Society in the second half of the 1790s: Rowan, Butler and Drennan all had second thoughts by or after mid-decade.

Apart from Rowan Hamilton, owner of a purchased estate in Kildare and heir to one in County Down, these men belonged to the professional classes. They were didactic in approach, abstract in reasoning, and curiously sweeping in some of their views. Thus, Emmet declared that all the laws passed for establishment of the government were illegal; while prepared to go along with a more discreetly worded resolution, he wanted the society to retain the right of deciding 'the expediency of resorting to *arms* if necessity required the measure'. In November 1793 Butler maintained that he was 'not only ready when necessary to *act* but to *bleed* for his *country*, and he feared that the time was not far distant when such *exertions* would be *expedient*'.[22]

According to Collins, at the meeting on 21 December members were told to support the cause 'not only with their fortunes but with their *lives*, which was not much relished by some of the leading papists'. However, the verbal posturing contained in this language by the leading Protestants was evidenced in the fact that two days later, in opposing the idea of qualifying the concept of resistance in a resolution, they maintained that 'nothing more was intended than legally resisting'. Behind the Brutus-like language, the purpose was somewhat less revolutionary. It was to discredit government by taking up radical issues. When Lewins declared on 7 March 1794 that 'he thought it beneath the *dignity* of the Society to notice so infamous a set of scoundrels as the members of that den (i.e. parliament)', he was supported by Drennan. But they were never very clear in their ideas as to how to go about replacing the government. In an address drawn up on the release of Butler and Bond, Drennan lamented 'the torpor of the *people* in submitting to the exercise of undefined privilege, and allowing their few remaining liberties to be frittered away...and then as a dernier resource to the people in case they do not choose to *act*, it advises them to emigrate from a land where they are compelled to wear the most ignominious of chains'. Drennan's contributions were invariably bombastic. It was one thing to call for action; it was quite another to define it. One of their few practical ideas was their publication programme, itself rather bookish, arranged by Rowan, Drennan and McNally.[23]

Emmet affords an instructive contrast with this clique. At the first meeting at which he is known to have spoken, he proposed a resolution similar to that put by the Duke of Leinster at the Association of the Friends of the Constitution (which the Duke had just founded). On 4 January 1793 he even represented the Duke of Leinster as having 'the most profound respect for them, and wished to coalesce and act with them in all their *pursuits*'. Emmet had been proposed for membership by both Drennan and Rowan Hamilton, but in his ideas about possible political allies among the Whigs, he was proceeding beyond the empty verbalising of Butler or Drennan. Moreover, on 23 December he had declared a readiness to accommodate Captain Edward Sweetman's amendment on resistance. In the recurring divide Collins was surprised by Emmet's stance five months later: 'it's wonderful that Emmet should have agreed to it'.[24]

The aim of the Rowan-Butler-Drennan group was to find issues which would enlarge the political conflict with government. This is quite evident in relation to the question of the Volunteers. Both sides in the Society were sympathetic to the Volunteer ideal, but in the second half of 1792 there was a contrast between those who wanted to play down the issue of revival lest it prejudice political advance in distraught districts at politically sensitive moments, and those who wanted to turn the revival of Volunteer corps, something of a hot potato, into a central issue of current politics. In contrast to the Neilson-Tone-Keogh line displayed during July and August of playing down armed parades in Down-shire-controlled Down, the Volunteers were resurrected by the ruling clique as an issue in November and December at the very moment when it could imperil the Catholic Convention and its outcome. Rowan was the prime mover.[25] On 23 December, resolutions triggered by the prosecution of Rowan and Tandy led to a debate on the proposal to insert the word 'legally' before the word 'resist' in a resolution. This proposal came from Chambers, Russell, Sweetman, Warren, McCormick 'and several other papists'. Those who opposed included Butler, McNally, and also Rowan, who wanted debate deferred altogether. Sweetman strengthened the amendment further from 'legally' to 'legally and constitutionally'.[26]

In the wake of tension which emerged in January between Edward Sweetman and Emmet on this issue, Sweetman proposed that the objectives of the society should be stated to be for governance by a king, lords and commons, and that for that purpose and emancipation alone and no other purpose did they associate. Drennan and Emmet opposed Sweetman. Emmet made a very strong speech, and got his way in appointing a committee to enquire into the war, and into the militia and gunpowder bills.[27] In other words the purpose was to make political capital. Sweetman sought to resign in February. There were semantics on both sides in the debate: it simply reflected a much larger issue. Sweetman's letter of resignation read on 15 February stated that he would adhere to the test but that 'he could promote the interests thereof much better than by continuing a member'; this is a clear hint that the future of the Society lay outside the Dublin talking-shop.[28]

Sweetman's concern related to the 'pending of the Catholic business in parliament'. Indeed, the opinions of his friend Tone seem to have been as strong.[29] Drennan failed to come to grips with Catholic (and northern radical) attitudes on the Volunteers. Because they had supported the Volunteers even in the immediate past, he was critical of the Catholics for not now supporting their reactivation in the capital in November at the very time the Convention was due to sit. Drennan's letter of 25 November 1792 to his sister is particularly illuminating on his attitude of Catholic betrayal at this time.[30] Catholic attitudes had been consistent since the time the convention had been mooted, and one of the objectives of Keogh, Neilson and Tone in County Down in July and September was to eliminate provocation by armed Catholics in the region where the largest coalition of anti-Catholic politicians existed. Hence their ventures in July and August into the marching areas of Down were combined efforts to cool supporters and woo Presbyterians in the only strongly Presbyterian county in which magnate power was working effectively on the side of government. Even a year later Drennan, in the course of noting how Neilson's *Northern Star* and the Belfast Society had remained low-key, gave vent to his anti-Catholic obsession: 'yours [the Belfast Society] has been silent all along, because your leading men are more under Catholic influence than ours'.[31] Years later, after the 1803 rebellion, his sister noted retrospectively Russell's reticence in expressing his political opinions.[32]

Things really came to a head on 19 April 1793 when Emmet gave notice that he would bring in an address to the Catholics asserting that Catholic relief had been 'in part obtained through the exertions of the *society* and the Protestants in general'. This was a response to what Sweetman had said earlier on 8 February: 'save and except some late exertions of the Presbyterians, the Catholics were the only people that ever contended for the independence of Ireland'. Collins's observation that 'I think the Presbyterians are heartily sorry and ashamed for the exertions that they made for the papists who they now see will only act for *themselves*',[33] reflects the attitude of Drennan, as the address originally promised by Emmet finally made its appearance in Drennan's hands on 3 May. The fact that Emmet, ever the diplomatist in divisive matters, had ceased to be publicly associated with it is itself significant. Debate on it was protracted over the month of May.

At this point a sustained challenge had arisen to the Butler-Drennan-Rowan hegemony. On 3 May Henry Sheares was elected president and a rival address to Drennan's gradually took shape. Two meetings later John Sheares headed opposition to Drennan's address, 'on the former grounds of inexpediancy [*sic*] at this time, and that the Catholics are not now a distinct body, but melted into the general mass of the people'. By contrast the Drennan side maintained that they were 'a separate class of people'. Little progress was made on the address, and a vote was lost by the Drennan side. The address was thus deferred to later meetings, and Drennan was further wrongfooted as Sheares got his way in appointing a committee to draw up his own address. This committee of five with the two Sheares and Tone on it had a majority for the new address; Emmet and Drennan were the minority, and Emmet himself was not wholly in the Drennan camp. At the meeting on 25 May 'the papists though they opposed Drennan's address because its title was to them [*sic*] fully approved of Mr Sheares'.' In all there were three hotly contested votes on the Drennan motion on 17, 25 and 31 May: the consequence was that Drennan's address was watered down to 'a very *dull, fulsome* poor production greatly inferior to what might be expected from him'. It was opposed even when finished, encountering 'a good deal of opposition from some of that body who threaten to secede if it goes to the public'. In mid-June Sheares's address was passed but, with Sheares's opponents eager to get their own back, they found enough support to postpone publication. This was a very fraught meeting: according to Collins, 'on Friday night the *lads* in Back Lane were near cutting each other's throats'.[34] Unfortunately Collins's information on this meeting was at second hand: in June and July he was largely absent from the Society because of his need to avoid his creditors. If we had more evidence on what happened, this would emerge as the key month in the story of the first Society in 1791–4. It is from this period that attendance fell. It was also at this stage, arising out of the Drennan address, that Tone withdrew altogether from attendance at meetings.[35] Writing on 24 August, after attending only his second meeting since his return, Collins commented that committees had not been filled at the quarterly meeting because the attendance had been insufficient and that 'the spirit of the society is totally lost'.[36]

On the occasion of the election of Rowan as president and

Butler as secretary on 1 November 1793, Henry Sheares proposed
a motion that the only appellation should be that of citizen 'in
place of Mr or any other title'.[37] As later events revealed, this was
an attack on Rowan. It marked a further stage in the deterioration
of the Society: two of the succeeding presidents, Bagenal Harvey
and James Reynolds, were far distant in outlook from the leadership clique. However, though they no longer held office, members of the clique attended consistently when they were in town
and, with many radical members absenting themselves, still had
their way in its proceedings on the whole. For instance they were
prominent in the committee to study the best ways of petitioning
parliament constitutionally, and in the group of stewards to
arrange the dinner for Rowan's birthday. But opposition was now
persistent. In the debate on political reform on 10 January 1794,
Emmet, Butler and McNally plus the two Sheares opposed a proposal to replace *voice* voting by ballot.[38] Though the Sheares supported the Rowan group on this occasion, the issue yet again represented a real divide between the ruling faction and others, all
the more so as Ulster supported the idea of a ballot.

A full-blown attack on the Society as it stood followed on 31 January 1794, led by Neilson who adverted to traitors in the society
'who constantly conveyed whatever passed in it, within a few
hours after, nay a few moments to the *castle*', and he proposed a
committee of public welfare to transact the business of the Society. The Society would meet only when summoned by the committee. In the succeeding debate 'others', in effect John Sheares,
also sought a purge of suspicious members. Neilson was opposed
by Butler, who declared that 'he wished the hall to be uncovered,
and all the people of Dublin, of all Ireland to be present at their
debates'.[39] Three weeks later the committee which had compiled
an address to Rowan was charged with having mutilated it in the
printing and 'also with having added the word Esqr to Mr
Rowan's name'.[40] Attendance slumped after 7 February when
attendance at only one of eleven successive meetings exceeded 35.
     A unique feature of the Dublin Society was its out-of-town
membership. While some were recruited in the course of the
Catholic Convention in December 1792, the bulk came earlier or
later. As early as October 1792, in regard to the committee of correspondence, it was 'ordered that the committee of correspon-

dence do immediately write to the different societies of United Irishmen throughout the kingdom in order to fix on a *plan* of *general union*, and to *organize* the whole so as that they may be able to *act together*'.[41] There was a thin scatter of members from across the country, but they centred on three locations: Wexford, north Connacht and the Ulster border region. The Wexford interest was a gentry or professional interest in the main, though in the vital Anthony Perry-Edward Sweetman association it ran deeper and also led to a local society in Gorey. Sweetman was the individual United Irishman who was closest to Tone; in February 1793, he emphasised that he was a republican. North Connacht membership arose out of old Volunteer politics and the recent opposition there to Catholic claims. Tone was well-disposed to two of the members, Plunkett and McDonnell. Plunkett was to be found in 1797 in both east Ulster and in Dublin; and in an obscure way this fits into the ties between Dublin and Belfast in these years.[42]

Neilson, Russell and Tone, quite distinct in outlook from the ruling clique, played a key role in the evolution of radical politics: they devised a common Dublin-Belfast strategy for the stormy border region. Belfast, Down and Antrim were not represented in the first Dublin Society, apart from Neilson and Russell, intermittent visitors to the capital. Moreover, the Belfast societies were not vocal, a contrast with the Dublin Society. In February 1794 Drennan, proponent of the public talking-shop principle, had to confess that 'I don't understand Neilson's system of eternal silence in Belfast and his expectations from it'.[43] Drennan's sister disapprovingly saw in the Belfast group a New Light dissenter group (this is a revealing insight into Drennan's own lack of sympathy with New Light thought, but not an accurate assessment of the composition of northern radicalism). The public profile of the Society in Dublin and its opting for a single forum (in contrast to four societies in Belfast) was a consequence of the central role in its first years of a group of would-be politicians or power brokers. The running was made by the Society's lawyers. So important were they that attendance fell during the two annual circuits of the Irish bar.

The little north-south axis, undistracted by either the high or assize politics of the age, developed wider contacts. Contacts with the Defenders were first identified on 20 February 1793 in the case of Thomas Warren and Richard McCormick: 'the last two are very hard mouthed, and I am satisfied correspond with the Defenders'. Neilson, Hazlett and two other members of the *Northern Star* were at a meeting on 11 January 1793. Two months later, at a meeting at which Russell acted as secretary, 'the only business done' was reading a letter from the Templepatrick United Irishmen.[44] Templepatrick was a key location in Antrim radicalism: Hope and others were from there, and they were successful in 1798 in bringing Defenders onto the field in County Antrim. In April 1793 Neilson was again in Dublin, this time attending the dinner for Burke.[45] In May Edward Carolan of Carrickmacross attended to take the test.[46] He was to be active in defence of United Irishmen and Defenders,[47] as was a second Carolan, John.

The secret elements

The Society, or at least the most radical element within it, was becoming secretive during 1793. This was already implicit in the links established with the Defenders in July and August 1792 which were handled by Tone, Neilson and Keogh. This action was not authorised by the Society: it has been seen by modern commentators as a Catholic Committee initiative, but the key figures were Lowry and Neilson, and Neilson himself was the catalyst. It involved attempts both to found further societies of United Irishmen and to create a union of Catholics and Presbyterians. Keogh's address, *Common Sense*, of 28 September, a follow-through intended for the northern counties, was highly political in content, and it is clear that Drennan found it uncongenial. It was read out at a meeting on 21 September, significantly by Tandy, the chairman that night. Drennan complained of its being left on the table. On another night when Drennan was not present Tandy moved that 3,000 copies be printed.[48] This occasion seems to have been the 28 September which, according to Collins, was 'a very thin meeting, all the *city people absent* and scarce a Protestant face to be seen'.[49]

A secret coterie may therefore have already existed in late 1792. In the wake of the May 1793 debates on the competing Drennan and Sheares motions, it was certainly in existence. Tone at this stage disappeared from the public meetings: by May 1794 Drennan noted that 'Tone I never see'.[50] McCormick and Sweetman also ceased to be attenders. On 4 June 1793 Collins complained for the first time that 'I have every reason to think that there is something going forward amongst the *private junto* that is not easy come at'. Almost three months later his suspicions had become better defined: 'I have very good reason to think that there are private meetings of some of the members, if not a select number bound by some particular obligations, who meet for the original *purposes* of the *society.*' By 27 September he believed that 'there never will be a numerous meeting, though I am also satisfied that several of the individuals are working privately to do all the mischief that is within their power.'[51] Indeed from the end of 1793 new members had virtually ceased to be proposed: after 3 December only one new proposal was made. Collins, out of touch with the private meetings and inaccurately assuming in his ignorance that quite incompatible figures had common cause in them, was from an even earlier date reduced to drawing up lists to represent the effective membership of the Society in changing circumstances: one list appeared after February 1793, another on 15 February 1794, and a third one after May 1794.[52]

At the meeting of 31 January 1794 Neilson raised the question of secrecy. John Sheares proposed a purge of suspicious members and then on 14 February he gave notice of proposing a new ballot of members to remove doubtful members, or else dissolve the society. This proposal was attributed by Collins to fright, but fright is more a feature of the Drennan axis than of the others. The meetings since December had, with three exceptions, drawn a mere rump of orthodox members including the wretched Drennan. Given the fact that some radicals were avoiding the meetings, it was now difficult to count on sufficient support for radical steps from those in attendance: this is why John Sheares on 28 February declared that in acting on the advice of friends he would not bring his motion forward. Rightly, Collins interpreted Sheares's move as one toward secrecy, observing that 'I am therefore convinced that in future every measure of any consequence will be agitated by the select party.'[53]

Drennan had tried in January 1794 to reanimate the Dublin Society on his terms. Not quite comprehending the significance of Neilson's low profile, he boasted to Sam McTier in that month that 'your societies appear extinct and have merely served as Catholic instruments, have served a turn, but ours lives, and will live…'[54] At that time he had made an approach to the Catholics.[55] Apparently he approached Tone, and received a dusty answer.[56] Given Drennan's unsuitability for the task and his total failure to elicit a response from the radicals, the effort on the part of the Society's conservatives to revitalise it passed to the more acceptable Emmet,[57] who as Drennan had already recognised was along with Russell and Tone 'entwined with Catholic trammels'.[58] Drennan's antics even at this stage put the revival of the Society at risk, and may have prolonged the time-span needed to achieve reorganisation. Sulking in August, he was still an active attender in October. He supported the readmission of McNally and as a result both Emmet and McCormick threatened that they would not attend.[59] With readmissions on this principle promising to keep the old-style Society in existence, the long-standing demand for a more secret organisation now gathered pace, though the lingering participation of members like Drennan and McNally in the re-balloted society must have greatly deferred a final decision on its reorganisation. From October 1794 there is evidence of the nature of the radical proposals: a society of sections of fifteen members, each section returning one representative to a central committee.[60]

These events suggest that Sheares in Dublin and Neilson in Belfast were proceeding on parallel lines on this issue. Proposals in Dublin were in the field as early as in the North; only in May 1795 did the delegates of 72 Ulster societies meeting in Belfast create a federation of committees.[61] These events, north and south, give added emphasis to the travels Russell undertook in 1793 and 1794. As the Defenders had a lodge system, they can even be seen as precursors of the later United Irishmen. Tone in his comments moreover had become upbeat: 'the Catholics…have, within these two years, received a great degree of information…there seems to be a spirit rising among the people, which never appeared before, but which is spreading most rapidly, as will appear by the Defenders and other insurgents'.[62] The Society itself never ended even in Dublin: it simply went underground, and part of its membership had effectively done so before 1794. Reorganisation in the North in May 1795 and Tone's presence in Belfast later in the same month were scarcely coincidental.

Nothing changed in one sense from the old to the new. Not only did a pattern of three-monthly elections continue, but the months of election were unchanged: February, May, August,

November. The major change was that, with some delay occasioned in part by difficulties in overcoming the persistent Drennan, the Society had finally shed him and the rest of the small coterie of ambitious politicians and prating ideologues. It also shed McNally, whom Drennan in 1794 had clearly perceived as a supporter of his concept of the Society. Distrusted by the radicals, McNally could henceforth only hang on the coat-tails of the Society; as an informer in the second half of the 1790s, he had little more than general information from sources such as 'my friend' and Tandy's ineffective and timid son to pass on. His exclusion was no doubt responsible, in his incomprehension of later events, for his emphasis on the distinction between a 'first' and a later Society.[63]

As things came to a head in 1794, the divide between the two wings gradually became more explicit and more open. As late as August, Drennan saw himself as still making the running, but two months later he was on the defensive, reduced to declaring that he would 'not attend these petty private plotting meetings, which, though they may multiply members, will...annihilate the Society itself'.[64] Butler shared his views, and severed his links with the movement, McNally's reports leaving a fleeting vignette of his new-found isolation.[65] Drennan left the movement at a more indeterminate point between 1794 and 1796. Emmet however favoured the move.

At the end of 1794 the Dublin radicals were so well organised that in the committee which spearheaded the Fitzwilliam agitation in Dublin, a majority (five of nine) were past or present United Irishmen. When delegates reported on their return from London on 9 April 1795, MacNeven and Ryan proposed to drop emancipation and unite with Protestants for parliamentary reform. Burke in London was quick to detect what was afoot: 'the tone was wholly Jacobinical...the language of the day went plainly to a separation of the two kingdoms. God forbid, that anything like it should ever happen'.[66] MacNeven, inactive in the old organisation, was prominent in the new structure. Bond and Jackson, who had supported the Butler axis and who between them held office on three occasions in 1793, transferred to the new structure: they were Presbyterians, free from rancour; McNally, when he distinguished between the two groups in the later Society, was unable to identify their attitudes.[67] They were not 'politicos', participating

little in the tedious debates of the old organisation. MacNeven
and Emmet, the only professional men among the survivors, had
larger public ambitions.

In the autumn of 1796 O'Connor and Edward Fitzgerald were
recruited into the organisation. The joint memorandum of Mac-
Neven, Emmet and O'Connor in August 1798 stated that they
had become United Irishmen in September/October 1796. While
this is plausible enough for O'Connor and Fitzgerald, the assertion is economical with the truth for both Emmet and MacNeven.
It disregards their role in the transitional arrangements in Dublin,
by dating their membership formalistically from the adoption in
Dublin of the new constitution of 10 May 1795 at the end of protracted debate.[68] Dublin's tardiness in the effective implementation of a cell structure, a concept which had been broached in
Dublin as early as in Belfast, arose from persistent attempts to
draw unaceptable members into it. As late as August 1796 a
Catholic of 'some consequence' asked Drennan that 'I should
enter into some small society they are instituting, of a nature similar, I believe, to many in the north.'[69] This was the end of dialogue with Drennan, and may have now left the radicals free to
organise as they wished. The large northern presence in Dublin
in 1796 hints too at northern supporters coming to Dublin to
help local radicals in their final tussles with the moderates.[70]

The northern radicals, 1796–8

These northerners were not simply United Irishmen, but the men
who had already been active in cultivating close ties with the
Defenders. That makes it all the easier to appreciate the depth of
the divide in Dublin and Drennan's revulsion for the new mode of
organisation. Moreover, if the Defender alliance was early and
political, it is easier to understand how the Orange Order was a
quite formal organisation from the start in September 1795, political, not agrarian, in its gentry-backed purpose of marshalling a
response to a growing and perceived Defender challenge. The by-
election in Armagh in January 1795, fortuitously occurring at a
delicate stage, had already been turned into a test of the strength
of country radicalism. Facing an incongruous dynastic alliance of
convenience consisting of Brownlow, Gosford and Charlemont,
Cope gathered the radical votes that a Charlemont candidate
would normally have captured, and lost the election by only some

thirty votes in a contest lasting a month. That emphasised the alarming radicalisation of the county before the founding of the Order, and radical strength was evident again in the meeting of freeholders in April 1797 at which most of the county grandees, aware of the approaching general election, were keen not to run foul of radical opinion.[71]

For the government the key political struggle in 1796 and 1797 was to contain the spread of radicalism in Down and Armagh. Arthur O'Connor's proposal to run as a candidate in County Antrim in the upcoming elections, and its timing in late 1796, was the logical thrust of this alliance, and was seen as a way of regaining the momentum threatened by the autumn arrests. Even Mrs McTier, whose dislike for O'Connor may reflect the political pusillanimity of her brother, conceded that electoral apathy 'may be blown up by such a spark as this'.[72] The idea is all the more interesting in that a plan to run Fitzgerald for Down was also in the air.[73] The immense importance of the countryside in the eyes of the northern leaders has been underestimated in modern understanding, because two events in 1796-7 have led us to appraise the strength of the organisation as it stood in their wake rather than on their eve. The first is the impact of the arrests in late 1796 of Neilson, McCracken and Russell and the flight in mid-1797 of Lowry to France and of Magennis to Scotland, which was most felt in the Armagh-south Down region, and which magnified the problems of restoring the Society's fortunes there. With the loss of many of the leaders Coigley's role was now greater; even the ill-informed McNally was aware of his growing prominence. This new role accounts for his several visits abroad (which further reduced local leadership along the Dundalk-Armagh corridor), and for his closeness not only to O'Connor, but to Fitzgerald: after his arrest a letter of Coigley's was found in Leinster House.[74] The subscriptions for Corry's book of verse in 1797 reflect the tie-up between the Fitzgerald-O'Connor faction in Dublin and Kildare and, in the North, a Belfast and Ulster border group.

The second event was the success of Downshire in the wake of the arrests in pressurising many in west Down to break with the Society. The crucial split was achieved in June 1797 when the machinations of Downshire and Annesley produced a split in the United Irishmen at a meeting near Newry.[75] Moreover the split made it easier to recruit spies, all the more so as propaganda, systematically stressing the unnatural character of a Catholic-Presbyterian alliance, could stir up latent anti-Catholic feeling. Samuel Turner, for whom a strong dislike and fear of Catholics was a motivating force, was recruited out of contacts with the Downshire interest that went as far back as May 1797. However, even into 1798, given much support on the ground, the United Irishmen had hopes of reviving their south Ulster fortunes. Lowry and Magennis apparently returned to the region on the eve of the Ulster rising, although in mid-June they were on the border with Leinster trying to raise the standard of rebellion there.[76] Teeling was remarkably vague in his *Narrative* (published in 1828) about the rebellion in Down, as he was clearly anxious to gloss over a sequence of failures in the county and on its borders: accounting in part for the failure at Ballynahinch by 700 armed men when they left the romantic Monroe because they wanted more immediate action, he stumbled into unintentionally making a statement which could be interpreted as confirming the old saga of a split with the Defenders. Hence in the *Sequel* published in 1832, he had to identify his role in a central division at Rathfriland (i.e. between Monroe's forces at Ballynahinch and Magennis and Lowry on the border), and to admit to the inglorious indecisiveness and inaction of the forces among whom he was personally cast.[77]

Emmet v. O'Connor

In the conflict within the Dublin Society, especially between Emmet and O'Connor, one of the key themes of the later organisation, there was more than personality involved. At issue was a struggle between the north-south axis, spearheaded by O'Connor and Fitzgerald, and a Dublin-based interest, represented by Emmet and MacNeven. McNally on the fringes saw the divide as one between the O'Connor faction 'whose other associates are mostly men in the lower orders of society, a few priests and a number of mechanics', and the moderate party, consisting 'of the men of education and of wealth'.[78] The *Union Star* was one of the objects of dispute, the moderates claiming that 'O'Connor's associates among the lowest orders are those who diffuse it. Emmet in particular is exerting himself to suppress this execrable publication.'[79] By way of contrast, when the moderates had been in the ascendant in 1791–4, divisions had made it impossible to sustain a radical newspaper in Dublin.

The spread of the organisation farther afield came from a two-fold thrust from Dublin, drawing on the two competing interests. The early impetus for the spread of the organisation had come from a central group revolving around the attorney Mathew Dowling with ties, for instance in the case of Wexford, with Perry, Harvey and Edward Fitzgerald of Newpark. Increasingly in 1797 the spread of organisation came from the pace-setting O'Connor faction and from lower-level radicals, now the main activists in the organisation. When released from jail in February 1798, Neilson remained in Dublin. His intention can only have been to reinforce the radical interest in the Dublin power struggle.[80] Supplementing the recruiting drive in the southern countryside were James Hope and William Putnam McCabe.

In the power struggle between the O'Connor-Fitzgerald-Neilson axis and a Dublin-based, more narrowly political group, headed by Emmet and MacNeven, MacNeven was seen with McNally's frequent inaccuracy as a tool of O'Connor. He was in fact close to Emmet.[81] The divide revolved around the extent to which the rebellion would rely on mass recruitment in the field (including explicit acceptance of Defender alliance), or whether it would be a more select rebellion which would have to await French forces. Thus, the clash of opinion on the question of whether to await the French was in the last analysis not a strategic issue but a larger issue of the reliability of mass democracy and ultimately the desirability of more thoroughgoing revolution. The attitude of the moderate faction is very evident in MacNeven's book which plays down both the Defender role and the north-south axis, and especially in the cross-questioning of Emmet which reveals an arresting mixture of doctrinaire rationalism, and a belief in bloodless revolution.

Even if the United Irishmen were to rebel before a French invasion, a further divide came into the open as the great day approached, as to whether a rebellion should be mounted by relying on the United Irishmen's own resources of men in city and country, or by relying primarily on the militia declaring for the republic.[82] That was the thrust of the divide between Sheares and Neilson at the last moment. The arrests in March, which jailed most of the moderates in the leadership, strengthened Neilson's hand. That in turn put the conflicting Neilson-Sheares perceptions of how to organise a rebellion without waiting for the

French at the centre of debate, and three restructurings of the directory in May reflected its intensity. Fitzgerald's arrest provided the excuse for John Sheares, apparently the loser in these struggles, to assert his leadership. His concern that Neilson's plan put Fitzgerald's life at risk seemed a plausible pose as Fitzgerald's military leadership was accepted by all, and hence presumably all loyal United Irishmen had his welfare at heart. The later rumour that Neilson had informed on Fitzgerald may conceivably have had Sheares-inspired origins at this stage. The gulf between Neilson and Sheares was not of recent origin. While the Sheares, opposed to the Drennan-Butler-Rowan clique, found themselves on the same side as the Neilson-Tone camp in the politics of the Society in 1792–4, they were not strictly speaking allies. The Sheares continued to attend when the others, a few isolated appearances apart, withdrew in mid-1793. Tone at the time expressed a dislike for the doctrinaire obsession of the Sheares with the use of the style of 'citizen'.[83] Given Neilson's reliance on mass-organisation, it is not surprising that the Sheares, who were not closely involved in the execution of the organisational principles they had supported in 1794, opted for a rising based more on a military coup.

The Emmet-MacNeven-O'Connor document drawn up for the government after the rising and Emmet's statements to the Lords Secret Committee threw doubts on all the military plans for the interval after their arrest, and Emmet even seems to criticise Fitzgerald by implication.[84] These should not be viewed as authoritative inside statements, simply the verdict of one faction on their rivals, whether those rivals were from the Fitzgerald-O'Connor-Neilson camp or from the Sheares one. The three signatories of the document, despite O'Connor's differences with his fellow signatories, could find common cause in claiming that no general plan for the insurrection which proved so disastrous had existed in March, and in putting the onus on 'some individuals' who had acted in their absence.[85] MacNeven himself, despite his opposition to the Fitzgerald-O'Connor axis, could stress in his *Account of the Treaty between the United Irishmen and the Government*, both 'the interruption of all system' from March 1798 and the consequences of the loss of Lord Edward, a man of 'distinguished military talents'.[86]

(left) Charles Lucas (1713–71), celebrated Dublin radical leader of the mid-century (*National Gallery of Ireland*); *(right)* Sir Edward Newenham (1732–1814) MP, reformer, outspoken supporter of the American Revolution (*NGI*)

(left) Rev. John Thomas Troy (1739–1823), Archbishop of Dublin and intellectual leader of the Irish Catholic episcopacy in the 1790s (portrait by T.C. Thompson, *NGI*); *(right)* Rev. Samuel Barber (1738–1811), leading Presbyterian minister, Moderator of the General Synod of Ulster 1792, and United Irishman (*Ulster Museum*)

(left) John Giffard (1745–1819), editor of *Faulkner's Dublin Journal,* High Sheriff of Dublin, leading Orangeman and radicals' *bête noire* under sobriquet 'The Dog in Office' *(NGI)*; *(right)* John FitzGibbon, Earl of Clare (1749–1802), Attorney-General and Lord Chancellor, member of the inner circle of government policy-makers, and leading conservative in the 1790s *(NGI)*

Theobald Wolfe Tone (1763–98), founder member of the United Irishmen, diplomat and French army officer (*National Library of Ireland*)

Archibald Hamilton Rowan (1751–1834), President of the first Society of
United Irishmen in Dublin (*NGI*)

Volunteer medal of the
Ballymascanlon (Co.
Louth) Corps, 1782,
showing Masonic
insignia (*Journal of the
Royal Society of Anti-
quaries of Ireland*)

Napper Tandy's
bookplate (*NLI*)

(left) Samuel Neilson (1761–1803), principal organiser of the Belfast United Irishmen, *Northern Star* editor *(UM)*; *(right)* Arthur O'Connor (1763–1852) MP, United Irishman, editor of *The Press*, intellectual, French general *(NGI)*

John Sheares (1766–98), barrister, President of the Dublin Society of The United Irishmen, executed 1798 *(NGI)*

NAPPER TANDY.

— Taken from Life in Newgate. Novemʳ 2ᵈ 1799.

James Napper Tandy (1740–1803), veteran Dublin radical politician,
founding member of the Dublin Society of The United Irishmen,
and French army officer (*NGI*)

15

THE FITZWILLIAM EPISODE REVISITED

Deirdre Lindsay

The two-month-long tenure of the viceroyalty by Lord Fitz-william in 1795 was notable for the unceremonious removal from office of several leading Castle figures and the accompanying promise (or threat) of Catholic emancipation, followed in quick succession by the recall of Fitzwilliam by the British cabinet, the reinstatement of the sacked officials, and the defeat of the Catholic bill by the Irish government. A full account of these events can be found in Lecky, McDowell, and (for details of the events in Whitehall) Ehrmann.[1] Lecky's measured judgment of the consequences of this episode was that:

Great classes who were as yet very slightly disaffected now passed rapidly into republicanism, and Catholic opinion, which had been raised to the highest point of excited hope experienced a complete, a sudden and a most dangerous revulsion.[2]

This view of the Fitzwilliam episode as a 'tragic turning-point' in Irish history has been endorsed in many histories since, but few have given any consideration as to what actual political changes occurred, if any.

When Earl Fitzwilliam was appointed to the Lord Lieutenancy, the most immediate impact was on the Irish Whig opposition. As with all parliamentary oppositions in time of war, the Irish opposition had been floundering since hostilities had begun. But the ascent into coalition of their Whig friends in Britain, under the leadership of the Duke of Portland, seemed to promise a similar return to power and influence for them. By the time that Fitzwilliam arrived to take up his position in Ireland on 4 January 1795, most of the Irish parliamentary opposition had, to quote O'Brien, moved 'effortlessly into the Portland camp and onto the gravy train'. They immediately made it clear to the new viceroy that they now wanted positions of power, not just profitable government places. When parliament opened on 22 January, Grattan, the Ponsonbys, Curran and Hardy all took seats on the Treasury Bench, an indication that they were in the confidence of the new administration.[3] Grattan was careful to decline an office for himself, but his speech in reply to Fitzwilliam's address to parliament expressed whole-hearted support for the war against France, thereby identifying himself with the government. Some weeks later, when Grattan moved for the introduction of a new Catholic relief measure, it was naturally assumed that he had viceregal support.[4]

The prospect for Catholics of favourable treatment under the new viceroy stimulated renewed activity among their leaders. Despite the apparent dissolution of the Catholic Committee in 1793, an organisational skeleton had remained in place – a committee of seven (appointed by the general committee) to look after its outstanding financial affairs. This Dublin-based body was meeting at least as late as October 1794.[5] Around this time a decision was made by 'some members of the late Committee' to hold an anniversary dinner on 3 December, to commemorate the Catholic Convention held two years previously. A dispute arose, however, over whether to include among the toasts one in favour of parliamentary reform. Although the dinner was postponed until 8 December, no prior agreement could be reached. Therefore a vote was taken on the issue at the dinner itself, which was attended by sixty-three leading Catholics and former delegates to the convention, and the proposed toast was defeated. According to Leonard McNally, who reported the incident to the Marquis of Downshire, arguments against the toast were based on prudence rather than principle:

that the Catholics should not renew the publication of any political principles until the determination of the new ministers in respect to them should be known...The necessity of parliamentary reform was not denied: on the contrary most of those who voted against the toast declared their resolution to support a reform whenever a denial was given to a 'restitution of their rights' or whenever they were in possession of them.

The minority of twenty-five withdrew to dine separately from the rest because 'they could not with consistency remain in any company, public or private, where parliamentary reform as a toast, would be declined on any pretence whatsoever'. Their subsequent toasts included tributes to the citizens of Belfast, to Fox and Sheridan (the anti-coalition Whigs in Britain), and the prayer that 'the peculiar grievances of Catholics [may] never suppress the sense of their sufferings as Irishmen'.[6] The controversy reveals the well-established division among leading Catholics on the eve of Fitzwilliam's viceroyalty between those who primarily sought political equality under the existing constitution with their Protestant counterparts, and those who were prepared to abandon a separate Catholic campaign to join Protestant (especially dissenting) reformists in seeking radical parliamentary reform.

For Catholics the situation changed dramatically a few days later when Grattan, returning from London on 13 December, brought news of the 'full consent on the part of the British government, that Roman Catholics were to be relieved of all their remaining disabilities'.[7] Some days later on 23 December another meeting of Catholics took place in Dublin, marked by unity and a sense of purpose. A committee of nine men, appointed by the meeting, drew up a petition seeking Catholic emancipation, and this was unanimously adopted. This Dublin committee comprised six of the seven men who had hitherto supervised the former Catholic Committee's finances, namely Edward Byrne, John Keogh, Richard McCormick, John Sweetman, Thomas Braughall and Hugh Hamill. The other three members were Randall McDonnell, William J. MacNeven and Charles Ryan. This committee was instructed to circulate their petition as an example and precedent to 'the different counties and great cities' of Ireland.[8] The Dublin Committee immediately complied and their hurried mobilisation of Catholic opinion was facilitated by both the remnants of the old General Committee and Convention, and also the Catholic clergy at diocesan and parish level.[9] The result was a succession of Catholic meetings in January and February throughout the country, and a stream of fifty-six petitions into parliament representing almost every county, all adopting the wording of the Dublin petition. Despite the fact that it was the Dublin radicals who had taken the lead, the agitation was supported by the nobility, landed gentry and clergy.[10] Clearly, whatever tensions may have existed among the Catholic party in 1794, differences were left aside when there was a prospect of a real change in their fortunes.

Apart from the specific impact of the Castle dismissals, the effect of the change of régime on the pre-Fitzwilliam government party has often been overlooked. This is partly due to the lack of public criticism of the new administration by prominent figures during January and February 1795. Such silence was dictated by the immediate need for discretion among Fitzwilliam's Irish opponents. Yet the evidence points to a great deal of confusion. At the start of the session, Sir John Blaquiere expressed privately the dilemma of many members of the Commons who usually supported government:

I know not what to do – my principles are the King's government – they can be no other – but I would like to know whether this can be the King's government or not.

As for the proposed Catholic emancipation, Blaquiere was convinced that it would lead to parliamentary reform, and sensed he was not alone in his anxiety: 'moderate men [are] alarmed and frightened though nobody speaks'.[11] Even the Marquis of Downshire, one of the country's most powerful magnates, displayed an uncharacteristic loss of self-assurance in his letters at this time:

I confess I do not know what these new governors are about, but if what I hear is true, I don't like their proceedings. You, I hope, agree with me and see the reason why nothing should be suspected, much more declared on our part.

And there was the dilemma of a staunch government man faced with unwelcome policy change:

Support the government in matters of Empire I am decided, but as to internal regulation which must affect the Empire I am against. Popery reform, no consideration can induce me to approve, much more to support.

Moreover, Downshire's letters to Dublin reveal the nature of the clandestine opposition to Fitzwilliam's Catholic policy. Downshire issued 'private and confidential' instructions to his own members of the Commons, and through them messages to a network of like-minded Protestant hardliners.[12] A correspondent of Lord Westmoreland, Fitzwilliam's predecessor as viceroy, later claimed that a general committee had been formed against the Catholic relief bill

in which the friends of the noble marquis [of Downshire]…were active and zealous. Lord Shannon, all the Beresfords (except Lord Waterford), the Archbishop of Cashel, the Chancellor, Speaker, Lord Enniskillen, Lord Kingsborough, the Wynne's etc, etc, joined them boldly…120 good men and true were ready to oppose Mr Grattan in the House of Commons, and there was a strong possibility it would go to 140.

This letter, written as it was after Fitzwilliam's recall, may contain some exaggeration and a touch of bravado, but its claim is partially corroborated by Thomas Hussey's report on 29 January that 'some round robins were signed at [Patrick] Duigenan's against the [Catholic] bill...'[13] The evidence seems to point to a government party, disorientated by the appointment of an avowed political opponent as viceroy, reeling under the speedy dismissal of their colleagues in the Castle, and attempting, covertly and with some success, to organise opposition to one of the main planks of the new administration's policy. The Downshire-Beresford group did not however have to endure this unaccustomed role of opposition for long. The ousted officials who had been quietly and successfully lobbying their friends in the English government for their reinstatement found a favourable reception. By the end of February, news was reaching Dublin of Fitzwilliam's recall.[14]

The most immediate reaction to the recall came, not surprisingly, from the Catholics. The Dublin committee called an immediate meeting in the Francis Street chapel on 27 February, which 'noted the present crisis and the expected removal of our beloved viceroy'. The assembly voted to address the king, by means of a delegation, in an effort to reverse the decision. As before, Dublin's sentiments were echoed throughout the country in a series of Catholic meetings which protested at the recall and the effective veto this gave to Grattan's Catholic bill.[15]

In parliament reaction to the recall was muted. Fitzwilliam's advisers maintained a silence which indicated their acute political embarrassment, and it was only when the House readjourned after an unscheduled month-long break that they resumed their roles in opposition. Again, as so often in the 1790s, the paucity of Commons' discussion masks considerable and widespread political activity that was going on outside parliament. A total of thirty-one public meetings (apart from the distinctively Catholic meetings), held throughout eighteen counties in March and April, indicates a high level of local political dialogue and action.[16] This political lobbying by liberal and radical Protestants, united with Catholics at the local level, seems to have been motivated as much by anger at the return of the Beresford party to their former political ascendancy, as by the effective cancellation of Catholic relief. In this instance party considerations coincided smoothly with a popular

political issue to produce a national outcry against the recall of
Fitzwilliam.

Grattan and his colleagues shared the political martyrdom of
their unfortunate patron, Fitzwilliam. The display of public
approval may have been gratifying but it scarcely compensated for
the loss of influence and prospective employment which the recall
occasioned. But attempts by the new Chief Secretary, Thomas
Pelham, to woo Grattan and the Ponsonbys to support Camden's
government were unsuccessful. With the Catholic bill still pending, Grattan opted to make the most of Catholic disappointment
and of the wave of sympathy for Fitzwilliam among liberals and
independents to stage a comeback at the helm of the opposition.
He launched himself into the Catholic camp, associating and co-
operating quite openly with the Dublin Catholic committee.[17] In
reply to an address voted to him on 27 February, he encouraged
them in terms which some of his opposition colleagues thought
inadvisable:

I tremble at the return to power of your old task-masters – that combination
which galled the country with its tyranny, insulted her by its manner, exhausted
her by its rapacity and slandered her by its malice...I have no hesitation to say that
they will extinguish Ireland or Ireland must remove them.

Grattan's statement to Catholics, although sanctioned by the
Whig Club, was nonetheless rejected in favour of the more moderate replies to similar Catholic addresses by George Knox,
Thomas Conolly and George Ponsonby; Knox claimed that they
'in effect gave Grattan a slap in the face'. He added that 'the truth
is, [Grattan] bitterly resents what he has done'.[18]

Despite efforts to retain the confidence of the Catholics, Grattan and his colleagues found themselves compromised by their
conduct in support of government. On the opening of
Fitzwilliam's parliamentary session, they had been taunted by Sir
Laurence Parsons and Henry Duquery, who remained in opposition, for their neglect of their former political concerns. Before
Fitzwilliam's recall, only two reform measures were in progress –
Grattan's proposed repeal of the police bill, and Forbes's reform
of Castle accountability by means of the Treasury Board.[19] The
brevity of the Grattan group's term in power makes it difficult to
assess the extent of their reformist intentions, but their unqualified support given for the war haunted their efforts at opposition
during the subsequent administration. Having isolated themselves

from the moderate patrons of the parliamentary opposition and lost the trust of Catholics in Dublin, they found their attempts at opposition increasingly futile; frustrated by this political impotence, their attacks on the Castle party became ever more bitter until they finally withdrew 'in protest' from the Commons in June 1797. A handful of members of the Commons maintained a fragmented independent opposition, but in a Commons firmly under government control after May 1795 their role was limited to attempts at modifying aspects of government policy, rather than forming any opposition in principle.

The sense of betrayal and disappointment expressed by Catholics at their meetings in March-April 1795 was soon compounded by other factors. When the news of the recall was confirmed, Dublin Corporation drew up a petition to the King against any further Catholic relief, which passed amid some controversy in the Common Council on 13 March. A similar address by Drogheda's Corporation was defeated. Furthermore the cool reception given to the Catholic delegates by the King, and the revelations (in Fitzwilliam's letters to Lord Carlisle) that a political union of Ireland with Great Britain had been discussed by the British cabinet, contributed to the anger and resentment felt by many Catholics against the intervention of the British government.[20] The mood of Dublin city was reflected in the contrasting scenes which marked the departure of Lord Fitzwilliam and the arrival of his successor, the Earl of Camden.[21] It was in this atmosphere of crisis that the Catholic committee of Dublin called a second meeting in Francis Street to receive formally the report of the Catholic delegation and discuss other business relative to emancipation.

The meeting at Francis Street on 9 April 'not only consisted of all the principal Catholics of Dublin, but was attended by a great many leading men of that persuasion from all parts of Ireland'. With John Sweetman in the chair, the speakers included Keogh, MacNeven, Ryan and Lewins; through all of their speeches ran the themes of the unity and harmony of Catholics and Protestants in favour of Catholic emancipation, their betrayal by England, their unequivocal opposition to the idea of a legislative union with Britain, and the need (if this last application as a Catholic body were to fail) to lay aside any sectional demand and to unite with their Protestant brethren in the cause of a radical reform of parliament.[22] The language and tone of the speeches and resolutions marked a change of mood from the previous public statements by Catholics, and the proceedings shocked contemporary observers. Edmund Burke complained of the 'wholly Jacobinical' tone of the meeting and commented that 'the language of the day went plainly to a separation of the two kingdoms'. Some weeks later, in the Commons debate on the Catholic bill, the speeches of 'the Francis Street orators' and the evident influence of United Irish ideas on their committee were condemned and used as a justification for withholding the franchise from Catholics.[23]

The Francis Street meeting has recently been described as announcing the 'merger of Catholics with United Irishmen',[24] and to the extent that the meeting was representative of the Catholics of Dublin, this is a valid point. It is, however, necessary to place the meeting in the context of concurrent events. The meeting claimed, perhaps with justification, to represent the Catholics of Ireland, but its proceedings were nonetheless firmly under the auspices not only of the Dublin Catholics, but of the most radical among them. The influence of United Irish thinking was certainly to the fore, particularly in the speeches of MacNeven and Lewins. Some of their declarations however must be seen more as aspirations rather than intentions: for example, their extravagant claims regarding Protestant and Catholic unanimity in the cause of Catholic emancipation are questionable in the light of the evidence of Protestant opposition to the demand. Given the long association of many of the Dublin committee with the United Irish Society, which pre-dated the Fitzwilliam viceroyalty, their espousal of such ideas, and with such force of conviction, is not in itself remarkable. However, the apparent unanimity of sentiment at the meeting in favour of extremist ideas is noteworthy. In the changed atmosphere of spring 1795, Catholics in general were much more susceptible to the radical, if still nebulous, agenda of the Society of United Irishmen. Events since the start of the year had altered the basis upon which the Catholic question rested, and dispelled one of the main assumptions which underlay Catholic campaigns until then – the belief in the benevolent intentions of the British Prime Minister and the British Whigs toward Catholic political aspirations. The recall of Fitzwilliam by his colleagues, at the behest of the anti-Catholic party in the Castle, cleared the way for and indeed gave credibility to separa-

tionist arguments, if not perhaps to the republican ideals of
United Irish Catholics. However, the Catholic meetings through-
out the country were in general moderate in tone, although stead-
fast in their support of reform. Only the 31 March meeting of the
Antrim Catholics approached the radicalism of Francis Street in
April.[25]

Defenderism was an ongoing and autonomous feature of rural
Irish politics both before and during Fitzwilliam's viceroyalty, but
some connection between events in Dublin and the upsurge in
Defender violence in parts of Connacht and north Leinster at this
time seems likely. In Sligo, for example, a printed Defender handbill, circulating at this time, vilified the 'oppressors of the
poor...the monopolists' and declared:

We thank our friends in both houses of parliament for their strenuous exertions in
our favour, and had their petition met with the success it deserved, we would
instead of crowded dungeons and blood spilled on the information of perjurers, we
would we say, enjoy peace, tranquillity and the cultivation of the arts and sciences.

In accordance with its policy of playing down the success of the
Catholic campaign and the extent of Fitzwilliam's support, the
government took note of such developments but tended to cast
doubt as to the origins of the political discontent. Camden decided that the renewed Defender violence had been promoted by
agents from Dublin, in an attempt to intimidate government on
the question of the Catholic bill.[26]

The stance taken by the new administration is a central consideration in assessing the character of the political transformation in
1795. The old Castle party returned to official employment with a
new sense of purpose, consolidated in their positions and confident of their role in directing Irish policy. Pitt's choice of Lord
Camden as viceroy was a major factor in strengthening the 'Castle
junto'. Before leaving for Ireland, the new Lord Lieutenant was
given explicit instructions to resist the Catholic bill, to take a
stand against any further Catholic claims, and to give 'the most
decided and unreserved support to the Protestants'.[27] Upon his
arrival Camden duly surrounded himself with a narrow circle of
Protestant hardliners and this group remained his advisers for the
next three years. With only slight variation they included Fitzgibbon, Foster, the Beresfords, the Archbishop of Cashel, the law
officers Wolfe and Toler, Robert Stewart (later Lord Castlereagh)
and (often by correspondence) the Marquis of Downshire. The

close working relationship established between Pelham, as Chief Secretary, and the Under-Secretary, Edward Cooke, reaffirmed the position of the latter as a key anti-Catholic, anti-reform figure. Camden also had instructions to counteract the deep and bitter divisions which had developed in the course of the Fitzwilliam affair between the old Castle party and the Irish Whigs. Portland advised his colleague 'It will be one of the most difficult parts of your duty to moderate, to soothe, conciliate and reconcile these jarring spirits.'[28] Camden's limited talents proved unequal to accomplishing this somewhat naive aspiration of the British Cabinet.

The immediate side-effects of the restoration of the Castle junto were to be seen in the summer of 1795, in both the vigorous military campaign by Lord Carhampton against Defender activity in parts of Connacht and Leinster, and in the emergence in Armagh of the Orange Order, embodying the triumphalist Protestantism which became manifest earlier in that troubled county than in any other part of Ireland. These developments underlined the significance for Catholics and radical Protestants alike of the return to power of those they termed 'their enemies'. This point was emphasised by the Catholic delegates in their interview with the Duke of Portland in March, and also privately at that time to Edmund Burke, whom they also visited. They insisted that 'they did not look on their lives or properties to be in safety' if the ministry in London 'was governed by the intemperate counsels of such a man as Lord Downshire, and operated in Ireland through the power of the Chancellor, the Speaker, Mr Cooke, Mr Hamilton and Mr Beresford'. Although the Catholic party was whole-heartedly in support of the Catholic bill, Edward Byrne admitted that, if it was put to the alternative, 'he would rather have Lord Fitzwilliam without the Bill, than the Bill without Lord Fitzwilliam'.[29]

In the event the Catholics were to have neither the bill nor Lord Fitzwilliam. The episode certainly put the Catholic question off the political agenda for the foreseeable future. Moreover, political Catholics and radical reformists found that their day-to-day situation had deteriorated in the wake of the political turmoil. In the space of six months, their options for improvement had narrowed considerably and much bitterness resulted. Catholics in Dublin and its environs seem to have been particularly affected.

There were several contributory factors: Dublin Catholics had taken an early and prominent role in the recent agitation; the high-profile contribution of Grattan, MP for the city, had been a focus for political controversy; and the sheer physical proximity of the high political drama had given them an immediacy and significance for the citizens of Dublin that was lacking elsewhere. There is evidence, however, that in parts of Ulster also the Fitzwilliam affair may have been a catalyst in the radicalisation of Catholic opinion. The influence of strong United Irish societies in this process may be presumed.

Yet, to argue that the radicalisation of Catholics was either immediate or universal in the wake of the Fitzwilliam episode would be misleading. Evidence of the persistence of loyalty to the British Crown, however muted, belies any suggestion of a complete transformation in Catholic opinion. Catholic reactions to the threat of a French landing in 1796 tend to suggest regional and social contrasts in the pattern of Catholic loyalty and disaffection. The appearance of the French fleet in Bantry Bay prompted so little reaction among local inhabitants, apart from displays of loyalty to the king, that the Castle remained confident of success in the event of a landing taking place.[30] Yet any such incident off a northern coast at this time would have posed immeasurably more serious problems for the government. Moreover, at this time a petition was raised by a group of conservative Catholics, among them Lords Fingall and Kenmare, in which expressions of loyalty were accompanied by a renewed request for further Catholic relief. The main representatives of the Catholic party, true to their Francis Street resolutions, were not associated with this petition and presumably were opposed to it. Indeed the conservative petition seems to have been initiated by Camden for party political purposes; it was quickly abandoned when it was shown to be a non-starter with the majority of influential Catholics.[31] Yet the incident highlights the persistence of Catholic divisions in attitude towards the government and the British crown. Similarly the Catholic response to the establishment and recruiting of the yeomanry in the late summer of 1796 and after varied considerably throughout the country and depended to a large extent upon the political hue of the gentry who were raising the corps locally. The intense build-up to the general election of 1797 and the local electoral contests which were fought out, despite government attempts to forestall them, add to the evidence of the survival of a political opposition, outside parliament, up to the eve of the 1798 insurrection. The spotty survival of constitutional opposition is crucial to understanding the mixed fortunes of the United Irishmen in these years.

The Fitzwilliam débâcle, although an important political landmark for many Catholics, did not in itself transform the mass of the populace into revolutionary republicans. Its impact on the Grattanite Whigs was dramatic and damaging, but it only accelerated the decline of a coherent parliamentary opposition. The brief Fitzwilliam viceroyalty was a unique chapter in the 1790s for it turned on its head, however briefly, the established political order. The overall effect was a destabilisation of the structures of power and of the accepted forms of challenging that power, in which all kinds of change seemed possible. It was a period when the volatility of Irish politics was starkly displayed, in a power struggle whose outcome was only briefly in doubt. In the development and spread of political radicalism in Ireland during the 1790s, these events, however sensational, were only part of a long and complex story. In the event the most immediate transformation effected by the episode was to strengthen the reactionary party in the Castle, under a new and malleable viceroy, Lord Camden, and to give an unmistakable message of support from Whitehall to the hardline Protestant elements of Irish society. The basis upon which government policy was formulated had been transformed, and the fruits of such a transformation were to be seen in the years which followed.

16

THE UNITED IRISH ORGANISATION
IN ULSTER: 1795–8

Nancy J. Curtin

United Irish organisation in Ulster in the years after 1795 reflected the tension between ideological and pragmatic impulses; what
emerged was a seeming contradiction in terms, a mass-based
secret society. Attempts to imbue this organisational structure
with democratic and republican forms was not always successful,
as the requirements of secrecy often conflicted with the desire for
widespread informed participation. The tensions thus produced
created structural strains which weakened the organisation as an
efficient revolutionary tool. However, these tensions also produced strengths which stood the challenge when the Irish government launched its campaign to root out sedition in Ulster. The
combined effects of mass arrests, judicial activism, martial law, and
especially General Lake's 'dragooning' of Ulster seem to have
succeeded in subduing revolutionary ardour in the North,
accounting, so it has been argued, for the pathetic showing of the
northern United Irishmen in the rebellion in Antrim and Down in
June 1798.[1] Yet while these events may have had a chilling effect
on some leaders and on many casual supporters of the United
Irish movement, the organisational structure survived intact and
in some ways may have been strengthened by defections of the
weakly committed.

The failure of the rebellion in Antrim and Down needs less
explanation than the fact that a great many United Irishmen did
turn out – despite disillusionment with the French, draconian
policies implemented so zealously by Lake and the military
authorities from 1797, defection of many of the leaders, and
uneasiness about the course of the rebellion in Wexford. It is the
persistence of revolutionary ardour in the face of such obstacles
that needs to be addressed. An important but by no means sole

explanation for this persistence is the structure within which the republicans mobilised. The United Irishmen offered their followers the status of citizen. Citizenship meant active commitment to the public good. 'The full and free enjoyment of our rights', wrote William Drennan, 'is absolutely necessary to the performance of our duties, and the unequal distribution of the former preventing the accomplishment of the latter, the freedom of the public must be necessarily connected with their *virtue* as well as their happiness.'[2] Such civic virtue must be nurtured by providing the citizen with opportunities to exercise it, and these the United Irish organisation provided.

Within the first year of their formation the United Irishmen succeeded in extending their organisation into three of the four provinces of Ireland, but outside Ulster their numbers were hardly significant.[3] It was in the Presbyterian north-east, however, that the new movement took deepest root, but even there it was unimpressive. I have found references to only nine societies in the North outside of Belfast – one in the town of Armagh,[4] two in County Down (at Saintfield and Newry),[5] and six in County Antrim (at Lisburn, Templepatrick, Sixmilewater, Randalstown, Killead and Muckamore).[6] In Belfast the United Irishmen were divided into many societies: there were at least four such clubs by the autumn of 1792, and each of these contained no more than thirty-six members.[7]

'I am somewhat surprised they do not multiply more', observed a puzzled William Drennan to his brother-in-law in Belfast, 'and I think your societies should exert themselves individually and by circular letter through all the towns about.'[8] Yet despite Drennan's admonition there is no real evidence that the Belfast or indeed the Dublin movement took his advice to heart. This was because the purpose of the founding societies was not to replicate themselves throughout the countryside as such. Rather, their function was largely propagandist – to disseminate political information and to co-ordinate whenever possible the activities of other like-minded reform groups, especially the Volunteers.[9] Thus the early United Irishmen were content to keep their own numbers relatively small as long as they could use Volunteer corps, the Catholic Committee, Masonic lodges, Presbyterian congregations, and town, parish and county meetings to pronounce critically on current political arrangements.[10] With so many vehicles for popular expression, United Irish clubs were free to concentrate on the dissemination of a radical political discourse through which popular criticism could thrive. They could direct and manipulate political education in Ireland and could even offer their own public pronouncements, but ultimately they were content to allow other organisations of a more established or representative nature to conduct the challenge to government.

Prior to 1794 the informal direction of the affiliated northern clubs was provided by a committee of public welfare in Belfast.[11] But once the United Irishmen adopted insurrectionary aims they required a tighter organisational structure. By May 1795 there were about 5000 members in the northern United Irish organisation, concentrated in clubs within a twenty-mile radius of Belfast.[12] In Belfast alone there were as many as sixteen societies.[13] If the United Irishmen were to move from their narrow base of support in the Belfast neighbourhood to become the provincial and eventually national movement that their strategy required, they had to devise an organisational model which would immediately provide for the proliferation of new societies all over the country under centralised leadership. Late in 1794 the Belfast leaders drafted a new constitution which offered the means to achieve these ends.[14] Now, so read the constitution,

the societies of United Irishmen, ardently desiring that the *unawed, unhired,* and *honest* part of the community should become one great Society of United Irishmen, are of opinion that a general code of regulations is absolutely necessary to accomplish that important end. For this purpose they have, after mature deliberation, adopted the following *constitution* and *test,* the adoption of which is necessary for such societies as wish to enter into communication and correspondence with those already established.[15]

Each local club or remnant Volunteer corps was urged to affiliate itself with the United Irishmen and to register with the Belfast committee. The committee in turn would provide each affiliated club with an identification number. When any local society reached a total membership of thirty-six, the club was to split in two, forming a senior and a junior society, with the junior applying to Belfast for a new number. 'When a new society is intended in any place', reported the informer John Smith (alias Bird), 'printed instructions are given by the Belfast committee – constitutions, copies of the test, etc. When the society is full, they give notice to the Belfast committee and are then empowered to form other clubs.'[16] Each town or half-baronial society was to send three elected representatives to the baronial committee. When more than eight local societies were represented in this superior committee, the committee itself would then split. Once three or more baronial committees were established within a county, the baronial representatives would elect delegates to a county committee. And once two or more county committees had been formed in a province, delegates from them would form the provincial committee. A national committee would then be established once five persons from each of at least two provincial committees were so delegated.[17]

This new system, devised by the Belfast leaders, could not be imposed on existing United Irish clubs; they had to vote to accept it. Societies were urged to hold baronial meetings on 9 May 1795 to appoint representatives to a general committee meeting in Belfast the following day. The United Irishmen officially approved the new constitution in Belfast on 10 May; present at this meeting were numerous delegates from Antrim and Down, representing seventy-two local societies.[18] A few months later, in August 1795, an Ulster provincial committee was formed, representing over 8000 United Irishmen from Counties Antrim, Down, Armagh and Tyrone.[19]

Local societies met monthly, generally on a Sunday evening. All members were required to pay dues, a shilling on being sworn and a shilling every month thereafter, though reductions based on inability to pay could be arranged.[20] A secretary and treasurer constituted the chief officers of each local club, and these served for a term of three months.[21] The treasurer and two or three elected representatives formed the committee of finance, responsible for collecting and dispensing the society's funds. The bulk of these funds were passed on to superior committees in order to finance United Irish emissaries, defray publication costs, purchase arms, and provide legal fees. Each local society was also required to have a committee of public safety, the chief responsibility of which was to correspond with other clubs and oversee the conduct of members. Members of this committee were not however elected, the first four persons on the seniority list of members constituting the committee. Every fortnight the two most senior members would give way to the next two on the list.[22] This at any rate was how the committee was supposed to work, but in practice membership on the committees tended to be of much longer duration.[23] Election of delegates to superior committees was supervised by 'two confidential men' who were chosen to count the ballots and, in an effort to preserve secrecy as far as possible, were sworn to inform only those elected of the results.[24]

The enrolment of new members formed the first order of business at each local meeting. These new members were required to swear the test and the oath of secrecy publicly before the assembled United Irishmen, who stood to attention, with their hats off, in recognition of this solemn ceremony. After the secretary had read the minutes of the previous meeting, the main business was undertaken – committee reports. These came not only from the internal committees of finance and public safety but more importantly from the committees of the United Irish structure.[25] Special attention was paid to the county returns of men and arms available to the organisation, designed to encourage members with somewhat inflated accounts of the movement's rapid advance.[26] Local United Irishmen might then ask their officers for further information or raise questions which would be referred to the superior committee for consideration. But in many ways these local meetings merely acted to rubber-stamp decisions already taken by the leadership.

This relationship between local and superior committees tended to belie the much-lauded democratic and representative structure of the United Irish movement, which was to serve as the model for the independent Irish republic to come. We must not, however, overrate the submissiveness of local societies to the central leadership, as these clubs would often ignore the instructions of their superior committees. One of the widest cleavages between theory and practice was opened when the leadership prohibited members from participating in arms raids. The leaders rightly reasoned that such activity would only call the attention of local authorities to the movement. It was vitally important to preserve the secrecy and energy of the movement until such time as the membership and organisation were sufficiently advanced to take the initiative, either to coerce the government into granting reform and emancipation or to carry through these objectives in one swift and relatively bloodless rising. The leadership assured its followers that arms would be available to all when the time came to use them. The rank and file were often too impatient to heed such promises and the accompanying pleas for caution and discretion.[27]

Thus, although prohibited by the provincial executive, nocturnal arms raids were a constant feature of United Irish activity in
Ulster. Lord Cavan reported that in the neighbourhood of Derry
alone, over 400 families had been robbed of their weapons in a
single night.[28] Matthew Hood, land agent to the Marquis of Abercorn, laconically informed his employer of similar activity by the
United Irishmen in the vicinity of his estate in west Tyrone: 'as
they keep their excursions a profound secret, I have little hopes of
procuring any previous intelligence in case of a visit; as the greatest part of the arms are now taken up, their excursions have
become less frequent'.[29] James Stewart, another of Abercorn's cor-
respondents, observed that although every house on his lordship's
east Donegal estate had been robbed of arms, nothing else had
been taken.[30] The geographical distribution of these incidents
suggests a direct relationship between breaches of discipline and
distance from Belfast.

A further example of lower-committee insubordination was
provided in the latter part of 1796 when the United Irishmen
committed themselves to grafting a military organisation onto
their civil one. Again, the system was in theory representative. A
local society would elect a sergeant. Three such societies would
elect a captain, and ten captains, representing thirty societies
which constituted a regiment, would elect their superior officers.[31]
A military committee was constituted in Belfast by the leaders.
One of its members, the infamous informer Edward Newell, complained that it had 'done little but consider plans for discipline'. In
overseeing the implementation of military organisation, Newell
and his comrades were pleased with the progress underway in
County Down, but they ran into obstacles in Belfast and in
County Antrim. In Belfast, Newell observed, 'the idea is that discipline is not necessary – that they need only give one fire and
rush out with the bayonet'.[32] The independent-minded artisans
and merchants of Belfast may well have bridled at this attempt to
regiment them under military discipline, but some local leaders in
the Antrim countryside were alarmed at the insurrectionary militancy implicit in such an initiative. 'The report of the last county
committee abounds with contradiction, absurdity, and nonsense,'
complained one baronial society:

We are called upon to march well as if a knowledge of military tactics could be acquired in a closet or by night. We look upon such a report as unworthy of men who are fit to represent a county and as offering an insult to our understanding.

Furthermore, the Antrim local leaders regarded the imposition of a military system as 'premature and highly improper...because it would be attended with the utmost danger, for there is nothing but a pretext wanting to declare us out of the king's peace'. Not only would such a plan call down upon them the severest repression by government, but it was clearly 'evident that a few counties in Ulster would be unable by force of arms to accomplish an object of such magnitude until our principles are more generally known and better understood'.[33] In this case the leadership was being condemned for being too militant.

The rank and file also proved restive under central direction when it came to finances. Rumours abounded, triggered by repeated requests for subscriptions made by superior committees, that the leaders were misappropriating society funds. No doubt there were a number of treasurers at all levels in the organisation who pocketed a few shillings for themselves. The accusations became so widespread, at least in Down, that the county committee felt obliged to issue a formal declaration in May 1797:

We are astonished that they [the rank and file] can trust us with their lives and cannot with a penny or two pence. We have had a great deal of trouble this last assizes and the expense has been immense – our affairs in consequence has [*sic*] been rather deranged. However, you may depend upon a regular account being given at the next county meeting. At present we urge you, as you value the cause you are engaged in, not to withhold the usual subscription.[34]

The entire system depended on the willingness of local societies to accept direction and discipline, but the organisation had few means to enforce its decisions. An informer or traitor within the movement could be assassinated, but what was to be done with a local society which refused to accept the executive's prohibition against arms raids? How could the leadership deal with United Irish captains who refused to call out their followers when summoned? During the rebellion in the North many erstwhile captains failed to summon their men to do what they themselves now thought better of – risking their lives in an armed contest with seasoned government troops.

The United Irish leaders could not afford to discipline their followers, for there was always the danger that they might lose them. Paradoxically, that most serious flaw in the United Irish system was

also its source of greatest strength – its numbers. The more extensively the system spread, the more vulnerable it became to informers, lack of discipline, confusion, and the half-hearted commitment
of many loosely recruited members. Nevertheless, as it turned out,
the most serious breaches of secrecy and defections came not from
the rank and file but from the leaders.

The system was also designed to facilitate communication
between a central leadership and rank-and-file societies through
the medium of delegates and representatives on an hierarchy of
committees. Although this was certainly an improvement over the
loose network of clubs which characterised the early years of the
United Irish movement, it was still fundamentally flawed. As far
as possible, the United Irishmen avoided putting anything on
paper and consequently relied on messengers. Such a mode of
communication suited the smaller organisation that had operated
within a twenty-mile radius of Belfast, where information could
be relayed speedily and efficiently. But as the organisation grew,
communications became a real problem. During times of special
government vigilance the executive ordered subordinate committees to cease meeting, thus cutting off that particular channel of
communication. Even when effective, however, these county and
provincial meetings met only once a month. A speedy and efficient mode of issuing orders to subordinate committees eluded an
organisation which tried to keep its activities as secret as possible
and relied for its success on a nation-wide and consequently dispersed network of local societies. If leaders were frustrated in
their inability to issue direct orders instantly to subordinate societies, local societies themselves were often discouraged by their
inability to secure reliable information from the leadership. A
farm labourer, Charles McFillin, described such a situation in
north County Derry at the end of 1796: 'It was rumoured that the
French had arrived, and a member rode instantly to Belfast to
know the truth; on his return he expressed much surprise that the
executive directory had no intelligence of the coming of the
French.'[35] This was in reference to the invasion attempt at Bantry
Bay in December 1796.

Yet despite such organisational flaws and the fitful challenges
offered by the rank and file, the central leadership remained in
control of the organisation, at least to the extent that control was
possible over the increasingly vast network of clubs. This central

leadership was embodied not in the provincial committee, but within an executive directory, which was referred to variously as the 'grand committee', the 'committee of elders' (suggestive of the Presbyterian tone of the movement), and the 'committee of public welfare' in Belfast, which gave orders to local clubs through the provincial and county committees.[36] It was this committee which arranged for and financed United Irish emissaries to carry the system through the rest of the country. The executive directory also approved the formation of new societies and in general over-saw all organisational matters relating to the movement. It sent out representatives to local clubs to collect money and 'to examine the societies and to confirm them in their republican career'.[37] Most importantly, the Belfast committee decided all major policy and tactical questions confronting the organisation. 'All business of the greatest importance originated in an executive directory, who communicated with their provincial committee,' reported a County Down informer in August 1797.[38] Negotiations with the French, for example, were supervised by the executive directory.[39] And in the summer of 1797, when Lake's troops were ravaging the countryside, the executive directory ordered all committees, from the provincial down to local societies, to cease meeting tem-porarily.[40] The provincial committee elected five members to the executive directory, but the directors themselves were empowered to co-opt additional members if needed.[41] This made the directory only partially accountable to the network of clubs and committees that they represented and directed. Therefore if the collective wisdom of the inferior societies failed to push forward men of talent and ability (or men judged thus by the Belfast leaders), the executive directors could rectify the deficiency as well as ensure a continuity of leadership, which, though disrupted by government arrests, would be immune from the interference of lower commit-tees. As Camden observed to Portland in June 1797, the origina-tors of the United Irishmen 'still remain in great degree the direc-tors'.[42]

In 1797, when the organisation began to take on that national dimension essential to United Irish strategy, the Ulster leadership found itself increasingly isolated from the central direction of the conspiracy. The ablest leaders in the North had been detained since September 1796, and the baton of command had passed to less capable and less courageous men. As the calibre of the new northern leaders was not such as to place them in the forefront of the movement, so the initiative easily passed to the Dublin republicans where a national executive was formed in November 1797, consisting of five members, one from each of the four provinces of Ireland and one director-at-large.[43]

It was not the calibre of the leadership, however, nor its geographical base, that alarmed the government. Rather it was the fact that the arrest of the northern leaders, beginning in the autumn of 1796, failed to throw the United Irish movement into disarray, prompting Camden to tell Portland in June 1797 that 'it is therefore the regularity of their system which is to be dreaded more than any individual ability'.[44] The strength of the United Irish organisation lay in this ability to withstand frequent crises: the arrest of the northern leaders, the dragooning of Ulster in 1797, the imposition of martial law under the Insurrection Act. If the aim of the United Irishmen was to establish that contradiction in terms, a mass-based conspiracy, they succeeded to a remarkable degree.

The rebellions in Antrim and Down in 1798 are often regarded as a classic example of too little and too late. The emphasis is placed on the vessel that is half empty. Yet the vessel in fact held far more substance than could reasonably be expected under such disadvantageous circumstances. How strong, then, was the United Irish organisation on the eve of the rebellion in Ulster? Official returns from Antrim and Down counted about 49,000 United Irishmen (22,716 in Antrim, 26,153 in Down) which may or may not have included about 8500 Defenders in the former county.[45] But the United Irish leaders deliberately exaggerated the numbers of their followers. After all, republican organisation should be considered not only as an expression of political theory and strategy, but also as a form of propaganda. By cultivating the impression of widespread participation, United Irish leaders heartened their followers, attracted new recruits drawn to the republicans' apparent strength, and intimidated the forces of loyalism. The leaders themselves displayed a more realistic grasp of their numerical strength. In March 1798 the republicans claimed a national network of at least 600,000 supporters. This boastful figure included soldiers and militiamen, Defenders, and the 280,000 counted in official returns; of these only about 40,000 were expected to take the field immediately when called.[46]

What proportion of the paper strength of 49,000 in the Antrim and Down organisations actually participated in at least one engagement in June 1798? Estimates of insurgents involved in the battle of Antrim range from three to seven thousand, and for the battle of Ballynahinch, five to seven thousand.[47] Charles Dickson has suggested that two or three thousand who arrived at Donegore Hill too late to engage in the battle for Antrim town should be added.[48] There were also a number of other engagements before defeat in these two battles put the last nail in the coffin of the northern rebellion. As Samuel McSkimin observed, 'in almost every town, village, or hamlet in the county of Antrim, hostile movements in a greater or lesser degree took place'. He estimated that nine thousand rebels took part at the battle of Randalstown, and another ten thousand at Ballymena.[49] Furthermore, an indeterminate number of rebels rose in the Ards peninsula, and there were also reputedly several thousands mobilised and ready for battle in south Down.[50] The most conservative figure obtained from these estimates of insurgent forces at the battles of Randalstown, Ballymena, Antrim, and Ballynahinch (excluding the late arrivals at Donegore Hill) is 27,000. In Antrim alone, if we add 8500 Defenders to the official returns of nearly 23,000, we might conclude that 22,000 of a possible 31,500 'turned out' in 1798. These figures, rough as they might be, clearly challenge the view of the United Irish organisation in the North as merely a hollow shell, ravaged by Lake's campaign, and pathetically asserting itself in a disorganised frenzy of desperation and bravado. Those who were engaged in minor skirmishes, or who arrived too late for battle, or who failed to link up with the main force, or who waited, like the men of the Mourne, to join the expected march south to Dublin, are not included in these perhaps exaggerated estimates of insurgent strength in Antrim and Down. The numbers were there; it was leadership and opportunity that was wanting.[51]

The failure of revolutionary zeal to manifest itself on a sustained and massive scale was hardly therefore the result of organisational breakdown. Northern revolutionary enthusiasm persisted after Lake's dragooning of Ulster and even through the confusion that followed the outbreak of the rebellion in the South, but many northern militants were denied the opportunity for action because of faulty communications and the refusal of their leaders to mobilise them. The hurried state of preparations for the rising after the ousting of the passive Ulster directory meant that these counties were unprepared for the call to arms when it came. Indeed, the persistence of rank-and-file militancy under such circumstances suggests that the organisation was far more successful in producing revolutionary citizens than disciplined soldiers.

There is another way of looking at the organisational strength of the northern United Irishmen on the eve of rebellion in 1798. Leaders like Robert Hunter and Robert Simms who resisted the call to rise seem to have been primarily concerned to protect an organisation which had shown itself able to absorb and politicise thousands of their fellow citizens. Convinced that success would elude them unless the French appeared in force, they refused to hazard their organisation in what they regarded as a premature and partial rising. 'Violent young men', among whom Hunter counted Henry Joy McCracken, Henry Munro, Samuel Orr (brother to the celebrated martyr William), and James Dickey, 'who had not the confidential communications, attempted to bring out the people', despite the fact that many colonels had resolved not to rise unless there was a French invasion. Realistically appraising the situation, Hunter and his like-minded comrades decided that they could not in good conscience lead their followers to certain defeat, a defeat which would, as the counter-revolutionary terror of the previous year confirmed, have only the most tragic consequences for the people of the North.[52]

As a model for an underground revolutionary organisation, the United Irish movement was wanting in several respects. Its networks were too vulnerable to infiltration, confusion and insubordination. The larger the organisation became, the more difficult it was to manage. Such vulnerabilities were the price of the ideological and propagandistic functions of the organisation itself. For a chief priority of the republicans was to educate the citizen or, as Thomas Addis Emmet put it, to 'make every man a politician'.[53] This involved embracing mass participation and instituting, as far as circumstances permitted, democratic and republican practices. The movement lingered on after 1798 as a tiny conspiracy until Emmet's insurrectionary outburst in 1803, when it was reconstituted in such a way as to eliminate its perceived major weakness, its mass-participatory and quasi-democratic character.[54] Never again did an underground republican movement enjoy so massive a following or as formidable and extensive an organisation as it did in the 1790s. Indeed, in respect to organisation, the United Irish network suggests much stronger similarities with the Catholic emancipation movement than with its republican counterparts of the nineteenth and early twentieth centuries.[55]

Is this to suggest that we should cease to look to the United Irishmen for the origins of an authoritarian, physical-force, republican tradition in Irish history and instead see them as the progenitors of the modern, democratic political party? The United Irishmen, with an organisation torn between functional needs for secrecy and central control, and ideological preferences for mass participation and political education, can claim parentage for both offspring.

17

THE DEFENDERS IN ULSTER

Marianne Elliott

The Defenders are no longer seen as just another Irish agrarian movement,[1] but considerable puzzlement remains as to their character and at least one historian has challenged the view that they were in any way politicised.[2] The sources themselves – dependent as we are on them – may actually present a barrier to a better understanding of this enigmatic movement, Edward Cooke's admission of bafflement in 1793 finding echoes throughout government sources.[3] In any event we can be sure that the homogeneity of rural Catholic communities in Ulster and the difficulty of communications in the hilly terrain where they often lived would have deterred information-gathering and would have distorted the official map of Defenderism. This paper is based on a continuing belief that we can approach a better understanding of Defenderism only by taking a longer historical view and by combining it with detailed local studies, notably in the heartland of Defenderism: south-east Ulster and north Leinster. What follows are merely suggestions towards such an approach and the airing of some preliminary findings.

The context of Defenderism

Although Defenderism spread far afield during the anti-militia riots of 1793, and again after the Armagh outrages of 1795, its original and most enduring heartland was south-east Ulster and north Leinster – most particularly south Armagh and south Down, and somewhat later the northernmost parts of Louth, Monaghan and Cavan. They were areas of hilly scrubland and mountain passes, the kind of rebelly 'fastnesses' referred to so frequently during the Elizabethan conquest of Ulster, and in the 1790s identifiable Defender territory.[4] It was a drumlin landscape of tiny farms, where a long tradition of subsidiary occupations laid the basis for Catholic involvement in the linen prosperity of the eighteenth century. Much of the barren and rocky terrain was reclaimed in this period through hard labour, then frequently turned to flax-growing, which in turn supplied the raw material for domestic weaving on the same farm. It is the affrays at the regular fairs and markets which define the early map of Defenderism, the domestic cloth industry and the remarkable mobility associated with it facilitating expansion, the cloth-merchants acting as its agents.[5] Land once thought uneconomic was assuming greater potential, a tendency further intensified by a population increase significantly higher than anywhere else in Europe, or in most of Ireland for that matter.[6] Areas where Catholics were traditionally settled were experiencing in-migration of Protestant settlers from districts further north, often onto lands whose very remoteness had deterred settlement from outsiders until the eighteenth century.[7]

The cultural geography of this area and Catholic attitudes to the land are fundamental to any understanding of Defenderism. Before the Tudor conquest, outright ownership of land was not the norm in Gaelic society. But centuries of encroachment by dominant lineages had given rise to an acute awareness as to who had rights to what, and to a concept of landholding defined by tradition and customary right.[8] From the Middle Ages to the late seventeenth century, families like the Magennises controlled the uplands of mid- and south Down. They were typical of kin-groups with a long-standing stake in identifiable land; this sense of territory was a factor which undoubtedly contributed to that reluctance to move and the willingness to pay exorbitant rents and thereby outbid Protestant tenants so noted by eighteenth-century commentators. Local studies elsewhere in Ulster have shown the persistence of traditional settlement patterns and the tenacity with which kin-groups clung to certain areas – a tenacity noted by the authorities in the 1790s and one of the chief causes cited for the anti-militia riots of 1793.[9] The sectarian tensions of the 1780s and 1790s were unusual in eighteenth-century Ulster, and it would appear that the kind of Protestant encroachment on traditional 'Catholic' territory, 'invasion' across internal cultural frontiers, was one of the elements shattering an uneasy *modus vivendi*.

This south Ulster/north Leinster area is what the contributors to the invaluable Gillespie/O'Sullivan volume, *Borderlands*, consid-

er a continuing frontier zone and cultural interface between Prot-
estant/Catholic, native Irish/settler traditions. It had been a traditional Irish enclave for centuries and in the eighteenth century
still hosted an important school of south Ulster poets. In mid-
and south Down (one of the areas where Defenderism was most
pervasive and enduring) this same cultural interface can be seen
operating in a number of more contained localities, particularly in
the barony of Mourne and the areas around Downpatrick, Lough-
brickland and Ballynahinch. Here the continuing influence of
once-prominent Catholic families like the Magennises seems to
have been an important factor in the assertiveness of local
Catholics. Proud descendants of the ancient Ulaid, they had sustained a bardic school long after such institutions had disappeared
elsewhere. Their territorial ascendancy in mid- and south Down
was only finally lost in the late seventeenth century through
indebtedness to the Hill family, whose descendants in the 1790s
were Lords Downshire and Hillsborough – notable hate-figures
for the Catholics.[10]

Gaelic society had been an intensely status-conscious one and
in the eighteenth-century poems of the Creggan poet, Art Mac-
Cooey, it is the 'upstarts', 'churls' and 'hucksters', with their
linen-generated wealth, who are lashed as much as the planter.[11]
Travelling through the remoter parts of Meath and Louth in
1798, Charles Teeling displayed a deference towards the descendants of the ancient families, now sunk in status, according to his
personal account.[12] Even more prominent than land in Defender
aspirations was the restoration of lost status, often crudely
expressed as a desired reversal of contemporary Catholic-Protes-
tant roles.[13] It is surely no accident that the names of those most
notably identified with the Defenders in these 'borderlands' were
members of such families – the Teelings (Antrim), the Magennises and Lowrys (Down), the McCanns (Louth), and the MacArdles
(south Armagh and Down). Not all were of native Irish stock –
the McCabes had been gallowglasses from the Western Isles, the
Teelings Anglo-Norman. Not all had remained Catholic. But all
would have enjoyed high rank in the Gaelic order, and most had
only lost the last of their freehold land at the close of the seventeenth century.[14] The case of such prominent local figures steeling
the cottiers on the Downshire estates with assurances that they
could not be dispossessed for their activities, cannot have been an

isolated incident. Their 'refractory disposition', complained Downshire's agent, 'had arisen from the contumaceous example of the McArdells, Magenises and Byrnes ...this junto of d - d United Papists...instilling into the minds of a numerous banditti of cottiers under them, that you are only entitled to a chiefry upon the lands, and cannot dispossess them'.[15] The list of Ulster delegates elected to the Catholic Convention of 1792 reveals a high percentage of old family names – a reflection of continuing status, whatever their contemporary economic position.[16] By the 1790s some would have become members of the growing Catholic middle class. Two of the Monaghan militiamen executed at Blaris camp in 1797 were sons of a Catholic innkeeper of radical sympathies whose forebears had been minor Gaelic chieftains in Monaghan since at least the thirteenth century.[17] The sons of such families appear to have been an important element in the Defender-United Irishmen alliance after 1795 and, like James Coigley, they may well have been nurtured on family traditions of lost status and glorious ancestry.[18]

These then were some of the local conditions conducive to the development of Defenderism: relatively recent losses of land, a sense of lost status, unusually rapid growth of population, economic competition between Protestant and Catholic, Protestant incursion into traditional Catholic 'territory'. But the worst Defender disturbances occurred in areas where the leading gentry were noted anti-papists, and such activities cannot be separated from Catholic Committee campaigning in these years. Most Defenders were not peculiarly anti-landlord. 'Tho' they are often riotous, disorderly and impatient of regular law', wrote Westmorland in 1792, 'I have not heard of any symptoms of disaffection to their landlords.'[19] Their nocturnal visitations were arms-raids, involving little destruction of property or life.[20] This makes the attacks on the Hill family property and persons unusual. It is perhaps no coincidence that the only serious disturbance in Ulster during the anti-militia riots of 1793 involved an attack on Lord Hillsborough while he was in the process of raising a company at Castlereagh.[21] The anti-popery of Lord Annesley – the major landlord in the most affected area around Rathfriland and Castlewellan – and of the leading county family, the Hills, was well-known and considered a chief cause of the disturbances, even by the government itself.[22]

Although the Defenders were usually Catholic, they were not
always motivated by anti-Protestantism, otherwise the alliance
with the United Irishmen would not have succeeded. But there
was a frequently voiced resentment at the blanket Protestant control of society from parliament to parish, particularly the domi-
nance of local life and justice by that very Ascendancy which was
the focus of Catholic Committee and United Irish attack. Given
the 1792 war of words between the Catholic Committee and the
grand juries in almost every county, and the latter's strident
defence of 'Protestant Ascendancy', the Committee's condemna-
tion of a narrow Ascendancy monopoly of power against the
interests of the people would have struck a chord of recognition at
local level. 'The Catholics have been attacked for years back,'
wrote John Keogh of the Rathfriland area; 'they contented themselves with shewing their wounds, and crying for protection; but
in vain...their alarms are increased beyond measure at perceiving
the Monopolists now arming their people, as they fear, to extir-
pate them'.[23] There were just as many complaints on the other
side of the argument. But there can be no doubt that in those
counties where justice was thought to be administered impartially
and where relations with the local gentry were good, Defenderism
was weak.[24] The stand taken by John Foster against the 1793
Catholic Relief Bill and his heavy-handed treatment of Defenderism in Louth was considered part of the same system and helps
explain the particularly violent history of Defenderism in that
county.[25]

The Defenders and the Catholic Committee

Defenderism in the south Ulster/north Leinster area lacked the
murderous notoriety of Defenderism in Armagh, and in consequence sources are rarer.[26] Although there were similar Defender-
Peep O'Day Boy disturbances in Antrim, Down and Louth by the
late 1780s,[27] Defenderism there did not assume its more militant
form nor begin to spread widely until 1792.[28] Much has been said
on the success of both the Catholic Committee and the United
Irishmen as propagandists, notably on their ability to transmit
some political understanding, however rudimentary, to less elevated social sectors.[29] 'At every cabin around us you will see them
reading the *Northern Star* (a paper which has sharpened them all
for rebellion)', remarked one English visitor to Ulster in 1796–7,

'and I often meet Sir John's labourers walking to work, and reading this paper as they move along.'[30] Like most observers, he
found a contempt for existing government and expectations of
major change, geographical remoteness being no deterrent to the
rapid politicisation of the Catholic population which occurred in
the 1790s. Walking through south Fermanagh in April 1793,
Thomas Russell fell in with a Methodist who claimed frequent
contact 'with people that others cannot thro bogs, mountains
etc...where you could not conceive that any news could reach'.
He found them perfectly well aware of political developments,
generally pro-French and supporters of reform.[31] Whatever the
long-term cultural and economic roots of Defenderism, its extension and politicisation in these years cannot be considered separately from the reform campaign, particularly that of the Catholic
Committee.

The revamped Catholic Committee of 1791–3 conducted its
business in a blaze of publicity, the elections to the Catholic Convention spreading an expectation of dramatic change to Catholics
at every level. Information relating to the progress of these elections on the ground is singularly lacking. But with the backing of
the clergy they involved all the male parishioners gathering in the
Catholic chapel, delegating one to two electors to a county meeting, which in turn forwarded one to four delegates to the Convention.[32] The elections progressed through the summer and autumn
months of 1792, and Catholic communities all over the country
can have been left in little doubt as to the momentousness of the
occasion.[33] In County Down alone a large print-run of the Committee's August 1792 address to the Defenders was distributed,
urging calm, yes, but also promising imminent success in the campaign to win legal equality with Protestants.[34] The unrealistic
expectations of radical change – so central to Defenderism – only
began to surface at this time and were undoubtedly generated by
these elections and the publicity surrounding the Convention.
'The Catholics make use of improper expressions such as "it will
be our turn next...we shall pay no tithes after xmas",' reported
Westmorland on 20 October 1792,[35] adding some weeks later:
'political discussions have raised very much the expectations of the
lower Catholics. They have been taught that the elective franchise
will improve their condition and they connect with it the non-
payment of rents, tythes and taxes.' The Committee's members

and the delegates to the Convention enjoyed considerable prestige with the Catholic populace and quickly acquired the status of
legitimate representatives. 'They had already exercised most of
the functions of a Government,' Westmorland continued, 'their
declarations taken as law by the people.'[36]

The attempt by government to implicate Catholic Committee
members with the Defenders rather backfired, and prior to 1795
there is little evidence of members encouraging the Defenders.[37]
But given their local esteem, Committee men do appear to have
been the bridge over which United Irishmen and Defenders later
joined forces. Luke Teeling – a prominent Catholic linen merchant in Lisburn – was elected to the Convention and was viewed
as the chief spokesman for the northern Catholics. His role in the
Convention of December 1792 and in subsequent months was
pivotal. He had been briefed by the Belfast United Irishmen and
helped break down the Catholic Committee's lingering reluctance
to associate with them. He was one of those who dominated proceedings, and it was he who shifted this largely moderate body in
a radical direction by proposing that nothing short of complete
emancipation should be demanded.[38] Teeling was widely recognised as one of the leaders of Catholic society in the North and
was later reputed to have been chosen to sit on the new republican executive in the event of independence.[39] His son-in-law, John
Magennis, was also elected to the Convention, and he too was to
be active in cementing the alliance between Defenders and
United Irishmen.[40]

At the outset the Defenders were a purely defensive movement
against Peep O'Day Boy attacks, which in turn were provoked by
signs of greater Catholic assertiveness.[41] 'The Protestants think
the XX [Catholics] are to murder them' and stay armed all night,
Russell was informed by the Methodist traveller in spring 1793.
'The XX [Catholics] equally frightened and fly to the mountains
with their goods.'[42] In areas where local magistrates appeared
unable or unwilling to check such attacks, Defender mobilisation
had become more organised by the early 1790s. In July 1792 the
Defenders were reported to be 'in regular companies, as well
armed as the Volunteers, and…better provided with ammunition'
around Mourne, Newcastle, Castlewellan and Rathfriland, and
were drilled by army deserters 'in the mountains [where] it is not
possible to get at them'.[43] The Catholic Committee intervened,

securing an introduction to the Rathfriland-Downpatrick area, where tensions were greatest, through the Lowry family. All with whom they met agreed that 'the Protestants were the aggressors', having taken 'great offence...at the Catholics marching about in military array'.[44] The Catholic clergy seemed to have had little control and generally condemned them, notwithstanding the isolated case of the parish priest of Kilcoo, who was encouraging the Defenders in the Rathfriland region.[45] The delegates were told that local Catholics did not believe they could expect equal justice with Protestants, the tendency of Lord Downshire and his son to see all the wrong on the Catholic side dictating the outlook of the local gentry. Keogh considered 'their petty tyrannies' part of a corrupt monopoly of power by a bigoted ascendancy – Lord Annesley's relationship with the Beresford clan confirming his view. Instead of offering protection, he complained, they permitted attacks on 'innocent and peaceable Catholics, driving them from a churchyard when only burying their dead – goading them to despair...reporting they do not pay rents, and yet compelling them to pay the dead half-year contrary to custom... arming the poorest Protestants, the very wretches who are reported to be the "Peep of Day-Boys" – and in this state threatening to disarm the Catholics, so as to leave them at the mercy of ignorant and enraged bigots'.[46] Tone's account – though less heated – confirms the basic details of Keogh's.[47] They were based on information gathered during that summer visit, and even allowing for bias and exaggeration, they give a fair picture of the kind of local polarisation and alienation from the governing process which lay behind the politicisation of Defenderism by 1792. The process was hastened further once the disappointment of leading Catholics and radicals at the incomplete nature of the 1793 Catholic Relief Act filtered down the social scale, a disappointment which was to figure in the militia riots of that summer.[48] It also robbed the Catholic Committee of its power and stature – a power which had been used to calm Defenderism at the close of the previous year. It is no accident that 1793 was to witness a major resurgence.

The Defenders and the United Irishmen

The Rathfriland delegation was told by local magistrates of arms having been sent from France for the Catholics. Tone and Keogh were incensed by this effort of government, as they thought, at 'spreading the vilest calumnies and falsehoods, to exasperate the two sects against each other, that they may with the greatest ease and security plunder both'.[49] They were right to discredit claims of arms being supplied by France. But the Dublin authorities were genuinely alarmed and there is evidence that the Defenders were purchasing arms in England and on the Continent – many reported to be arriving via the traditional smuggler community on the south Down coast.[50] This undoubted venture into the arms market raises yet more questions about the social status of the Defenders and of those supporting them. We have far too readily accepted government sources describing the lowly social status of Defenders. The 1793 Secret Committee report into Defender disturbances described the Defenders as 'in general poor, ignorant labouring men, sworn to secrecy and impressed with an opinion that they are assisting the Catholic cause'. But the aim of the report was to discredit the Catholic Committee by implying that such lowly social elements must surely have been 'directed by men of a superior rank'.[51] The term 'farmer' is loosely used in government information. But it could and did encompass everything from a quite substantial manufacturer to a labourer.[52] Certainly the Teelings and Joseph Cuthbert, frequently cited as leaders of the Defenders, were well-off, the former prosperous linen merchants, the latter 'a tailor of some property and influence'.[53] Who then were the Defender negotiators in the post-1795 merger with the United Irishmen? Are we really talking about two separate sets of leaders, and were the Defenders always necessarily socially inferior to the United Irishmen?

Unlike the Society of United Irishmen in the South, that in Ulster had always had a more popular base. But it was only in 1795 that recruitment of Catholic Defenders became policy. The exact nature of the effective merger of the two is shrouded in mystery and is usually considered more apparent than real. Much has been made of the United Irishmen and Defenders fighting under different banners and squabbling during the Ulster rising of 1798.[54] But Hope, who fought at the battle of Antrim, says nothing of it. There is evidence of former Defenders actually becoming United Irishmen, only reverting as the United Irish Society collapsed. The differences referred to in 1798 might reflect this deterioration after the military suppression of Ulster in 1797 and 1798. Certainly all the information reaching the Castle convinced

Lord Castlereagh that this was happening. He found a general falling away of Protestants from the movement after 1798, and Defenderism reviving to replace the United Irish system as the chief organiser of treason.[55]

In 1795, however, the Ulster United Irishmen had embarked on a recruitment campaign among the Defenders with considerable enthusiasm and success, utilising their economic power as linen manufacturers and farmers to enlist recruits. Thus in July 1795 a United Irish meeting in Antrim, attended by a number of linen manufacturers, drapers and shopkeepers, proposed paying weavers one shilling above the normal price per web and waiving various small debts to encourage enlistment, while a farmer from Kells in County Antrim undertook at another meeting the following month to use his influence with the Defenders in Armagh to the same end. 'This plan of union', wrote James Hope, 'was projected by Neilson [a native of Lisburn], assisted by Luke Teeling of Lisburn, and his family and connection', notably his seventeen-year-old son, Charles, who 'was labouring to unite the Defenders and Catholics of the smaller towns of Ulster'. [56] Madden has a vivid description of such a recruitment mission, undertaken by Hope and William Putnam McCabe in Monaghan, Cavan, Armagh, Leitrim and Fermanagh, one of their tactics being to pose as recruiting sergeants and intercept convicted Defenders, giving them the choice of prison or the army.[57] The point is that one-time Defenders *were* being sworn into the United Irish system and we need to treat reports about separate Defender and United movements thereafter with some caution. Defenders who became United Irishmen re-surfaced as Defenders in the revival of Defenderism after 1799, a revival which occurred in the same pre-1795 strongholds. But it was a more actively republican movement which emerged after 1798, sworn in not by the motley pre-1795 collection of Defender oaths but by that of the United Irishmen.[58]

The Ulster United Irish leaders regarded the recruitment of Defenders (and especially Defenders in the militia) as the key to their revolutionary potential after 1795. In the summer of 1796, William Bird – one of Dublin Castle's more useful informants – returned to Belfast after an absence of some months. At Barclay's Tavern he was told by several leaders (including Henry Joy McCracken) 'that there had been a junction between the leaders

of the United Irishmen and the Defenders since his last
visit...that the army was with them, particularly the Limerick City
militia...that messengers had been sent to Connaught...to further
the connection between the UI and the Defenders...that emancipation was not far off...[that] if they could organise the Defenders
they could defy government...[and that now] there was a complete union between the Defenders and the United Irishmen'.[59]
Luke Teeling was given as a toast. Daniel Shanahan – one of the
Catholic leaders in Belfast who, like many others, had thrown in
his lot with the United Irishmen after Fitzwilliam's departure –
was also there. He and Cuthbert had been the main instruments
in turning Defenders among the militia into United Irishmen,
while in County Down, Lowry and Magennis were the chief
organisers.[60] In an atmosphere of impending crisis during 1795–6,
Protestant attacks on Catholics in south Ulster escalated. The
Armagh outrages were mirrored in neighbouring counties, while
recruitment into the yeomanry in 1796 reactivated local religious
feuds.[61] They provided the backdrop to the widely reported readiness of Defenders to join with the United Irish organisation that
summer, permitting it to claim a membership of some 50,000 by
November.[62] We do not hear again of a separate Defender organisation in Ulster until after the collapse of the 1798 rebellion. It
was into the United Irishmen that frightened Catholics flooded
after General Lake's disarming of Ulster, making them a majority
in the lower committees.

Such recruitment of Defenders gave the northern United
Irishmen an early numerical superiority over its counterparts elsewhere. It also sharpened differences with the Dublin executive,
which had been far less enthusiastic about the enlistment of thousands of lower-class Catholics. There had always been tensions
between the United Irishmen in the North and those in Dublin.
The confidence and strength which the Defender alliance afforded the northern movement – but also the difficulties of holding
lower-rank restiveness in check – pushed the two further apart.
The northern leaders called for a rising early in 1797, even without French assistance. Dublin refused. It was at this stage that
those northern United Irishmen who had helped bring the United
Irish/Defender merger to such a pitch and who appear time and
time again in government documentation as Defender leaders
(the Teelings, Alexander Lowry, James Coigley, Anthony

McCann among them) began to force the pace, conducting their own missions to France independent of that mounted by the Dublin Directory. It may well have been the Defender links which prompted another development that was sponsored almost exclusively by the northern wing: the expansion of the United movement into England and Scotland. Joseph Cuthbert was in Scotland as early as 1795 distributing the new United Irish constitutions and, with few exceptions, those United Irishmen involved in spreading the United movement to the northern English cities were northerners like James Coigley, Arthur MacMahon, John Magennis, William Putnam McCabe, all closely associated with the United Irish/Defender merger in Ulster, and they moved along well-established migratory routes for Ulster weavers into the north of England.[63]

Conclusion

This paper has raised more questions than it answers. But I hope to have at least partly demonstrated that the Defenders were not always the lowly peasantry and labourers of government propaganda. Nor was Defender involvement in the northern United Irishmen simply a case of giving a head to a less co-ordinated body. Rather there would appear to have been elements of common membership from the earliest stages of United Irish organisation, and co-operation after 1795 may have been more a merger and less the uneasy alliance of previous perception. Sectarian tensions within the allied movements should not be over-played. They do not seem to have fundamentally jeopardised relations in the years of most intensive organisation up to 1797. Indeed the two movements had a good deal more in common than the northern United Irishmen had with those elsewhere in the country. Most of all, however, the paper points to some of the long-term economic, cultural and historical roots of Defenderism, which in the specific circumstances of the 1790s provided such a fertile ground for popular politicisation.

18

THE SOCIAL AND POLITICAL IMPLICATIONS OF THE RAISING OF THE YEOMANRY IN ULSTER: 1796–8

Allan Blackstock

'The first up will carry the day!' So asserted Thomas Knox MP when he and the Reverend William Richardson were promoting the Dungannon Association, one of the prototypes of the Irish yeomanry. Knox's competitors in the race to be 'up' were the local United Irishmen, who in 1796 were effecting an alliance with the Defenders, greatly increasing their numbers.[1] 'Up' was the United Irish code-word to indicate the establishment of a military organisation. 'Up and up' signified the alliance between United Irishmen and Defenders.[2] Looking back after almost 200 years, the concept of being 'up' is a useful device for historians trying to interpret the 1790s, a decade when social and political pressures forced a plethora of combinations and associations to rise up from Irish society.

The yeomanry were raised as part of the war effort against revolutionary France. It was a time of very real fear for government. Not only was there a probability of a French invasion in 1796, but it was well known that the United Irishmen were in close contact with the Directory.[3] This dual threat is reflected in the Dungannon Association resolutions of June 1796 which declared their resistance to all enemies 'foreign and domestic'.[4] The scenario haunting anxious ministers and alarmed magistrates was of an invasion which could not be resisted by the regular army garrison in its depleted wartime state. Many regulars were scattered through the countryside on 'peace-keeping' duties. Invasion could be confronted only if these could be drawn in and concentrated into a solid force. This in turn would leave only the militia for local peace-keeping. Because these were mostly Catholic in rank and file, they were therefore suspected of having been infiltrated by the United Irishmen.

The Irish yeomanry created in 1796 was a territorially based, part-time, auxiliary organisation, established by parliamentary statute for the duration of the war.⁵ They were raised by land-owning gentry in the countryside and by professional bodies in the capital. Yeomanry corps averaged 100 men for infantry and around 40–50 for cavalry; they covered the whole country but were most concentrated in Ulster. The first levy in 1796 raised 20,000.⁶ By 1798 this had increased to 39,000.⁷ They were administered centrally by the Yeomanry Office, a branch of the Irish War Office in Dublin Castle; their make-up and character, however, were determined locally.

Yeomanry had two main roles, roughly corresponding with their civil and military functions. They could do garrison duty to free regular troops for anti-invasion activity, or they could be used to 'beef-up' the authority of local magistrates, who would otherwise have had to request detachments of valuable regulars. In normal times they were a latent though highly visible force. They carried out parade and exercise duty on one or two days per week, and could be called out by magistrates (who were often yeomanry officers) to assist with local problems and to help make arrests. But in disturbed times they were put on permanent duty. This meant that they voluntarily submitted themselves to the military discipline of the Mutiny Act, acted as a military corps under the control of the District General and received daily pay.⁸ This type of duty involved regular patrolling, guarding and carrying despatches, utilising their local knowledge so valued by the generals.

A typical yeomanry corps had the landlord or his agent as captain, smaller land-owners as commissioned officers and tenants or servants in the ranks. All commissions were issued from the crown via the Lord Lieutenant as royal representative. Officers were chosen by a delicate and extremely idiosyncratic system that could include recommendation by the local magnate, election by the rank and file and sanction by Dublin Castle. There was no actual provision for wives and families but if yeomen were required to move any distance from their area single men were chosen. Widows were entitled to a provision from the Concordatum Fund. In the wake of the rebellion there was no shortage of applications.⁹

The religious make-up was predominantly Protestant, though there were Catholic yeomen in the south and west. In areas, such as parts of County Derry, where many Presbyterians were radical, there is evidence that they did not countenance yeomanry membership until after the failure of Emmet's rising in 1803.[10] The word yeomanry had social and political connotations. This was reflected in the original plan which stated they were to be of 'the most respectable and loyal inhabitants residing within certain districts'.[11] Within the yeomanry itself, there was considerable social variation; cavalry corps were of a higher status than infantry as they could afford to maintain their own horses. However, the guiding principle was that all yeomen should have some stake in the country. It was reckoned that people defended better if they had something to lose.

The records of the Yeomanry Office were destroyed in 1922, but one set of evidence stands out as being especially useful as a starting-point; the private correspondence of the viceroy, Earl Camden, who had to try to anticipate the social and political consequences of the institution he was just about to create. Camden feared that he ran the risk of losing control by creating the volunteers anew, and that he would be seen to be damaging relations between Protestant and Catholic.

The yeomanry measure was proposed in early July 1796, but not formally agreed until September.[12] To landlords and magistrates, terrified by the growth of the United Irish organisation in Ulster, government appeared to prevaricate; in reality, Camden was agonising over the decision. His dilemma was not whether to have additional forces, but rather what form they should take. Ideally, he would have liked regulars, but reinforcements could not be spared in wartime. The Irish militia was generally suspected of having been infiltrated by the Defenders and United Irishmen. The ordinary parish officers were hopelessly inadequate and the more recent measure of baronial constables (debilitatingly nicknamed 'Barnies') covered only four counties, none in the North.

For locally raised defence, Camden had Irish and British precedents on which to draw. The most recent Irish one was the Volunteers; the English precedent was the Yeoman Cavalry and Volunteer Infantry Associations, raised in 1794. The idea of an Irish volunteer cavalry scared Camden, given the volatile political conditions of the late 1790s. He had received offers of armed loyal associations from Lords Mountjoy and Carhampton in 1795 but refused them, fearing 'a new system of volunteering'.[13] The British yeoman cavalry were organised by the county lords lieutenant and paid for by county subscription.[14] To have delegated this sort of power to the Irish county equivalents, the governors, would have been decidedly risky; those opposed to government could have followed the volunteering example and used their power for political ends; and in counties where there were multiple governors, there was the unsavoury prospect of military power and patronage being used for electioneering.[15] In short, there was a major dilemma as to how to control a nation-wide yeomanry force; if the government got it wrong the ensuing difficulties would call into question its ability to govern even the governable section of Irish society. Attempts to overcome this problem reveal the political implications of the yeomanry most clearly.

The Irish government in the event adapted the British yeomanry model to Irish conditions, permitting a mixture of cavalry and infantry collectively known in Ireland as 'yeomanry'; it was paid for by central government in Ireland, not by the county. Moreover, commissions to recruit yeomanry were in the gift of the Castle rather than the county governors, as in England. There were still, however, many difficulties: local influence was necessary for recruitment; if government allowed only their supporters to raise corps, the strategic purpose of the measure would be defeated. These problems were solved by using magnates with the most local influence in a county, leaving it a non-political decision as to who was entitled to recruit yeomanry. Even so, once enrolled for recruitment, Camden dictated the manner in which corps were raised and manipulated the status they were accorded for political ends. A comparison between two of the magnates he used, the Duke of Leinster and the Marquis of Downshire, brings this out clearly.

Leinster was an ex-Volunteer and a strong Whig opposition figure whose brother was Lord Edward Fitzgerald. Leinster was deliberately difficult in the negotiations over raising a yeomanry; he claimed that his gentlemen objected to taking pay and clothing from government.[16] Camden suffered him to raise the yeomanry in Kildare, but when he aspired to the honorific position of Captain Commandant to which his social position entitled him, it was Camden's turn to be difficult, delivering a snubbing, calculated refusal.[17]

Downshire controlled both seats for County Down, was governor of the county, and its wealthiest land-owner. He was a politi-

cal conservative who was moving closer to the Castle. Rather than
risk weakening his attachment, Camden allowed him unprecedented latitude when it came to raising a yeomanry. He was
allowed to proceed on a cavalry-only basis, like the English
county aristocracy, raising a subscription from church and laity.[18]
Expediency and local conditions were given as the explanation for
this exception, but the real logic behind this and the snubbing of
Leinster is unmistakable. Once government had gained the
advantage of having a nation-wide law-and-order organisation
with which to confront the United Irishmen, it could utilise the
opportunities its administration presented to strengthen or
weaken county political interests as required. Ironically, Downshire's prejudice against infantry badly delayed the establishment
of a mixed yeomanry in his county.

When yeomanry administration is examined at a local level, a
second political factor emerges: as well as hooking gentry and
politicians, the new system cast a net over important sections of
the northern Protestant people. It may be stretching a point to
claim that the government actually planned this, but in retrospect
it is clear that the yeomanry institution provided a structure which
could contain dangerously divided opinion.

The Castle's treatment of Charlemont on the yeomanry issue
in the Armagh area highlights these political points. The decision
to allow him to raise yeomanry in the North was a decision of
critical importance. He was ex-commander-in-chief of the northern Volunteers and a principled reformer who put defence of his
country before his dislike of its government's policies – while still
retaining the right to criticise.[19] Camden hesitated over
Charlemont at first, but was convinced by his pragmatic Chief
Secretary Pelham that this move was 'particularly calculated to
reconcile all those persons who were eager promoters of the Old
Volunteers'.[20] This was a decision which had far-reaching consequences. William Richardson of the Dungannon Association
reported that 'schisms and feuds' had broken out in Armagh over
the yeomanry issue. He noted there had always been two parties
there, 'the old royalists and the republican reformists now disposed to loyalty, amongst whom were Lord Charlemont's old volunteers'. Apparently Charlemont had tried to enrol both parties
together but the 'royalists' protested: 'shall we who always fought
the battle of loyalty be dispersed and taken place of by the very

men who three years ago erected the Tree of Liberty in Armagh Street, and since Lord Charlemont came to Armagh debated an hour whether they should take the Oath of Allegiance or not'.[21] The resolution of the 'schism' shows how the yeomanry administrative system could be manipulated. Richardson suggested a way out. Charlemont could use the printed regulations about maximum numbers per corps as a pretext for enrolling his old Volunteers in a separate corps.[22] The 1797 Yeomanry lists show that he did just that. Two cavalry troops are shown for Armagh city. The Neighbourhood of Armagh Cavalry were commanded by Johnston, his old volunteer lieutenant. The Armagh Cavalry were headed by the leader of the other party, the city sovereign Macan.[23] Government had prevented the old Dublin Volunteers from having a separate corps, but they bent the rules for Charlemont.

Yeomanry therefore provided a rallying-point for important groups among Irish Protestants, whereby they could be attached to government at a critical period when their predisposition for reform meant they could have gone either way. Moreover, the yeomanry system could be flexibly administered to accommodate political differences and to prevent the build-up of dangerous tensions.

Pádraig Ó Snodaigh, in his valuable studies of the muster rolls for yeomanry, militia and volunteers[24] of various counties, has argued that in the officer ranks strong family and kinship ties connected all three forces and indeed go back to the old militia of the mid-eighteenth century. This implies a sort of genetic inevitability in yeomanry membership. The evidence from Armagh shows this was not quite as predestined as subsequent history makes it appear. Not only were the United Irishmen quite realistic in hoping to attach the northern Volunteers, but the 1793 suppression of Volunteering could have rebounded against government insofar as it created a dangerous self-defence vacuum in frightening times.

The phenomenon of yeomanry created an ideological dilemma for many old Volunteers of the Whiggish tradition. The right of the citizen to arm in self-defence was central to the classical republican tradition. On the other hand, the Yeomanry Act came in tandem with one suspending Habeas Corpus. However, by using Charlemont and implementing the rules flexibly, government were able to attach quite disparate northern opinion on the basis of the lowest common denominator: having something to lose.

A further example of the way the yeomanry could be administered flexibly and advantageously to government came in mid–1797. In rural Armagh yeomen were being heavily outnumbered by United Irishmen, and some yeomanry corps were actually being infiltrated. Thomas Knox's brother, General John Knox, devised a test to be put to the corps to purge 'a nest of traitors'.[25] Those corps belonging to Charlemont were so enraged by this perceived slight on their loyalty that they went straight to Pelham, over Knox's head.[26] The fact that the yeomanry was both a civil and a military institution facilitated this, but it is of paramount importance that the yeomen themselves felt the system was friendly and could work 'on the nod' as it were. And it did work, as Pelham felt it politic to except Charlemont's corps from the test.[27] There are other examples of government's sensitivity to Charlemont. He once threatened to resign his yeomanry command in protest at the city of Armagh being proclaimed under the Insurrection Act. The proclamation was immediately rescinded.[28]

It would be overstating the point to assert that, with one deft move, government got control over that section of society which produced the Volunteers. The Volunteer cannon which was pointed at government forces, including yeomanry, in the Battle of Antrim explodes that theory. However, they did create the potential for control. The military historian P.C. Stoddart has argued that the irregular localised formation of the yeomanry was a structural and strategic defect.[29] This may be true militarily but the ad hoc structure was a real political strength. It was responsive to local problems and had the added benefit of altering the pattern of tensions from local versus central to gentry versus generals. In the longer term it controlled and contained sentiment long enough, and through tumultuous times, to produce a simplified loyalty. However, the other side of this coin was, as Camden feared, polarisation and alienation of the Catholics.

In any discussion of the Irish yeomanry there is the temptation to categorise the yeomanry and their effects on society in simple sectarian terms. In some areas Presbyterians were involved from the start and there were many Catholic yeomen in the south and west of the country. Even amongst Protestant yeomen there was much diversity of sentiment. The standard opinion is that the Irish yeomanry were virulently anti-Catholic and were recruited from strong Protestant families and Orangemen. Hereward Senior, historian of the Orange Order, supports this analysis, arguing that the Dungannon Association represented a de facto alliance between government and early Orangemen.[30] The sources contain many references which appear to confirm this: an early Orange song-book contains a song entitled 'The Orange Yeomanry' to be sung to the tune of 'Rule, Britannia'.[31] The impression is that the yeomanry started life as an exclusive sectarian organisation. However, the reality was more complex. Sectarianism and alienation came in distinct stages.

The Irish yeomanry system got off to a bad start as far as Catholics were concerned. Camden was concerned about this. He told Portland that he feared that arming the men of property would be construed as 'arming the Protestant against the papist'.[32] However, the prehistory of the yeomanry ensured that this construction was inevitable. Camden's predecessor, Fitzwilliam, had intended to introduce a bill granting full Catholic relief in 1795, and to establish a yeomanry which would include middle-class Catholics. Fitzwilliam intended to make the rule of law more effective by including such Catholics in the polity, recognising their property and their right to defend it.[33] He had felt that the only way to protect the status quo in an age of revolution was to broaden its social base. He hoped to attach such Catholics to government, and thus bring their under-tenants, employees and cottiers under control, arguing that a socially inclusive yeomanry would be dangerous only if Catholics were denied their rights.[34] Camden's brief was to resist further pressure for Catholic relief.[35] Therefore when he came to raise yeomanry it was inevitable that many would associate it with the Catholics' failure. It was a very public business. Grattan dubbed the new force an 'Ascendancy army' in parliament.[36] Outside parliament, others made political capital of Catholic disappointment. John Keogh disingenuously suggested that government were only arming Anglicans and ignoring Catholics and dissenters.[37] Richard McCormick travelled as far as Cork to prevent Catholics from enlisting.[38] The United Irishmen took a similar line.[39]

Yet in 1796 there was no official policy to exclude any religious group. Camden told Downshire, 'I confess I should think it would

be wise to admit those Catholics and dissenters upon whom you
can rely, into these corps.'[40] He had also suggested to Lord
Waterford not to refuse Catholics, saying he had encouraged
Lord Kenmare, a Catholic aristocrat, to form a corps.[41] However,
the ultimate decision regarding membership was left to local discretion. This militated against large-scale Catholic participation.
The words 'upon whom you can rely' in the letter to Downshire
are critical. This gave the local gentry a veto which left the door
open for yeomanry to reflect prevailing prejudices at a time when
the United Irish-Defender alliance was at its least quantifiable and
most frightening, and when parts of central Ulster still lay under
the shadow of Orange disturbances. A potentially constructive
and conciliatory new measure came increasingly to be built on old
foundations.

It can be argued that the United Irish-Defender alliance was
the beginning of a polarising process whereby republicanism
became Catholic and loyalism Protestant. This implies a negative,
reactive role to the yeomanry in the formation of this loyalism.
However, contemporaries considered the yeomanry to be a posi-
tive, dynamic force in this moulding. Castlereagh told Wellesley
in 1807: 'we may reckon fairly on an increase in the numbers of
zealous loyalists since the start of the Yeomanry, and from no
cause more decidedly than from the influence of that institution'.[42]

How did this happen? Was it that their foundation simply represented another arming of the Protestant 'garrison'? The truth
in Castlereagh's statement lies more in the evolution of the yeomanry than in its formation. The Orange factor was critical in
1796, but not, as Senior suggested, paramount. The *de facto* alliance between Castle and Orangemen did not start until May
1797, when General John Knox got permission to use Orangemen
militarily. Knox asked that 'protection may be given silently by
permission to enrol themselves in the District Corps, provided
they refrain from outrage'.[43] Cohesive groups of Orangemen, such
as those who enlisted under James Verner, now came into the
yeomanry as Orangemen *en masse*, rather than as the selected
individual Orangemen that some, but by no means all, supporters
of the Dungannon Association were enrolling, unknown to government, in 1796. These 1797 enrolments were small-scale ones,
but they set a precedent for the spring of 1798; then Castlereagh
himself instigated a major linkage with the Orangemen when he

permitted thousands of them to enrol as emergency supplementary yeomen.[44]

The rubicon was crossed. The rebellions of 1798 and 1803, and Union without emancipation, meant there was no going back. Grattan may have formed a yeomanry corps on his Wicklow estate in 1803 with so many Catholics that it was nicknamed 'the Virgin Mary Corps', but the tide had turned against this socially inclusive type of yeomanry.[45] More typical was the reaction reported by Wickham to Castlereagh, after Emmet's rising, that so strong was the general determination not to have Catholics in yeomanry corps, that government must either reject the services of loyal Catholics altogether, or enrol purely Catholic corps, which, he said, 'would not be cried, but roared out against throughout all Ireland'.[46] This meant, as surely as Fitzwilliam's recall, a reaffirmation of Catholic exclusion from the polity and, conversely, that Protestantism equalled loyalty, and membership of the yeomanry symbolised inclusion, in the political and social *status quo.*

The novelist Michael Banim had childhood memories of yeomanry parades in his home town of Kilkenny, describing them as objects of amusement to the poor children who taunted them, being either decrepit with age, or comically un-military. However, he made a telling point when he noted that they joined, not to use their guns, but to identify themselves with the *status quo.*[47] This was the inevitable consequence of the policy trends of 1796–8. By the early nineteenth century the 'first up' were carrying the day socially and politically, as they had previously done militarily.

Acknowledgments
I would like to thank the following individuals and institutions for permission to quote from the various collections used in this article: the Keeper of the Public Records, London, for the Home Office Papers, War Office Papers and Colchester Papers (all Crown Copyright); the Director of the National Archives, Dublin, for the Rebellion Papers and State of the Country Papers; the Marquess of Downshire and the Deputy Keeper of the Records, PRONI, for the Downshire Papers; the Keeper of Manuscripts, the National Library of Ireland, for the Lake Papers; the Dept of Archives, the National Army Museum, London, for the Nugent Papers; the County Archivist, Kent Archives Office, for the Camden Papers; the British Library and the Deputy Keeper of the Records, PRONI, for the Pelham Transcripts.

19

'AN UNION OF POWER'?
THE UNITED IRISH ORGANISATION: 1795–1798

Thomas Graham

The first article of the constitution of the Society of United Irishmen stated as its purpose, the 'forwarding a brotherhood of affection, a communion of rights, and an union of power among Irishmen of every religious persuasion'.[1] To what extent was a credible national organisation, 'an union of power', actually forged? How close did it come to achieving its objective which, after 1795, was separation from England?

During the legal phase of its existence, until May 1794, it was only in Ulster, predominantly in Antrim and Down, that the 'affiliated system', laid down in the Society's written constitution, actually took shape.[2] This allowed for 35-member parish-based cells, or simple societies, which were to send delegates to ascending baronial, county and provincial assemblies. Outside of Ulster no serious attempt was made to establish a genuinely national network, although there were fleeting references to societies in Limerick, Gorey, Tullamore, Clonmel and Nenagh.[3] Activity centred on the Dublin Society, which had a total membership of about four hundred; the active membership was about half of that, but the Society had extensive out-of-town connections.[4] Instead, organisation and mobilisation were carried on through surrogate bodies in which the United Irishmen played a significant role – the Volunteers, Masonic lodges, the Catholic Convention of 1792, and the Ulster Convention of 1793.[5] One by one these organisational surrogates were blocked off by government counter-measures, and the Society itself was finally suppressed in May 1794.

However, the main strength of the legal Society was not in its organisation, but in the power of its propaganda and the consequent politicisation of the population at large. The success of the

various United Irish propaganda campaigns of the early 1790s –
for Catholic emancipation and parliamentary reform, against the
Militia Act and government coercion – in transforming the
Defenders into a much more politicised and widespread revolutionary force cannot be overestimated.[6] By 1795 Defender organisation and activity had spread beyond south Ulster into Connacht,
north Leinster and Dublin itself, where it blended with the capital's already-established artisan Jacobin clubs, such as the Telegraphic and the Philanthropic, many of which had a significant
Protestant membership. By the summer of 1795 the greatest
threat to government appeared to come, not from the United
Irishmen, but from the Defenders. It was a threat more apparent
than real; by 1796 Carhampton's repressive campaign in Connacht and the much-publicised Defender trials and executions in
Dublin put paid to it. Only the United Irishmen stood by the
Defenders, being especially active in organising their legal defence.

From 1796 increasing numbers of Defenders joined the expanding network of United Irish cells. Elliott has claimed that it
was this phenomenon alone that 'gave the impression of an
expanding United movement after 1795'.[7] This appears to have
been the case in mid- and south Ulster but not in the rest of the
country. In Dublin, for example, there is hardly any mention of
Defenders after 1796; the fact that Kildare and Meath, where
Defenders were also conspicuous in mid-decade, subsequently
proved themselves comparatively well organised and disciplined
under the United system, belies the impression of undigested
Defender elements within the new organisation. Furthermore, in
Wicklow, Wexford and Carlow, where the United Irish organisation expanded with greatest success in 1797 and the early months
of 1798, there had never been Defender organisation (as opposed
to reports of 'Defenderism', a catch-all label indiscriminately
applied to outbreaks of unrest by over-anxious Castle correspon-
dents).

The recall of Fitzwilliam in the spring of 1795 dashed any lingering hopes of constitutional reform. The consequent escalation
and spread of uncoordinated Defender activity convinced United
Irish leaders of the necessity for a credible alternative strategy.
Externally this would involve the solicitation of French military
aid; in April it was agreed that Tone would be the agent.[8] Inter-

nally it would involve building a single, uniform, mass-based revolutionary movement or 'Union' throughout the country. The basis for this type of structure had continued in existence throughout the vicissitudes of the previous years in Ulster, and particularly in the immediate Belfast area. The rapid transformation of these societies into just such an organisation was feasible because in Ulster, unlike Dublin, the organisation had adhered to the cell-structure of the original written constitution. They had kept a lower public profile and had a more determined and radical cadre of leaders, especially Samuel Neilson, Thomas Russell and Henry Joy McCracken.[9]

On 10 May 1795 the 'Union' was formalised in a new constitution by delegates representing United societies in Antrim and Down; its structure differed little from the 1791 prototype.[10] It is surely no coincidence that the Catholic Committee dissolved itself in the same month.[11] Equally significant, Tone was sworn a member in June 1795, a month before departure on his foreign mission; despite this, claims that he had no official sanction and lacked organisational backing still persist.[12]

Over the following two years, the strengths and weaknesses of the new strategy were demonstrated. Elliott has comprehensively outlined the spectacular success of Tone's foreign mission.[13] Had Hoche's force landed at Bantry Bay in December 1796 it would in all likelihood have liberated the country, not least because the spread of the United Irish organisation resulted in the extreme dispersal of government forces. According to a detailed return of men and arms made at the end of April 1797, United membership had expanded to 128,000, spread across the nine counties of Ulster and five counties in Leinster – Louth, Meath, Westmeath, Kildare and Dublin.[14] The spread of membership was extremely uneven, however. The Leinster counties accounted for 16,000 men or only 12.5 per cent of the total membership, and United leaders had only just managed to set up a provincial committee. Organisation in Ulster was concentrated in Antrim and Down, which between them accounted for 49,000 men or 44 per cent of the province's 112,000 total. A military organisation had been adopted, with clusters of three societies forming companies of 100 to 120 men led by captains. Each captain commanded ten sergeants who commanded platoons of ten or eleven men. The captains within each barony elected at least one colonel, and these commanded regiments of roughly a thousand men. Each county was under the command of an adjutant-general appointed by the central leadership from a short-list submitted by the county's colonels.

By 1797 the organisation was on the defensive. Arrests in the autumn of 1796 had decapitated the Ulster movement by removing the most able and determined leaders (Neilson, Russell, etc.); this allowed unreliable elements to pass up through the ranks, one of whom, Nicholas Maguan of Saintfield, became a member of the provincial committee and thereafter supplied the Castle with details of its transactions.[15] The April 1797 report to the Castle also reveals the effect of General Lake's disarming campaign. Most Ulster counties were unable to file any returns of arms; Antrim, one of the few that did, could muster fewer than 9,000 weapons of various sorts for its 23,000 men.

In mid- and south Ulster, an area racked by sectarian conflict, the United Irishmen organised separate Catholic (usually Defender) and Presbyterian units, but they were under a unified command structure.[16] Although an understandable and practical expedient, it left the organisation vulnerable to the incitement of sectarianism, particularly through the agency of the Orange Order. A more subtle technique was described by the Tyrone magistrate Andrew Newton. He induced the Catholics of Arboe parish to adopt resolutions swearing allegiance and claiming that they had been led into error by the Presbyterians. The Presbyterians in turn were immediately informed and the desired effect was achieved:

The resolutions enclosed [those adopted by the Catholics] are beginning to show the best effects – the two parties are now afraid of each other and both are flocking in with their arms.[17]

Thereafter the Ulster movement receded to its original heartland in Antrim and Down.

Moreover, the failure of the French to follow up their Bantry effort exposed the limitations of United Irish military strategy. In June 1797, when the hard-pressed Ulster leaders called on their Dublin counterparts for action, there was simply no credible alternative strategy nor the military capacity (outside of Ulster) to put any into effect. The Leinster movement was numerically weak, and also lacked both arms and military organisation.[18] The crisis brought on by the government's offensive in the spring and summer of 1797 also exposed the weakness of the organisation's leadership structure. According to the constitution five members from each organised province were to form a national committee which was to exercise authority over the whole body. In fact no such committee was ever established; authority was instead split between two separate five-man 'executives', elected by their respective provincial committees, one in Belfast and one in Dublin. A national committee of sorts, comprising the two executives and twelve additional co-options, twenty-two in all, met in Dublin in June 1797 to consider the Ulster movement's demands for an immediate rising. This meeting broke up in disarray. Many of the Ulster delegates, fearing arrest, subsequently fled abroad, including Samuel Turner who later turned informer.[19] The Ulster movement never fully recovered from this second decapitation and from Lake's venomous assault upon the organisation on the ground.

Given this organisational collapse in 1797, the arrest of the Leinster leadership in the following March, and the chaos and apparent lack of co-ordination of the rebellion itself, it is easy to understand why Elliott has stated so categorically that

the United Irish movement was declining in 1798. The rebellion was not a United Irish one as it would have been a year earlier, but a protective popular uprising which a spent United Irish leadership failed to harness.[20]

In fact the Leinster organisation staged a remarkable comeback in late 1797 and early 1798. Not only was organisation consolidated and membership increased in existing strongholds such as Dublin, Meath and Kildare, but it was successfully extended into Wicklow, Carlow and Wexford, and to a lesser extent into the midland counties of Westmeath, King's and Queen's. Moreover it was a reorganisation and expansion according to a new constitution drawn up in August 1797, something which has drawn surprisingly little comment from historians. The maximum size of the primary cells was reduced from thirty-five to twelve to make them more adaptable to military organisation; only one delegate rather than the previous two or three would ascend to the higher committees; and security and financial control were generally tightened up.[21]

Elliott's assertion that 'the rebellion was not a United Irish one...but a protective popular uprising' refers, presumably, to

Wexford where it has long been assumed there was little or no United Irish organisation.[22] There were good grounds for this assumption, and the very few references to County Wexford in the Rebellion Papers for late 1797 and early 1798 give the impression of quietude. In fact this was largely the result of an attempt by Mountnorris, a local grandee, to carve out a political space for himself in Wexford between the United Irishmen on one hand and the Orange ultras on the other, by persuading the populace to swear oaths of allegiance. Since there was no middle ground in Wexford this proved futile, but it did have the effect of temporarily suspending United Irish activity. No return of arms or men for Wexford was ever forwarded to the leadership in Dublin nor did a Wexford delegate ever sit on the Leinster provincial committee. This was due to the United Irishmen's formalistic approach to organisation. Under the 1795 constitution at least three baronies within a county had to be organised to qualify for representation on the provincial committee. The Wexford organisation passed that threshold in the autumn of 1797 only to find that the new constitution now demanded that four baronies had to be organised. Mountnorris's campaign intervened and it was not until the following March, at the fateful meeting in Oliver Bond's house in Dublin, that Wexford qualified for representation. Its delegate, Robert Graham, arrived late, avoiding arrest. Wexford's returns were accordingly never submitted; the Castle (and historians ever since) remained oblivious to the extent of the county's United Irish organisation.[23]

The higher levels of the Leinster organisation were never penetrated by Castle spies and informers to the same extent as in Ulster. Established entirely in conditions of illegality, it was thus more security-conscious. In particular, its five-man executive was never penetrated by Castle spies, contrary to the claim advanced by Pakenham on behalf of Francis Magan, the man who betrayed Lord Edward Fitzgerald.[24] Magan, in fact, got no higher than the Dublin City committee. At least thirteen different people sat on the five Leinster executives, elected every quarter, which held office between early 1797 and the rebellion in May 1798. Yet none of their names crops up in the organisation's lower committees in either Dublin or Leinster. In particular none of the Leinster provincial committee arrested at Bond's was a member of the executive. They elected a rotating five-man executive, not from their own number, but from a pool of recognised leaders who otherwise held no official position. Therefore Magan, who was active in the lower city committees, could not possibly have been a member.[25] With great frustration the spy-master Francis Higgins reported to the Castle in January 1798 that 'not one of the heads or leaders will allow themselves to be returned to either baronial or provincial associations. They now select the most active, dangerous and desperate incendiaries to fill these situations...and when affairs shall be ripe...then the leaders and ringleaders are to come forward and drive these lower order of banditti from their political situations'.[26]

The inability of the United Irishmen to establish a truly national committee or executive with authority for the whole organisation was not such a handicap in 1798. From a security point of view the lack of co-ordination between the two provinces probably saved the Leinster organisation from contamination at the top by its spy-ridden Ulster counterpart. From a military perspective Ulster became strategically less important as it became clear that an insurrection without the French must be attempted immediately or not at all. Such a strategy demanded that the initial and decisive blow be struck in and around Dublin, the country's capital and its centre of communications. What really mattered for the prospect of success was the state of the Leinster organisation and that of Dublin in particular.

Thus the arrests on 12 March 1798 at Oliver Bond's were a cruel blow to the organisation. Almost the entire Leinster provincial committee was arrested, along with two members of the executive, William James MacNeven and Thomas Addis Emmet, in separate swoops. A third, Richard McCormick, fled. It is important to note that the arrests were not the result of Castle penetration from without but of betrayal from within, and the culprit, Thomas Reynolds, was not a reluctant and gullible recruit, the impression given in the apologetic biography by his son, but a long-standing and bona fide member.[27]

It was a measure of the resilience of the organisation that the March arrests did not stop it in its tracks entirely. The arrested delegates were simply replaced.[28] From the point of view of decisive leadership, the arrest of MacNeven and Emmet and the flight of McCormick may have been a blessing in disguise: they had all been reluctant to sanction a purely domestic rising. They were replaced by Neilson and the Sheares brothers who, along with the executive members who had escaped arrest, Lord Edward Fitzgerald and William Lawless, were at one in supporting the strategy of a purely domestic rising, though they were to differ later on tactical questions.

Emmet, O'Connor and MacNeven claimed that before the March arrests the 'military committee' with responsibility for drawing up a general plan of insurrection did nothing. They did admit, somewhat disingenuously, that 'some of its members' on their own initiative may have drawn up such plans.[29] One of them happened to be the insurgent commander-in-chief, Lord Edward Fitzgerald. A paper seized at Bond's, in his hand, outlined tactics for urban warfare.[30] Pakenham has asserted that the leaders 'adopted a bewildering variety of ideas' and that the plan that was eventually decided upon was 'hurried' and 'a last desperate throw'.[31] In fact the broad strategic outline, hints of which began to trickle into the Castle's intelligence network from as early as March 1798, remained more or less consistent. The Dublin United army was to seize various important buildings within the city – notably the Castle, the Customs House, Trinity College, and the banks. At the same time the armies of the counties immediately adjacent were to establish a cordon of positions outside Dublin, deal with local government forces, and then advance into the city. As soon as they got word of these developments the United Irishmen in the rest of the country were to rise and tie down government forces in their own areas.[32]

The seizure of positions within the metropolis by Dublin's United men was the keystone of the plan, but in early 1798 its city organisation lagged behind the surrounding counties. Pakenham has suggested that its strength had 'been falling before even the arrests at Bond's'.[33] In fact its numbers had been steadily *increasing* up to and beyond the March arrests to 10,000 for the city and 9000 for the county on the eve of the rebellion.[34] This would make sense of the decision to delay the insurrection for a further two-and-a-half months, contrary to Pakenham's impression of indecision and procrastination.[35] By the middle of May government counter-measures were beginning to bite, particularly in Kildare and Wicklow; yet Samuel Sproule, usually a reliable spy, reported that although the 'violent' lamented the delay because of the weakening of the organisation overall, it was still gaining in and around Dublin.[36] Further, it was only in April and May that the military chain of command was completed with the election of colonels.

The Leinster executive was fully involved in these preparations and was not isolated from the lower organisation.[37] While the Sheares brothers and Lawless toured the provinces, Neilson and Lord Edward Fitzgerald supervised the military preparations in and around Dublin. Neilson in particular has been underestimated by historians. Pakenham, for example, dismisses him as 'a harmless alcoholic'.[38] In fact he was one of the most effective of all the leaders. For five years until his arrest in the autumn of 1796, he had edited and published the most successful commercial and propaganda newspaper of the day, the *Northern Star*. It was he who first recognised the necessity for a properly structured and disciplined organisation. He was involved in the crucial link-up with the Defenders and helped keep the northern United Irish organisation going during the mid-decade hiatus. Although his health was impaired by his imprisonment in the autumn of 1796, he immediately threw himself into the task of organising when he was released from custody in early 1798. Thomas Boyle, the spy, reported that he was 'constantly riding to different parts of the county Dublin, west, north and south, Fingal, Drumcondra, Ballybough, Raheny, Clontarf, etc., delivering instructions' and that 'the lower orders much admire him'. According to the information of a rebel captain, Dennis Ryan, Neilson had ridden 387 miles through Ulster and Munster since his release and helped formulate the military plan.[39]

If the United Irishmen's organisation and preparation for a rising were more credible than has usually been conceded, how can the apparent lack of co-ordination of the rising and indeed the military chaos be explained? The arrests of the leaders on the very eve of the rising proved its undoing. In early May the Sheares brothers split or were removed from the Leinster executive. Disagreement had arisen on the question of tactics. Neilson and Lord Edward wanted to stick to the original plan, but the Sheares preferred disaffected militia stationed at Loughlinstown to effect the internal seizure of the city rather than trust the rank-and-file Dublin organisation. Their subsequent maverick activity has added greatly to the impression of complete chaos and disintegration yet, according to Samuel Sproule, after their secession they knew nothing of the real counsels of the organisation. This was confirmed by McNally. Their liaison with Captain Armstrong of the King's County Militia, who reported all to the Castle, had no bearing on the official preparations for the rising and their arrest on 21 May was, according to Sproule, 'all a sham'.[40] The real disaster had struck two days before when the arrest of Lord Edward Fitzgerald left Neilson as the only leader of national stature prepared to act.

The day of the rising, Wednesday, 23 May 1798, dawned with the Castle still unclear as to its timing, its rendezvous points or even its form. It was expecting a rising the following day according to the Sheares's plan. At nine o'clock that evening Neilson assembled fifteen Dublin colonels in Church Lane, produced a map and assigned each a post to occupy.[41] However, an hour earlier Thomas Boyle had already informed the Castle that the rising was due to commence at ten o'clock; by nine, yeomanry corps were already occupying rendezvous points such as Smithfield and setting up checkpoints on the bridges and on the approach roads.[42] Neilson, meanwhile, left the meeting of colonels and headed towards Newgate in order to reconnoitre it for an attack to liberate its prisoners, where he was arrested. Not only had the rising been pre-empted but it was now leaderless as well. Nevertheless it was a close call. According to Musgrave,

The rebel drums were to have beaten to arms an hour after ours...if they had preceded us by ever so small a space of time, the fate of the city and its loyal inhabitants would have been decided; for the mass of the people, armed with pikes and other weapons, were lurking in lanes, alleys and bye-places, ready to start forth on the first beat of their drums, and would have occupied all the streets and assassinated the yeomen before they could have reached their respective stations.[43]

According to the Rev. William Bennet, former private secretary to Westmorland and later Bishop of Cloyne: 'after sunrise the lanes and alleys to Smithfield and other posts were found full of pikes and muskets which they [the rebels] had dropped and thrown away in their precipitate retreat'.[44] He gave a slightly more sober assessment than Musgrave of the potential threat the rebels represented:

Neilson was one of the most determined and intelligent of all the rebel leaders, and it was entirely owing to his and Lord Edward Fitzgerald being apprehended that the night of the 23rd passed over so quietly. The columns of the rebels which surrounded the town waited one for the other to begin, and had any daring officer

been found to lead his men under fire, the others from Ringsend, Eccles St, Clontarf and Harold's Cross in all which places were large bodies of them, would have
probably followed the example, which might have been of the worst consequences
as the garrison was so weak, and the troops from Loughlinstown Camp did not
arrive till two in the morning.[45]

Considered within the framework of an organised rising, albeit
one that had gone wrong, events in the surrounding county and
beyond begin to make more sense. Contrary to Pakenham's claim
that the rebels constituted a 'great mob of peasants' without a
coherent military strategy, the United forces did attempt to effect
the agreed plan.[46] Rebel armies began to mobilise on the night of
23 May in the surrounding counties – Wicklow, Kildare, Meath
and north County Dublin – and by the morning of 24 May held a
crescent of positions within a twenty- to twenty-five-mile radius
of the capital, effectively sealing it off from the rest of the country. Mail coaches had been stopped, which was the signal to rouse
the counties beyond – in Munster, south Leinster and Ulster.
This would explain the delay before rebellion broke out in the
'outer counties' – King's County, Queen's County and Carlow on
25 May, and Wexford on 26 May. Within the framework of the
intended rising, the orders given to the various rebel commanders
were as adequate as they had to be and were not without a certain
strategic ingenuity. However, the failure of the initial rising in
Dublin city, its keystone, brought the whole edifice crashing
down, and gave the rising that appearance of chaos, spontaneity
and improvisation which has so confounded historians of it ever
since.

The organisational achievements of the United Irishmen were
considerable. During the first phase of their existence, in the early
1790s, they politicised broad sections of the population to an
extent and to a level never before witnessed. From 1795 onwards
they welded this consciousness into a formidable political and
military organisation, 'an union of power', which at one time or
another had a presence through Ulster, Leinster, east Munster
and parts of Connacht. From late in 1796 it was faced with the
combined pressures of severe government repression, repeated
disappointment of hopes of French assistance, arrest or defection
of its ablest leaders, and internal dissension. Yet it continued to
pose a real threat to the English connection until its defeat in the
insurrection of 1798. Those who with the benefit of hindsight are

tempted to regard this defeat as 'inevitable' should bear in mind Castlereagh's admonition to Chief Secretary Pelham in June 1798:

I understand…you are rather inclined to hold the insurrection cheap. Rely upon it there never was in any country so formidable an effort on the part of the people.⁴⁷

20

IRISH NEWS IN THE FRENCH PRESS: 1789–98

Gilles Le Biez

How much was known in France during the 1790s about events in Ireland, and what role did the Irish situation play in French political life during the Revolution? Until now, the sources used to answer these questions have been official documents or memoirs of the main Irish and French personalities of the period. The press however provides a different perspective which reflects not alone the official government viewpoint but the full range of public opinion, permitting an analysis of the development of attitudes over time, and revealing a real enthusiasm in France for the United Irishmen when the 1798 insurrection took place. This study is not exhaustive; it is based on the 'official' French press of the time, various newspapers published by the Cercle Social and Girondin presses, the Jacobin press, newspapers hostile to England in 1797–8, the popular press, and the most important newspapers published during the Directory.[1]

News items were most frequently sourced from the English press, from other French newspapers favourable to the government, or from official despatches. The most important source until the end of 1792 was the *Courrier de l'Europe* and the *Gazette franco-angloise* of Cox. Others cited are the *Morning Herald*, the *Morning Post*, the *Morning Chronicle*, the *Dublin Journal*, the *Sun*, the *Courrier* and *The Times*. Some books were also made use of, notably Edward Ledwich's *Antiquities of Ireland*, William Crawford's *History of Ireland*, and Arthur Young's *Travels in Ireland*.[2] Newspapers tended to copy English articles word for word, and when they included commentary, usually put it between brackets in the main body of the article. Reports usually appeared some two weeks after the events to which they refer – and up to a month in some cases during 1798 – and they always showed a dogged trust in the accuracy of the printed word that provided their source. Thus one newspaper in 1798, while defending the insurrection, published an article in June which detailed massacres allegedly carried out by the United Irishmen, noting that 'old people, women and children were not spared'. But it took a perverse pride in doing this, going on to note that:

From the moment when the English committee found a way to stop eight or ten direct and valuable pieces of correspondence reaching us, we have at least shown that we love truth even more than these United Irishmen whose cause was so dear to us.[3]

The *Moniteur* was, however, wary of the accuracy of foreign news, and in particular of the German newspapers – 'always in a hurry to publish, and to exaggerate anything disadvantageous to the French, and to anyone fighting for liberty'.[4]

News from Ireland was frequently published in Lebrun's *Journal Général de l'Europe* in 1791–2, in the *Bulletin des Amis de la Vérité* published by the Cercle Social in early 1793, and in *Le Bien Informé*, which in 1798 was published by the Cercle Social.[5] Direct statements or declarations from the United Irishmen, the Catholic Committee or the Defenders were only rarely published in the French press, and then mainly in the period 1791–2. These included speeches made at the celebrations marking the fall of the Bastille in 1791 and 1792, the United Irish circular letter of 31 December 1791, the 1792 circular from the Catholic Committee, and the United Irish pamphlet of early 1793 which compared the Secret Committee of the House of Lords to the Inquisition. Declarations or pamphlets of this type were not published again until the spring of 1798. Articles on the economic and political situation in Ireland were also rare. The first such account, published early in 1792, painted a picture of an Ireland which could be 'leading the second line powers of Europe if the situation were different'. But instead Ireland is just 'a humble dinghy moored beside a high-sided vessel'. The same article went on to define the four parties in Ireland:

the court, which wields influence; Catholics, who have numbers and misfortunes on their side, and are opposed to the French Revolution; the whigs, made up of the large landowners who are looking for places; and the true patriots, the Presbyterians, who keep and nourish the sacred flame of freedom.[6]

Two lengthy articles, published in 1797, present a poetic version of the early history of Ireland, its independence and its

national characteristics. They give a somewhat exaggerated description of Irish history and geography, and 'the robustness of its
inhabitants [whose] extremely simple manners are close to the
barbaric...the poor unfortunates need religion to save them from
despair'.[7]

This survey of ten years' output by the Parisian press, from
1789 to 1799, can be divided into three phases: the first up to the
spring of 1793, corresponding to the expansionist phase of the
Revolution; the second from the summer of 1793 to the autumn
of 1797, when reform came to an end in Ireland and repression
was used against the United Irishmen and Defenders; the final
phase covering the insurrection and Humbert's expedition.

Phase I: 1789 – spring 1793

The Irish issue first taken up by the Parisian press was the religious question. On 28 November 1791 the *Moniteur* published a
private letter, calling for Irish Catholics to be allowed 'enjoyment
of the same rights that Parliament has granted to the Roman
Catholics of Great Britain'. On 17 January 1792 it published
details of a petition from the Catholic Society of Dublin. The
Catholic question was subsequently taken up in articles published
in the *Courrier de l'Europe* and in *Le Patriote Français* which cited
Burke: 'Irish Catholics will obtain what they are seeking; they
must get it, for who would have the right to oppose the will of
three million people?'[8]

The Girondin press quickly grasped the link between the
Catholic question and parliamentary representation. Clavière
summarised perfectly the issues at stake in an article pointing out
that union, liberty and peace were the aims of Irish Catholics, and
parliamentary reform and civic equality their means of attaining
them:

The disagreements currently agitating Ireland are not about separation. They are
about giving Catholics back their political status. If the court of London opposes
it, this can only be because of the strength that this decision will give to the leaders
of Ireland once reform has taken place.[9]

Nevertheless, opinion in Paris was doubtful about the commitment and real aims of Irish Catholics. Like the Ministry of Foreign Affairs, the press was wary of the religious fanaticism 'of
Popish priests who fly into a rage at the very word reform',[10] and
of certain Protestants who talked 'with the same fanaticism that

Catholics used against them in the fifteenth century [*sic*]'.[11] Similar criticism was levelled against the 'fanaticism' of the Irish parliament.[12] On the other hand, in response to a newspaper article which claimed that 'Catholics have always been the most vile abusers of absolute power', and that the prospect of civic equality was alarming for Protestants,[13] the *Moniteur* published a letter which painted an idealistic picture of the relationships being forged between the various religious groups.[14] Regular articles on the way in which the Volunteers, led by Hamilton Rowan and James Napper Tandy, were active in support of Catholics in 1791–2, as well as events such as the establishment of the first societies of United Irishmen, the campaign of the Catholic Committee, and the holding of the Dungannon Convention, all provided grounds for hope in Paris that religious hostility in Ireland was on the wane.[15]

Political developments in Ireland, and especially the ceremonies to commemorate the fall of the Bastille, were used as evidence that the French Revolution was not an isolated event, but one of wider significance that was supported and understood by other countries in Europe: 'The French Revolution is not regarded with horror in all parts of England,' one paper noted, going on to say that declarations of support for France were published because they were 'worthy of a people which knows the price of the duties and the rights of man'.[16] After the declaration of war in April 1792, Irish reactions were widely publicised and they helped Parisians to come to terms with their early defeats: the French flag, it was claimed, was cheered in Waterford,[17] gifts and money were being sent to the National Assembly,[18] Irishmen were joining the French armies,[19] and an Irish corsair was being equipped to sail to France.[20] In October 1792 the newspapers reported on celebrations held in Dublin, Ballyclare and Belfast to mark French military victories.[21] They also publicised the banquet in White's Hotel in Paris, where the toasts voiced hopes for a future 'agreement between France, England and Ireland', and for the union of France and England, which 'will be the glory of Europe and establish universal peace in its midst'.[22] It also published details of the address sent to the National Convention and the reply of the Abbé Grégoire.

The first three months of 1793 were also a time of hope, when the Parisian press reflected the belief that revolution was brewing in Ireland as England prepared to enter the war against France. Thus significance was given to the Dungannon Convention with its brief to look at the state of political representation in the country, and to discuss whether Ireland should join the war against France.[23] 'Everything here points to revolution,' noted one paper, because the principle of popular sovereignty 'founded on the law of nature' was generally accepted.[24] Another paper noted: 'if the revolution has not yet taken place, we are nevertheless witnessing its beginnings'.[25] This hope was encouraged by the rural agitation stirred up by the Defenders – 'banditti (for that is what our tyrants call good citizens who want reform of abuses and equal representation for the people) who are searching for arms'.[26] The Defenders were usually called 'patriots' or 'sans-culottes' in articles, although the *Bulletin des Amis de la Vérité* initially portrayed them as Catholics 'led astray by fanaticism', adopting the term 'patriots' only at a later stage.[27]

Hopes for Ireland were, however, dashed in May – for two reasons. The first was the beginning of political repression: two of Dumouriez's officers were arrested in County Clare, the army was taking control of the streets in Belfast, the Dublin Volunteers had surrendered their arms while those in Belfast hid them, and some of the leaders of the United Irishmen were imprisoned and put on trial. The second was growing evidence that Catholics were putting their trust in George III and his government to change their legal position. Nevertheless, at a time when France found itself at war with almost the whole of Europe, *Le Patriote Français* wrote that 'if there is a nation whose inhabitants should be treated as brothers, it is the Irish'.[28]

During these years Irish affairs were reported and publicised in France by the Girondin and Cercle Social newspapers which were edited by Brissot, Clavière, Roland, Lebrun, Mercier, Nicolas de Bonneville and Louvet. There were several reasons for this. In the first place, many of them had lived in London during the 1780s. Secondly, as members of the Cercle Social, many of them held liberal political views very similar to those of the United Irishmen, and they hoped to 'found the universal republic in which men of letters would be the legislators'.[29] They also knew many of the English and Irish living in Paris, including Paine, Oswald, Lord Edward Fitzgerald, Caesar Colclough, Duckett, William Jackson, Thomas Muir and the Sheares brothers. Finally, devel-

opments in Ireland justified their view of the necessity of a pre-
ventative war against *ancien régime* Europe, in order to defend and
spread the revolution.

Phase II: 1793–7

From the spring of 1793 until the autumn of 1796 several Parisian
newspapers continued to provide a basic coverage of Irish events.
Early in 1794, newspapers stated that 'the revolutionary tempera-
ture is rising' and that the 'reunited Irish' had been accepted into
the ranks of the English Convention.[30] The arrest of William
Jackson was published in the *Journal de la Montagne* on 4 *prairial* II
(23 May 1794), as was the banning of the United Irishmen and the
confiscation of their papers.[31] On 8 *prairial* the same newspaper
announced Hamilton Rowan's departure from Morlaix to meet
Jeanbon Saint-André at Brest, while five days later other papers
announced the arrest of Rowan – or his escape – in Dublin.

The nomination of Earl Fitzwilliam to review 'the intolerant
laws enacted against Catholics' was duly reported at the end of
1794, as was his recall. So too were the petitions and mobilisation
of opinion carried out in his support throughout Ireland, supposedly by Catholics and Protestants alike, as well as what were
termed 'partial' insurrections in many counties. The growing mili-
tarisation of the country was emphasised each time news of the
arrival of more English troops there was reported, and when the
yeomanry was established – 'a type of National Guard selected by
property owners'[32] – the *Sentinelle* predicted that 'Ireland could
become the Vendée of Great Britain'.[33] Many reports dealt with
Defender trials, and they introduced Parisian readers to the
Defenders' use of oaths and catechisms, and to the government's
use of spies whose uncorroborated testimony was sufficient to condemn suspects to death, as well as commenting generally on the
cruelty of British justice.[34] The sectarian aspect of the conflict in
Ulster was noted once or twice. The *Annales Patriotiques* believed
that Catholics had acted provocatively against Protestants in
County Armagh,[35] while another source placed the responsibility
for the troubles there on 'government supporters'.[36] In general, the
sectarian aspect was almost totally ignored until the events of 1798.

Hoche's expedition in December 1796 was preceded by a
French press campaign which began on 19 *brumaire* (10 November) with the communiqué from the Minister of the Navy,

Truguet, announcing that an insurrection had driven 10,000 English soldiers out of Ireland.[37] Only one journal threw doubt on this news, noting that 'we have been soothed with sweet stories for so long', but the story was never officially withdrawn.[38] Right until the time of the fleet's departure, the press listed parishes proclaimed under martial law, or subjected to military rule and arrests. In a long article, Mercier encouraged Hoche on his mission to Ireland:

towards an island whose oppressed people have been calling for French liberty for six years. Towards an island where a proconsul, feudal lords and the Anglican clergy are for ever fleecing the skin of a people who are unfortunate enough to add a belief in hell to their bitter resentment against the suffering imposed on them.[39]

The real aim of the expedition was revealed only on 6 *nivôse* (26 December). French papers initially published accounts of a successful landing. Once Hoche had returned, however, Bouvet was accused of cowardice for having turned down Grouchy's suggestion of a landing with 6000 men; details of what had taken place were taken from the English press.[40] Parisian editors were to find some consolation in the argument that 'the expedition which has just taken place, in the middle of winter...should prove to both nations how easy such expeditions would be, when planned on a larger scale and utilising all the resources of the republic'.[41] This kind of argument was used again after the defeat of the Dutch navy at Texel in September 1797, and indeed after the failure of the 1798 expeditions as well.

As in the spring of 1793, Irish news then disappeared from the press for several weeks, reappearing only when Pelham's report on the activities of the United Irishmen and Wolfe Tone was published, or when a major discovery of arms and uniforms was made 'on whose buttons a harp was engraved, with this inscription: National Guard of Belfast; on a chest which contained guns, an upside-down crown was painted, with a tree of liberty on either side'.[42] There was also an article announcing that Lord Edward Fitzgerald was not standing in the 1797 elections, as 'there can be no such thing as free elections in Ireland. Nominations can only be made with the permission of the incoming military commander.'[43]

From November 1797 to January 1798 a press campaign developed around the planned invasion of England, using all possible forms of propaganda, ranging from books and articles to songs and plays.[44] War against Britain was not aimed at either Scotland or Ireland:

> Let the French flag
> Flutter above the debris of Carthage,
> And let age after age read on it the words,
> 'Here perished the last of the English'.
> Spare their victims, the Scots and the Irish,
> For they will support your aims.[45]

Articles called for 'the destruction of the English government, [and] the independence of England, Scotland and Ireland' to be proclaimed official policy.[46] The idea even spread to the French provinces; in Toulouse there were celebrations for 'these generous Irish defenders, who share all our principles, who have fallen by the thousand, martyrs for their love of sacred equality'.[47] The British residents in Paris played their part too, with Paine contributing to the collection made for the *armée d'Angleterre*, and Muir warning that the 'heart of patriots will bring them to co-operate with the French; but even if the invasion fails, it will divert their eyes away from America and focus them on France'.[48] During 1798 a jeweller in Paris marketed jewellery carrying the emblems of the Irish Union.[49]

Phase III: 1798

From the winter of 1797–8 *Le Bien Informé* played a central role in disseminating Irish news in France, and its files are the main source used in what follows on press coverage of the insurrection and of the subsequent French expedition. In its early numbers it picked out its adversaries quite clearly: 'so-called loyalists, who call themselves Orangemen, [and who] have hunted down several thousand Catholic families. The terror that these loyalist brigands have caused has ensured that no one will dare testify against them.'[50] It also picked out its allies – men such as Napper Tandy, whom it welcomed to Paris as

one of these rare men who, unlike most of his fellow countrymen, has not spoken in the kind of ambiguous terms that can mean different things in different circumstances; for fourteen years, ever since the first day that men spoke of fighting for liberty, he has thrown himself wholeheartedly into the enterprise.[51]

The United Irishmen were portrayed as men eager for liberty: 'the appalling government of the court of St James would like to ignite a new religious war...but the United Irish thirst after liberty, and are neither Protestant nor Catholic'.[52] It reported on the arrest and trial of the Rev. James Coigley and Arthur O'Connor, as well as on the political repression which was steadily filling up Irish prisons.[53] It claimed that the United Irishmen were 'gaining in strength and unity every day. The militia is wholly on their side.'[54] Political repression was aimed at 'anyone with short cropped hair in the Jacobin style, [who is being] hunted down as a United Irishman, like a wild beast'. In Naas, County Kildare it was reported that people were being condemned to death for treason, 'and that, as our own Montesquieu stated, is the crime of men who are innocent'.[55]

Between May and July 1798 *Le Bien Informé* carried news of the insurrection on its front page in every issue, and at the height of the fighting up to a quarter of its entire page space was devoted to it.[56] It always raised doubts about any news that was unfavourable to the rebels: 'do not believe news of a total defeat of the rebel forces at Vinegar Hill; it is quite possible that they have just moved camp to another hillside'.[57] On 22 *messidor* it printed on its first page an article from England that described several defeats suffered by the United Irishmen, but on the following page reiterated its belief in a voluntary retreat from Wexford. It criticised French papers such as the *Messager des Relations Extérieures*, 'which for six months now have been describing the defeat of the United Irish as a *fait accompli*, or publishing anything that could be harmful to their cause'.[58]

Two United Irish songs were published, as were some of their slogans and poems.[59] On 14 July 1798 a long article described the United Irishmen as republicans drawn from both sides of the religious divide. Some days later, *Le Bien Informé* parodied the classics to publish a modern version of the 'tirade of Galgacus' dedicated to 'the children of Erin and of Caledonia'.[60] The *Ami des Lois* also drew on the inspiration of classical poetry in a long editorial entitled 'To the United Irishmen', which called on the French to support the efforts being made by the

valiant Irish, the first to respond to liberty's call for the freedom of your country, who are undeterred by the vagaries of war. The spirit of liberty binds varying fortunes to its flags, but those who confront misfortune are invincible; let our example and our shouts encourage you: SOON OUR ARMS WILL COME TO YOUR AID.[61]

The Irish insurrection was mentioned in the official celebrations commemorating the sixth anniversary of the fall of the monarchy on 23 *thermidor* Year VI (10 August 1798). The president of the Council of Five Hundred, Lecointre Puyraveau, claimed:

The independence of Ireland is necessary for the world. The French Revolution spread the seeds of liberty throughout the continent of Europe; perhaps the Irish revolution will soon provide us with the liberty of the seas.[62]

In a speech delivered on the same day one of the Directors, Merlin, stressed the universality of the message of 10 August: 'may your name echo to the farthest corners of warlike Ireland, and give to the minds of its worthy children courage...perseverance...hatred of tyranny'.[63] News of the fighting gradually became more infrequent from mid-August onwards, and news of executions took its place: the execution of Roche – 'this Catholic priest was an excellent republican'[64] – Byrne and O'Connor, at whose last breath 'the harp of Erin still softly murmured songs of victory: his triumph, immortal gods, is the tomb!' Unlike other journals – and notably the *Ami des Lois* which published a letter from a member of the United Scotsmen, Doctor Watson – *Le Bien Informé* placed no credence in the alleged treason of Bond, O'Connor, Emmet, Sampson and MacNeven, who were accused of having sold out to 'the Beresford party'.[65] Later *Le Bien Informé* published the section of the secret report on the conspiracy, which covered the history of the links with France since 1796.

The insurrection had evidently failed, despite reports of the help that was still being prepared in French ports. On 10 *messidor* *Le Patriote Français* carried the following note:

Brest. 3 messidor: a small secret expedition is being prepared here with all possible haste, and will soon set sail. Oh Ireland! is this to help you? We would like to think so.

But not all papers gave as much detail, and *Le Bien Informé* hinted that there were good security reasons for this: 'we know what cannot be said; but we also know what can and must be said'.[66] In mid-August 1798 several newspapers published an appeal to the United Irishmen:

The national flag, the sacred green, is now fluttering above the ruins of despotism. Awake, brave people of Ireland; unite, rise, assume an attitude suitable for a great and generous people, determined to live free or die...Inactivity is cowardice when the sacred cause of liberty needs to be defended, and those who are cowards deserve to lose the very property that they fear to defend.[67]

Another such appeal was addressed to all the Irish living in Paris.[68]

The French expedition to Ireland was wished success: 'Irish patriots will be helped. Let us hope we do not arrive too late!'

> Let them go to avenge this perfidious monster,
> Who alone in the universe, avid for massacres,
> Sheds human blood with impunity.
> Frenchmen, you shudder when thinking of Ireland;
> So you give the order to descend there,
> To avenge nature and vexed heaven.[69]

But events in Ireland moved too swiftly for the French press to keep up with them. The news of Humbert's landing was published on 29 *fructidor*, along with his letter of 6 *fructidor* to the Minister of the Navy. Yet by then he had already been defeated. The details of the landing and the subsequent campaign were reported after his defeat, using official documentation provided to the editors by the Directory, or articles from the English press.[70] Newspapers then listed the executions of Bagenal Harvey, Cornelius Grogan, John Henry Colclough, Edward Crosbie, Henry Munroe, the Sheares brothers – 'who took an extremely active part in the French Revolution [and who] were executed on the day of its anniversary'[71] – 'the unfortunate Teeling whom we loved so dearly', and the younger Tone. *Le Bien Informé* announced the death sentences, while other journals gave detail of the trials and executions. The only trial reported by *Le Bien Informé* was that of Tone. To save the Irish who had taken part in the French invasion, Paine asked the Directory to pledge their lives against those of Irish officers from the British forces who were prisoners in France.[72] From then on, whenever Ireland was reported in newspapers, it was to tell of the exploits of Joseph Holt, who became the symbol of Irish resistance.[73] As for Wolfe Tone, he featured in the press only after his arrest and during his trial:

Tone, whose fate is now of interest to so many people, is the same man who went to London at Fitzwilliam's request to present the remonstrances of the Roman Catholics; he himself wrote their petition, and had taken upon himself to support their rights to political emancipation. Yet he is a Protestant.[74]

An account of his trial was given in *Le Bien Informé*, which announced his death in a few short lines in its centre pages, under the rubric of 'News from Leyden':

News that we have received from London, dated the 7th of this month, tells us that Theobald Wolfe Tone is dead from his wounds, in Dublin, on 28 *brumaire*. He had been condemned to death and was to be executed on 22 *brumaire*, but on the day set for his execution he cut his own throat: he was too seriously wounded to be taken to the scaffold.[75]

L'Ami des Lois noted that 'the penniless' Tone had left '30 livres in écus, and 6 francs for his wife; his sword and uniform went to his father, and his ring, which contained strands of Hoche's hair, to Emmet'.[76]

Once the insurrection had been defeated, news from Ireland became rare. The capture of Malta and the initial successes of the Egyptian expedition led by Bonaparte quickly took over front-page news, and Ireland was relegated to short articles of a few lines or so in the inside pages. In the months which followed, if news from Ireland appeared in the press, it related mainly to the Union; *Le Bien Informé* reported that the Orangemen were going to oppose the Act of Union and that 'Irish republicans [are] close to uniting with Orangeists to proclaim Irish independence, and to separate permanently from England'.[77] However, some days later, the paper blithely contradicted itself by reporting that Orangemen were also said to be violently opposed to patriots.[78] The Declaration of the Republic of Connaught, the Pardon Bill and the Amnesty Bill which applied to ninety Irishmen, excluding Napper Tandy, Lewins and McMahon, were also published by journals linked to the Directory.

In 1799, once the whole invasion of 1798 was well and truly over, some of the difficulties surrounding the departure of the expedition began to be made public. The problems that it had created, and the personal rivalries it engendered, resulted in several of those involved settling their scores through the columns of the press. *Le Patriote Français* took Humbert's side, highlighting the role of individuals whose help had been vital to the whole expedition.[79] Sarrazin's journal of the expedition, published from his notes and personal journal, appeared in *L'Ami des Lois*.[80] General Hesse summarised the whole experience in his *Refléxions politiques et instantes sur les expéditions d'Irlande*, apportioning blame for the failure of the insurrection partly to France, insofar as the French pretence of preparations for an invasion of England had been misunderstood in Ireland.[81]

Conclusion

Throughout the 1790s, the volume of Irish political news in the French press followed the rhythm of political developments in

Ireland. News from Ireland played a political role in France by showing that the French were not alone in their passion for revolution. Girondins in particular used Ireland to justify their policy of preventive war and to show that the Revolution enjoyed support elsewhere, and that countries such as England could never be sure of their own security. The Irish situation also revealed the political dangers of religion, and showed that London had its Vendée in Ireland; it was noted that the means used to tackle it were similar to those of the Terror. Finally, for the Directory, Ireland became the secret door through which to pass to the conquest of England. This study also confirms the results of our previous research, based on the archives of the Ministry of Foreign Affairs in Paris, which revealed that political support for the United Irishmen in France was orchestrated by the leaders of the Girondins, of the Cercle Social, and above all by Thomas Paine.

21

THE UNITED IRISHMEN, THE ENLIGHTENMENT AND POPULAR CULTURE

Kevin Whelan

The United Irishmen, the Enlightenment and the Defenders

The United Irishmen were bearers of the European Enlightenment, freely importing ideas from England, Scotland and France. They believed that they were moving in tandem politically with the inevitable laws of historical evolution, which would sweep away the existing medieval political situation. Tone observed, in characteristic imagery, that 'a new age had dawned. These were the days of illumination at the close of the eighteenth century.'[1] Samuel Barber, moderator of the Presbyterian General Synod of Ulster, claimed: 'before science, sooner or later, all tyranny will fall'.[2] Very conscious of the French Revolution's claim to have annihilated history, the United Irishmen subscribed to the revolutionary orthodoxy of repudiating the past, and specifically the Irish past: 'we have thought much about our posterity, little about our ancestors. Are we forever to walk like beasts of prey over the fields which these ancestors stained with blood?' 'Mankind have been too retrospective, canonized antiquity and undervalued themselves.' 'It [the Society of United Irishmen] will not by views merely retrospective stop the march of mankind or force them back into the lanes and alleys of their ancestors.'[3] They adopted the relentlessly modernising rhetoric of the Enlightenment, suffused with images of light, of rationality, of progress, of Utopia. In a typical flourish, the *Northern Star* claimed:

The present is an age of revolution. Everything is changing, every system is improving and mankind appear to become more wise and virtuous, as they become more informed. This is the consequence of knowledge, the effect of intelligence, the result of truth and reason.[4]

They accepted the Enlightenment's claim to eliminate particularism in favour of universalism; the United Irishmen's function would merely be to spread this message from European core to European periphery and from top to bottom of the Irish political spectrum. Once Enlightenment principles had permeated the Irish body politic, they would result in clear, simple, unambiguous law, in line with the modern spirit of the age. These laws would allow cosmopolitan Enlightenment principles to achieve their correct dispositions; benevolence, civic virtue, beauty would come into play and there would be a synchronicity between national character (Montesquieu's *l'esprit*) and its laws (*les lois*), between *res* and *publica*. This repudiation of the divisiveness of the Irish past had also a pragmatic political value; the United Irishmen wished to indulge in collective amnesia, in order to stress the enabling rather than disabling forces in Irish history. Thus they consciously agreed to develop a political programme solely on agreed issues, and tacitly to ignore divisive ones. 'Our principal rule of conduct has been to attend to those things in which we agree, to exclude from our thoughts those on which we differ.'[5] It is, however, necessary to note that the United Irish repudiation of the past was different from the standard radical reading, which saw the past in Burkean terms as a stabilising, and therefore sedative, political agent. In the Irish context, the United Irishmen wished to repudiate the past for precisely the opposite reason – its potentially destabilising effect.

In Montesquieu's classic Enlightenment statement of the relationship between *l'esprit* and *les lois*, every society had its own innate characteristics (dictated by climate, geography, diet), which determined its *esprit*, or national character.[6] Thus, the historical evolution of every society is inscribed in its origin and development, and this should be crystallised in its laws. The central problem for the Irish Enlightenment was that this simple equation between *l'esprit* and *les lois* did not exist: the calculus was fundamentally disturbed by the position of Catholic Ireland. This could represent itself (especially from the mid-eighteenth-century historiographical innovations initiated by Charles O'Conor) as a legitimate cultural entity, with its own specific *esprit* derived from a lengthy and authentic history, but which was excluded from political power as *incapax libertatis*. Ireland was therefore not a simple *tabula rasa*, on which Enlightenment principles could be unproblematically inscribed. Until Catholics were admitted to the polity, there could be no consonance between *l'esprit* and *les lois*. Two options then presented themselves to Irish politicians: to reform the people (i.e. the Catholics) so that *l'esprit* became congruous with *les lois*; or to change *les lois* to make them reflect the Irish *esprit*. The option of reforming the laws only presented itself as feasible once the French Revolution seemed to demonstrate that Catholics (having shaken off their addiction to despotism and priestcraft) were now *capaces libertatis*. Thus, for the late eighteenth-century bearers of the European Enlightenment in Ireland, reform of the laws and system of government, not reform of the people, became the preferred option, as projected by the United Irishmen. These reforms would create a natural consonance between cultural identity and government practice, generating a harmony which would allow for the unimpeded expression of beauty, benevolence and civic virtue. Without this consonance, only a disjointed, corrupt, unrepresentative politics could operate. William Michael Byrne, in his dying declaration from 'Newgate Bastille' on 24 July 1798, highlighted the centrality of the concept of virtue to the United Irishmen: 'no one political action or sentiment of my life has ever been actuated by any other motive than a wish to promote the cause of virtue'.[7]

In practical political terms, the United Irishmen had identified the lack of a natural relationship between *l'esprit* and *les lois* as the principal irritant in Irish life, causing inevitable and recurrent conflict. In particular, the exclusion of Catholics guaranteed the unrepresentative nature of Irish government. In the United Irish analysis, a narrow handful could thereby run the country in their own corrupt and self-serving interest, facilitated and copperfastened in so doing by the English connection which propped up this same unnatural handful to ensure that English policies could be smoothly implemented in Ireland. This arrangement created a logjam which stymied reform, denied a representative, reformed parliament, and left the country in the hands of a junta. The United Irishmen identified the junta as straw men, buttressed solely by the English connection; remove that connection and they would topple overnight, without bloodshed or anarchy. This is what Tone meant when he referred to 'breaking the connection with England, the never-failing source of all our political evils'.[8]

When this despotic and arbitrary government had been removed, the new representative Irish parliament would enact legislation which would bind the nation together, bringing *l'esprit* and *les lois* into harmony again. In the United Irish view, divisions within Irish society were artificial, deliberately exacerbated by the junta (or faction) to maintain their own corrupt régime. William Drennan, the most self-conscious Enlightenment figure among the United Irishmen, observed: 'The faction traduces one half of the nation to cajole the other and by keeping up distrust and division wishes to continue the proud arbitrators of the fate of Ireland.'[9] Arthur O'Connor asked rhetorically: 'has it not been by sowing, maintaining and fomenting division that Irish administrations have governed Ireland?'[10] Thus, in classic Hutchesonian terms, the United Irishmen attacked despotism, which destroyed the internal cohesiveness of society, and thereby prevented the exercise of virtue. The United Irishmen believed that the balance could be rectified by simply changing the mode of government, and their programme was anchored insistently on this point. 'With a parliament thus reformed, everything is possible.'[11] There is accordingly only a muted articulation of social, economic or cultural reforms within early United Irish rhetoric. Such issues could safely be left to a reformed, representative parliament, which would, because it represented the national *esprit*, inevitably enact suitable legislation in these arenas.

Thus, the United Irishmen felt that there was no need to recast the people, to reform them in advance of the laws; no need therefore to adopt a cultural nationalist position, although by the end of the eighteenth century, Romanticism was already beginning to undermine the Enlightenment's faith in law as the sole vector of historical change. By then, early Romantics were beginning to valorise societies with a long past, and to claim that such societies produced citizens who practised traditional uncorrupted virtue. They queried the universality of law when confronted by cultural heterogeneity, questioned the imperatives of a cosmopolitan future when confronted by the primacy of a particularist past. They asked whether a renovated society could be achieved by law alone, or whether one needed instead to recreate the people, by recuperating their cultural identity, as expressed through *les moeurs* (customs, habits, tradition). Romanticism, and its political offshoot cultural nationalism, therefore reversed the horse and cart in the motor of historical change. If *l'esprit* of the people was nurtured, fortified and stabilised, *les lois* would inevitably yield to the pressure of its insistent presence. Cultural nationalism there-

fore valorised the past, the customary, the regional, the particularist, at the expense of the new, the cosmopolitan, the universal.
Despite a few decorative gestures in this direction – such as the
Belfast Harp Festival and the publication of *Bolg an tSolair* in 1795
– the United Irishmen simply did not represent this intellectual
tradition in Ireland. William Drennan sneered in 1795 at Bishop
Thomas Hussey's and General Maurice O'Connell's brogue,
which 'kept its native broadness and vulgarity', surprised to find
that both men, despite their European experience, should 'smack
so strongly of the bogtrotter'.[12] The United Irishmen's necks were
set in concrete, staring relentlessly forward. They saw their project in Ireland as simply to accelerate the reception of Enlightenment principles. Their relationship with popular culture therefore
was radically different from a cultural nationalist programme: they
wished not to valorise but to politicise it.

While the United Irishmen rode the cusp of an Enlightenment
wave, and saw themselves as moving purposefully and inexorably
forward with the momentum of inevitable historical progress, the
Defenders, the other great movement of the late eighteenth century, had no desire to repudiate history but rather to re-immerse
themselves in it. They wished to use their shared history to create
an imagined community with a common identity. Their claims to
authenticity derived from their self-perception as the aboriginal
inhabitants of the island. Time's arrow for them was not uncomplicated, untroubled or progressive; they wished to flex time, to
bend it back to a pre-plantation, pre-lapsarian idyll, to suture the
earlier lesions inflicted on the Irish body politic. Their potent
sense of dispossession expressed itself in hopes of reversing the
land settlement, overturning the church establishment and avenging their seventeenth-century set-backs. 'They can never forget
that they have been the proprietors of this country.'[13] Theirs was
fundamentally an historical explanation of traditional grievances –
tithes, rents, taxes, labour and living conditions. Their millenarianism could also be interpreted in this way: apocalyptic change
would be equally subversive of time, again eliding the present.
Their levelling tendencies – 'the cobbler and the Caesar made
level' – was derived from an historically based sense of social
injustice, applicable to the obvious disparities in eighteenth-century Irish life. 'We have lived long enough upon potatoes and salt;
it is our turn now to eat beef and mutton.'[14]

The message of the French Revolution could be easily absorbed within these parameters: it was now possible to cast off old oppressions, and revert to a version of the *status quo ante*. It was also easy to give a sectarian gloss to these readings of Irish history. The Defenders' sense of ethnic allegiance and identity was sharpened by the abrupt juxtapositions of Catholic, Presbyterian and Anglican (or Irish, Scotch and English) in Ulster, and especially in the cockpit of county Armagh. The Defenders could also practise the politics of the grudge, develop an adversarial sense of collective awareness, and unify themselves through their hostilities. Because of the compressed social range of Ulster Catholicism, it was much easier to maintain solidarity there than in the more class-based Catholic communities of the south and east. Indeed, this may be one of the reasons why Defenderism never penetrated into the old heartlands of the secret societies in east Munster and south Leinster. Catholics in Ulster, with very few exceptions, were at the bottom of the social hierarchy: thus, the only available leadership of the Defenders there came from 'alehouse keepers, artisans, low schoolmasters and a few middling farmers'.[15]

In a sense then, Defenderism represented the democratisation of the political culture of Catholics, and a definitive break with the century-old Catholic strategy of supplication. Thus, Defenderism could be simultaneously reactive and proactive and it was this Janus-headed character which gave it its protean and resilient qualities. But its impulse of solidarity at the demotic level also led to a proto-cultural nationalism. The events of the 1780s and 1790s gave Defenders a heightened sense of nationality. Thomas Bartlett has stressed their anti-state, anti-settler, anti-Protestant animus. 'They look upon or talk of the English settlers as not of their nation.' They wished 'to plant the true religion that was lost since the Reformation'. They were encouraged 'by the hope of being what they called uppermost'.[16] A consciousness of dispossession, latent or overt, was widely diffused at the popular level.

In an inchoate way, Defenders groped towards a cultural nationalist statement, but lacked the vocabulary to articulate it. Only the widespread reception of Romanticism would facilitate its expression. Appealing to history for authenticity and legitimacy, Defenderism sought to use the past to create the future, to utilise (or invent) tradition as the binding force shaping and perpetuating the nation. Particularists not universalists, emotionalists not rationalists, exclusive not inclusive, realists not Utopians, Defenderism articulated a different world view to that of the United Irishmen. The classic Enlightenment project, as represented by the United Irishmen, reached Ireland late, and at a period when it was already being redefined elsewhere by Romanticism. The United Irishmen in this sense represented the end, not the beginning, of a political tradition. The O'Connell campaign, for example, inherited from Defenderism (not from the United Irishmen) the concept that the Catholics were 'the people of Ireland'. The Young Irelanders gave a coherent and refined version of the ill-defined but deeply felt cultural nationalist project of Defenderism.

Bringing the republic to the village

Looking at the United Irishmen in the light of this analysis, one can claim that they were simply not interested in popular culture *per se*, but only in politicising it, in using it as one more weapon in the battle for public opinion and especially in 'the race for the Catholic' that was being run at breakneck speed in the early 1790s. The central (and novel) achievement of the United Irishmen was the creation of public opinion as the pivotal political force. As in revolutionary France, the press was the seminal architect of the arena of public opinion, a novel public space in which competing claims and discourses were mediated. In Habermas's terms, the United Irishmen were intent on creating a culturally produced social sphere, in which public opinion acted as the arbiter of political rectitude, and in which the press could plausibly pretend to represent a diversified public. The United Irishmen were equally keen to place their ideological imprint on public opinion. Their literature therefore could not transcend the partisan pressure of politics; art for the United Irishmen was a mould, not a mirror, hence the strongly didactic tone of all their productions. For United Irishmen, therefore, the Republic of Letters offered the precondition for a political republic, a school where republicans could be shaped internally prior to their political incarnation.

Arthur O'Connor made the point forcefully, while invoking a typical litany of Enlightenment figures and placing the Irish experience firmly within the American and French fold.

The Press is the palladium of Liberty. What has heretofore made England celebrated over the nations of Europe? – the Press. What overturned the Catholic despotism of France? – the Press, by the writings of Montesquieu, Voltaire, Rousseau, Diderot, Seyes, Raynal, and Condorcet. What has electrified England, and called down its curses on a Pitt? that Press he in vain attempted to silence. What illumined Belfast, the Athens of Ireland? – the *Press* and the *Northern Star*. Why did America triumph over tyranny? – a journeyman printer fulminated the decree of nature against the giants of England – and the pen of a Franklin routed the armies of a King.[17]

To achieve similar effects in Ireland, the United Irishmen relied on the power of print (suitably customised) to shape politics out of doors. For their literature to fulfil its proleptic role as antenna of the political future, its message needed to be transmitted as widely as possible. Thus, the United Irishmen made impressive and successful efforts to disseminate their ideas at the ground level. O'Connor claimed that 'the increase of information and improvement of intellect among the poor, not being accompanied by a proportionate amendment of their condition, they became fully sensible of the wretchedness of their state'.[18]

Especially successful were populist, scaled-down versions in pamphlet form of classic Enlightenment authors. One commentator noted how two such pamphlets had been 'industriously distributed to the peasantry of the north' between 1795 and 1797 – the first 'compiled chiefly from Goodwin [*sic*], Locke, Paine etc.', the second 'a compilation from Voltaire, Volney and other atheistical writers'.[19] Nor did these activities stop at mere distribution. In 1795 it was reported from Belfast that William Putnam McCabe, the charismatic United Irish emissary and organiser, was distributing Paine's *Age of Reason* among mill workers there, following that by discussions in which he 'answered their several objections to any part of it'.[20]

Belfast, and more especially Dublin, United Irishmen had access to a well-established printing, publishing, journalistic and distribution network, many of whose practitioners were sympathetic to the United Irish message. In the 1790s there was a minimum of fifty printers in Dublin, thirty-four provincial presses (especially concentrated in north-east Ulster) and at least forty newspapers in print. There were fifteen booksellers and printers in the Dublin Society of United Irishmen (1791–4), including such leading figures as John Chambers, Patrick Byrne, Richard Cross, Randal McAllister, Thomas McDonnell and John Stockdale.[21] A minimum of five Dublin printers were arrested as United Irishmen in 1798 – Patrick Byrne, Arthur Loughlin, John Blyth,

Timothy Byrne and Robert Connolly.[22] Publishers had well-defined networks for disseminating their products, and the executive watched aghast as Dublin and Belfast-printed propaganda circulated widely. Fitzgibbon claimed that 'the press had been used with signal success as an engine of rebellion. Sedition and treason have been circulated with increasing industry, in newspapers and pamphlets, handbills and speeches, republican songs and political manifestos', while in 1794 the Attorney-General claimed: 'Great pains are taken to disperse their publications and besides the newspapers, there were handbills dispersed to the number of many thousand over the whole kingdom, by every shopkeeper in their society, packed in his bales, by every merchant enveloped in his correspondence.'[23] Pedlars, carmen, country dealers, chapmen and emissaries constantly spread these publications.

By as early as 1793 Denis Browne was already attributing the changed political spirit of the ordinary people to the stream of paper emanating from Dublin, a spirit 'produced by the circulation of Paine's *Rights of Man*, of seditious newspapers, and by shopkeepers who having been in Dublin to buy goods have formed connections with some of the United Irishmen.'[24] In County Kildare at the same time, James Alexander considered as an explanation for the changing political atmosphere that 'newspapers went a good way into the business: for I never knew the people in [this] neighbourhood anything like so attached to these vehicles of information and political sentiment'.[25] By September 1795 the spy Leonard McNally observed the effects of this paper deluge:

So sudden a revolution in the Catholic mind is easily accounted for. I impute it to the press. The publication of political disquisitions, addresses and resolutions by the Societies of United Irishmen of Belfast and Dublin written to the passions and feelings of the multitude filled them with electrical celerity; these papers prepared the way for Paine's politics and theology.[26]

Dillon, chief constable of police in the Athlone district, agreed: 'the press is destroying the minds of the people in this country for they wish for nothing else'.[27] A Limerick correspondent of Dublin Castle in 1797 was surprised to find that in the remoter parts of County Tipperary 'great numbers of printed papers on half sheets had been dispersed all over the hills'. Closer enquiry showed that 'these papers were mostly distributed by persons appearing as pedlars, whose boxes had underdrawers to them'.[28] An English visitor was struck by the number of political pamphlets on sale in Dublin bookshops.[29]

The United Irishmen reached the limits of contemporary literacy by using public readings. From Ross barony in County Galway, Walter Bermingham, a local landowner, voiced his suspicions of William Hamilton to Dublin Castle, claiming that he was 'a great politician' who 'spent his time reading newspapers to the common people'.[30] Lord Viscount Dillon was convinced that the United Irishmen had 'paid interpreters in remote parts to translate for the ignorant'.[31] FitzGibbon expressed the establishment assessment of the United Irish movement as a conspiracy composed of 'a deluded peasantry aided by more intelligent treason'.[32] The most articulate exponent of 'intelligent treason' was the *Northern Star* newspaper – 'its paragraphs exquisitely adapted to the taste and understanding of the northerns' who could be seen reading it 'in clusters'.[33] The *Northern Star* reckoned that each of its 4200 print run reached at least six people in this fashion.[34] Its penetration is suggested in a vignette in Thomas Russell's diary: when traversing the high Mournes, he 'saw a little girl in quite a wild part near Ballynahinch with a paper in her hand. Ask her what it was. Answered the *Northern Star*.'[35] Radicals and conservatives alike were agreed that the exceptionally high literacy in east Ulster was conducive to the reception of radical propaganda. Arthur O'Connor claimed that the people of Ulster were 'the best educated peasantry in Europe', while Richard Musgrave associated Presbyterianism, literacy and radicalism, noting that in Counties Antrim and Down 'the mass of the people are Presbyterians, can read and write and are fond of speculating on religion and politics'.[36]

The *Press*, lent credibility by Arthur O'Connor's name, took over the *Northern Star* mantle in September 1797. Hostile commentators noted that it 'had immediately a more extensive circulation than many papers long established'.[37] It soon had an unprecedented print run of 6000 copies, and a crowd on the night of publication in Church Lane to read each new issue, amidst 'a revelry of sedition'.[38] The newspaper was aggressively marketed, eventually provoking a clampdown on its vendors, accused of 'bellowing at every corner their treasonable publications'.[39] Even possession of a copy became a serious misdemeanour, and an Offaly priest, Fr John Brookes of Shinrone, was courtmartialled for having one in his house.[40] A United Irishman in Dublin was confined after the rebellion 'for the *horrid* crime of swearing that there never was a paper printed worth reading but the *Press*, that he had every number of it and by J...s would have them bound in the most elegant manner possible'.[41] The *Press* was so popular, even after its suppression, that three collected editions were published (under the title *Beauties of the Press*) in London, Dublin and Philadelphia.[42]

Another favoured ploy was the printing of broadsheets, whose reverse side was left blank; these were then pinned in public places (chapel, church and meeting-house doors, trees, pubs) for public perusal. In February 1794 the United Irish plans for parliamentary reform were ordered to be published 'on a single sheet for the purpose of hanging up in cabins'.[43] The *Union Star*, printed on one side only, was ideally suited to public display. One magistrate, who had dispersed a seditious meeting under the guise of a boxing match at Sallins, County Kildare, was disappointed that he could not send the Castle a copy of the *Union Star* which had been posted upon the canal stores there: 'in taking it down, it has been too much torn to send to you'.[44] A May 1797 report from Baltinglass, County Wicklow, shows clearly how the republic reached the village. 'Our town is overrun with disorder by the means of a republic newspaper now done in Carlow where every Sunday two fellows come after mass is over and read what they please to the ignorant country people.'[45] In the same year a report on the taproom of Lennon's pub in Arran Street, Dublin, commented on the avidity with which the clientele listened to public readings of the *Union Star* by a United Irish organiser, Joseph Davis.[46]

As in revolutionary France, the paper flood had two principal effects.[47] One was to diminish the authority of élite culture, by displacing expensive books in favour of cheap pamphlets, newspapers, ballads, songbooks, prints and broadsheets, thereby democratising the printed word itself. The second was to challenge the very style of political discourse. Paine, in particular, illustrated the possibility of creating a vernacular prose, adequate to political discourse, social responsibility and moral seriousness, in a way which had previously been thought possible only in the classical style.[48] This broke the inherently élitist link between a classical education and political life, and made available a fundamental democratisation of style itself. This enhanced the accessibility of the radical message and constituted Paine's greatest achievement. Inspired by this breakthrough, the United Irishmen cultivated a plain, blunt style, whose muscular rhythms approximated the spoken voice, and which was designed to be read by the many rather than admired by the few. Avoiding the conventional Ciceronian flourishes of established political discourse, Paine's *Rights of Man* and Tone's *Argument*, the two most successful pamphlets of the early 1790s in Ireland, were a stylistic as much as a political triumph, and set the tone for a flood of populist polemical writing. The *Poor Man's Catechism* mocked the notion of aristocracy in a conceit drawn from Paine, claiming that aristocrats should be immediately recognisable at birth: 'they would come into the world finished statesmen, orators, mathematicians, generals, dancing masters, hairdressers, taylors etc., nay, they would come from the womb covered with embroidery, ribbons, stars and coronets'.[49] That same iconoclastic style lay behind the success of the United Irishmen's prose satires, especially *Billy Bluff and Squire Firebrand*, with its subversive mimicry of Lord Castlereagh and the Ards magistrate, John Cleland.

Conservative critics were quick to denounce this new style of political discourse: Judge Day described it as 'composed in all the jargon, phraseology and pompous vulgar slang of the Jacobin school, made up of the stolen shreds and scraps of their vile vocabulary'.[50] They were equally quick to denounce its cheapness: 'The United Irishmen, by publishing at a penny-a-piece and sending through the country in thousands and ten thousands Paine's detestable book have cut asunder in many instances those bonds of amity which united persons of every rank.'[51] The effectiveness of this propaganda drive depended on a literate populace, and the United Irishmen also encouraged popular education, and were instrumental in founding Sunday schools and plebeian book clubs in east Ulster in the 1780s and 1790s. By 1795 the well-informed Captain McNevin reported from Carrickfergus how these book clubs were being used: 'The United Irishmen, being prevented from meeting publicly, have established clandestine societies who are well supplied with inflammatory publications, some calling themselves Book-Clubs, Literary Societies and Reading Societies.'[52] According to Musgrave:

these meetings, formed after the model of the Jacobin clubs in France, were usually held in barns and schoolhouses, and were liberally furnished with inflammatory publications, composed by the literati of the United Irishmen, or extracted from larger treatises of a similar tendency in both kingdoms and published in the form of pamphlets for more general circulation. The pretext of meeting for mutual information and improvement was considered as a plausible motive for the lower class of people to assemble...The rustic orators declaimed, with much vociferation and zeal, to the great edification of admiring audiences. The most fluent speakers went from one society to another, to display their talents and make proselytes to the new philosophy.[53]

It is no surprise then that the book clubs ('seminaries of sedition') were viewed with undisguised alarm by conservatives, as mimicked by James Porter in the words of Squire Firebrand:

Oh, how times are changed and all for the worse. Your Catholic College, your Catholic schools, your Catholic emancipation, your Sunday schools, your charter schools, your book societies, your pamphlets, your books and your one hell or another are all turning the people's heads and setting them athinking about this, that and the other.[54]

Indeed national education was one of the few practical suggestions on the United Irish agenda; they constantly encouraged reading as the most salutary weapon against corruption in Irish government. The *Union Doctrine or Poor Man's Catechism* suggested that the Irish people were deliberately kept poor to restrain them from thought:

By being poor, we must be on the alert to procure the necessaries of life, which makes true the old maxim 'they keep us poor and busy'. Our time will be spent studying to avoid want, instead of enquiring the cause of it, for inquiry is dangerous to tyranny.[55]

Text, context

To overcome the literacy barrier, the United Irishmen developed a series of genres designed to be permeable across the reading/speech divide. These included ballads, prophecies, speeches, toasts, oaths, catechisms, sermons and jokes, all of which privileged the individual voice, and which appealed especially to the evangelical and dissenting tradition. This material was also composed with a close eye to scriptural exegesis, and the cadences of the King James Bible can frequently be heard in it. The Scriptures offered an available model of a language that could involve and transcend a variety of social classes and linguistic competences. Consider this passage from the radical handbill *The Cry of the Poor for Bread*, produced in Dublin in 1795:

Oh! lords of manors, and other men of landed property, as you have monopolised
to yourselves the land, its vegetation and its game, the fish of the rivers and the
fowls of heaven...in the present condition of things can the labourer who culti-
vates your land with the sweat of his brow, the working manufacturer, or the
mechanic, support himself, a wife and five or six children? How much comfort do
you extort from their misery, by places, offices and pensions and consume in idleness, dissipation, riot and luxury?[56]

The dissenting and evangelical imagination, nourished on the
Book of Revelations, tended to react to extreme pressure by evok-
ing images of apocalypse, purgation and the advent of a new
order.[57]

Such millenarian perspectives were given added potency by the
American and especially French Revolutions. In 1792 the Quaker
Abraham Shackleton anxiously sent a 'prophecy said to be found
in the vault of a druid' to a colleague in Dublin, soliciting his
opinion of what he described as 'an awful alarm'.[58] By the mid-
1790s such prophecies were being extensively used by the United
Irishmen and Defenders, and inserted into the popular consciousness. Little described 'false prophecies' as one of the principal
stratagems of the Connacht United Irishmen, who had 'established a mint for coinage of false prophecies, from whence new
ones were to issue as fast as old ones should fail'.[59] In 1796 John
Beresford complained: 'they have songs and prophecies, just written, stating all late events and what is to happen, as if made several
years ago, in order to persuade the people that as a great part of
them had already come to pass, so the remainder will certainly
happen'.[60] 'Prophecy men' circulated in Ulster and Connacht, carrying with them new radical publications.[61] In 1795 alone, three
books of prophecies were published in Belfast, two in Strabane
and one in Monaghan.[62] All used millenarian perspectives to
explain the French Revolution and to give ideological impetus to
the struggle. The County Down United Irishman and New Light
Presbyterian minister, William Staveley, added an introduction to
the *Northern Star*'s reprint of Robert Fleming's *A Discourse on the
Rise and Fall of Anti Christ wherein the Revolution in France and the
Downfall of Monarchy in this Kingdom are Distinctly Pointed out.*
Staveley was keen to make the political message stick: 'that mil-
lennium state [is] now fast advancing, when men will cast far off
the chains of slavery'.[63] It was relatively easy to transmit levelling
principles under the aegis of eschatology. Andrew Gamble in
Strabane produced a small millenarian chapbook for circulation

by pedlars at fairs – *Christ in Triumph Coming to Judgement*:

and what happy times will succeed to many people when the poor will be had in equal (or perhaps superior) estimation with the rich. The courts of Kings, the seats and palaces of noblemen, the banqueting halls of the luxurious, the full barns of farmers, the cottages of husbandmen and the stalls under which beggars lie will be as one and come to nothing.⁶⁴

This biblical eschatology formed the substratum for a blending of millenial, Enlightenment and republican ideas about the future, a blend which has been identified as an important ingredient in the development of the American and French Revolutions.⁶⁵

Like prophecies, tunes could be customised to fit a newly politicised context. A military riot was initiated in Belfast in March 1793 by a blind fiddler playing the 'Ça ira'.⁶⁶ In the same year Thomas Russell recorded an incident at the Fermanagh grand jury meeting where the MP Arthur Cole-Hamilton threw his glass at another blind fiddler's head for inadvertently playing the Jacobite air 'The White Cockades'.⁶⁷ The 'Rights of Man' entered the traditional repertoire as a slow air in the 1790s and the United Irishmen also produced a trenchant parody of 'God Save the King' called 'God Save the Rights of Man'. They often disrupted public performances of the loyal version – hissing it at the theatre in Wexford in 1792, refusing to take off their hats as a military band performed it in Kells in 1796, and inciting full-scale riots in Astley's Hippodrome and the Fishamble Street theatre in 1797 when the bands there tried to play it.⁶⁸ During the short-lived Wexford Republic, the radical version was immediately substituted for the loyal version on public occasions.⁶⁹

The United Irishmen also published a series of songbooks, including at least four separate editions of *Paddy's Resource*.⁷⁰ This book was sufficiently popular (so successful in 'galloping about the country' that Squire Firebrand's servant thought its name was 'Paddy's Race-Horse') to provoke Squire Firebrand's ire:

T'is songs that is most to be dreaded of all things. Singing, Billy, is a damned bad custom: it infects a whole country and makes them half mad, because they rejoice and forget their cares, and forgets their duty, and forget their betters. By heavens, I'll put an end to singing in this part of the country in a short time. And there's whistling is near as bad: do you hear much whistling nowadays?⁷¹

The content of these ballads was not their only revolutionary message. Failure to join in the chorus of a popular radical song was a sure sign of disaffection from the popular cause. Songs had a

symbolic as well as ideological freight. Thomas Handcock, a clerical Wexford magistrate, was conscious of the defiant symbolism
of a condemned United Irishman, 'a desperate rebel, [who] when
taken sang a wicked rebel song, which he declared he would sing
at the gallows if required and I do not doubt it'.[72] Rebels gathering
on the Wicklow/Kildare border on the eve of the insurrection are
described as singing 'horrible songs never before heard by any
loyalist to excite the rebellion'.[73]

Taken together, all these genres were interfaces where authoritative forms of the written word penetrated oral culture and
imprinted their shape on it; assimilated in this public (oral) fashion, rather than in a private (written) way, they created a communal store of knowledge, accessible to all, and hence were inherently democratic modes of communication. Such genres were
essentially performance-driven, enacted in contexts of sociability.
They were also fluid, portable and malleable, capable of being
given a topical or local inflection as occasion demanded, through,
for example, the alteration of place or personal names. Because of
the heavy emphasis on orality in Irish popular culture, these
United Irish strategies were successful in 'making every man a
politician', as Thomas Addis Emmet expressed it.[74] In January
1798, for example, a traveller on the Roscrea to Limerick road
noted that there was 'not a village on the road in which the name
of William Orr and the cause for which he died is not as well
known as in the town of Carrickfergus'.[75] Such awareness was created by popular journalism, by memorial cards, by the dissemination of gold rings with the motto 'Remember Orr', by songs and
by Drennan's poem 'The Wake of William Orr'. In the case of
effective politicisation of this type, the medium was also the message. Historians have paid more attention to text than to context
in assessing the impact of these performance genres. Above all,
they signified solidarity, public affirmation and a means of assessing the political spirit of any gathering. Finally, the most striking
feature of all these genres is their assumption that the culture
which they addressed was a shared one. Adams's conclusions from
a survey of a wide range of this late eighteenth-century popular
literature in Ulster is that 'it is impossible to assign material to a
Protestant or a Catholic tradition'.[76]

From edition to sedition

The emphasis on the power of the printed word to alter public perceptions and thereby initiate political change was especially pronounced in the early phase of the United Irishmen, in which William Drennan, a quintessential Enlightenment figure, was the dominant ideologue and drafter of documents. However, once the war with France had altered the political climate to a situation where the United Irish organisation was heavily repressed, high-flown rhetoric had an increasingly hollow and bombastic ring. By the mid-1790s, social radicals within the movement, like Samuel Neilson in Belfast and John Burk in Dublin, took the initiative, arguing that the paper war had to be supported by a revolutionary mass movement, capable of seizing the power which, it now seemed, would never be voluntarily relinquished to them through the normal political process. Such a mass movement could only be constructed by politicising poverty, by building bridges into existing organisations such as the Defenders, the combinations, the Freemasons and the popular political clubs, and by accelerating the ideological trajectory of the United Irishmen towards pragmatic and politically subversive issues like taxes, tithes, living conditions and the class structure. This would necessitate addressing, even appealing to, the glaring inequalities in Irish life, and having recourse to the past in order to interpret them. Such a perspective was obviously more closely aligned to the Defender position, and made feasible the merger of the two organisations in 1795–6. This merger was orchestrated and implemented by the social radicals within the United Irish movement – Samuel Neilson, Thomas Russell, Henry Joy McCracken, James Hope, James Coigley, William Putnam McCabe, Richard Dry, Alexander Lowry, Charles Teeling and Bernard Coyle. The success of the radicalisation project created the great establishment nightmare of the eighteenth century – the Jacobinising of the secret societies, leading to an educated Whiteboyism linked to 'intelligent treason'. For the first time, the grievances of the secret societies were joined to an effective national programme for sweeping political change.

To implement this new policy, the United Irishmen needed to advance beyond empty rhetoric and beyond the print medium itself. United Irish radical rhetoric skilfully blended international, national and local issues, increasingly addressing long-nurtured feelings of exclusion and historical injustice, radicalising pre-existing cleavages. The United Irishmen also moved to incorporate pre-existing clubs in the capital. As early as 1791, a newspaper report commented on 'the great tendency to form into clubs – annuity clubs, drinking clubs, hunting clubs, gambling clubs, eating clubs, smoking clubs, singing clubs and political clubs'.[77] Wolfe Tone had formed such a club in 1790 as a forum for advanced political thought but had been disappointed on seeing it dwindle into a mere 'oyster club'.[78] In 1796, John Scott, Lord Clonmell, described the attractiveness of convivial clubs to lawyers in particular (almost one-fifth of the first society of Dublin United Irishmen were lawyers):

Afterwards during his first years, which are years of leisure, he gets into knots and clubs of barristers and young men, who pass their evenings not unpleasantly over a bottle and gay conversation, now and then regaled by a good song: from this way of life, he rarely emerges. These are the men that overstock and crowd the profession. I see acres of their wigs daily before me in the courts.[79]

Clonmell referred sarcastically to the 'nests of clubs in the city of Dublin'.[80] In these clubs, ideals of fraternity and sociability were blended with occupational solidarity and territoriality. The United Irishmen in Dublin in the mid-1790s colonised these clubs, using them as forcing houses for the revolutionary movement. In 1794, immediately after the 'open' United Irish movement had been suppressed, John Burk set to work to build a network of these clubs: 'I formed the Athenian, Telegraph and Philanthropic societies as nurseries from which to procure men of full intellectual growth and patriotism, and in addition to these, I set on foot an armed secret organisation divided into tens.'[81]

Other societies of similar tendencies followed, including the Strugglers (so called from the tavern where they met), the Society for Eating and Drinking, Democratic Citizens, Real United Traders, and the Clady, Cold Bone Dexter, Huguenot, Shamrock and Shoe Clubs. Surveying the range of societies in Dublin in the mid-1790s, Musgrave described the city as 'a great shell, fraught with various combustibles and ready to explode on the application of a match'.[82] Others noted the great attractiveness of such clubs to young artisans:

The younger part of the tradesmen, and in general all the apprentices of the city of Dublin (lads from 15 to 25 years of age) by the abominable custom adopted by masters of keeping only outdoor apprentices, in their leisure hours after work, which should be spent in the society of their masters or parents, where they might hope to improve in intellect and morality, have now the mischievous alternative of devoting themselves to youthful intemperance, in assembling in clubs instituted for the specious purpose of improvement, under the name of reading clubs, but designed for the corruption of their members. Such clubs the emissaries of sedition have fatally succeeded in establishing.[83]

This observer considered these clubs as 'preparatory schools to the fraternity of Defenders', while Judge Day claimed that their 'army of advocates' included 'neglected apprentices, needy journeymen, seditious masters hoping to ride in the whirlwind' who 'familiarly discoursed on rebellion as the sacred birthright of the people'.[84] *Faulkner's Dublin Journal* concurred in designating their leaders as 'profligate, unprincipled men who hang loose on society', keeping up the 'fainting hopes' of their members 'by Paine and the *Evening Post*'.[85]

Masonic lodges, confraternities, burial societies and lottery clubs could all be pressed into service. The United Irishmen even organised their own clandestine lottery, running parallel to and subversive of the state lottery. Whole organs of the state were systematically undermined. By 1796, the United Irishmen had infiltrated the watch, described in the *Freeman's Journal* as 'a democratical army in the metropolis under near 200 republican directors'.[86] In the build-up to the rebellion, the United Irishmen also utilised pre-existing groupings as a necessary cover for political mobilisation, given the restrictions imposed by the Insurrection and Convention Acts which prohibited political meetings. Thus, clandestine United Irish meetings were held under the aegis of sporting meetings and communal festivities – cockfights, wrestling matches, horse races, patterns, dinner parties, pilgrimages, bonfires, wakes, turf-cuttings, dances, balls, spinning bees, Masonic lodges, confraternities. The informer Thomas Boyle describes a typical example – a cockfight in a barn at Clonard on the Meath/Kildare border, attended by one hundred men, ninety of whom took the United Irish oath, under the tutelage of Flynn and Tuite, the chairman and secretary of the local corps.[87] From the Kildare/Wicklow border in June 1797, a spy reported that United Irish organisation was proceeding under the cloak of cockfighting in the Ballymore Eustace, Dunlavin, Donard and Hollywood areas. The fights attracted a crowd which was then proselytised by Dublin and northern emissaries.[88] Confraternities were also considered suspicious: Caesar Colclough wrote to Dublin Castle in January 1799 deprecating their episcopal encouragement, on the basis that 'prior to the rebellion in the county of Wexford, the effects of such societies were very destructive'.[89] Rev. James Little in County Mayo was especially critical of the Carmelite confraternity and its promotion of the scapular: 'I have no doubt this institution was resorted to as a political engine...designed for the mere purpose of organising the people, now rendered difficult by the laws prohibiting all popular assemblies.'[90]

In circumstances in which their activities were closely monitored, United Irish emissaries became adept at disguise: the Presbyterian clergyman James Porter posed as an itinerant astronomer, James Hope organised a fictive linen market to gather a crowd in the Creggan area of south Armagh. The Antrim man James Cochran, while on United Irish business in Tyrone, carried three forged Freemasons' seals and medals and a stolen brown linen seal, to facilitate his ease of movement. William Putnam McCabe, their most effective, ubiquitous, protean and resourceful emissary, used his acting and mimic powers to become a preacher, a recruiting sergeant, a yeoman, a travelling hedge schoolmaster, a pedlar, as occasion demanded.[91] In June 1797, 'a man named O'Kelly, who styled himself a travelling poet' was arrested at Termonfeckin on suspicion of being a United Irishman.[92]

The politicisation of popular culture

The United Irishmen attempted to politicise popular culture, whether this be in sport, calendar custom or communal festivities. They also sought to channel pre-existing factions into their organisation. Collections of young adult males (already group-bonded) would form tight and cohesive United Irish cells. In Carlow town, William Farrell described how the five Mayboy 'factions' (The Quarry Boys, The Clash Boys, The Burren Boys, The Castle Hill Boys and The Potato Market Boys), each rooted in a particular area of the town, were recruited into the United Irish organisation in 1797.[93] In Dublin, it is likely that similar faction groups (The Cross-Lane Boys, The Newmarket Boys, The Marybone Lane Boys, The Light Horse) were similarly absorbed.[94]

In the rebellion of 1798 such groups formed the backbone of whole United Irish units. In Wexford, for example, the Duffry, Mulrankin and Kilmallock (Bogtown) units were based around pre-existing hurling teams and in Dublin the Donnybrook hurlers were a revolutionary front.[95] Given the predominant role of young, unmarried adult males in the rebel ranks, this is understandable and gave cohesion and *esprit de corps* to non-professional fighting men. Miles Byrne describes with feeling how localism acted as a bonding agent in the United Irish camps: 'the sweet cry of the name of their native barony or village roused them at once'.[96] At Gorey Hill, the 300-strong Ballymanus corps, led by Billy Byrne, marched into the camp, chanting 'Ballymanus, Ballymanus'.[97]

By the spring of '98, the architects of the United Irish organisational structure sought to build in the advantages of localism in revamped, more streamlined cells. 'No society should consist of more than twelve members and these as nearly as possible of the same street or neighbourhood, whereby they may be all thoroughly well known to each other and their conduct be subject to the censorial check of all.'[98] The new structures worked well in practice. For example, the 'Macamore Boys', from the coastlands east of Gorey, maintained a strong fighting corps right through the rebellion. In Wexford town, the rebel corps were derived from the age-old sectors of the town – the artisanal John Street corps, the mercantile Selskar corps, and the fisherman Faythe corps.[99] Feeding on the pervasive and intimate localism of Irish life, this territoriality principle stiffened morale, and allowed ersatz soldiers to perform competently in an arduous and protracted campaign. In such settings, the inherited leadership role of locally potent families came into play, and these families disproportionately supplied the officer corps of the United Irish army; the kinship ties which bound together these endogamous families provided a powerful cementing force in the leadership of the United Irishmen.[100]

The fusion of high politics and quotidian life was exemplified by Lord Edward Fitzgerald. An account from 1793 noted that 'he is turned a complete Frenchman, crops his hair, despises his title, walks the streets instead of riding and thence says he feels more pride in being on a level with his fellow citizens'.[101] Such activities brought instant recognition of his role as a tribune of the people. Anne, Countess of Roden, describes a Dublin theatrical scene in 1793:

One of the actors brought in of himself, 'Damn the French!', upon which there was a moderate clap and Lord Edward Fitzgerald stood up in his box and hissed singly; upon which you would have thought they would have tore the house down

with clapping, men, women and every creature. He looked bursting with rage and
venom. I never saw anything so delighted as they were with it.[102]

In Kildare, he participated enthusiastically in local life and is
described there in 1796 as 'dancing among the rustics at bonfires
and in short [conducting] himself among them with such uncom-
mon condescension, freedom and affability that, like Absalom of
old, he stole away the hearts of the people'.[103] With Michael
Reynolds, Fitzgerald used handball matches to spread the United
Irish organisation in County Kildare and he made a vigorous
effort to interact with the ordinary people. *Faulkner's Dublin Journal* describes how 'he used to mix with and participate in the
breakfasts and dinners of the meanest peasantry in the
county...that he used to hold the plough in order to obtain the
confidence (i.e. for the purpose of abusing it) of the unsuspecting
and ignorant tillers of the land'.[104]

The most striking example of United Irish success in the field
of popular culture is the use of the Tree of Liberty. This could
easily be grafted onto the indigenous May Bush tradition, the fes-
tive, decorative bush which welcomed the summer. The transna-
tional and demotic symbols of optimistic regeneration were fused
in a potent cumulative symbol, in which the green colour also had
a powerful resonance. In August 1795 the soldiers had to be called
out from Cork to Blarney, 'to prevent the planting of a tree of liberty, adorned with ribbons and mounted with the red cap by Irish
carmagnoles'. The tree was 'a finely grown birch tree, the most
stately found in the wood' and its planting was to be accompanied
by 'the playing of the Marseillaise, Réveil le Peuple, Ça Ira etc' by
a specially requisitioned group of blind pipers.[105]

Public displays were also used by the United Irishmen to make
explicit the power of numbers: political funerals, potato diggings,
harvestings and turf-cuttings were not simply solidarity demonstrations, but a celebration of the local strength of adherence to
the cause and a calculated, intimidatory gesture of defiance.
Henry Echlin, returning from Balbriggan to Dublin in the spring
of 1798, was 'much surprised at seeing at least 200 men on horse-
back, almost all cropped, pass by me. I found they were going to
Lusk to the funeral of a man called Wade, a tanner from Dublin. I
have seldom seen such an assemblage.'[106]

All gatherings became suspect in this 1790s numbers game.
They were seen by conservatives as provocations, a public display

of insolent democracy requiring to be kept down. Any public display of Catholic religious observance (patterns, pilgrimages, funerals) fell under similar suspicion. A proclamation of the Lord Lieutenant of 6 November 1796 observed the dangers of

the disaffected having adapted a practice of marching in military array, and assembling in large bodies, in some instances to the number of several thousands, under pretence of saving corn, and digging potatoes; but in fact to terrify the peaceable and well-disposed, and to compel them to enter into treasonable associations. The same system has since frequently been had recourse to by the United Irishmen in other parts of the Kingdom under various pretences, such as funerals, football meetings, etc with a view of displaying their strength, giving the people the habit of assembling from great distances upon an order being issued, and making them more accustomed to show themselves openly in support of the cause.[107]

This theatrical sense of political expression could draw on a long-established repertoire. Elaborate mock funerals bearing a fleece had been organised by unemployed weavers to dramatise their distress. In August 1782, for example, 'a number of broad loom weavers have, for these days past, perambulated the streets of this city, preceded by the effigy of a golden fleece, borne on a pole covered with crepe, symbolical of the distress they suffer from the stagnation of their business'.[108] Other examples of United Irishmen use of this tactic can be illustrated. In the eighteenth century the price of a loaf remained fixed, but its size fluctuated in response to market conditions. In May 1795 a procession from the Liberties paraded to the Parliament House, Dublin Castle and the Lord Mayor's mansion,

preceded by a loaf hung with crepe and sable to signify the distress of the time. This procession was followed by a lean, wretched horse, on which was mounted a chief mourner, who ever and anon looked at the loaf, and then, with no ill-acted shew of horror, applied his handkerchief to his face in token of grief for its diminutive appearance.[109]

In the same year the Dublin United Irishmen were planning to decapitate the three royal statues in the city, which were throughout the eighteenth century a target for popular opprobrium in politically tense situations.[110] In 1796 a gallows was erected outside the house of the rector of Ardboe in County Derry who had been active against the United Irishmen.[111] In 1797, when specie (coinage) was in short supply in Dublin,

one of these ambulatory wags with which this city abounds exhibited as a practical and profitable jeu d'esprit a show box with glasses, [covers?] etc., etc. on Essex

Bridge to which all persons were loudly invited at the moderate premium of one penny to behold one of the greatest curiosities that could be exhibited. The opening box displayed on inspection a solitary guinea suspended by a black ribbon under the scroll of – a real, original, golden guinea.[112]

This essentially subversive sense of humour was demonstrated at the funeral of John FitzGibbon, when a dead cat was hurled at the coffin – an ironic reminder of Lord Clare's boast that he would 'make the seditious as tame as domestic cats'.[113] A similar cast of mind can be seen in the use of 'Sir John Doe' as a pseudonym on threatening letters – a parody of the conventional name for the typical citizen used in legal textbooks.

Public houses loomed large in loyalist perceptions of sedition. A Cork commentator claimed that every porter house 'could boast a set of statesmen who without the aid of education or experience conceived themselves competent in every branch of legislative occupation'.[114] At the Kilmainham quarter sessions in January 1796 Judge Robert Day conjured up a horrifying vision of public houses seething with sedition:

it is in the dead of night, when all nature seeks repose, all but creatures of prey, that conspirators assemble and hatch dark and bloody treasons and other atrocious crimes. And it is in these hotbeds of corruption and debauchery that the first seeds of vice and criminality are sown, which afterwards ripen into full-blown guilt.[115]

Such clubs were frequently pub-based – because the crowded tenements of the Liberties, for example, allowed no scope for domestic socialising. In the 1790s there were at least fifty pubs in Thomas Street, the spine of the Liberties.[116] The city as a whole had 1300 public houses (one for every eight houses paying the hearth tax) in 1791.[117] In 1789 a newspaper claimed that one in four houses in the Liberties was a dram shop and an 1804 visitor to the 'St Giles of Dublin, in Meath Street and Thomas Street' noted 'the drunkenness, noise, beatings of drums and fifes at the door of alehouses'.[118] As in late eighteenth-century Paris (with its 3000 bars in 1789), the poorer areas of the city bristled with pubs, where journeymen and immigrants escaped their crowded, cramped rooms.[119] The pub then became a key arena of masculine sociability. Not just the clientele, but even the names and signboards of public houses could carry the revolutionary message. In Belfast in 1793 drunken soldiers of the 17th Light Dragoons pulled down the signs of Dr Franklin, Mirabeau and General Dumouriez, commander of the French northern army, at the public house of the father of the celebrated William Putnam McCabe; he retaliated by putting his own portrait on the signboard under the title 'McCabe – an Irish slave'.[120]

Yet, by the spring of 1798, the tightened United Irish organisation was eschewing the use of public houses as meeting places. 'Avoid as much as possible meetings in public houses, either of societies or committees, because they might be attended with much danger and the occasions of meetings induce no such necessity: a few minutes in any convenient place will be sufficient for a small number of men to confer on the objects of their deliberation.'[121] Two reasons were advanced for avoiding public houses; as well as increasing discipline, it would simultaneously depress government excise revenue. The movement therefore laid great stress on avoiding excessive drinking (a potential source of indiscipline). 'In the pursuit of these great and valuable objects, let not drink and idleness dishonour United Irishmen.' 'Be discreet and avoid drunkenness. Be firm but be patient, and avoid riots.'[122]

So successful were the United Irishmen in disciplining their followers that the absence of heavy drinking and faction-fighting was taken as a sign that an area was very well organised. Musgrave considered 'the abstinence of the lower class of people from spirituous liquors to a degree of sobriety too unusual and general not to be systematic' as a symptom of the approaching insurrection, while Judge Day noted that in both 1798 and 1803 'it was observed that the people were never more peaceable, orderly or sober than while the preparations were going forward for the rising'.[123]

While the United Irishmen accentuated some elements in the repertoire of popular culture, they sought to discard others, in particular, sectarianism, faction-fighting and excessive alcohol consumption. They invested a considerable degree of organisational energy attempting to stem the spread of sectarianism in mid-Ulster in the mid-1790s, in line with their own often stated aim of concentrating attention on issues which could be supported by all the Irish people. Thus, United Irish rhetoric, as in this example from a 1796 ballad about the Armagh expulsions, stressed the necessity of repudiating sterile, historically based sectarianism. 'We'll throw by all distinctions, what's past never mention,/join hands with our neighbours, and let all agree'.[124] Accordingly, loyalist observers could be equally shaken by 'infernal calm' as by outright lawlessness; both betokened a dangerous level of organi-sation.[125] Only a customary level of violence was reassuring. In 1804 a conservative commentator noted with satisfaction that in Wexford and Kilkenny,

never was there a greater number of broken heads known at any former period, as all the barony bullies headed their respective factions and every evening closed with drunken quarrels. For some time before 1798, a quarrel was not known at any fair or patron and my barometer for the political state of the country is the parish and barony factions fighting with each other. Every fair in the country ends at pre-sent with a general engagement between rival factions.[126]

Conclusions

The successful penetration of popular culture by the United Irish-men was possible because Irish élite groups, in common with their European counterparts, had begun to disengage from it in the second half of the eighteenth century. Common ties, which had united the classes vertically in the informal intimacy of collective engagement in popular culture, had snapped. A more formal, dis-tant relationship replaced them. As the gentry adopted metropoli-tan standards of taste, propriety and refinement, their patronage of hurling, of traditional music, of mumming groups, and their involvement in sociable (dancing, drinking) activities with their tenants withered and faded.[127] In the late eighteenth century this withdrawal from popular culture was accelerated by assaults on its degenerate and lawless character. Under such conditions there was no competitor to the United Irishmen in their quest to colonise popular culture, with the notable exception of the gentry-led eff-ort to support popular loyalism in mid-Ulster in the mid-1790s.[128]

Given this broader cultural change, government distrust of popular culture was strong. It is remarkable how many flash-points in the 1790s revolved around communal festivities, as, for example, the John Foster-inspired military assaults on patterns in County Louth. As early as 1788, in an effort to prevent the spread of the Defender movement into the county, Foster had headed a troop of soldiers, attacked a pattern at Oldbridge on the Boyne, 'cut up the tents, charged the mob and totally dispersed them', and announced his intention of doing the same at every other pat-tern and fair.[129] In 1792, in a controversial reprise of this policy, soldiers under Foster's control first fired into, and then charged with drawn swords, a pattern at Tallanstown believed to be a

Defender display of strength.[130] This disengagement of the gentry was echoed by the institutional Catholic church, with episcopal condemnations mirroring government ones: Bishop Caulfield wished 'to most earnestly recommend and conjure you... to avoid all unnecessary meetings, associations, places of pilgrimage, or patrons, of diversions and dissipation which can tend to no good'. He itemised these as 'dancing, ball-playing, hurling, and assembling in alehouses'.[131]

The disengagement of the gentry from popular culture also completely transformed the administration of law and order, which had been indulgent and personalised, operating within the softening ambit of the moral economy. Given the sectarian nature of the eighteenth-century Irish state, there was always a brittle and queasy relationship between authority and alienation. There was also a communal ambivalence towards the law, and considerable hostility to its agents – the tithe proctor, the gauger, the crimping sergeant, the police, the pressgang, the soldier. It was relatively easy to politicise those feelings in the volatile 1790s.

However, there were three main failures in the United Irish colonisation of popular culture. Firstly, systematic recourse to the printed word as its political cutting edge had the effect of concentrating its most effective penetration in anglophone and literate areas, which had close links to the main publishing centres of the period, Dublin and Belfast. United Irish strength was greatest in the Anglicised east coast area stretching from Antrim to Wexford. This obvious correlation is a warning against the facile splitting of the east Ulster/south Leinster rebellion in 1798. The weakness of the United Irishmen was their inability to penetrate significantly Irish-speaking areas. Even in counties with an internal linguistic frontier, such as Donegal and Wexford, the United Irishmen's limits of organisation fell neatly astride the linguistic boundaries. Predominantly Irish-speaking counties, even those with a major city such as Kilkenny, Waterford, Cork, Limerick and Galway, remained largely impervious to the new radicalism.

Secondly, the United Irishmen did not see popular culture as the basis for a political project – one in which, for example, a sense of a communal Irish identity might be created by recourse to a shared culture. Universally grounded cosmopolitan appeals to benevolence, virtue and other displays of moral fortitude rang increasingly hollow as the local situation deteriorated in the mid-

1790s. Rooting these in the narrow ground of Ulster, for example, required a carefully thought out politics of culture. The United Irishmen's simply instrumental view of popular culture did not encourage such an approach. Finally, the United Irishmen overestimated their ability to transcend the inherited politics of religion in Ireland. The United Irishmen's elaborate efforts to elide the divisiveness of the Irish past and religious differences concealed the popular potency of both and conceded them to conservatives as a political weapon. Once government explicitly endorsed the sectarian card in the post-Fitzwilliam period, popular Protestantism, notably through the Orange Order, was wrapped with a tough ideological carapace. The appeal to disunited rather than united Irishmen had an atavistic, visceral attraction for communities who were encouraged to see themselves as threatened.

The central strategic mistake of the United Irishmen was their incredulity that there could be a genuinely popular counter-revolutionary impetus of this type; in their reading, it could only be artifically induced by government and Ascendancy connivance. Once the people's eyes were opened and they could see how they were being cynically duped by self-serving politicians, they would abandon their political stance. The United Irishmen fundamentally misjudged the depth of popular counter-revolutionary sentiment, unrealistically expecting massive defections from the militia and yeomanry once the rebellion actually started. It was to be a fatal mistake; underestimating popular support for the régime, the United Irish revolution failed.

Acknowledgments
I would like to thank Kevin Barry, Tom Bartlett, Bernard Browne, Seamus Deane, Tom Dunne, Luke Gibbons, Brian MacDonald and Mary Helen Thuente for their assistance.

22

PIECING TOGETHER A SHATTERED PAST: THE HISTORICAL WRITINGS OF THE UNITED IRISH EXILES IN AMERICA

Martin Burke

In the course of his narration of the lives and times of the United Irishmen, Richard Robert Madden identified at least one chapter in their collective history that was not marked by political upheaval or personal tragedy. Among those who had sought exile in America – in New York City in particular – Madden found a 'little Irish community' bound together by ties of friendship and marriage, and enjoying the blessings of liberty and property that fate had denied them at home.[1] While Madden's favourable assessment of their circumstances might not be applicable to everyone who sought refuge in the United States, it applies to the great majority of the sixty or so members of United Irish societies who can be located in the historical record.[2] The larger research project from which these comments are drawn examines the institutional and interpersonal configurations of these 'little communities', their relations with the larger Irish emigrant population, and the cultural and political activities of these *émigrés* in the United States during the late eighteenth and early nineteenth centuries.[3]

This essay addresses one aspect of these activities, that is the writing of Irish history. After the failure of the rising of 1798, the United Irishmen John Daly Burk, William James MacNeven, Thomas Addis Emmet and William Sampson composed narratives to explain the political goals of their movement, and to defend the character of the emigrant communities of which they were now a part from charges of disloyalty and barbarity. Their writings helped shape the convention in Irish and American-Irish nationalist historiography that the significance of 1798 could be interpreted in terms of 1789, and both could be domesticated under the sign of 1776. Instead of celebrating the Glorious Revolution and the rights of Englishmen, the Irish could look instead to the French and American Revolutions and the rights of all men. For each of these *émigrés*, the history of Ireland served as a 'narrow ground' of political and cultural contestation, one in which a battle of the books had more than bibliographic implications.[4]

Of these texts, John Daly Burk's *The History of the Late War in Ireland* in 1799 was the first to appear, and was the most emphatic in its identification of the Irish, French and American causes.[5] Though details of his biography are unclear, Burk was most probably from a Cork middle-class, Protestant family. He entered Trinity as a sizar in 1792, and was dismissed from the College in 1794 for espousing heterodox religious principles. Soon after his dismissal he produced a pamphlet dramatising his 'trial for heresy and blasphemy', as well as contributing pieces to the *Dublin Evening Post*. In politics Burk's opinions were as radical as his religious ones; his associates in Dublin included Dr James Reynolds, Oliver Bond, Denis Driscol, Bagenal Harvey and the brothers Sheares. With them he was engaged in establishing such clandestine groups as the Strugglers, and the Athenian, Telegraphic and Philanthropic societies, and in reorganising a far more militant Society of United Irishmen. In his *History*, Burk claimed to be the first person to 'conform to the constitution of the present society'. But given the precarious legal situation of these Dublin radicals, Burk fled to America, arriving in Boston in the autumn of 1796.[6]

Once in the United States he began a career as an author, editor and playwright for the cause of 'republicanism' – a concept which for him embraced the politics of Thomas Jefferson, the Jacobins and the United Irish societies. Burk was soon numbered among those 'Wild Irishmen' whose strident attacks against the presidency of John Adams (in such party organs as the *Polar Star* of Boston and the *Time Piece* of New York) led to prosecutions for criminal sedition, and helped to provoke a major American political crisis in the years 1797 and 1798. This turn towards political journalism was not untypical of United Irish *émigrés* and their American-Irish compatriots. Along with Burk, such figures as John Binns, Patrick Byrne, John Chambers, James and Mathew Carey, Denis Driscol, William Duane, and perhaps – had he lived – Samuel Neilson, edited and published partisan newspapers with a strong Jeffersonian flavour.

In addition to Burk's journalistic work, his writings include a quartet of historical dramas, an essay on ancient Irish music and song, and a multi-volume *History of Virginia*. Burk's plays, especially *Bunker Hill*, were among the first and most popular of the 'republican theatricals' on the American stage. Within these various spaces he sketched out a linear model of history with a decidedly secular eschatology. Burk wrote of an inexorable republican progression from America to France to the British Isles, of 'an epoch of general revolution' that was reconstituting the world.[7]

The History of the Late War in Ireland combines a topical and chronological narrative of events in Ireland from the 1780s onward, with large quotes from a range of contemporary sources and a smattering of Burk's own poetry and song. Despite its disjointed composition, the text is a useful source of information about Burk and his fellow Dublin radicals, especially for the mid-1790s. *The History* was hastily composed in 1799 as a response to the depiction of those events by members of the Federalist party. To such pamphleteers and publicists as William Cobbett and John Fenno, the risings in Leinster and Ulster were nothing but squalid *jacqueries*; its leaders were brutal, if inept, agents of the Jacobin conspiracy. These charges were more than exercises in vitriolic political rhetoric or anti-Irish prejudice, however; they were written in support of the Alien and Sedition legislation and the pro-British foreign policy of the Adams administration. Burk's task, then, was to offer a counter-interpretation of recent Irish history, one representing the United Irishmen not as savage, subversive enemies, but as heroes and martyrs in the cause of international republicanism.[8]

At the centre of that interpretation is an impassioned defence of the alliance between the United Irishmen and France. To Burk, the significance of the French Revolution for Ireland was twofold: it provided both the ideological impetus and the military aid necessary for the genesis and the triumph of Irish republicanism. The 'explosion' of the Revolution had drawn the Irish people out of a collective political inertia and drawn them into extended conversations on the meaning of the changes in France: farmers, mechanics, merchants, and men of letters formed their own class-specific understandings, insightful yet incomplete. This plurality of interpretations was reduced to one, however, by the organisation of the United Irishmen in 1791. In Burk's analysis, only that society was able to adapt the call for *liberté, égalité, fraternité* to a suitably Irish idiom; only that society – with its non-sectarian politics – could claim to speak for the entire nation. Burk was careful to note that the founding of the United Irishmen took place in the wake of the commemoration in Belfast of the fourteenth of July; by celebrating the fall of the Bastille, Burk's Irish were also celebrating the rise of their national consciousness. Hence for him that date marked the intersection of two lines of historical development, the Irish and the French.[9]

If in Burk's estimation the Revolution had been a pervasive ideological force in Ireland since its inception, it became a material one in 1796, and again in 1798, with the French incursions of those years. Although each of these ended in failure, Burk was ready to find in them portents of ultimate success. The willingness of the French to intervene in Ireland was indicative of their fidelity to internationalism; the brief victories enjoyed by Humbert's troops were suggestive of the ease with which a more substantial expedition would prevail. With this confidence in the military feasibility of a French invasion, and in the revolutionary potential of the Irish people, Burk's judgment is closer to that of a number of late twentieth-century historians than it is to the writings of many of his contemporaries. In Burk's analysis of the dynamics of six hundred years of Ireland's history, the achievement of independence was a necessary not a contingent event, and the United Irish alliance with the Directory remained the best way of realising the republic. Each of these bodies was but a manifestation of the spirit of liberty, the calumnies of Fenno and Cobbett notwithstanding.[10]

While William James MacNeven held in common with Burk a commitment to Irish independence, he was not willing to posit a simple equivalence between Irish and French needs. Burk had participated in the Revolution and the Rising only through his writings whereas MacNeven, as a member of the United Irish executive, had engaged in the often difficult negotiations with the Directory – and subsequently with the Consulate – on matters of military intervention. After his imprisonment at Fort George, MacNeven returned to France in 1803 and served there with the Irish Brigade; in the autumn of 1805 he emigrated to America.[11] Once established in New York city, MacNeven resumed the practice of medicine, pursuing a very successful career as a physician and professor of chemistry, obstetrics and *materia medica*. But unlike a number of the professionally trained United Irish *émigrés* who rapidly assimilated into American society – Robert Adrian or Harman Blennerhasset for example – MacNeven continued to identify himself publicly with Irish affairs, and assumed a position of leadership within the emigrant community in New York and in the country at large.[12]

A significant moment in that leadership occurred during spring 1807, in the course of an election campaign for the Assembly of the State of New York. At the head of the Federalist party's list of candidates was Rufus King, the former minister to Great Britain who in 1798 had been involved in preventing the Irish state prisoners from settling in the United States. King now found himself opposed by an American-Irish electorate that was in general hostile to the Federalists, numbering among its more influential members the former prisoners MacNeven, Emmet and Sampson, as well as John Chambers, Joseph Cuthbert and Thomas Traynor. A characteristic episode of New York ethnic politics ensued, as the Federalists once more conjured up images of murderous and cowardly French and Irish Jacobins in the pages of the *Evening Post*, while the Jeffersonians responded with a rhetoric of virtuous American and Irish republicanism in their organ, the *American Citizen*.[13]

Among the results of this campaign – in addition to the defeat of King – was the appearance in 1807 of *Pieces of Irish History*. That volume, edited by MacNeven, included essays by him and by Thomas Addis Emmet, as well as a collection of state papers, memoirs and letters relevant to the history of the United Irishmen. For MacNeven, the publication of this text was necessitated by the 'abusive misrepresentation' that he and his fellow exiles were subjected to by the 'hirelings' of the British crown: the accusations that they had been and still were the agents of France, traitors in Ireland and subversives in the United States.[14] These charges were to be found both in certain party organs and in such ostensibly 'impartial' histories of the insurrection as those of James Gordon, John Jones and Sir Richard Musgrave.[15]

To answer these accusations, MacNeven turned to an examination of the relations between the United Irishmen and the French, relations which for him were more a matter of expedience than of revolutionary affinity. In his calculations, the Irish on their own could never hope to overcome English domination; they were obliged to seek support wherever that might be found. Just as the Americans had to rely on French assistance, so too did the Irish. But the irony – if not the tragedy – of Irish history could be seen in the efficacy of these respective alliances. The Americans, aided by a self-interested monarchy, were able to gain independence; the Irish, aided by a self-professed republic, were not. Here Mac-Neven distanced both himself and the United Irish movement from the French, while not being prepared to break completely with them. From his perspective, the dynamics of European geo-politics were such that the English would meliorate conditions in Ireland only when faced with the threat of foreign incursion. Thus as long as the French were England's adversaries, they would remain Ireland's friends.[16]

If courting invasion was evidence of disloyalty, MacNeven wondered, what of England's past. Since the invitation to William of Orange constituted a 'Glorious Revolution', why then did the invitation to the Directory constitute treason? The answer, he suggests, is to be found in the power to assign such labels: a power exercised in Irish and English public discourse only by the com-posers of supposedly impartial texts favourable to the British con-nection. Fortunately, circumstances were different in America, especially Jeffersonian America.[17]

As its title suggests, *Pieces of Irish History* was an attempt to con-struct a history of the late incidents in Ireland, but one freed from the assumptions of a Whiggish, loyalist tradition. These pieces were written in anticipation of a more substantial United Irish interpretation of history. Although the United Society may have lost the fight over political reformation, its members might still win in the struggle over Irish historical representation. Mac-Neven, however, never completed his projected Irish history, rough notes for which Madden found in the doctor's papers.[18]

The need to gain control over the past as a precondition of future political action was also stressed by MacNeven's close friend and fellow contributor to the *Pieces*, Thomas Addis Emmet. Emmet had arrived in New York in 1804 – one year earlier than MacNeven – and reverted to the practice of law. Emmet, too, enjoyed a great deal of professional success in America. He became a prominent member of the bar, and in 1812 was appoint-ed as the Attorney-General of New York State. Like MacNeven, Sampson and Chambers, he was actively engaged in the affairs of

the emigrant community and in the promotion of Irish independence. Emmet's personal and political connections in New York
are also suggestive of the limits of such labels as 'moderate', 'radical', 'Jacobin' or 'Painite' in Irish and American circumstances.
While certainly a 'moderate' in the intricate, internecine politics
of Dublin and Paris, Emmet was suspected of being a francophile
in New York; and while far from the late twentieth-century category of 'Painite', Emmet was one of the few in New York to
remain personally loyal to the international radical, and was the
executor of Paine's last will and testament.[19]

As one of the leaders of the United Irish movement, Emmet
had had extensive contact with successive régimes in Paris; like
MacNeven he was far more circumspect in identifying the interests of Ireland with France than was John Daly Burk. In his essay
'Towards the History of Ireland', Emmet argued that the
'immense importance' of the French Revolution was to be found
in its exemplary, rather than its practical, effect on Irish affairs. In
demonstrating that a Catholic people could overthrow a despot,
the French had contradicted that favourite Whiggish dogma that
Catholics were unfit for freedom – a charge still made by some in
the Federalist camp. By abolishing tithes and legal disabilities for
religious minorities, the French had earned the admiration of
Irish dissenters and Catholics alike. The example of France had
helped, in effect, to weaken those cultural barriers used by the
English to separate the peoples of Ireland, and to subvert the logic
of that celebrated British constitution under which the civil liberties of one religious community were maintained at the expense of
the other's. Even if these outcomes were unanticipated, the Revolution had served to reconcile the Protestant reformer to his
Catholic countrymen, and to enhance the articulation of a new,
more inclusive, Irish nationalism – that of the United Irishmen.[20]

Not all examples from France were so helpful in promoting
that Society's original goals of parliamentary reform and Catholic
emancipation, however. The execution of Louis and the outbreak
of hostilities between England and France in 1793 gave a new
urgency to Dublin Castle's policy of promoting sectarian rivalries.
The public revulsion against the Terror and the Revolution's
assault on organised religion bolstered the opponents of reform.
If, as the latter insisted, such 'outrages' as regicide and anti-clericalism were produced by the spread of democracy, preservation of

the existing order was preferable to radical change. Here Emmet's comparison between intransigent Irish loyalism and recalcitrant American Federalism came to the fore. In Emmet's analysis, events in France could promote reformist and republican sentiments, but they could also provoke reaction.[21]

The forging of a national identity from so divided a population and in so contentious an ideological context was no simple matter, and the United Irishmen realised what was at best an ephemeral success. Emmet's narrative ends before the disasters of 1798; but in order to make sense of those defeats, the essay interweaves chronology with a careful attention to the social and political conditions of Ireland in the years 1789 to 1795, and with an evaluation of the strengths and weaknesses of that movement. Emmet was writing to defend the leadership of the United Irishmen from the accusation that they were visionaries who had deluded their followers with schemes for an unattainable, impractical republic. For Emmet, the writing of Irish history was a means of both political analysis and political apologetic.[22]

MacNeven's and Emmet's concern with the Irish and American implications of historical interpretation was shared by the final member of this quartet of *émigré* writers, William Sampson. As a result of the turmoil of 1798 he too was subjected to arrest, imprisonment and eventual banishment. Before that year Sampson had been an influential member of the Irish bar, and after settling in New York in 1806, he returned to the profession. Like Emmet, counsellor Sampson did quite well in the legal and political circles of that city. With the publication of his *Memoirs* in 1807 he joined in the domestic debate over the meaning of the rising, the consequences of the revolution, and the character of Irish republicanism.[23]

In his 'Preface', Sampson noted that for the past ten years the only accounts of the late rebellion were either loyalist tracts, or less partisan pieces whose accuracy had nonetheless been compromised: 'the printing presses of Ireland have been lawlessly demolished, and all who dare to write or speak the truth, have been hunted to destruction'. Part of the suppression of republicanism in Great Britain and Ireland, then, had been the suppression of the truth of the recent past. For Sampson, this pattern of conceptual distortion could be found in the terms used to represent these events. If by 'rebellion' was meant open, armed resistance to the law, were not those in the government who breached the king's peace to maintain their ascendancy in rebellion as well? If within the concept of 'crime' were included arson, pillage, and murder, could these be so easily redefined as 'vigour beyond the law' when committed by Irish authorities? If the phrase 'the Terror' evoked the bloody theatricals of a state turned upon its own citizenry, had not Ireland been subject to a terror as well?[24]

Sampson's emphasis on terminology was more than simply a flourish of his considerable rhetorical skills. It was part of a larger effort at reinterpreting the history of Ireland from the perspective of the vanquished, not the victors, an effort which in the *Memoirs* led him to a sustained examination of conditions in France in 1793 and '94 and those in Ireland in 1797 and '98. When placed in a comparative perspective, the excesses of the British in first disarming the countryside and then crushing the 'rebellion' were far worse than those carried out under the orders of the Committee for Public Safety. Only in Ireland were prisoners and members of the clergy summarily executed; only in Ireland were women regularly violated; only in Ireland did the authorities stand to gain in fortune and favour from such outrages. Yet, Sampson argued, 'every historian who has treated of them, seems more or less tinctured with the spirit of the times, and to crouch under the sentiments we deplore'. In his analysis, those rights to life, liberty and property supposedly guaranteed to all British subjects were rights systematically denied to Irishmen. In the name of upholding the constitution, the government of Ireland had, in effect, overturned it.[25]

Contrasted with John Daly Burk's enthusiastic endorsement, or with MacNeven's and Emmet's more balanced views of the alliance with France, Sampson's was heavily critical of France and the French. He made it quite clear that he had no foreknowledge of the negotiations with the Directory, an undertaking whose wisdom he seriously doubted. Nor did he wish to engage himself in the defence of the patently indefensible activities of Robespierre or Bonaparte. Like Emmet and MacNeven, Sampson much preferred his fellow Americans' efforts at employing the principles of the political philosophers to those of the French. Rather, Sampson hoped that by exposing the oppression of the Irish, and by establishing an equivalence between the two 'Reigns of Terror', he could help undermine English pretensions to moral superiority over the French and to political authority over the Irish. In so doing, he wished, as did his fellow *émigrés*, to generate a more comprehensive nationalist discourse on Irish history and identity, to recover the 'character of the Irish from English historians'. Though the terms and assumptions of these nationalist emplotments of Ireland's history might appear to be self-evident one hundred years later, their efforts at displacing the discourse of loyalism in the barren period after 1798 were ambitious undertakings.[26]

If held to late twentieth-century standards of professional historical competence and objectivity, each of these texts can, to a certain degree, be found wanting. Burk's *History*, for example, is marred by its hasty composition and by its repression of the narratives of the 'outrages' committed by Catholic against Protestant. It suffers, too, from a unilateral partisanship similar in form to the loyalist and Federalist accounts he wished to disprove. Though his mixing of genres might appeal to a literary critic concerned with the 'instability' of texts, it is an impediment to other readers. Burk's lengthy quotes and extracts from sources do lend an air of authenticity to his claims, but this evidence often reads like a legal brief. The writings of MacNeven, Emmet and Sampson can be faulted as well for their lack of balance and distance. None of these works comes close to fulfilling the promise of Emmet's prospectus. In 1841 Sampson did make emendations to the American edition of William Cooke Taylor's *History of Ireland*, but he died before he could publish his own study on the subject.[27]

However, these are not perhaps the relevant criteria with which to evaluate such texts; a more modest standard is appropriate. Miles Byrne, in his *Notes of an Irish Exile of 1798*, remarked upon the 'misfortune' of a nation unable to 'produce one historian who could boast that he was neither a place-hunter, placeman, or pensioner of the English government'. Sampson, Emmet, MacNeven and Burk were many things, but certainly not these; their histories may have been self-serving, but they were not self-interested. In his survey of the histories of Ireland in the last years of the eighteenth century, Richard Robert Madden observed that while the 'Musgraves, the Duigenans, and Reynoldses...have had their hearing', justice demanded that the men of '98 have their turn as well. While far from comprehensive, these emigrants' attempts at piecing together a shattered past did address the demands of justice and historical memory.[28]

NOTES

The following abbreviations are used below:

Arch. Hib.	*Archivium Hibernicum*
BL	British Library
BNL	*Belfast Newsletter*
Bartlett, 'Defenders'	Thomas Bartlett, 'Defenders and Defenderism in 1795', *Irish Historical Studies*, XXIV (1984–5), pp. 373–94
Beresford Corr.	*The Correspondence of…John Beresford*, William Beresford (ed.) (2 vols, London 1854)
[Bergeron & Cullen], *Culture et pratiques*	
	[Louis Bergeron & L.M. Cullen (eds)], *Culture et pratiques politiques en France et en Irlande XVI–XVIIIe siècles* (Paris 1991)
Burke Corr.	*The Correspondence of…Edmund Burke*, Thomas Copeland et al. (eds) (10 vols, Cambridge 1958–78)
Burke Works	*The Works of…Edmund Burke*, Bohn edn (8 vols, London 1883–1911)
Burke Speeches	*The Writings and Speeches of Edmund Burke*, Paul Langford et al. (eds) (Oxford 1973–[ongoing])
Castlereagh Corr.	*Correspondence of Viscount Castlereagh*, Marquis of Londonderry (ed.) (12 vols, HMC 1848–53)
Charlemont MSS	*The Manuscripts and Correspondence of James, first Earl of Charlemont* (2 vols, HMC 1891–4)
Chart, *Drennan Letters*	*The Drennan Letters*, D.A. Chart (ed.) (Belfast 1931)
Cogan, *Meath*	Anthony Cogan, *The Diocese of Meath, Ancient and Modern* (3 vols, Dublin 1862–70; reissued Dublin 1992)
Curtin, 'United Irishmen'	
	Nancy Curtin, 'The Origins of Irish Republicanism: the United Irishmen in Dublin and Ulster, 1791–98' (Ph.D. thesis, University of Wisconsin 1988)
Curtin, 'Transformation of U.I.'	
	Nancy Curtin, 'The Transformation of the United Irishmen into a Mass-Based Organization, 1794–96', *Irish Historical Studies*, XXIV (1984–5), pp. 463–92
DCHAH	Dublin City Archives, City Hall
DDA	Dublin Diocesan Archives
DEP	*Dublin Evening Post*
DNB	*Dictionary of National Biography*

D'Alton, *Archbps of Dublin*
      John D'Alton, *Memoirs of the Archbishops of Dublin* (Dublin 1838)

Elliott, *Partners*
      Marianne Elliott, *Partners in Revolution: The United Irishmen and France* (Yale 1982)

Elliott, *Tone*
      Marianne Elliott, *Wolfe Tone: Prophet of Irish Independence* (Yale 1989)

FDJ   *Faulkner's Dublin Journal*

F. Jnl   *Freeman's Journal*

Froude, *Ire.*   J.A. Froude, *The English in Ireland in the Eighteenth Century* (3 vols, London 1872–4)

Gough & Dickson, *Ire. and the Fr. Rev.*
      Hugh Gough & David Dickson (eds), *Ireland and the French Revolution* (Dublin 1990)

Hayes, *Ir. and the Fr. Rev.*
      Richard Hayes, *Ireland and Irishmen in the French Revolution* (Dublin 1932)

Hib. Chron./Hib. Jnl   *Hibernian Chronicle /Hibernial Journal*

Jnl H.C. Irl.   *Journal of the House of Commons of Ireland*

KAO   Kent Archives Office

Lecky, *Ire.*   W.E.H. Lecky, *History of Ireland in the Eighteenth Century* (5 vols, London 1892)

M. Post   *Morning Post*

McDowell, *Age of Imperialism*
      R.B. McDowell, *Ireland in the Age of Imperialism and Revolution* (Oxford 1979)

McDowell, *Public Opinion*
      R.B. McDowell, *Irish Public Opinion, 1750–1800* (London 1944)

McDowell, 'Personnel of U.I.'
      R.B. McDowell, 'The Personnel of the Dublin Society of United Irishmen', *Irish Historical Studies*, II (1940–1), pp.12–53

McDowell, 'Proceedings of U.I.'
      R.B. McDowell, 'The Proceedings of the Dublin Society of United Irishmen', *Analecta Hibernica*, XVII (1949), pp.1–143

MacNeven, *Pieces*   W.J. MacNeven, *Pieces of Irish History, Illustrative of the Condition of the Catholics...* (New York 1807)

Madden, *U.I.* (1860)   R.R. Madden, *The United Irishmen, their Lives and Times* (rev. ed., 4 vols, London 1857–60)

Madden Papers   Trinity College Dublin, MS 873, Madden Papers

Musgrave, *Rebellions*   Sir Richard Musgrave, *Memoirs of the Different Rebellions in Ireland...* (Dublin 1801)

Nat. Archives   National Archives of Ireland

New Hist. Irl. IV   T.W. Moody & W.E. Vaughan (eds), *A New History of Ireland*, IV, *Eighteenth-Century Ireland 1691–1800* (Oxford 1986)

Nat. Archives	National Archives of Ireland
NLI	National Library of Ireland
N. Star	*Northern Star*
NUI	National University of Ireland
O'Brien, *Tone Autobiography*	
	R. Barry O'Brien (ed.), *The Autobiography of Theobald Wolfe Tone, 1763–98* (2 vols, London 1893)
Pakenham, *Year of Liberty*	
	Thomas Pakenham, *The Year of Liberty: The Great Irish Rebellion of 1798* (London 1969)
PRIA	*Proceedings of the Royal Irish Academy*
PRO(L.)	Public Record Office (London)
PRONI	Public Record Office of Northern Ireland
Palmer, *Democratic Rev.*	R.R. Palmer, *The Age of Democratic Revolutions* (2 vols, Oxford 1959–64)
Parl. Reg. Irl.	*The Parliamentary Register: or, History and Debates of the House of Commons of Ireland, 1781–97* (17 vols, Dublin 1782–1801)
Rep. Comm. Sec.	*Reports of the Committees of Secrecy of the House of Commons and the House of Lords of Ireland, with appendices* (Dublin 1798)
Reb. Papers	National Archives, Rebellion Papers
SNL	*Saunder's Newsletter*
SOC	National Archives, State of the Country Papers
SRO	Scottish Record Office
Sirr Papers	Trinity College Dublin MSS 868–9, Sirr Papers
Stud. Hib.	*Studia Hibernica*
Tone, *Life*	W.T.W. Tone (ed.), *The Life of Theobald Wolfe Tone* (2 vols, Washington 1826)
Troy Papers	Dublin Diocesan Archives, Archbishop Troy Papers
TCD	Trinity College, Dublin
UCD	University College, Dublin
UJA	*Ulster Journal of Archaeology*
Woods, *Russell*	C.J. Woods (ed.), *Journals and Memoirs of Thomas Russell, 1791–5* (Dublin 1991)

Chapter 1

1. My thanks to Nicholas Canny, Steven Ellis, Gearóid Ó Tuathaigh and Niall Ó Ciosáin for advice and comments on an earlier draft of this article. My thanks also to Hiram Morgan for allowing me to see in advance of publication a copy of his article 'Hugh O'Neill and the Nine Years War in Tudor Ireland'.
2. Tone, *Life*, I, pp.51–2.
3. Cork, 1982 and New Haven & London, 1989, respectively.
4. Tom Dunne, *Theobald Wolfe Tone: Colonial Outsider* (Cork 1984), pp.16–17, 23, 47.
5. Elliott, *Tone*, pp.4, 37.

6. Ibid., pp.84, 93, 106, 128.

7. Dunne, *Colonial Outsider, passim*; Elliott, *Tone*, p.85.

8. Tom Paine, *The Rights of Man* (new ed., New York 1961), p.413. See also Tone's defensive remarks: 'I am sure a great many of us make use of those words [republicans and levellers] that do not know the meaning of them...but suppose...that these words mean everything that is wicked and abominable, still I say, what is that to us?' ('A Liberty Weaver' [Wolfe Tone], 'To the Manufacturers of Dublin' [Mar. 1793], in Tone, *Life*, I, p.370).

9. Quoted in Gordon S. Wood, *The Creation of the American Republic* (Williamsburg, Va. 1969), p.48.

10. Isaac Kramnick (ed.), *James Madison, Alexander Hamilton and John Jay: the Federalist Papers* (new ed.: London 1987), Letter no. IX: 'The Utility of the Union as a Safeguard Against Faction and Insurrection', pp.119–20.

11. J.G.A. Pocock (ed.), *The Political Works of James Harrington* (Cambridge 1977), p.113; [Hamilton], *Federalist*, no. IX, pp.120–2.

12. Kramnick, *Federalist Papers, passim*. For Montesquieu, see Judith Sklar, 'Montesquieu and the New Republicanism', in Gisele Bock, Quentin Skinner and Maurizio Vivoli (eds), *Machiavelli and Republicanism* (Cambridge 1991), p.266.

13. Tom Paine, *Common Sense*, Isaac Kramnick (ed.) (London 1986), pp.72, 95.

14. Max Lerner (ed.), *The Prince and the Discourses by Niccolo Machiavelli* (New York 1950), pp.290–6; Pocock, *Harrington Works*, pp.18, 71. And see Algernon Sidney's remark: commonwealths are 'various, according to the different tempers of nations and times...if some of them seem to have been principally constituted for war, others have much delighted in peace', and he concluded that the superiority of a republic over a monarchy lay in the fact that the former was more effective at making war (Jonathan Scott, *Algernon Sidney and the Restoration Crisis, 1677–1683* [Cambridge 1991], pp.235–6).

15. Pocock, *Harrington Works*, p.146; Wood, *Creation*, pp.53, 419.

16. Quoted in J.G.A. Pocock, *Virtue, Commerce and History* (Cambridge 1986), p.131; Pocock, *Harrington's Works*, p.148. See also, for a detailed discussion of the various strands in republican thought in the late eighteenth century, J.G.A. Pocock, *The Machiavellian Moment: Florentine Political Thought and the Atlantic Republican Tradition* (Princeton 1975).

17. Maurizio Vivoli, 'Machiavelli and the Republican Idea of Politics', in Bock et al., *Machiavelli and Republicanism*, p.155; Blair Worden, 'The Revolution of 1688–9 and the English Republican Tradition' in J.I. Israel (ed.), *The Anglo-Dutch Moment: Essays on the Glorious Revolution and its World Impact* (Cambridge 1991), p.259.

18. Wood, *Creation*, p.479.

19. Quoted in Sklar, 'Montesquieu and the New Republicanism', p.271. Madison's ideal republic, according to his editor, was 'government by representative officials as opposed to by the people themselves': Kramnick, *Federalist Papers*, p.41.

20. Quentin Skinner, 'The Republican Idea of Political Liberty', in Bock et al., *Machiavelli and Republicanism*, p.303.

21. Worden, 'English Republican Tradition', in Israel (ed.), *Anglo-Dutch*

Moment, p.245; Pocock, *Harrington's Works*, pp.298–9; Blair Worden, 'Milton's Republicanism and the Tyranny of Heaven', in Bock et al., *Machiavelli and Republicanism*, p.228; for Sidney, see Jonathan Scott's masterly *Algernon Sidney*.

22. Montesquieu was undoubtedly reacting against the 'Augustan charade' of seeing the prince as the exemplar of 'the republican virtues of selfless patriotism, abnegation of all personal inclinations in favour of the public good [and] stern repression of all ambitions other than public ones' : Sklar, 'Montesquieu and the New Republicanism', p.266; and Paine, *Rights of Man*, pp.406–11, for his attack on hereditary rule.

23. Wood, *Creation*, pp.202, 586–7.

24. Adams wrote that 'the uncorrupted British constitution is nothing more or less than a republic in which the king is first magistrate' (quoted in Wood, *Creation*, p.206). The author of *Cato's Letters* (1720) claimed that England was 'the best republic in the world with a Prince at the head of it', quoted in Worden, 'English Republic Tradition', p.264; Sklar, 'Montesquieu and the New Republicanism', p.269.

25. Cf. Wolfe Tone: 'It has always been a principle of mine that if a people choose a bad government they ought to have it for I acknowledge no foundation of empire but their choice' (Tone, *Life*, I, p.508).

26. Worden, 'English Republican Tradition', p.250.

27. Pocock, *Harrington's Works*, p.15.

28. Quoted in Wood, *Creation*, p.585.

29. James Madison, Letter no. XXXIX (Kramnick, *Federalist Papers*, p.256).

30. Quoted in Wood, *Creation*, p.263.

31. Ibid., p.570.

32. Tone, 'Reply to "The Protestant Interest in Ireland Ascertained"', in *Life*, I, p.394.

33. Dunne, *Colonial Outsider*, p.15.

34. See Caroline Robbins, *The Eighteenth-Century Commonwealthman* (New York 1968), *passim*, esp. p.174; Sean Murphy, 'Irish Republicanism before the United Irishmen (paper given to United Irish Bicentennial Conference, Dublin). On Toland, see the rather slight piece by J.G. Simms, 'John Toland (1670–1722): a Donegal heretic', in *IHS*, XVI, pp.304–20, and the remarks by Pocock, in *Harrington's Works*, pp.141–3.

35. 'Declaration and Resolutions of the Society of United Irishmen of Belfast, Oct. 1791', in Tone, *Life*, I, p.368.

36. *Life*, II, p.482. But note that Tone contemplated the confiscation, and redistribution to needy families, of land belonging to the Church of Ireland which he estimated at 30 per cent of all Irish land (*Life*, II, p.312).

37. *Life*, II, p.375; see also Wood, *Creation*, p.64.

38. Elliott, *Tone*, p.56.

39. It would not be too much to say that anti-Catholicism was a central tenet of republican thought since Machiavelli's time. See Sklar, 'Montesquieu and the New Republicanism', p.265; Scott, *Sidney, passim*; Paine, *Common Sense*, p.76; Tone, *Life*, I, p.162; II, p.161.

40. Elliott, *Tone*, p.206; Tone, *Life*, I, p.246.

41. 'For my own part', wrote Tone in 1796, 'I think it right to mention that at

this time [1791] the establishment of a republic was not the immediate object of my speculations. My object was to secure the independence of my country under any form of government': Tone, *Life*, I, p.55.

42. Tone, *Life*, II, p.498. For an up-to-date survey of sixteenth-century Ireland, see S.G. Ellis, *Tudor Ireland* (London 1985).

43. Patrick Corish, *The Origins of Catholic Nationalism: A History of Irish Catholicism*, III, fasc. viii (Dublin 1968), p.10; T.W. Moody et al. (eds.), A *New History of Ireland*, III (Oxford 1976), p.122; M. Kerney Walsh (ed.), '*Destruction by Peace': Hugh O'Neill After Kinsale* (Armagh 1986), p.4.

44. 'Answer to O. Roe O'Neill's Proposal', 27 Dec. 1627, in Brian Jennings (ed.), *Wild Geese in Spanish Flanders, 1582–1700* (Dublin 1964), pp.230–3. There is a useful discussion of this document in Tomás Ó Fiaich, 'Republicanism and Separatism in the Seventeenth Century', in *Leachtaí Cholm Cille*, IX, pp.74– 87; see also Jerrold Casway, *Owen Roe O'Neill and the Struggle for Catholic Ireland* (Philadelphia 1984), pp.33–4.

45. Ó Fiaich, 'Republicanism and Separatism', pp.82–3.

46. Cited by M. Perceval-Maxwell, 'Ireland and Scotland, 1638–48', in John Morrill (ed.), *The Scottish National Covenant in its British Context, 1635–1651* (Edinburgh 1990), p.207. For the influence of the Dutch revolt as both model and inspiration, see Hiram Morgan, 'Hugh O'Neill and the Nine Years War', *Historical Journal*, XXXVI (1993), pp.1–17.

47. Ó Fiaich, 'Republicanism and Separatism', p.85.

48. Tone, *Life*, I, p.32.

49. See Bartlett, 'The Rise and Fall of the Protestant Nation, 1690–1800', *Éire-Ireland* (Summer 1991).

50. 'Lord Holland's Memoir' in Countess of Ilchester and Lord Stavordale (eds), *The Life and Letters of Lady Sarah Lennox, 1745–1826* (2 vols, London 1901), I, p.18.

51. Tone, *Life*, I, p.551.

52. Archbp Hugh Boulter to Duke of Newcastle, 19 Jan. 1724 in *Letters Written by His Excellency, Hugh Boulter, DD* (2 vols, Dublin 1770), I, p.7.

53. Archbp Stone to Henry Pelham, 25 July 1752 in *Stopford Sackville* MSS (HMC 1904), I, p.185; Stone to Newcastle, 14 Jan. 1754, in C.L. Falkiner (ed.), 'Correspondence of Archbishop Stone and the Duke of Newcastle', *Eng. Hist. Rev.*, XX (1905), p.738.

54. Quoted in David Hayton, 'Walpole and Ireland', in Jeremy Black (ed.), *Britain in the Age of Walpole* (London 1984), p.98.

55. Even Edmund Burke – scarcely English – could claim that the mild Absentee Tax proposed by the Irish parliament would in fact lead to 'the separation and derangement of the whole contexture of this empire' (Burke to Rockingham, 29 Sept. 1773, in *Burke Corr.* II, p.468).

56. *An Inquiry into Some of the Causes of the Ill Situation of Affairs in Ireland* (Dublin 1731), p.11.

57. For Protestant nationalism in eighteenth-century Ireland, see Thomas Bartlett, '"A people made rather for copies than originals": The Anglo-Irish, 1760–1800' in *International History Review*, XII (Feb. 1990), pp.11–25.

58. Bartlett, 'Rise and Fall of the Protestant Nation'; Walpole quotation from Hayton, 'Walpole and Ireland', p.105.

59. *The Cork Surgeon's Antidote to Lucas's Poison*, no. 4 (Dublin 1749), p.6.
60. Pollock's letters are collected in John Lawless (ed.), *The Belfast Politics Enlarged* (Belfast 1818), pp.112–53. Pollock's fierce anti-English rhetoric and his demand for an end to the connection could easily make one classify him as an early Protestant separatist; but Pollock was merely a more extreme example of those radicals who wanted Ireland 'separate' from the English *parliament*, but still connected to the English *crown*.
61. Tone, 'An Argument on behalf of the Catholics of Ireland' in *Life*, I, pp.346–7.
62. See James Kelly, 'The Origins of the Act of Union: an Examination of Unionist Opinion in Britain and Ireland, 1650–1800' in *IHS*, XXV, 99 (May 1987), pp.236–63.
63. McDowell, *Public Opinion*, pp.115–16. See also Kelly, 'The Search for a Commercial Arrangement: Anglo-Irish Politics in the 1780s' (Ph.D. thesis, UCD), pp.410–14, for similar examples drawn from the Dublin press, and for similar scepticism regarding their separatist quality.
64. Tone, 'Letter to the Editor of *Faulkner's Journal*, 11 July 1793' in Tone, *Life*, I, p.500. Tone and FitzGibbon can be seen as the living embodiment of that phrase 'union or separation', and both were intensely conscious of the other's existence. The first word in Tone's published works is 'FitzGibbon', and FitzGibbon was a relative of Tone's wife, Matilda. At various points in Tone's career, his path and that of FitzGibbon crossed, and both can be seen as embittered radicals. Neither, however, had much regard for the other: Tone may have acknowledged FitzGibbon as 'at least an open and avowed enemy', but FitzGibbon was furious that Tone's execution had been postponed merely because of 'the opinion of a surgeon's mate that a man whose throat was cut could not die of hanging': Elliott, *Tone*, p.69; Tone, *Life*, II, p.468; Clare to Auckland, 26 Nov. 1798 (PRONI, T3287/7/24) – this passage from Clare's letter was omitted in the published version of the letter, presumably because of the squeamishness of the nineteenth-century editor (Bp of Bath and Wells [eds], *The Journal and Correspondence of William, Lord Auckland* [4 vols, London 1861–2], IV, p.71).
65. See D.G. Boyce, 'Separatism and the Irish National Tradition' in C.H. Williams (ed.), *National Separatism* (Cardiff 1982), pp.75–103, for a discussion of late eighteenth- and nineteenth-century Irish separatism.
66. Tone, *Life*, I, p.33. *Spanish War!* is reprinted in Tone, *Life*, I, pp.327–40. It is perhaps significant that when the demand for a separate Irish navy was raised at the time of the constitutional crisis in 1781, the British government were firmly opposed to it: Hillsborough, the Secretary of State, declared that such a suggestion 'opens a door to I cannot tell what': Hillsborough to Carlisle, 3 Dec. 1781 (PRO[L.], SP63/477/133–5).
67. Tone, 'Argument' in *Life*, I, p.359.
68. Tone's letter is reprinted in *Report from the Secret Committee of the House of Lords* (Dublin 1793), p.43.
69. Tone, 'Letter' in Tone, *Life*, I, p.499.
70. For the equation of reform with separation, see Bartlett, *The Fall and Rise of the Irish Nation: a History of the Catholic Question, 1690–1830* (Dublin 1992), pp.131, 140, 159.

71. On Drennan, see John Larkin (ed.), *The Trial of William Drennan* (Dublin 1991), and Ian MacBride, below.
72. Tone, 'Argument' in Tone, *Life*, I, pp.358–9.

Chapter 2

1. *Recherches sur la Révolution, bilan des travaux scientifiques: textes rassemblés par A. de Baecque, sous la direction de Michel Vovelle* (Paris 1991); *Les colloques du bicentenaire, présentés par Michel Vovelle, avec la collaboration de Danielle Lemonnier* (Paris 1991).
2. Roger Chartier, *Les origines culturelles de la Révolution française* (Paris 1990). More immediately relevant for this paper is Keith Michael Baker (ed.), *The French Revolution and the Creation of Modern Political Culture*, I: *The Political Culture of the Old Régime* (Oxford 1988); see the important introduction by Baker, and the review in *Annales historiques de la Révolution française* (1989); L. Hunt, *Politics, Culture and Class in the French Revolution* (California 1984), introduction; C. Mazauric, *Jacobinisme et Révolution, autour du bicentenaire* (Paris 1984).
3. *L'Image de la Révolution française* (4 vols, Oxford & Paris 1990), iv: Rapports by J. Revel and R. Chartier, *passim*.
4. On the use and significance of the word 'revolution' see Michel Peronnet, 'Les révolutions avant la Révolution' in C. Mazauric (ed.), *La Révolution française et l'homme moderne* (Paris 1990), pp.215–33.
5. See Gérard Gingembre, *La contre-Révolution ou l'histoire désespérante* (Paris 1989), and my review in *Cahiers d'Histoire de l'Institut de Recherches Marxistes*, iv (1991); also J. Tulard (ed.), *La contre-Révolution – origines, histoire, postérité* (Paris 1990).
6. F. Furet & M. Ozouf, *Dictionnaire critique de la Révolution, 1789–1799* (Paris 1989), intro. and pp.35–7; see also Antoine de Baecque in *Recherches sur la Révolution*, p.18.
7. See Vovelle in *Recherches sur la Révolution*, p.10.
8. Robert Derathe, *Jean-Jacques Rousseau et la science politique de son temps* (2nd ed., Paris 1988), pp.142ff.
9. Maurice Agulhon, *Pénitents et franc-maçons de l'ancienne Provence: essai sur la sociabilité méridionale* (Paris 1984); see in particular the methodology outlined in the preface. Also Agulhon, 'Classe ouvrière et sociabilité avant 1848', in *Histoire vagabonde: ethnologie et politique dans la France contemporaine* (Paris 1988), I, 60ff. Also Agulhon, 'D'un colloque à l'autre', in *Aux sources de la puissance, sociabilité et parenté, Colloque du GRHIS 1987* (Rouen 1989), pp.7–9; and 'Sociabilité normande' in *Etudes Normandes*, I (1991) which has a collection of articles on this whole question relating to Normandy.
10. J.J. Rousseau, *Discours sur l'origine et les fondements de l'inégalité parmi les hommes* (new edn, Paris 1964), p.156.
11. Derathé, *Rousseau*, pp.148–9.
12. *La Révolution française et les processus de socialisation de l'homme moderne: Colloque de Rouen, 1988* (Paris 1989), introduction by C. Mazauric, commentary by X. Martin, pp.11, 77.
13. See Rousseau, *Social Contract*, civ.1, ch.1; 'Kant', in *Dictionnaire critique*,

pp.1008–12.

14. Here we follow the views of Mona Ozouf, *L'Homme régénéré: essai sur la Révolution française* (Paris 1989), *passim*; and de Baecque, 'La Révolution accueille la régénération: naissance, éducation et prétention d'un nouvel homme' in *La révolution et les processus de socialisation*, pp.662–9.

15. Agulhon, *Pénitents*; N. Gauthier, P. Goujard, R. Montel, J.P. Rioux, G. Lemarchand et al., in *Sociabilité, pouvoirs et société*.

16. See the recent synthesis of Michel Winock: *1789, l'année sans pareille* (Paris 1988), esp. ch. IV.

17. G. Lefebvre, *Quatre-vingt neuf* (new ed., Paris 1988).

18. C. Mazauric, 'Sur trois champs d'étude de l'histoire politique de la Révolution', *Recherches sur la révolution*, pp.55–60.

19. On the Amis des Noirs, Y. Benot, *La Révolution et la fin des colonies* (Paris 1988); *Révolution française* (Paris 1989), p.22. On the Cordeliers Club, see J. Guilhaumou's article in ibid., p.293, and the collection *Existe-t-il un fédéralisme Jacobin?* (Paris 1986).

20. See Marcel Dorigny, 'Le cercle social' in Soboul (ed.), *Dictionnaire historique*, p.196; on the idea of 'France in revolution', see my own 'Revolutionary France, Revolutionised France, France in Revolution: for a Clarification of Rhythms and Concepts' in G. Levitine (ed.), *Culture and Revolution* (University of Maryland 1989).

21. See my 'Voies nouvelles pour l'histoire politique de la Révolution française', in *Jacobinisme et Révolution*, and 'Quelques perspectives nouvelles sur l'histoire politique de la Révolution française', forthcoming in *Recueil de l'Accademia dei Lincei*. See also the standard sources cited by de Baecque in *Recherches sur la Révolution*, p.33 fn.37; Rann Halévy & Patrice Gueniffey, 'Clubs et sociétés populaires' in Furet (ed.), *Dictionnaire critique*, p.492; and my own 'Jacobins, Jacobinisme' in Soboul (ed.), *Dictionnaire historique*, pp.585–92.

22. K. Baker, 'Politiques et opinion publique sous l'ancien régime', *Annales ESC*, XLII (1987), p.41; and *Inventing the French Revolution* (Cambridge 1990); see also Baker, Lucas & Furet (eds), *The French Revolution and the Creation of Modern Political Culture* (3 vols, Oxford 1988–90). Vol. III contains a controversial analysis of this question, relating to 1793, by Paola Viola, 'Mécanismes de formation de l'opinion publique en révolution' (pp.88–93).

23. On the decisive importance of the decree of 14 *frimaire*, see Albert Soboul, *Les sans-culottes parisiens en l'An II: mouvement populaire et gouvernement révolutionaire (2 juin 1793–9 thermidor An II)* (2nd ed., Paris 1962), 3e partie. See also my article 'Jacobins, Jacobinisme' (*loc. cit.*), and G. Maintenant, *Les Jacobins* (Paris 1984); M. Kennedy, *The Jacobin Clubs in the French Revolution: the First Years* (Princeton 1984); M. Vovelle (ed.), *Paris et la Révolution* (Paris 1989).

24. For an endorsement of this chronology of development, see Vovelle, *La mentalité révolutionnaire* (Paris 1984).

25. See my papers 'Anatomie et physiologie du Jacobinisme', and 'Dans quelle mesure peut-on parler d'un parti Jacobin?', given at Colloquia in Leipzig, October 1987 and October 1989 (A.K. Verlag 1988 & 1990); see also Michel Peronnet, *Les Jacobins du Midi* (Montpellier 1990).

26. J. Boutier & P. Boutry, 'La diffusion des sociétés politiques en France

(1789–An III): une enquête nationale', *AHRF*, III (1986); *idem*, 'Les sociétés politiques en France de 1789 à l'An III: une machine?' in *Revue d'Histoire Moderne et Contemporaine*, I (1989); *idem.*, 'La sociabilité politique en Europe et en Amérique à l'époque de la Révolution française' in *Congrès Mondial* (Actes), 1, 2, 53.

27. P. Higonnet, 'Sociability, Social Structure and the French Revolution' in *Social Research*, I (1989), p.99.

28. Danielle Pingué is completing a doctoral thesis on Jacobinism and the popular societies of Haute-Normandie (eastern Normandy); see her 'Un Jacobinisme de masse: les sociétés populaires en Haute-Normandie' in *Annales de Normandie*, II (1989); and 'Les Jacobins haut-normands face à la crise fédéraliste' in *Révolution et mouvements révolutionnaires en Normandie, actes du 24e Congrès des Sociétés Historiques et Archéologiques de Normandie* (Le Havre 1983), pp.321ff.

29. J.P. Jessenne, *Pouvoir au village et Révolution: Artois, 1760–1848* (Lille 1987).

30. Christine Peyrard, 'Peut-on parler de Jacobinisme rural?' in *La Révolution française et le monde rural* (Paris 1989); *idem*, 'La géopolitique Jacobine à l'épreuve de l'Ouest' in *AHRF*, III (1986), p.448.

31. See the acts of the conference, *Les pratiques politiques en Provence à l'époque de la Révolution française* (Montpellier 1990).

32. *Existe-t-il un fédéralisme Jacobin?* (*op. cit.*): see contributions of Dorigny, Monnier and Guilhaumou.

33. H. Gough, *The Newspaper Press in the French Revolution* (London 1989); J. D. Popkin, *Revolutionary News: the Press in France, 1789–1799* (Durham, N.C. 1990); E. Wauters, *Journaux et journalistes normands pendant la Révolution française* (Doctoral thesis, University of Rouen 1990).

34. See my article 'Jacobins, Jacobinisme' (*op. cit.*); and Boutier & Boutry, 'Sociétés politiques en France' (*op. cit.*).

35. The concept of acculturation was first raised at the XII International Congress of Historical Sciences in Vienna (1965), but has not since then attracted the interest that might have been expected. But see the proceedings of the Rouen conference, *La Révolution française et les processus de sociabilisation de l'homme moderne* (*op. cit.*).

36. M.-H. Froesle-Chopard, 'Pénitents et sociétés populaires du sud-est' in *AHRF*, III (1987), p.117; *Jacobins du midi* (*op. cit.*); E. Francois & R. Reichardt, 'Les formes de sociabilité en France du milieu du XVIIIe siècle au milieu du XIXe siècle' in *Revue d'Histoire Moderne et Contemporaine* (1987), p.452.

37. Kare Tonnesson, *La défaite des sans-culottes: mouvement populaire et révolution bourgeoise en l'An III* (Paris 1959).

38. Noted by Boutier & Boutry, 'Sociétés politiques en France' (*op. cit.*): 'Under the *ancien régime* politics was not part of collective life; on the contrary, it was expressly excluded from it...What importance, compared with the massive force (of 5,500–6,000 popular societies) had some fifty academics, several hundred reading clubs and the 850 or so masonic lodges (655 of which were linked to the Grand Orient) during the 1780s?' It should be added that many of these *ancien régime* societies, and especially masonic lodges, were dead and inactive in 1789 (see E. Saunier & C. Mazauric, 'Sur la fin de la

franc-maçonnerie normande' in *Pratiques politiques en Provence* (cited in n.31).

39. C. Mazauric, *Robespierre: écrits* (Paris 1989).

40. Hannah Arendt, *Essai sur la Révolution* (Paris 1963); Mazauric, 'La terreur: un compromis légaliste' in M.J. Vellaverde (ed.), *Alcance y Legado de la Revolucion francese* (Madrid 1989).

41. Rossitze Tacheva, 'Recherches sur les membres du club des Jacobins de Paris (Sept. 1792 – thermidor An II)' in *Etudes Balkaniques*, III (1988), pp.40–53; idem., *Les Jacobins dans la Révolution française (1789–1794)* (Sofia 1989).

42. Francoise Brunel, 'Images et approches des Montagnards: une histoire de la montagne est-elle possible?' in *L'image de la Révolution française*, I, 10, 504–11; see also her article in A. Soboul (ed.), *Girondins et Montagnards* (Paris 1975).

43. For Gramsci, see *Dialectique*, nos 4–5, 1974 (articles by C. Buci-Gluckman, H. Portelli, L. Gruppi); also *Gramsci dans le texte* (Paris 1975); C. Buci-Gluckman, *Gramsci et l'état* (Paris 1975), pp.145–52; A. Tosel (ed.), *Gramsci: textes* (Paris 1983).

44. K. Holzapfel & M. Middell (eds), *Die Franzosische Revolution 1789 – Geschichte und Wirkung* (Berlin 1989).

45. On 7 July 1917 Lenin wrote in *Pravda*: 'Twentieth-century Jacobinism would be the domination of the revolutionary class of the proletariat which, on the shoulders of the impoverished peasantry, would be able to achieve what eighteenth-century Jacobins did, in the way of great and indestructible acts': *Œuvres* (Paris 1957), XXV.

46. See Boutier, 'Les sociétés politiques', and my 'Jacobins, Jacobinisme'. See also Mona Ozouf, *L'Ecole de la France* (Paris 1984); F. Furet, *Penser la Révolution française* (Paris 1978), esp. 'Augustin Cochin: la théorie du Jacobinisme'.

47. A. Soboul, *La Révolution française* (Paris 1989), p.331.

48. As far as the French Revolution goes, Francoise Brunel has revised the idea of 'party', which French historiography has shied away from using since the first analyses made by Albert Mathiez; but she uses the term less in the sense of the creation of a political sociology and a structure of sociability than in the sense of the internal workings of opinion formation and group discipline within the National Convention (see her 'Partis politiques en révolution', *La Pensée*, ccxlvi [1985], p.113; and 'Les moments de la Révolution française et la synthèse politique' in *Recherches*, p.49). What we are considering here is different, and would lead us to take into consideration other groupings which often intermix, such as Jacobins, members of the 'Mountain', Robespierristes, etc., depending on whether we are analysing the upper or the lower levels of political sociability, or the heart or the periphery of the 'public space' of political communication – to use the formula of Habermas.

49. Raymond Huard, *La préhistoire des partis: le mouvement républicain en Bas-Languedoc, 1848–1881* (Paris 1982); see especially the bibliography (which I have used extensively here), pp.466–82.

50. Alphone Aulard (in 'La législation des clubs pendant la Révolution', published in *La Révolution française*, XII [1889], pp.255–67) was the first to publish basic texts and to produce an analysis of this attitude, hostile as it was to the development of an organised political sociability and seen as hostile to the self-determination of the sovereign people. His analysis has been taken

up by many authors since.

51. A term used by Michelet, cited in Boutier & Boutry, 'Les sociétés politiques', fn.19.

52. See my article in *Dictionnaire historique*, p.585, and the article 'Sans-culottes, sans-culotterie' in ibid., p.957.

Chapter 3

1. Cf, pp.59, 217.
2. R.L. Marshall, *Maghera in '98* (n.p., n.d.), pp.174–8.
3. A.T.Q. Stewart, 'The Transformation of Irish Presbyterianism in the North of Ireland, 1792–1825' (unpublished MA thesis, QUB 1956); Brendan Clifford, *Belfast in the French Revolution* (Belfast 1989), pp.139–44; R.F.G. Holmes, 'United Irishmen and Unionists: Irish Presbyterians 1791 and 1886', *Studies in Church History*, XXXV (1989), pp.171–89.
4. W.H. Crawford, 'Economy and Society in Eighteenth-Century Ulster' (unpublished Ph.D., QUB 1982), pp.101–13.
5. Peter Brooke, *Ulster Presbyterianism: the Historical Perspective* (Belfast 1987), pp.70–9.
6. Ibid., p.70.
7. W.D. Bailie, 'Rev. Samuel Barber, 1738–1811...' in J. Haire (ed.), *Challenge and Conflict...* (Antrim 1981), pp.79–80.
8. W.T. Latimer, *A History of Irish Presbyterians* (Belfast 1893), p.379.
9. Brooke, *Presbyterianism*, p.113.
10. H.A. Landsberger, *Rural Protest: Peasant Movements and Social Change* (London 1974), pp.7, 14.
11. Brooke, *Presbyterianism*, p.12.
12. Holmes, 'Irish Presbyterians', p.175.
13. Brooke, *Presbyterianism*, p.107.
14. Latimer, *History of Presbyterians*, pp.366–7.
15. D.W. Miller, 'Presbyterianism and "Modernization" in Ulster' in C.H. Philbin (ed.), *Nationalism and Popular Protest in Ireland* (Cambridge 1987), p.96.
16. Ibid., p.94.
17. J.M. Barkley, 'The Presbyterian Minister in the Eighteenth Century' in *Church and Change*, pp.48–9.
18. See Crawford, 'Ulster Economy', chaps 2, 3.
19. E.J. Hobsbawm, *Bandits* (Manchester 1972), p.22; ibid., *Rural Protest: Social Banditry* (London 1974), p.149.
20. David Dickson, *New Foundations: Ireland, 1660–1800* (Dublin 1987), pp.135–6; Pieter Tesch, 'Rural Unrest in Eighteenth-Century Ireland' (unpublished MA thesis, Universiteit van Amsterdam 1987), chaps 2, 3, 4; Anthony Canavan, 'Hearts of Steel' (unpublished MA thesis, QUB 1982); J.S. Donnelly, 'Hearts of Oak, Hearts of Steel' in *Studia Hib.*, XXI (1981).
21. See Tesch, 'Rural Unrest', and Donnelly, 'Hearts', *passim*.
22. See Dickson, *New Foundations*, p.143; also Tesch, 'Rural Unrest', chap. 3; Canavan, 'Hearts of Steel', *passim*; W.A. Maguire, 'Lord Donegall and the Hearts of Steel' in *IHS*, XXI, 84 (1979), pp.351–76.

23. Dickson, *New Foundations*, p.143.
24. Latimer, *History of Presbyterians*, pp.359–60.
25. W.H. Crawford and B. Trainor, *Aspects of Irish Social History, 1750–1800* (Belfast 1969), pp.163–5.
26. Latimer, *History of Presbyterians*, p.361.
27. PRONI, Abercorn Papers, T2541/1A2/22/76.
28. Ibid., T2541/1A2/2/105.
29. Ibid., T2541/1A2/2/128.
30. Latimer, *History of Presbyterians*, pp.366–7.
31. PRONI, Pelham Transcripts, T2627/6/2/4.
32. Samuel Barber, MS sermon on Revelations 18:20 (in possession of the Presbyterian Historical Society, Belfast).
33. W.D. Bailie, *William Steel Dickson, DD* (Belfast 1976), p.14; Miller, 'Presbyterianism', p.94.
34. McDowell, *Age of Imperialism*, pp.427–9; Bailie, *Dickson*, p.15.
35. J. Gebbie, *An Introduction to the Abercorn Letters* (Omagh 1972), pp.175–6.
36. Bailie, *Dickson*, p.16; Clifford, *Belfast*, p.4; Brooke, *Presbyterianism*, pp.119, 124–5, 126–7; Holmes, 'Irish Presbyterians', p.181.

Chapter 4

1. Drennan to Samuel McTier, *c.*Nov. 1791, in Chart, *Drennan Letters*, p.64; Drennan to McTier, 28 Jan. 1792 PRONI, Drennan Papers, T765/321a; A.T.Q. Stewart, '"A Stable Unseen Power": Dr William Drennan and the Origins of the United Irishmen' in John Bossy and Peter Jupp (eds), *Essays Presented to Michael Roberts* (Belfast 1976), pp.80–92. The idea of an oath-bound association within the Volunteers was first suggested in [William Drennan], *An Address to the Volunteers by the Author of a Letter to Edmund Burke* (Dublin 1781).
2. Drennan to Samuel McTier, 21 May 1791, in Chart, *Drennan Letters*, p.54. The 'Brotherhood' paper can be found in *Rep. Comm. Sec.*, App. iv, pp.l–lvi.
3. 'Intended Defence', reprinted in John Larkin (ed.), *The Trial of William Drennan* (Dublin 1991), pp.124–5. Drennan later maintained that the defence had contributed to his acquittal: Drennan to Martha McTier, 21 Mar. 1806, in Chart, *Drennan Letters*, p.356.
4. Drennan to Martha McTier, 1 Dec. 1791, ibid., p.100.
5. *Belfast Monthly Magazine*, X (1813), p.152.
6. Caroline Robbins, *The Eighteenth-Century Commonwealthman* (Cambridge, Mass. 1959), pp.168–76.
7. For civic humanism see J.G.A. Pocock, *Virtue, Commerce and History* (Cambridge 1985), but also Isaac Kramnick, 'Republican Revisionism Revisited' in *American Historical Review*, LXXXVII (1982), pp.629–64.
8. James MacKay, *The Happiness of the Righteous in a Future State* (Belfast 1768), contains some biographical information.
9. I.M. Bishop, 'The Education of Ulster Students at Glasgow University during the Eighteenth Century' (unpublished MA thesis, Queen's University of Belfast 1987), pp.31–2. See also James and Samuel McConnell, *Fasti of the Irish Presbyterian Church, 1613–1840*, David Stewart (ed.) (Belfast 1951); W.

Innes Addison, *The Matriculation Albums of the University of Glasgow* (Glasgow 1913).

10. See Classon Porter, *The Seven Bruces* (repr. from the *Northern Whig*, Belfast 1885).

11. In addition to Abernethy's *Personal Persuasion*, see Samuel Haliday, *Reasons Against the Imposition of Subscription to the Westminster Confession of Faith* (Belfast 1724), and James Kirkpatrick, *A Defence of Christian Liberty* (Belfast 1743). For an account of the subscription controversy, see J.S. Reid, *History of the Presbyterian Church in Ireland* (3 vols, Belfast 1867), III, pp.110–211.

12. John Abernethy, *Persecution Contrary to Christianity* (Dublin 1735), p.25.

13. Abernethy, *Religious Obedience*, p.12.

14. John Abernethy, *Scarce and Valuable Tracts and Sermons* (London 1751).

15. James Duchal to William Bruce, 1 Oct. 1742, quoted in Thomas Dix Hincks, 'Notices of William Bruce, and of his Contemporaries and Friends, Hutcheson, Abernethy, Duchal and Others' in *Christian Teacher* (London 1843), new ser., V, pp.72–92.

16. Hincks, 'Notices of William Bruce', p.79.

17. Drennan to Martha McTier, *c.*Feb. 1796 and *c.*Oct. 1799, in Chart, *Drennan Letters*, pp.232, 293.

18. William Campbell, *The Presence of Christ with his Church in Every Age and Period of it, Explained and Improved* (Belfast 1774), esp. p.34.

19. Samuel Barber, MS sermon on Revelations 18:20 (in possession of the Presbyterian Historical Society, Belfast).

20. *Belfast Monthly Magazine*, VI (1811), p.496; Drennan, *Letters of Orellana, an Irish Helot* (Dublin 1785).

21. For a study of Hutcheson's life and teaching, see W.R. Scott, *Francis Hutcheson* (Cambridge 1900).

22. Hutcheson to Thomas Steward, 12 Feb. 1740 (Magee College, Derry, MS 46, Steward correspondence, 279f.); John Hill Burton (ed.), *The Autobiography of Dr Alexander Carlyle of Invernesk* (London 1910), p.94; William Hamilton (ed.), *The Collected Works of Dugald Stewart* (10 vols, Edinburgh 1854), X, p.105.

23. See James Moore, 'The Two Systems of Francis Hutcheson: on the Origins of the Scottish Enlightenment' in M.A. Stewart (ed.), *Studies in the Philosophy of the Scottish Enlightenment* (Oxford 1990), pp.37–59; Knud Haakonssen, 'Natural Law and Moral Realism: the Scottish Synthesis', ibid., pp.61–85.

24. Francis Hutcheson, *A System of Moral Philosophy* (2 vols, Glasgow & London 1755), II, pp.117–40.

25. Hutcheson, *System*, II, pp.270–7.

26. Samuel Kenrick to James Wodrow, 28 June 1794 (Dr Williams Library, London, Wodrow/Kenrick Correspondence, MS 24, 157, no. 192).

27. In addition to Robbins, *Commonwealthman*, see Pocock, 'Machiavelli, Harrington and English Political Ideologies in the Eighteenth Century' in *William and Mary Quarterly*, 3rd ser., XXII (1965), pp.549–83, for his original treatment of Harrington, since expanded in countless articles. William Bruce published an Irish edition of Harrington, together with another Commonwealthman classic by Henry Neville, in 1737: see *The Oceana of James Harrington esq. and his Other Works: with an Account of his Life Prefixed, by*

John Toland. To which is Added Plato Redivivus, or, a Discourse Concerning Government (Dublin 1737). Many Presbyterian ministers can be found among the subscribers.

28. James Arbuckle to Molesworth, 31 Oct. 1722, 13 Feb 1723, in *Report on Manuscripts in Various Collections*, VIII (HMC 1913), pp.351–2, 354–5. See also the letters from William Wishart and George Turnbull, ibid., pp.347–9, 352, 360–1, 366–7. Arbuckle is discussed in M.A. Stewart, 'John Smith and the Molesworth Circle' in *Eighteenth-Century Ireland*, II (1987), pp.89–102.

29. Drennan to Bruce, Mar. 1787 (PRONI, Drennan/Bruce Papers, D553/80).

30. [Henry Joy], *Historical Collections Relative to the Town of Belfast* (Belfast 1817), pp.100, 110.

31. For a rare exception, see Drennan's editorial in *Belfast Monthly Magazine*, XI (1813), p.148, and the biographical sketch of Hutcheson in the same issue, pp.110–14; D.F. Norton, 'Francis Hutcheson in America' in *Studies in Voltaire and the Eighteenth Century*, CLXIV (1976), pp.1547–68; James L. McAllister, jun., 'Francis Alison and John Witherspoon: Political Philosophers and Revolutionaries' in *Journal of Presbyterian History*, LIV (1976), pp.33–60.

32. William Bruce, 'The Progress of Non-Subscription' in *Christian Moderator*, II (1827), p.350.

33. Hutcheson to Drennan, 17 April 1738 (Queen's University, Belfast Library, MIC/B39); Bruce to Hutcheson, 9 Feb. 1737, 15 May 1738 (National Library of Scotland, MS 9252, Dunlop Papers, 106ff., 125).

34. Hutcheson to Lord Minto, 4 July 1744 (NLS, Minto papers, MS 11,004, 57f.).

35. Alexander Haliday to William Bruce, 27 Mar. 1754 (PRONI, Bruce Papers, T3041/1/D4).

36. [William Bruce], *Some Facts and Observations Relative to the Fate of the Late Linen Bill, Last Session of Parliament in this Kingdom* (Dublin 1753); [*idem*], *Remarks on a Pamphlet Entitled Considerations on the Late Bill for Paying the National Debt, etc.* (Dublin 1754).

37. *Advice to the Patriot Club of the County of Antrim* (Dublin 1756), p.14. See also *A Layman's Sermon, Preached at the Patriot Club of the County of Armagh, which Met at Armagh, the 3rd of Sept. 1755* (Dublin 1755); *Remarks on a Pamphlet Entitled, Advice to the Patriot Club of the County of Antrim* (Dublin 1756); *Will. Bruce's Ghost which Appeared Last Night, and Held the Following Dialogue with a Certain Eminent Politician* (n.d., n.p.).

38. A copy of the inscription can be found in PRONI, Bruce Papers D2673/2/1. This is probably the copy owned by Drennan: see Drennan to Martha McTier, 9 Aug. 1805 (Drennan Papers, T765/1174).

39. Alexander Haliday, 'Brutus, a Monody to the Memory of Mr Bruce' in *Monthly Review*, XIV (1756), pp.351–6.

40. [Gabriel Cornwall], *An Essay on the Character of the Late Mr William Bruce* (Dublin 1755), p.11.

41. James Bruce to William Bruce (n.d. *c.*1753), 15 July, 12 Nov. 1753, Bruce Papers, D2673/1/14–16).

42. Maclaine to Samuel Bruce, n.d. (PRONI, Bruce Papers, D2673). Hutcheson's *Short Introduction to Moral Philosophy* (Glasgow 1742) was commonly

referred to as the 'Compend'.

43. For Hutcheson's supervision of Irish students, see Hutcheson to Thomas Drennan, 31 Jan. 1737, 27 Feb. 1738, 1 June 1741 (QUB, MIC/B39).

44. Kenrick to Wodrow, 28 June 1794, 22 Mar. 1794 (DWL, Kenrick/Wodrow correspondence, MS 24, 157, nos 188, 192). Ironically the Scottish radical Thomas Muir was arrested for reading Drennan's 'Address from the Society of United Irishmen in Dublin to the Delegates for Promoting a Reform in Scotland'.

45. James Wodrow to the Earl of Buchan, 4 May 1808 (Mitchell Library, Glasgow, MS Baillie 32, 59–60ff., 225); see also *Autobiography of Dr Alexander Carlyle*, p.78.

46. Donald Winch, *Adam Smith's Politics* (Cambridge 1978), p.42; William Steele Dickson, *A Narrative of the Confinement and Exile of William Steele Dickson* (Dublin 1812), pp.3–5.

47. See Richard B. Sher, 'Professors of Virtue: the Social History of the Edinburgh Moral Philosophy Chair in the Eighteenth Century' in Stewart, *Philosophy of the Scottish Enlightenment*, pp.87–126.

48. According to Stewart, 'the metaphysical philosophy of Scotland, and, indeed, the literary taste in general, which so remarkably distinguished this country during the last century, may be dated from the lectures of Dr Francis Hutcheson in the University of Glasgow': *Collected Works*, X, p.428.

49. W. Crawford, *Regulations of the Strabane Academy and an Address to the Students in General* (Strabane 1785), *passim*.

50. Records of the Presbytery of Antrim, II, pp.37–8, and *passim* (PRONI, T1053/1).

51. Other authorities mentioned in the 'Intended Defence' include Locke, Priestley and Price.

52. See n.2.

53. Drennan to Samuel McTier, 1 Sept. 1793, in Chart, *Drennan Letters*, p.171.

54. See, for example, Drennan to Samuel McTier, 3 July 1791 (Drennan Papers, T765/303).

55. Drennan to William Bruce [early Nov. 1791] (PRONI, Drennan/Bruce Papers, D553/72).

Chapter 5

1. W.H. Crawford, 'Change in Ulster in the Late Eighteenth Century' in T. Bartlett and D.W. Hayton (eds), *Penal Era and Golden Age* (Belfast 1979), p.194; W.H. Crawford, *Domestic Industry in Ireland...* (Dublin 1972), pp.78–80.

2. P.J. Corfield, *The Impact of English Towns, 1700–1800* (Oxford 1982), p.1. See also C. Shammas, *The Pre-Industrial Consumer in England and America* (Oxford 1990), especially p.8.

3. G. Benn, *A History of the Town of Belfast* (London 1877), p.535.

4. P. Roebuck, 'The Donegall Family and the Development of Belfast, 1600–1850' in P. Butel and L.M. Cullen (eds), *Cities and Merchants...* (Dublin 1986), pp.132–3.

5. C.E.B. Brett, *Buildings of Belfast* (London 1967), pp.2–8.

6. *First Report of the Commissioners Appointed to Inquire into the Municipal Corporations in Ireland, Appendix*, Part I (H.C. 1835, XXVIII), 695–740; see Introduction by W.H. Crawford to W.H. Crawford and Peter Brooke (eds), *Problems of a Growing City: Belfast, 1780–1870* (Belfast 1973).
7. *Charlemont MSS*, II, p.58.
8. 40 Geo. III, *c*.37.
9. See S. Nenadic, 'The Rise of the Urban Middle Class' in T.M. Devine and R. Mitchison (eds), *People and Society in Scotland, I: 1760–1830* (Edinburgh 1988), ch. 6; P. Earle, *The Making of the English Middle Class* (London 1989); P. Borsay, *The English Urban Renaissance* (Oxford 1989).
10. G. Chambers, *Faces of Change: the Belfast and Northern Ireland Chambers of Commerce and Industry, 1783–1983* (Belfast 1984), chapters 3 and 4, based on N.E. Gamble, 'The Business Community and Trade of Belfast, 1767–1800' (unpublished Ph.D. thesis, University of Dublin 1978); T. Truxes, *Irish-American Trade, 1660–1783* (Cambridge 1988), pp.114–5, 119–20.
11. *BNL*, 2 Jan. 1776.
12. McDowell, *Age of Imperialism*, p.262.
13. P.D.H. Smyth, 'The Volunteers and Parliament, 1779–84' in Bartlett and Hayton, *Penal Era and Golden Age*, p.116.
14. Ibid., p.125.
15. S. Millin, *Sidelights on Belfast History* (Belfast 1932), p.5.
16. A. McClelland, 'Amyas Griffith' in *Irish Booklore*, II, 1 (Spring 1972).
17. [H. Joy], *Historical Collections Relative to the Town of Belfast* (Belfast 1817), p.233.
18. W.H. Crawford, 'Ulster Landowners and the Linen Industry' in J.T. Ward and R.G. Wilson (eds), *Land and Industry* (Newton Abbot 1971), pp.131–3. This struggle can be followed through the *BNL* files.
19. 'Anonymous Letter in Aug. 1782 from the North Threatening Me' (PRONI, Foster Papers D207/28/101).
20. *BNL*, 19 Nov. 1782, reporting resolutions adopted at Lisburn on 29 Oct. 1782.
21. Letter from Edward and Isaac Corry, Newry, to the *BNL*, dated 9 November 1782 and published in subsequent issues.
22. *BNL*, 29 November 1782.
23. 3 Geo. III, *c*.34. See also W.H. Crawford, 'The Evolution of the Linen Trade in Ulster before Industrialisation', *Irish Economic and Social History*, XV (1988), pp.39–40.
24. *BNL*, 21 Jan. 1783, letter from 'A Northern Draper', replying to letter from 'Reason and Common Sense' in earlier issue.
25. *London-Derry Journal*, 17 Dec. 1782.
26. *BNL*, advertisement dated 18 May 1785 and published in subsequent issues; S. Millin, 'Eighteenth-Century Banks' in *Sidelights*, pp.13–27.
27. Chambers, *Faces of Change*, pp.107–20.
28. R.B. McDowell, 'The Late Eighteenth Century' in J.C. Beckett and R.E. Glasscock (eds), *Belfast: the Origin and Growth of an Industrial City* (London 1967), p.61.
29. Smyth, 'Volunteers and Parliament', p.133.
30. Joy, *Historical Collections*, pp.329–31.

31. Ibid., pp.334–42.
32. Ibid., note on p.353.
33. Ibid,. p.358.
34. Ibid., p.364.
35. Ibid, p.365.
36. Tone, *Life*, I, pp.149–50.
37. McDowell, *Age of Imperialism*, pp.551–4.
38. Ibid., pp.557–62.
39. Ibid., pp.569–70.
40. Ibid., pp.589.
41. S. McSkimin, *Annals of Ulster*, E.J. McCrum (ed.) (Belfast 1906), p.54.
42. J.S. Donnelly, 'Hearts of Oak, Hearts of Steel', *Studia Hibernica*, XXI (1981), p.38.

Chapter 6

1. Coghill to Southwell, 21 Sept. 1727 (BL, Southwell Papers, Add. MS 21,122, 33f.; King to Southwell, 12 Sept. 1727 (TCD, King Papers, MS 750/9, 19f.).
2. *Universal Advertiser*, 8 Nov., 6, 9 Dec. 1760.
3. E. Snoddy, 'Some Notes on Parliament and its Limerick Members, 1767–71' in *North Munster Antiquarian Journal*, IX (1962–5), p.169; *F. Jnl*, 12 Nov. 1763, 26 May 1764, 20 May 1766, 2 May 1767.
4. *F. Jnl*, 20 May 1766, 13 Jan., 10 Feb. 1767; *Pue's Occurrences*, 21 Oct. 1769.
5. *Pue's Occ.*, 6 Aug. 1768, 2 Dec. 1769; Bernard Bailyn, *The Ideological Origins of the American Revolution* (Harvard 1967).
6. *Hib. Jnl*, 7 Feb. 1772, 21 April, 30 Oct., 13 Nov., 1773, 3, 5 Jan. 1774, 20 June 1777; James Kelly, 'Napper Tandy: Radical and Republican' in J. Kelly and Uáitéar MacGearailt (eds), *Dublin and Dubliners: Essays in the History and Literature of Dublin City* (Dublin 1990), pp.2–3.
7. *Finn's Leinster Journal*, 3, 27 Nov. 1773, 11 May 1774; 1 Nov., 27 Dec. 1773, 9 Feb., 2, 4, 25 Mar., 21 Oct. 1774.
8. *Hib. Jnl*, 25 Mar., 6 July, 7, 21 Oct., 12 Dec.; *FLJ*, 11 May, 25 June, 19 Nov., 2 Dec. 1774.
9. *FLJ*, 14 Jan.; *Hib. Jnl*, 16 Jan. 1775.
10. *Hib. Jnl*, 30 May, 1 July 1774, 20 Jan., 13 Feb., 17 May, 16 July, 16 Aug. 1775; *FLJ*, 28 Oct. 1775, 6 July 1776; G.O. Sayles, 'Contemporary Sketches of the Members of the Irish Parliament in 1782' in *PRIA*, LVI, C (1954), p.233.
11. *FLJ*, 15 Mar. 1775, 17 Feb. 1776; *Hib. Jnl*, 12 Dec. 1774, 3 July 1776; Sayles 'Contemporary Sketches', p.246.
12. *Hib. Jnl*, 9 July 1777, 21 Dec. 1781.
13. David Dickson, *New Foundations: Ireland 1660–1800* (Dublin 1987), p.152; W.R. Hutchinson, *Tyrone Precinct* (Belfast 1951), pp.97–8.
14. Oliver Snoddy, 'The Volunteers...of County Waterford' in *An Cosantóir*, XXXV (1975), p.342; *idem*, 'Notes on the Volunteers...of County Cavan' in *Breifne*, III (1968), p.327; *idem*, 'Notes on the Volunteers...of County Roscommon' in *Irish Sword*, XII (1975–6), p.26; J. Mitchell, 'Colonel William Persse' in *Journal of the Galway Archaeological and Historical Society*,

XXX (1963), pp.60–1; Hutchinson, *Tyrone Precinct*, p.99.

15. *Memoirs of R.L. Edgeworth* (2 vols, London 1820), II, pp.48–50; Jebb to Dobbs, 27 Jan. 1783 (NLI, Dobbs Papers, MS 2,251, 138–41ff.); John Larkin (ed.), *The Trial of William Drennan* (Dublin 1991), pp.126–7.
16. *DEP*, 15 Feb., 25 Mar. 1783; *A Letter to Henry Flood on the Present State of Representation in Ireland* (Belfast 1783), p.20; *Arguments to Prove the Interposition of the People to be Constitutional and Strictly Legal* (Dublin 1783), pp.13–17, 20.
17. *Jnl H.C. Irl*, X, p.378; XI, p.197; *DEP*, 17 Apr. 1783.
18. Larkin, *Drennan*, pp.126–7; *Proceedings Relative to the Ulster Assembly of Volunteer Delegates* (Belfast 1783), pp.1–4.
19. The correspondence of the Committee of Correspondence can be found in the Joy Papers, Linenhall Library, Belfast; see also *Proceedings...Ulster Assembly*, p.26ff.
20. James Kelly, 'The Irish Parliamentary Reform Movement: the Administration and Popular Politics, 1783–5' (MA thesis, NUI [UCD] 1981), pp.45–58.
21. *Proceedings...Ulster Assembly*, pp.7–14; *Charlemont MSS*, I, pp.116–18; *History of the Proceedings and Debates of the Volunteer Delegates of Ireland* (Dublin 1784), pp.16–26.
22. Drennan to Bruce, 30 Oct. 1783 (PRONI, Drennan-Bruce Papers, D553, no. 16); Chart, *Drennan Letters*, no. 17; James Kelly, 'The Parliamentary Reform Movement and the Catholic Question' in *Arch. Hib.*, XLIII (1988), pp.101–03; Lord John Russell (ed.), *Memorials and Correspondence of Charles James Fox* (4 vols, London 1853–7), II, pp.204–6.
23. *History of...Volunteer Delegates*, pp.48–52.
24. *Charlemont MSS*, I, pp.126–7; *Edgeworth's Memoirs*, II, pp.63–4; Kelly, 'Parliamentary Reform', pp.98–100.
25. Kelly, 'Parliamentary Reform', pp.100–33.
26. Kelly, 'Parliamentary Reform', pp.126–32, 160–79; James Kelly, 'Scarcity and Poor Relief in Eighteenth-Century Ireland: the Subsistence Crisis of 1782–4' in *IHS*, XLVIII (1992), pp.38–62; L.S. Benjamin (ed.), *The Windham Papers* (2 vols, London 1913), I, pp.73–4.
27. *Volunteer Journal* (Dublin), 9 June 1784; *DEP*, 10 June 1784.
28. 'Address to the People of Ireland from the Citizens of Dublin' (Oireachtais Library, Dublin, MS 8 H 10).
29. William Todd Jones, *A letter to the Electors of the Borough of Lisburn* (Dublin 1784), pp.48–55; Kelly, 'Parliamentary Reform', pp.212–8, 235–6.
30. Kelly, 'Parliamentary Reform', pp.285–90.
31. Bruce to Joy, 7 Oct. 1784 (Joy Papers, MS 14/19); Tandy to Tandy, 20 Oct. 1784 (PRO[L.], Chatham Papers, 30/8/330, 262f.).
32. Kelly, 'Parliamentary Reform', pp.285–90.
33. *Letters of Orellana, an Irish Helot to the Seven Northern Counties not Represented in the National Assembly of Delegates...* (Dublin 1785).
34. Kelly, 'Parliamentary Reform', pp.302–16; Drennan to Bruce, — Mar., 13 April (Drennan-Bruce Letters, nos 38, 40); *Parl. Reg. Irl.*, V, pp.150–65, 188–96; Rutland to Sydney, 14 May 1785 (PRO[L.], HO100/16, 362–3ff.).
35. W.R. Anson (ed.), *Autobiography and Political Correspondence of Augustus... Duke of Grafton* (London 1898), p.391; Orde to Pitt, 16 Aug., Pitt to Orde,

25 Sept. (NLI, Bolton Papers, MS 16, 355, 1–4ff., 33–6); Fitzgibbon to Eden, 29 Aug. 1784 (PRONI, T3229/1/2).

36. *Charlemont MSS*, I, p.136.

37. James Kelly, 'The Genesis of Protestant Ascendancy' in Gerard O'Brien (ed.), *Parliament, Politics and People* (Dublin 1989), pp.93–127; A.T.Q. Stewart, '"A Stable Unseen Power": William Drennan and the Origins of the United Irishmen' in John Bossy and Peter Jupp (eds), *Essays Presented to Michael Roberts* (Belfast 1976), pp.84–7.

38. McDowell, 'Personnel of U.I.', pp.12–53; Simon Davies, 'The *Northern Star* and the Propagation of Enlightened Ideas' in *Eighteenth-Century Ireland*, V (1990), p.148; Henry Joy, *Belfast Politics* (Belfast 1794), pp.130–5.

Chapter 7

1. R.B. McDowell, 'The Age of the United Irishmen' in *New Hist. Ire.: IV*, p.325.

2. J.T. and R. Gilbert (eds), *Calendar of Ancient Records of the City of Dublin* [*CARD*] (Dublin 1889–1944), XIV, pp.241, 243. Recent studies of the genesis and significance of the term 'Protestant ascendancy' are conveniently reviewed in James Kelly, 'Eighteenth-Century Ascendancy: A Commentary', *Eighteenth-Century Ireland*, V (1990), pp.173–87.

3. In the 1760s and 70s the guilds had lost the campaign to give statutory force to their historic claims to regulate the work of all who followed the handicraft trades in Dublin and certain other towns (see Maureen MacGeehin Wall, 'The Catholics of the Towns and the Quarterage Dispute in Eighteenth-Century Ireland', *IHS*, VIII [1952], pp.91–114). But their members were still for the most part associated with trade, and checking of guild representatives on the city commons in 1790 against trade directories reveals that at least four-fifths still followed the trade represented by their guild.

4. DCACH, Journal of the Sheriffs and Commons, 1791–5, pp.18–20; *Hib. Jnl*, 25 Jan. 1792.

5. There were two men named Binns in the city commons 1792; since George Binns was a United Irishman it seems reasonable to assume that he was the speaker in this case. Information on membership of the United Irishmen has been taken from McDowell, 'Personnel of U.I.', pp.12–53.

6. *Hib. Jnl*, 25 Jan. 1792.

7. Burke's response is discussed in W.J. Mc Cormack, *Ascendancy and Tradition in Anglo-Irish Literary History from 1789 to 1939* (Oxford 1985), pp.77–81.

8. *CARD*, XIV, pp.251, 284–7; *Dublin Chronicle*, 21 Jan 1792; *M. Post*, 21 Jan. 1792.

9. *M. Post*, 16 Mar. 1792. Note that admiration for King William (and hence the colour Orange) had not yet been entirely renounced by the Dublin radicals, and consequently was not available to be used exclusively by 'ascendancy' activists. See Jacqueline R. Hill, 'National Festivals, the State, and "Protestant Ascendancy" in Ireland, 1790–1829', *IHS*, XXIV (1984), pp.35–7.

10. Poor quality microfilm has meant that estimates of the total of votes cast vary by one or two, *DEP*, 21 Apr. 1792. The report in the commons' journal only

gives the votes of the successful candidates: DCACH, Jnl Sheriffs & Commons, 1791–5, p.27.

11. *M. Post*, 14 April 1792.

12. For the content of these ideologies, see J.G.A. Pocock, *The Ancient Constitution and the Feudal Law* (Cambridge 1957); *idem, The Machiavellian Moment: Florentine Political Thought and the Atlantic Republican Tradition* (Princeton & London 1975), chaps 11, 12; J.A.W. Gunn, *Beyond Liberty and Property: the Process of Self-Recognition in Eigteenth-Century Political Thought* (Kingston & Montreal 1983), chap. 1.

13. Nicholas Rogers, *Whigs and Cities* (Oxford 1989), chap. 1.

14. Charles Lucas, *Divilena Libera: an Apology for the Rights and Liberties of the Commons and Citizens of Dublin* (Dublin 1744), pp.17–26.

15. Lucas, *A Remonstrance Against Certain Infringements on the Rights and Liberties of the Commons and Citizens of Dublin* (Dublin 1743), pp.36–7. On Lucas's campaign see Sean Murphy, 'The Corporation of Dublin 1660–1760' in *Dublin Historical Record*, XXXVIII (1984), pp.22–35; *idem*, 'Charles Lucas and the Dublin Election of 1748–9', *Parliamentary History*, II (1983), pp.93–111.

16. Pearse Street Library, Gilbert Collection (PSLGC), Charters and Documents of the Guild of the Holy Trinity or Merchants Guild of Dublin, 1438–1824, transcribed for J.T. Gilbert, II, MS 79, p.219; DCACH, Jnl Sheriffs & Commons, 1781–6, p.31; *CARD*, XIII, p.53, 238.

17. An error in the wording of Article XXIII originally made it apply to members of both houses of the corporation, (*CARD*, XII, pp.555–6). Only freemen of the city were entitled to seek employment under the corporation; DCACH, Jn. Sheriffs & Commons, 1781–6, p.87.

18. E.g., *CARD*, XII, p.447; DCACH, Jnl Sheriffs & Commons, 1786–91. p.42.

19. Stanley H. Palmer, *Police and Protest in England and Ireland, 1780–1850* (Cambridge 1988) gives an account of the origins of the Act and the opposition it encountered; pp.79–104, 114–36.

20. DCACH, Jnl Sheriffs & Commons, 1781–6, p.185; 1786–91, pp.2, 23, 49, 59.

21. Palmer, *Police and Protest*, p.124.

22. DCACH, Jnl Sheriffs & Commons, 1786–91, pp.123, 138.

23. Ibid., pp.156–86; *CARD*, XIV, pp.489–99.

24. PSLGC, MS 79, p.285; National Archives, *Transactions of the Guild of St Loy*, M 2925, pp.65–6.

25. For details of the annual ballots, see DCACH, Jnl Sheriffs & Commons, 1786–91, pp.8, 46, 74, 108, 156, 215; 1791–5, p.27.

26. But see David Dickson, '"Centres of Motion": Irish Cities and the Origins of Popular Politics' in [Bergeron & Cullen], *Culture et pratiques*, pp.102–22.

27. *CARD*, XII, p.50.

28. See John R. Walsh, *Frederick Augustus Hervey, 1730–1803* (Maynooth 1972), chap. 2.

29. *CARD*, XII, pp.188, 241–2; XIII, pp.59, 421.

30. *CARD*, XIII, p.385.

31. DCACH, Jnl Sheriffs & Commons, 1781–6, p.141. For the reform congress see Moody & Vaughan, *New Hist Ire: IV*, chap. 10.

32. For a discussion of the enduring importancce of Erastianism in Protestant political thought, see Mark Goldie, 'The Civil Religion of James Harrington'

in Anthony Pagden (ed.), *The Languages of Political Theory in Early-Modern Europe* (Cambridge 1987), pp.197–222.

33. Walsh, *Hervey*, chaps 2–3. On the limits to the growth of toleration in the eighteenth century (England as well as Ireland), see Jacqueline Hill, 'Religious Toleration and the Relaxation of the Penal Laws: an Imperial Perspective' in *Archivium Hibernicum*, XLIV (1989), pp.98–109.

34. Douglas A. Leighton, 'The Meaning of the Catholic Question, 1750–1790: Religious Aspects of the Irish *Ancien Régime*' (Ph.D. thesis, University of Cambridge 1990), chap. 6.

35. On the religious composition of Dublin, see Dickson, 'Centres of Motion', pp.105–116.

36. The shocked reaction of the Irish administration to the British government's new Irish policy is reflected in viceregal correspondence. See e.g. National Archives, Westmorland Correspondence, Letterbrook I, Westmorland to Dundas, 26 December 1791, pp.25–41.

37. *Hib. Jnl*, 25 Jan. 1792.

38. *M. Post*, 22, 29 Mar. 1792.

39. *Hib. Jnl*, 16 Apr. 1792.

40. Ibid., 20 Apr. 1792.

41. *M. Post*, 21 Apr. 1792.

42. See Joseph W. Hammond, 'Mr William Cope's Petition, 1804', *Dub. Hist. Rec.*, VI (1943), pp.25–38. In 1798 Cope hadd been instrumental in inducing the United Irishman Thomas Reynolds to turn informer, for which Cope received a pension of £1000 for his wife and children. By 1804 his business had failed, and his petition to government (transcribed by Hammond) highlighted the plight of his son, an army officer then imprisoned in France, and asked government to fulfil an earlier pledge to do something for him. The petition recounted his role on the 'loyalist' side since 1792, but (while no doubt substantially reliable) it needs to be read with care, for Cope exaggerated the extent to which his 'ascendency' activities in January 1792 were prompted by government. For instance, he implies that he only stood for membership of the city commons in 1792 at John Lee's suggestion: in fact, Cope had been a member since 1784.

43. *M. Post*, 6, 31 Mar., 14, 19 Apr. 1792. On Giffard's reputation, see also Brian Inglis, *The Freedom of the Press in Ireland, 1784–1841* (London 1954), esp. pp.57–62.

44. Hammond, 'Cope's petition', p.25.

45. But see *M. Post*, 19 Apr. 1792.

46. *CARD*, XIV, pp.220–2. Founded in 1669, the school provided free education and maintenance for up to 200 boys, and was of great importance to the Protestant artisans who comprised the freemen of the guilds. Concern over its management had helped fuel Lucas's campaign in the 1740s. See Lesley Whiteside, *A History of the King's Hospital* (2nd ed., Dublin 1985), chaps 3–4.

47. *CARD*, XIV, pp.265–6. The three United Irishmen were Tandy, Ewing and Henry Jackson.

48. *M. Post*, 10 Apr. 1792.

49. Ibid., 5 Apr. 1792.

Chapter 8

1. Introduction to *On the Sublime and the Beautiful* (*Burke Works*, I, p.59).
2. *Burke Corr.*, IV, p.118.
3. Ibid., VIII, p.5.
4. *Parliamentary Register* (*G.B.*), XVI, pp.112–3; XVIII, p.333.
5. *Burke Works*, I. pp.448, 508–9; II, p.28.
6. *Burke Corr.*, IX, p.113.
7. Ibid., IX, p.277.
8. Ibid., II, p.336; III, p.386.
9. Ibid., VIII, p.207.
10. Ibid., IV, p.71.
11. *idem.*
12. Ibid., IV, p.225.
13. Ibid., V, p.50.
14. *Burke Works*, I, pp.484, 501.
15. *Burke Corr.*, I, p.140.
16. Ibid., III, pp.218, 244, 286–7.
17. Ibid., IV, p.359.
18. *Charlemont MSS*, I, p.400.
19. *Burke Corr.*, IV, p.440.
20. Ibid., IV, p.460; IX, pp.122, 166.
21. Ibid., IX, p.257.
22. Ibid., IX, pp.114, 190, 290.
23. *Burke Works*, II, p.33.
24. Ibid., III, p.79.
25. *Burke Speeches*, VIII, p.324.
26. *Burke Corr.*, III, p.438.
27. *Burke Speeches*, VI, p.305.
28. *Parliamentary History*, XXI, 710.
29. *Burke Corr.*, IV, pp.84, 218.
30. Ibid., IV, p.85.
31. Ibid., VI, p.215.
32. Ibid., VI, p.80.
33. Ibid., VI, p.270.
34. Ibid., VII, p.359.
35. *Burke Speeches*, IX.
36. *Burke Corr.*, VII, p.244.
37. Ibid., IV, p.9.
38. Ibid., III, p.457.
39. Ibid., VII, p.55.
40. *Parl. Reg.* (*G.B.*), XXVIII, p.468.
41. *Burke Corr.*, VII, p.9.
42. Ibid., VIII, p.255.
43. Ibid., VII, pp.40, 298.
44. Ibid., IX.
45. Ibid., VII, pp.11, 300.
46. Ibid., VII, p.342.

47. Ibid., VII, pp.40, 94, 283, 300; VIII, pp.34, 254.
48. *Burke Speeches*, VIII, p.176.
49. *Burke Corr.*, VII, p.510.
50. Ibid., VII, p.283. The Irish radicals in their publications ignored Burke's attack on the revolutionary creed. Drennan, however, in his *Letter to his Excellency Lord Fitzwilliam* (Dublin 1795), by emphasising how men in the humbler ranks of life could be turned into better citizens by education, implicitly replied to Burke (in a footnote he refers to the swinish multitude).
51. *Burke Corr.*, IV, p.71.
52. Ibid., VII, p.118.
53. Ibid., VII, p.360.
54. Ibid., IX, p.338.
55. Ibid., VIII, p.9.
56. Ibid., VIII, p.248; IX, p.356.
57. Ibid., VII, p.512.
58. Ibid., VIII, p.249.
59. Ibid., VIII, p.143; IX, pp.171–2.
60. Ibid., IX, pp.113, 165, 255, 330–1.
61. Ibid., IX, pp.139, 158.
62. Ibid., IX, pp.168–9, 368.
63. Ibid., IX, pp.117, 122, 168–9, 256.
64. Ibid., IX, pp.188–9.
65. A.P. Samuels, *Early Life, Correspondence and Writings of Edmund Burke* (Cambridge 1923), pp.306–7.
66. *Burke Corr.*, VII, p.443; VIII, p.101.
67. Ibid., IX, p.346.
68. Ibid., IX, pp.125, 301, 333.
69. Ibid., IX, p.356.
70. Ibid., IX, pp.149, 255, 283, 336, 373.

Chapter 9

1. Tone, *Life*, II, p.467.
2. Madden, *U.I.* (1860), p.226.
3. Madden, *op. cit.*
4. Elliot, *Tone*, p.227.
5. Reb. Papers, 620/20/28.
6. The Bishop of Bath and Wells (ed.), *The Journal and Correspondence of William, Lord Auckland III* (London 1862), p.422. In addition, FitzGibbon to Auckland, 26 Nov. 1798, BL Add. MS 34,455, 38–9ff.: 'after he [Tone] was brought up to be tried by a military tribunal in Dublin, upon what principle was his execution delayed from Saturday to Monday? Nay more, there was fully time to execute him on Monday, after it was known that an application would be made to the King's Bench and before it was made. And what of the opinion of a surgeon's mate that a man whose throat was cut could not die of hanging?' His Grace of Bath and Wells discreetly omitted this excerpt from the published version of this particular letter. My very grateful acknowledgment to Dr Anthony Malcomson for bringing this item to my attention.

7. FitzGibbon to Cooke, 13 August 1799, (Reb. Papers 620/47/41).

8. Jonah Barrington, *The Rise and Fall of the Irish Nation* (New York 1845), pp.356–7.

9. TCD, Madden Papers, 415f.

10. PRO(L.), HO/100/66, 350–1ff.

11. Compare, for example, MacNeven's comments on Catholic Emancipation with FitzGibbon's rendering in the report of the Committee of Secrecy; Madden, *U.I.* (1860), pp.223–4; Irish House of Lords, *Journals*, VIII, p.144.

12. See, for example, Henrietta Battier's superb satirical poem *The Gibbonade* (Dublin 1794), p.24. According to Mrs Battier, FitzGibbon's paternal grandmother, Honor, supported herself by hiring out as a wetnurse and by engaging in sharp dealings in livestock. His grandfather supposedly sold buttermilk door to door.

13. Constantine FitzGibbon, *Miss Finnegan's Fault* (London 1953), pp.80–3. John FitzGibbon, a cousin and namesake, wrote a long letter to Betham giving a romantic account of a collusive discovery that went awry. Although Constantine FitzGibbon claims that the original letter is in the Chief Herald's office, I have not been able to trace it.

14. P. Beryl Eustace (ed.), *Registry of Deeds, Abstracts of Wills* (Dublin 1956), I, pp.209–10; James Roche, *Critical and Miscellaneous Essays of an Octogenarian* (Cork 1850), II, p.116.

15. E. Keane, P.B. Phair, T.U. Sadleir (eds), *King's Inns Admission Papers 1607–1867* (Dublin 1982), p.168.

16. Ibid.; Eileen O'Byrne (ed.), *The Convert Rolls* (Dublin 1981), p.103.

17. John Ferrar, *History of Limerick* (Limerick 1787), p.364.

18. Henry Grattan, *Memoirs of the Life and Times of Henry Grattan* (London 1849), I, p.192.

19. *Burke Corr.*, VII, p.192.

20. E. MacLysaght (ed.), *The Kenmare Manuscripts* (Dublin 1942), pp.73–5, 288–315.

21. W.G. Hamilton to John Hely Hutchinson, 29 Jan. 1763 (TCD, Hutchinson Papers, C/1/16).

22. *Burke Corr.*, I, pp.275–6.

23. Idem.

24. Roche, *op. cit.*, II, pp.116/117.

25. Hamilton to Hutchinson, 4 December 1762 (Hutchinson Papers, C/1/13).

26. *Debates Relative to the Affairs of Ireland* (Dublin,1763), pp.208–21.

27. Hamilton (?) to Hutchinson, 6 August 1767 (Hutchinson Papers, C/1/45).

28. *Hib. Chron.*, 30 Nov.–4 Dec. 1775.

29. William Hunt (ed.), *The Irish Parliament: 1775* (London & Dublin 1907), p.20.

30. Tone, *Life*, I, p.138.

31. PRONI, T3244/11/1.

32. *The Character of the Late Earl of Clare* (Dublin 1802). This is a broadside sheet with no page numbers: 'Lord Clare' in *Dublin University Magazine*, XXX (1849), p.675.

33. See for example the published account of his speech in support of the Act of Union, *The Speech of the Right Honourable John, Earl of Clare, Lord High Chan-*

cellor of Ireland on a Motion by him on Monday, February 10, 1800 (Dublin 1800), pp.69–70.

34. Lord de Rosse to Lord Redesdale, 9 May 1822 (PRONI, Rosse Papers). My thanks to Kevin Whelan, who kindly sent me a copy of this particular letter.

35. This striking turn of phrase appears in the published version of his speech on the Act of Union, p.22.

36. Sir Edward Newenham to Sir John Gay Alleyne, 29 September 1784 (PRO(L.), Chatham Papers 30/8/329); *DEP*, 4 Dec. 1783; 2 Jan. 1795.

37. Act of Union speech, p.22.

38. Westmoreland to Pitt, 11 January 1793 (NLI, MS 886).

39. J. Ridgeway, *Reports of cases…* (Dublin 1795), III, pp.106–203; FitzGibbon to William Eden, 22 Aug. 1785 (University of Keele, Sneyd Muniments).

40. For his relations with his wife, see A. Aspinall (ed.), *The Later Correspondence of George III* (London 1962–70), IV, p.8, no. 2584, fn.; he was a very kind and attentive guardian to his young cousin Thomas FitzGibbon, later a persistent and tiresome suitor for an excise office. It is interesting that young Thomas waited until after FitzGibbon's death to approach government and that he made use of the good offices of the compliant Lady Clare. This circumstance suggests that FitzGibbon, while fond of young Thomas, did not consider him a very worthy or promising object of patronage. See NLI MS 7866 for the circumstances of FitzGibbon's guardianship. For Thomas FitzGibbon's pursuit of office, see Nat. Archives, Westmoreland Papers, Carton 1, 141ff., 142, 144.

41. C.L. Falkiner, *Studies in Irish History and Biography* (London 1902), p.145; FitzGibbon to Eden, 10 Jan. 1786; FitzGibbon to Roger Cashin, 21 November 1801 (letter in private collection). I am grateful to Dr Malcomson for bringing this letter to my attention. Also FitzGibbon to General Morrison, 29 June 1798 (NLI, MS 7333).

42. See, for example, Edmund Burke's very grudging acknowledgment: Burke to Captain Emperor John Alexander Woodford, 31 May 1797, in *Burke Corr.*, IX, p.363.

43. FitzGibbon to Cashin, 15 May, 1794 (NLI MS 8343/9).

44. There are endless and tedious examples which could be given to support this point. For FitzGibbon the avenging paternalist as judge, see *Hib. Jnl*, 30 Aug. 1791; for FitzGibbon the avenging paternalist in parliament, see *Hib. Jnl*, 24 Feb. 1791.

45. FitzGibbon to Lord Camden, 28 August 1796 (KAO, Camden Papers, C/183). FitzGibbon persistently referred to Presbyterians as 'Puritans'.

46. Madden, *U.I.* (1860) p.223.

47. Irish House of Lords, *Journals*, XI, p.144.

48. New York *Freeman's Journal*, 17 July 1841: quoted in Madden, *U.I.* (1860), pp.247–8.

49. For resistance to FitzGibbon's appointment as attorney general, see *Grattan Memoirs*, p.112; for opposition to his appointment as chancellor, see *HMC Dropmore*, I, pp.463–8.

50. FitzGibbon to Auckland, 17 Nov. 1801 (Sneyd Muniments).

Chapter 10

1. K. Whelan, 'Catholics, Politicisation and the 1798 Rebellion' in R. Ó Muiri (ed.), *Irish Church History Today* (Armagh 1991), pp.63–84; ibid., 'The Role of the Catholic Priest in the 1798 Rebellion in County Wexford' in Whelan (ed.), *Wexford: History and Society* (Dublin 1987), pp.296–316.

2. E. O'Flaherty, 'Irish Catholics and the French Revolution' in Gough & Dickson, *Ire. and the Fr. Rev.*, pp.52–68; L.M. Cullen, 'Late Eighteenth-Century Politicisation in Ireland ...' in [Bergeron & Cullen], *Culture et pratique*, pp.137–59.

3. T. Tackett, *Religion, Revolution and Regional Culture in Eighteenth-Century France* (Princeton 1986).

4. Preface, *Life of James Quigley* (London 1798).

5. Reb. Papers, 620/10/121/111, J.W., 6 June 1798.

6. *Burke Corr.*, IV, p.134.

7. Maureen Wall, 'The Penal Laws, 1691–1760' in G. O'Brien (ed.), *Catholic Ireland in the Eighteenth Century* (Dublin 1990), pp.1–61.

8. E. O'Flaherty, 'The Catholic Convention and Anglo-Irish Politics, 1791–93' in *Arch. Hib.*, XL (1985), p.18.

9. Cardinal Antonelli to Troy, 24 Dec. 1791; Antonelli to Charles O'Connor, 24 Dec. 1791 (Dublin Diocesan Archives, Troy Papers).

10. Troy to Major Hobart, 29 Nov. 1791 (PRO[L.], HO100/34/33).

11. Declaration of loyalty of the Catholics of Ireland, *FDJ*, 27 Dec. 1791. R.D. Edwards (ed.), 'The Minute Book of the Catholic Association, 1773–93' in *Arch. Hib.*, IX (1942), p.144.

12. Troy to Bp F. Moylan, 23 Dec. 1791 (Troy Papers).

13. *FDJ*, 15 Dec. 1791. This was soon matched by an anti-Kenmare petition from Kerry.

14. Bp Caulfield to Troy, 22 Apr. 1792 (Troy Papers); *Hib. Jnl*, 4 Jan. 1792; Whelan, 'Role of the Catholic Priest', p.297.

15. Caulfield to Troy, 27 Jan. 1792 (Troy Papers). By contrast the aggressively anti-Kenmare petition in Wexford was signed by 440 individuals and published in the *Hib. Jnl*.

16. Bp P. Plunkett to Troy, 29 Jan. 1792 (Cogan, *Meath*, III, pp.167–72); Elliott, *Tone*, p.153.

17. Edwards, 'Minute Book', pp.146–7.

18. 32 Geo. III, *c*.21.

19. Patrick Duigenan, *An Answer to the Address of the Rt. Hon. Henry Grattan to his Fellow Citizens* (Dublin 1798), p.24; *FDJ*, 14 Feb. 1792.

20. Edwards, 'Minute Book', p.157.

21. Ibid., pp.157–60.

22. D'Alton, *Archbps of Dublin*, II, p.484.

23. Troy to Brancadero, 18 May 1792 (Troy Papers); *Burke Corr.*, VII, pp.439–44.

24. Jim Smyth, 'Popular Politicisation in Ireland in the 1790s' (Ph.D. thesis, University of Cambridge 1989), p.43.

25. Caulfield to Troy, 31 March 1792 (Troy Papers); John Keogh to Hussey, 29 March 1792 (PRO[L.], HO100/38/243).

26. Caulfield to Troy, 31 March 1792 (Troy Papers); Edwards, 'Minute Book', pp.160, 167.
27. Hobart to Evean Nepean, 8 Oct. 1792 (Nat. Archives, Private Official Correspondence, cited in P. O'Donoghue, 'The Catholic Church in Ireland in the Age of Revolution and Rebellion, 1782–1803' [unpublished Ph.D. thesis, NUI (UCD) 1975], p.177). Cf. J.A. Murphy, 'The Support of the Catholic Clergy in Ireland, 1750–1850' in *Historical Studies* V (1985), pp.103–21.
28. Musgrave, *Rebellions*, p.63; *Burke Corr.*, VII, p.293.
29. *The Excommunication of the Rev. Robert McEvoy* (London 1798), p.9.
30. Keogh to — , 2 Oct. 1792 (PRO[L.], HO100/38/275–8); B. Egan to Troy, 3 Nov. 1792; Archbp Bray to Troy, 22 Oct. 1792 (Troy Papers).
31. Troy to Bray, 8 Dec. 1792 (Cashel Dio. Archives).
32. Ibid.
33. Smyth, 'Popular Politicisation', p.57.
34. 'Pastoral of the Four Metropolitans, 25 Jan. 1793' (Cashel Dio. Archives).
35. Troy to Bray, 16 March 1793 (Cashel Dio. Archives); P. Duigenan, *Fair Representation of the Present Political State of Ireland* (London 1799), p.18.
36. O'Donoghue, 'Catholic Church', p.206.
37. Anthony Thompson to Bray, 5 March 1793 (Cashel Dio. Archives).
38. John Troy, *Pastoral Instructions on the Duties of Christian Citizens* (2nd ed., Dublin 1793), pp.124–34.
39. Hobart to Nepean, 6 March 1793 (cited in O'Donoghue, 'Catholic Church', p.210).
40. Valentine Bodkin to Bray, 30 Aug. 1794 (Cashel Dio. Archives).
41. Tone, *Life*, I, p.101; Thomas Bartlett, 'The Origins and Progress of the Catholic Question in Ireland, 1690–1800' in Thomas Power and Kevin Whelan (eds), *Endurance and Emergence: Catholics in Eighteenth-Century Ireland* (Dublin 1990), p.14.
42. Troy to Bray, 19 Feb. 1793 (Cashel Dio. Archives); Musgrave, *Rebellions*, p.122; *Burke Corr.*, VII, p.361.

Chapter 11

1. McDowell, 'Proceedings of U.I.', pp.19, 23–4.
2. Moody & Vaughan, *New Hist. Ire.*: IV, p.290.
3. Bibliographical information is drawn (except where otherwise stated) from the *Eighteenth-Century Short Title Catalogue Database* (last search 14 Nov. 1991: Thomas Paine/printings in Ireland).
4. McDowell, 'Proceedings of U.I.', p.23.
5. R.C. Cole, *Irish Booksellers and English Writers, 1740–1800* (London 1986), p.175.
6. P.S. Foner (ed.), *The Complete Writings of Thomas Paine* (New York 1945), I, p.408.
7. Foner, *Paine Writings*, II, p.635. Patrick Byrne produced a Dublin edition of this essay in 1788.
8. Notably Oliver Goldsmith, Richard Brinsley Sheridan and Edmund Burke himself.
9. Paine to John Hall, 25 Nov. 1791 (Foner, *Paine Writings*, II, p.1,322).

Paine's friend Romilly, writing to a friend in France during 1791, commented that the impression which *The Rights of Man* 'has made in Ireland is, I am informed, hardly to be conceived': quoted in Hayes, *Ire. & Fr. Rev.*, p.8n.

10. *National Intelligencer*, 15 Nov. 1802, quoted in Foner, *Paine Writings*, II, pp.909–10.

11. Sackville Hamilton, Dublin Castle to Evan Nepean, 14 and 16 Sept. 1791 (PRO[L.], HO/100/34/305/307); *FDJ*, 19 July 1792; Gregory Claeys, *Thomas Paine: Social and Political Thought* (Boston 1989), p.27; Ann Thomson, 'Thomas Paine and the United Irishmen' in *Etudes Irlandaises*, XVI (juin 1991), pp.109–10.

12. *Hib. Jnl*, 21 March 1791.

13. O'Brien, *Tone Autobiography*, I, p.77. The Dublin editions/printings can be tentatively listed in order of appearance as follows: John Rice (March); 36 Dublin booksellers; Whigs of the Capital (May); Patrick Byrne; J.S. Jordan; re-issue of the Whigs of the Capital; Patrick Byrne '13th edition'. A systematic bibliography of the Irish printings is currently being constructed.

14. Elliott, *Tone*, p.123.

15. McDowell, *Age of Imperialism*, p.481. The publication committee was composed as follows: James Hartley and John Chambers (President and Secretary of the Whigs of the Capital); H. Crothers (Treasurer); O. Bond; J.N. Tandy; R. McAllister; W. Gilbert; J. Pasley; W. Humphries; R. Sheridan; H. Hutton; S. Rossbrough: *Hib. Jnl*, 6 April 1791.

16. Patrick Kelly, 'Irish Writers and the French Revolution' in *La Storia della Storiografia Europea sulla Rivoluzione Francese* (Rome 1990), p.338.

17. *Remarks on Mr Paine's Pamphlet, called The Rights of Man* (Dublin 1791), p.6.

18. Paine to Hall, 25 Nov. 1791 (Foner, *Paine Writings*, II, p.1,322); Olivia Smith, *The Politics of Language, 1791–1819* (Oxford 1984), p.64.

19. Edward Cooke, Dublin to Scrope Bernard, 21 Nov. 1791 (PRO[L.], HO/100/34/ 269).

20. [Henry Joy], *Historical Collections Relative to the Town of Belfast* (Belfast 1817), pp.350–1.

21. *Hib. Jnl*, 15 July 1791; *FDJ*, 16, 19 July 1791; Curtin, *United Irishmen*, p.119. The processional lantern also bore the message: 'We do not rejoice because we are slaves but we rejoice because of the French being free.'

22. *N. Star*, 25 Feb. 1792.

23. Martha McTier to William Drennan, 28 Oct. 1791, quoted in McDowell, *Public Opinion*, p.163.

24. *DEP*, 1 Aug. 1786.

25. Brian Inglis, *The Freedom of the Press in Ireland, 1784–1841* (London 1954), pp.64–5. The earliest issues of the *Rights of Irishmen* are in the RIA Library.

26. Elliott, *Tone*, pp.126–9.

27. *F. Jnl*, 17 March 1792. See appendix to Patrick Byrne's edition of *The Rights of Man*, Part II (Dublin 1792).

28. *N. Star*, 4–7 April 1792. Extracts were also published in the *Rights of Irishmen* in April and May.

29. Claeys, *Paine*, pp.88ff., 125; Senan Ensko, 'Thomas Paine and Ireland, 1791–4: the Reaction of Public Opinion' (UCD unpublished MA thesis 1990), pp.9–11.

30. Curtin, *United Irishmen*, pp.210–1.
31. *M. Post*, 26 May 1792; Claeys, *Paine*, p.118; Christina Bewley, *Muir of Huntershill* (Oxford 1981), p.24.
32. *F. Jnl*, 5 Jan. 1793.
33. Quoted in Kelly, 'Irish Writers', p.338.
34. R.J. Coughlan, *Napper Tandy* (Dublin 1976), pp.59–60.
35. Quoted in Curtin, *United Irishmen*, p.453; cf. ibid., p.57.
36. Claeys, *Paine*, p.82.
37. *F. Jnl*, 27 Dec. 1792.
38. Ensko, 'Paine and Ireland', pp.39–42.
39. Patrick Kelly, 'Perceptions of Locke in Eighteenth-Century Ireland' in *Proc. RIA*, LXXXIX, C (1989), pp.31–2.
40. McDowell, *Public Opinion*, pp.166–7; Ensko, 'Paine and Ireland', pp.28, 51.
41. William Downes, Dublin to Lord Sheffield, 4 Jan. 1793 (PRONI, Sheffield Corr., T3465/44).
42. Inglis, *Press*, pp.65–6, 82, 87, 94–5.
43. Coughlan, *Tandy*, pp.95–100.
44. *F. Jnl*, 18 July 1793, quoted in Curtin, *United Irishmen*, p.387; ibid, p.391.
45. George Knox to the Duke of Abercorn, 14 Feb. 1793 (PRONI, Abercorn MSS, T2541/1131/4/12). Cf. Jim Smyth, *The Men of No Property: Irish Radicals and Popular Politics in the Late Eighteenth Century* (London 1992), p.103.
46. *FDJ*, 13 Aug. 1793; Smyth, *Men of No Property*, p.143. Cf. Claeys, *Paine*, p.119.
47. [Thomas Collins] to John Giffard, 20 Nov. 1793 (Nat. Archives, Reb. Papers 620/20/78).
48. Caesar Colclough to John Colclough, 19 Nov. 1792 (PRONI, T3048/C/10); Thomas Moore, *The Memoirs of Lord Edward Fitzgerald* (London 1897), pp.126–9; McDowell, *Age of Imperialism*, p.478; Elliott, *Partners*, pp.54–62; D.V. Erdman, *Commerce des Lumières: John Oswald and the British in Paris, 1790–93* (Columbia, Mi. 1986), pp.216–7, 233–46, 305; Thomson, 'Paine and the U.I.', pp.110–2.
49. McDowell, *Public Opinion*, pp.173–7; Claeys, *Paine*, pp.177–95.
50. O'Brien, *Tone Autobiography*, I, p.246; John Anderson, *Catalogue of Early Belfast Printed Books, 1694 to 1830...* (Belfast 1890), p.42.
51. Rev. Thomas Hincks, *Letters to the Inhabitants of Cork, Occasioned by the Circulation of a Work Entitled* The Age of Reason *in that City* (Cork 1795); McDowell, *Public Opinion*, p.174; Michael Durey, 'Irish Deism and Jefferson's Republic', *Éire-Ireland*, XXV, 4 (1990), pp.58–61.
52. McDowell, *Public Opinion*, p.176.
53. Ibid., p.176; Woods, *Russell*, p.174.
54. Whitley Stokes, *A Reply to Mr Paine's Age of Reason...* (Dublin,1795).
55. Rev. William Jackson, *Observations in Answer to Mr Thomas Paine's Age of Reason* (Dublin 1795), pp.2, 92.
56. William Gahan, *Youth Instructed in the Grounds of the Christian Religion...* (Dublin 1798), pp.148, 151.
57. Information of Mr Smyth (Nat. Archives, Reb. Papers, 620/54/7).
58. Handbill, 'The Real Black List of the Members of the Corporation of Dublin' [March 1795] (Nat. Archives, Reb. Papers, 620/51/202).

59. T. Howell, *Complete Collection of State Trials*, XXVI (London 1819), col.430; Smyth, *Men of No Property*, pp.147–8.
60. Mary McCracken to R.R. Madden, 13 Nov. 1857 (TCD Madden Papers, MS 873/70).
61. 'J.W.' Cork to —, 13 Apr. 1795 (KAO, Camden Papers, MS U840/0144/10). Cf. 'J.W.' to —, 12 Sept. 1795, quoted Lecky, *Ireland*, III, p.382.
62. F. H[iggins] to Sackville Hamilton, 14 April 1795 (Camden Papers, MS U840/0143/3).
63. Deposition of Robert Cowan, 6 May 1796 (Nat. Archives, Reb. Papers 620/23/98). Stockdale was subsequently printer of *The Press*.
64. Claeys, *Paine*, pp.196–208.
65. Musgrave, *Rebellions*, append. xxi, p.9; Claeys, *Paine*, pp.120–2; Smyth, *Men of No Property*, pp.167–8.
66. Curtin, *United Irishmen*, p.317.
67. G.-D. Zimmermann, *Songs of Irish Rebellion...* (Dublin 1967), pp.37–40; R.B. Browne, 'The Paine-Burke Controversy in Eighteenth-Century Irish Popular Songs', in Browne et al. (eds), *The Celtic Cross: Studies in Irish Culture and Literature* (New York 1970), pp.83–6, 91–5; Tom Dunne, 'Popular Ballads, Revolutionary Rhetoric and Politicisation' in Gough & Dickson, *Ire. and the Fr. Rev.*, pp.139–55.
68. Maurice J. Bric, 'Ireland, Irishmen and the Broadening of the Late Eighteenth-Century Philadelphia Polity' (unpublished Ph.D. thesis, John Hopkins University 1991), p.531.
69. William Todd, Sligo to —, 5 June 1800 (Nat. Archives, Reb. Papers 620/9/100/4). But for evidence of the circulation of *The Rights of Man* in County Mayo some four years earlier, thanks to the activities of trade contact with Dublin, see Hayes, *Ire. & the Fr. Rev.* p.15.
70. Thomson, 'Paine and the U.I.', pp.115–7.
71. Bewley, *Muir*, p.166; Elliott, *Partners*, pp.170–1; Thomson, 'Paine and the U.I.', pp.113–7.
72. Sean Cronin, 'Thomas Paine and the United Irishmen' in *Thomas Paine Society Bulletin*, VI, 4 (1980), pp.94–5; Thomson, *op. cit.*, pp.117–8.
73. Audrey Williamson, *Thomas Paine, his Life, Work and Times* (London 1973), p.251.
74. Coughlan, *Tandy*, p.226.
75. See Martin Burke's paper below.
76. Claeys, *Paine*, p.113; Dickson, 'Taxation and Disaffection in Late Eighteenth-Century Ireland' in Samuel Clark and J.S. Donnelly (eds), *Irish Peasants: Violence and Political Unrest, 1780–1914* (Manchester 1983), pp.37–63.
77. Quoted in H.T. Dickinson, 'The Rights of Man – from John Locke to Tom Paine' in O.D. Edwards & George Shepperson (eds), *Scotland, Europe and the American Revolution* (Edinburgh 1976), p.46.
78. Zimmerman, *Songs*, pp.106, 256.
79. I am grateful to Niall Ó Ciosáin for information on the Association and its publishing activity in Ireland.
80. V. Kinane & C. Benson, 'Some Late 18th- and Early 19th-Century Dublin Printers' Account Books: the Graisberry Ledgers' in Peter Isaac (ed.), *Six Centuries of the Provincial Book Trade in Britain* (Winchester 1990), p.145.

81. I am very grateful to Tom Bartlett, Dáire Keogh, Vincent Kinane and Kevin Whelan in drawing to my attention a number of key pieces of evidence relevant to the reception of Paine in Ireland without which this paper would have been very different.

Chapter 12

1. *Rep. Comm. Sec.*, App. IV, p.91.
2. McDowell, *Age of Imperialism*, p.363.
3. *Rep. Comm. Sec.*, App IV, p.91.
4. H.W. Meikle, *Scotland and the French Revolution* (Glasgow 1912); J.D. Brims, 'From Reformers to "Jacobins": the Scottish Association of the Friends of the People' in T.M. Devine (ed.), *Conflict and Stability in Scottish Society, 1700–1850* (Edinburgh 1990), pp.31–5.
5. *Caledonian Mercury*, 28 July 1792.
6. *The Bee, or Literary Weekly Intelligencer*, 18 Apr. 1792.
7. *Glasgow Courier*, 9 Aug. 1792.
8. A. Fletcher, *Memoir Concerning the Origin and Progress of the Reform Proposed in the Internal Government of the Royal Burghs of Scotland* (Edinburgh 1819), *passim*; Meikle, *Scotland and the Fr. Rev.*, pp.8–12, 127–8.
9. Archibald Fletcher to Robert Grahame, 17 June 1792 (SRO, Cunninghame Graham Muniments, GD22/1/315).
10. *Caledonian Mercury*, 1 Sept., 4 Oct. 1792; Robert Watt to Henry Dundas, 21 Sept. 1792 (SRO, Home Office Corr. [Scotland], RH 2/4/64, 318–9ff.).
11. J.D. Brims, 'The Scottish Democratic Movement in the Age of the French Revolution' (unpublished Ph.D. thesis, University of Edinburgh 1983), pp.180–93.
12. Lord Bute to William Adam, 3 Nov. 1792 (SRO, Blair Adam Mun., Gen. Corr. 1792, A-Z).
13. John Fyffe to Robert Graham, 25 Nov. 1792 (SRO, H.O. Corr. [Sc.], RH 2/4/207, 413–8ff.).
14. *Caledonian Mercury*, 1 Dec. 1792.
15. *Second Report from the Committee of Secrecy of the House of Commons (G.B.) Respecting Seditious Practices*, 6 June 1794, App. IV: Printed Minutes of the First Convention; *Parliamentary History of England*, XXXI, col. 873–4.
16. SRO, H.O. Corr. (Sc.), RH 2/4/66, 354–5ff.
17. Ibid., 354f.
18. Ibid., 355f.
19. Thomas Muir, for example, 'was for a monarchy under proper restrictions [believing] that a republican form of government was the best but that monarchy had been so long established in this country...it would be improper to alter it': T.J. Howell, *Complete Collection of State Trials* (London 1817), XXIII, col. 151.
20. *Parl. Hist. Eng*, XXXI, col. 151.
21. SRO, H.O. Corr. (Sc.), RH 2/4/66, 388–9ff.
22. Ibid., 369f.
23. Ibid. Robert Fowler in SRO, H.O. Corr. (Sc.), RH 2/4/66, 368–9ff.
24. The address is printed in *Parl. Hist. Eng.*, XXXIV, col. 6157.

25. Vid. communication of an informer, 15 Dec. 1792 (Nat. Archives, Reb. Papers 620/19/120).
26. W.H. Drummond (ed.), *Autobiography of Archibald Hamilton Rowan...* (Dublin 1840), p.170.
27. Chart, *Drennan Letters*, pp.133–4.
28. For Muir's speech, vid. *Glasgow Advertiser...*, 23–6 Nov. 1792.
29. SRO, H.O. Corr. (Sc.), RH 2/4/66, 352–3ff.
30. Ibid., 356–7ff.
31. Brims, 'Democratic Movement', pp.303–10.
32. Ibid., pp.418, 420–1.
33. *Jnl H.C. G.B.*, XLVIII, pp.729–38.
34. *Parl. Hist. Eng.*, XXX, col. 925.
24. Brims, 'Democratic Movement', pp.419–20.
36. Howell, *Complete State Trials*, XXIV, col. 36.
37. Henry Shipley to William Shipley, 6 July 1793 and copy[?] reply to same, n.d. (SRO, Justiciary Papers, Main Series, JC26/280).
38. William Mitchell to Muir, 1 May 1793 (SRO, Justiciary Papers, Main Series, JC26/269).
39. *Edinburgh Gazetteer*, 5 Nov. 1793; Howell, *Complete State Trials*, XXXIII, col. 394, 413.
40. H. Cockburn, *An Examination of the Trials for Sedition which have Hitherto Occurred in Scotland* (Edinburgh 1888), I, p.223.
41. The address of the four Belfast Societies to the Assembly of Delegates can be found in SRO, Justiciary Papers, Main Series, JC26/276.
42. A.H. Rowan to Norman Macleod, 25 July 1793 (SRO, Justiciary Papers, Main Series, JC26/276).
43. William Skirving to [Mr Burn?], 16 Oct. 1793 (SRO, Justiciary Papers, Main Series, JC26/280).
44. Howell, *Complete State Trials*, XXIII, col. 427, 452.
45. 'J.B.' to William Scott, 23 Nov. 1793 (SRO, H.O. Corr. [Sc.], RH 2/4/73, 225–6ff.). It would seem that the informer J.B.'s reports to government were scrupulously accurate.
46. Ibid., 225–6ff.
47. 'J.B.' to Scott, 26 Nov. 1793 (Ibid., RH 2/4/72, 110–2ff.).
48. 'J.B.' to Scott, 26 Nov. 1793 (Ibid., RH 2/4/73, 232–5ff.); Howell, *Complete State Trials*, XXIII, col. 457.
49. Ibid., XXIII, col. 611–2.
50. Meikle, *Scotland and the Fr. Rev.*, p.146; Brims, 'Democratic Movement', pp.516–22.
51. Howell, *Complete State Trials*, XXIII, col. 1269–71, 1399.
52. Tone, *Life*, II, p.90.
53. PRO(L.), HO100/62, 142–3ff., 23 July 1796.
54. Ibid., HO100/62, 144–5ff., [July 1796].
55. Thomas Pelham to Charles Greville, 6 Dec. 1797 (PRO[L.], HO100/70, 327–8ff.).
56. Dundas to John King, 14 July 1797 (SRO, H.O. Corr. [Sc.] , Rh 2/4/80, 130f.).
57. Scott to Dundas, 22 July 1797 (SRO, Melville Castle Mun., GD51/5/30/1):

'The Irish system of uniting...among the disaffected is termed planting Irish potatoes'.

58. K.J. Logue, *Popular Disturbances in Scotland, 1780–1815* (Edinburgh 1979), pp.75–115.
59. P. Berresford Ellis & S. Mac A'Ghobhainn, *The Scottish Insurrection of 1820* (London 1970), pp.77–8.
60. Logue, *Popular Disturbances*, pp.108–14.
61. Vid. memorial of Thomas Muir, endorsed '1797 Ecosse' (Ministère des Relations Extérieures, Paris, Archives Diplomatiques, Mémoires et Documents, II, 153f. et seq.).
62. Muir estimated that 100,000 Scots would rise up and support a French invasion; another United Scotsmen delegate in Paris, Thomas Graham, claimed that 200,000 Scots were prepared to fight against the 'old regime': Muir memorial (*loc. cit.*); *Castlereagh Corr.*, I, p.309.

Chapter 13

1. William Drennan to Samuel McTier, 21 May 1791 (Chart, *Drennan Letters*, pp 54–5).
2. J. M. Roberts, *The Mythology of the Secret Societies* (London 1972).
3. Palmer, *Democratic Rev.*, II, p.282; J.P. Jenkins, 'Jacobites and Freemansons in Eighteenth-Century Wales' in *Welsh Historical Review*, IX, 4 (1979), p.405.
4. Musgrave refers to Catholics in County Armagh 'who assumed the name masons' and 'robbed Protestants of their arms', but is otherwise remarkably silent on the matter: *Rebellions*, p.67.
5. R. Clifford, *Application of Barruel's Memoirs of Jacobinism to the Secret Societies of Ireland and Great Britain* (London 1798), pp.1–5, 25.
6. J. Money, 'Freemasonry and the Fabric of Loyalism in Hanoverian England' in E. Hellmuth (ed.), *The Transformation of Political Culture: England and Germany in the Late Eighteenth Century* (Oxford 1990), pp.235–71.
7. *Cork Gazette*, 19 June 1796.
8. For instance, the 'Petition of the Protestant associations forming the loyal union of Orange' draws an explicit parallel between the Orange Order and the 'venerable...Brotherhood called Free Masons' (PRONI, T755/2).
9. Chart, *Drennan Letters*, pp.54–5.
10. Cf. D. Knoop, G.P. Jones & D. Hamer, *Early Masonic Catechisms* (Manchester 1943), and Bartlett, 'Defenders', pp.373–94. For Magennis, see Edward Cooke to Thomas Pelham, 4 Dec. 1795 (PRONI, T755/2, 253–5ff.).
11. J. Hamill, *The Craft: a History of English Freemasonry* (Cambridge 1986), p.22; J.H. Billington, *Fire in the Minds of Men: Origins of the Revolutionary Faith* (London 1980), p.92.
12. P. Crossle & J.H. Lepper, *History of the Grand Lodge of Free and Accepted Masons of Ireland*, I (Dublin 1925), p.423.
13. J. Pollock to Pelham, 23 Nov. 1798 (Reb. Papers, 620/35/152).
14. Hamill, *The Craft*, pp.50–1. Steven Bullock lays great stress on the artisan character of the ancients in eighteenth-century America: 'The Revolutionary Transformation of American Freemasonry' in *William and Mary Quarterly*, 3rd ser., XLVII, 3 (1990), pp.347–69.

15. George Knox to Lord Abercorn, 18 Sept. 1795 (PRONI, Abercorn Papers T2541/IbI/6/45); G. Soden, Maghera, 26 May 1796 (Reb. Papers 620/23/124); *SNL*, 20 July 1796; Philip Robinson, 'Hanging Roper and Buried Secrets' in *Ulster Folklife*, XXXII (1986), p.8.

16. Laurence Dermott, *Ahiman Rezon: or a Help to a Brother* (5th ed., Belfast 1783), p.viii.

17. Crossle & Lepper, *Grand Lodge*, pp.246–9. One Masonic toast proclaimed, 'May the gallant VOLUNTEERS OF IRELAND invariably unite in Brotherly ties, and be faithful to each other as free masons have ever been found to be': Dermott, *Ahiman Rezon*, p.xix.

18. C. Downes, *Downes List of Irish Masonic Lodges in 1804* (Comber 1908).

19. See Appendix, pp.174–5.

20. *BNL*, 18–22 Jan. 1793.

21. *Cork Gazette*, 29 June 1796.

22. Crossle & Lepper, *Grand Lodge*, pp.297–8.

23. *N. Star*, 5–9 and 9–12 Jan. 1793.

24. Tone, *Life*, I, p.73.

25. Patrick Rogers, *The Irish Volunteers and Catholic Emancipation, 1778–93* (London 1934), p.288.

26. Ibid., pp.61–2.

27. M.J. Bric, 'The Irish and the Evolution of the "New Politics" in America' in P.J. Drudy (ed.), *The Irish in America: Emigration, Assimilation and Impact* (Irish Studies 4: Cambridge 1985), pp.149–51, 154; T. Twomey, *Jacobins and Jeffersonians: Anglo-American Radicalism in the United States, 1790–1820* (New York & London 1989), pp.214–40. Driscol had previously edited the *Cork Gazette*.

28. See Appendix, pp.174–5.

29. John Bird to Edward Cooke, July 1796 (Nat. Archives, Frazer Papers 1A/40/111a/23); General Carhampton to Pelham, 15 Nov. 1796 (PRONI, T755/3); V. Mayne to J. Lees, 24 May 1798 (Reb. Papers, 620/37/144); E.J. Newell, *The Apostacy of Newell* (London 1798), p.29. For similar activities in County Meath, see W. Taylor to Pelham, 17 March 1798 (Reb. Papers, 620/36/17).

30. Information of Francis Higgins, 29 Nov. 1797 (Reb. Papers, 620/36/226). On the suspension of the Dublin lodges, see W. Geoghahan, *The History and Antiquities of the First Volunteer Lodge of Ireland* (Dublin 1912), p.23.

31. Knox to Cooke, 7 May and 6 June 1798 (Reb. Papers, 620/37/3; 620/38/61).

32. Pelham to the Earl of Donoughmore, 24 Oct. 1797 (Reb. Papers, 620/32/184).

33. Billington, *Fire in the Minds*, p.92.

34. Chart, *Drennan Letters*, p.122.

35. Abercorn to Knox, 27 Sept. 1795 (Abercorn Papers, T2541/1k/15/124F).

Chapter 14

1. Curtin, 'Transformation of U.I.'.

2. A.P.W. Malcomson, *John Foster: the Politics of the Anglo-Irish Ascendancy* (Oxford 1978), p.362.

3. See Eliott, *Tone*, pp.221–2, and *N. Star*, 29 May–1 June 1793, referred to in Elliott, *Tone*, p.447.

4. Fingall had hoped to sell his services to Fitzwilliam, and lost no time in representing his perception of the situation to him on his arrival in Ireland. See Fingall to the Duke of Portland, 15 Jan. 1795 (in Elliott, *Tone*, p.447 fn.50).

5. Chart, *Drennan Letters*, p.231.

6. The events are referred to in Edmund Burke's correspondence. They also received extensive newspaper coverage.

7. Sirr Papers, MS 869/8, 156f.; Reb. Papers, 620/10/121/61, 620/10/121/128, McNally, 27 May 1797, 17 Sept. 1800; Reb. Papers, 620/22/16, Sir Edward Newenham, Rathdrum, 14 July 1795; Reb. Papers, 620/11/130/45.

8. Chart, *Drennan Letters*, p.11.

9. See chaps by Woods and Cullen in Gough & Dickson, *Ire. and the Fr. Rev.*, pp.83–100, 117–38.

10. Chart, *Drennan Letters*, p.175.

11. Ibid., p.222.

12. Madden Papers, MS 873, no. 24.

13. McDowell, 'Proceedings of U.I.', pp.54, 55, 57, 58, 60. (As far as possible, page references to this source are indicated in sequence in a sole note to a paragraph. Collins usually indicated whether he was writing on the night of a meeting or the next day. When this is clear, the date of the meeting is employed in the text; on other occasions, the date of the letter is given).

14. Chart, *Drennan Letters*, p.117; PRONI, Drennan Papers, D591, undated letter from Newry, listed under 1786. For Drennan's revealing comments on Bishop Hussey, General Daniel O'Connell and Edmund Burke, see Chart, *Drennan Letters*, pp.228, 233.

15. Ibid., p.171. Drennan, in conceding the need for this accommodation, had noted that 'I see, though shortsighted, as far into the Catholic mind as others. I do not like it. It is a churlish soil...'; for an expression of his sister's fears, see ibid., p.213.

16. Reb. Papers, 620/10/121/35, 26 Sept. 1796, McNally.

17. Chart, *Drennan Letters*, p.212.

18. Tone, *Life*, I, pp.111, 113.

19. MacNeven, *Pieces*, pp.48, 71, 179.

20. Ibid., p.108.

21. The officers elected in May were continued from August onwards (because of poor attendance at the statutory August election meeting). As Sheares was much absent from Dublin, however, Butler presided at three of the four meetings in the Aug.-Sept. quarter for which the chairman is known. In the spring, after the arrests of Butler and Bond, president and secretary respectively, Drennan and Dowling had been elected to serve the remainder of the Feb.-April quarter. When Rowan and Butler declined to serve, after their election on 1 November 1793, Bagenal Harvey and Owen McDermott were elected in their stead.

22. McDowell, 'Proceedings of U.I.', pp.57, 59, 93.

23. Ibid., pp.51, 53, 85, 87, 115.

24. Ibid., pp.53, 54, 58, 79.

25. Ibid., p.43. Keogh and Drennan were seen by Collins, acute in observation

but often inaccurate in his surmises, as the 'grand movers'. This is doubtful, not only of Keogh, but of Drennan who had an ambivalent attitude towards the Volunteers.

26. McDowell, 'Proceedings of U.I.', pp.52–3; 57.
27. Emmet and Drennan were both on the committee to look into the question of the war, 'by which means' according to Collins, 'Emmet as being the only lawyer on the committee will have the whole management of the business': ibid., p.63.
28. Ibid., p.66.
29. Chart, *Drennan Letters*, pp.105–8.
30. Ibid., pp.96–8; see also pp.106–7.
31. Ibid., p.117.
32. Ibid., p.328.
33. McDowell, 'Proceedings of U.I.', pp.63, 75.
34. Ibid., pp.78, 79, 81, 82, 83.
35. Tone, *Life*, pp.121–2. On 20 Dec. 1793 Collins noted the attendance of 'several of the late Catholic committee, being their first attendance for some months past': McDowell, 'Proceedings of U.I.', p.99.
36. Ibid., p.86.
37. Ibid., p.92. Butler and Rowan who had been nominated in their absence (and who had other preoccupations on their minds) declined to serve.
38. Ibid., pp.104–5, 121; 123.
39. Ibid., p.108. John Sheares' role can be identified in later letters: ibid., pp.111, 112.
40. Ibid., p.112.
41. Ibid., p.36.
42. *Jnl H. C. Irl.*, XVII, append. dcccccxx.
43. Chart, *Drennan Letters*, p.188.
44. McDowell, 'Proceedings of U.I.', pp.58, 67, 69.
45. Chart, *Drennan Letters*, p.149.
46. McDowell, 'Proceedings of U.I.', p.78.
47. Ibid., p.25.
48. Chart, *Drennan Letters*, p.141.
49. McDowell, 'Proceedings of U.I.', p.32.
50. Chart, *Drennan Letters*, p.196.
51. McDowell, 'Proceeding of U.I.', pp.83, 86, 87.
52. There are effectively four lists: two undated ones, of which the first is a fuller copy of a preceding one (from internal evidence the document should be post-February 1793) (ibid., pp.133–7), a further one (pp.137–9) which can be dated to 15 February 1794 (see p.111), and a final one which is given a date after May 1794, dated by McDowell (pp.139–41). Another list (pp.130–1) simply refers to supporters for a request for a meeting of freeholders (see p.66, 16 Feb. 1793).
53. Ibid., pp.108, 111, 114.
54. Chart, *Drennan Letters*, p.181.
55. Ibid., p.212. The letter refers back to events in January 1794.
56. 'As for union with several of us, I believe Tone would and will ever prevent it': ibid., p.181.

57. Ibid., p.212.
58. Ibid., p.123.
59. Ibid., pp.213–14.
60. Ibid., pp.214–15.
61. MacNeven, *Pieces*, p.101.
62. Tone, *Life*, I, p.276.
63. Reb. Papers, 620/10/121/114, 13 June 1798; 620/10/121/155, no date; 620/10/121/161, no date.
64. Chart, *Drennan Letters*, pp.214–15. His almost proprietorial and patronising confidence as late as August 1794, in the course or reballotting the society, is evident in his statement at that time that 'we admit Tone, Russell, etc. but it is probable they will never attend or be of use, as Tone follows voluntarily or perforce, every turn of the Catholic mind': ibid., p.214.
65. Reb. Papers, 620/10/121/35, no date.
66. *Burke Corr.*, VIII, pp.245–6, Burke to Bp Hussey, 18 May 1795.
67. Reb. Papers, 620/10/121/149, no date.
68. In the Secret Committee Report (*Jnl H. C. Irl.*, XVII, append. dcccxxxviii), the constitution is dated simply 10 May without indication of year, but it clearly refers to 10 May 1795, the date cited by MacNeven.
69. Chart, *Drennan Letters*, p.238.
70. *Jnl H. C. Irl.*, XVII, append. dccclxvi, dccccxx. This would also make sense of the otherwise peculiar testimony of Oliver Bond that he had originally been associated with the northern executive (append. dccccxvii).
71. R. Ó Muiri, 'The Killing of Thomas Birch, United Irishman, March 1797...' in *Seanchas Ardmhacha*, X, 2 (1982), pp.267–319.
72. Chart, *Drennan Letters*, p.244.
73. Ibid., p.247.
74. Reb. Papers, 620/42/8.
75. Reb. Papers, 620/31/128, George Anderson, Newry, 20 June 1797.
76. Teeling is quite specific in stating that 'two of the most active and influential leaders of the province were at this moment absent – Lowry and Magenis': C.H. Teeling, *History of the Irish Rebellion of 1798: a Personal Narrative* (1876 ed., repr. Shannon 1972), pp.114–15. A possible attempted action of the Leinster border is hinted at elsewhere in Teeling's account (*Sequel to the History* ..., p.198).
77. This is a revision of the account in Cullen, 'Political Structures of the Defenders' in Gough & Dickson, *Ire. and the Fr. Rev.*, Teeling's account presents considerable difficulties: if Lowry had returned to Ireland (a fact consistent also with the tradition of his descendants that he came to Norway from Ireland, not apparently from Paris or Hamburg), the meeting with Magennis and Teeling described by Teeling (*History*..., pp.114–19) is clearly on the eve of the rebellion. Teeling is surprisingly coy about events after his own release (which took place, according to Madden, in 1797), and refers only to his meeting with Lowry and Magennis, apparently immediately prior to the Down rebellion (*History*..., pp.114–19), and later to his escape, by implication, from the battle at Ballynahinch (*Sequel to History*, pp.210–30). Remarkably, he has no personal account of the battle, or any precise details about its immediate background, which suggests deliberate and long-winded

evasion of some of the issues.

78. Reb. Papers, 620/10/121/149, no date.

79. The Emmett-MacNeven-O'Connor memorandum, in referring to a paper found 'on one of us' expressing opposition to a particular newspaper if it was not discontinued, clearly has this paper in mind, and skirts over the divide between the three signatories themselves: MacNeven, *Pieces*, p.180.

80. See reports from Ulster provincial meeetings, 1 and 17 April 1798 in *Jnl H. C. Irl.*, XVII, append. dccclxvi.

81. Mrs Jane Mary MacNeven, 22 Sept. 1842 (Madden Papers, MS 873, no. 526, p.6). McNally represented MacNeven as the 'subservient tool' of O'Connor and Fitzgerald: Reb. Papers, 620/10/121/149, no date.

82. I am indebted to my student Thomas Graham for his stress on the significance of this distinction. The point is also made in Pakenham, *Year of Liberty*, pp.91–2, 95.

83. Tone, *Life*, I, p.110. Tone's son does not mention the name Sheares in this regard, but it is clear from Collin's reports that this initiative stemmed from John Sheares.

84. MacNeven, *Pieces*, pp.184–5, 219–20, 233.

85. Ibid., pp.183–4.

86. Ibid., p.146.

Chapter 15

1. Lecky, *Ire.*, III, pp.238–324; McDowell, *Age of Imperialism*, ch. 13; John Ehrmann, *The Younger Pitt* (London 1983), ii.

2. Lecky, *Ire.*, III, p.323; Gerard O'Brien, *Anglo-Irish Politics in the Age of Grattan and Pitt* (Dublin 1987), pp.127–32; McDowell, *Age of Imperialism*, pp.450, 452.

3. *Parl. Reg. Irl.*, XV, pp.4–8, 99ff.

4. Braughall Papers, Circular from Catholic Finance Committee to former delegates, 10 October 1794 (Nat. Archives, Reb. Papers, 620/34/50).

5. 'J.W.', 'For Information of the Marquis of Downshire', December 1794 (PRONI, Downshire Papers, D607/C/56); *DEP*, 13 Dec. 1794.

6. *DEP*, 18 Dec. 1794.

7. *DEP*, 27 Dec. 1794. For text of Catholic petition, see *Jnl H.C. Irl.*, XVI, p.17.

8. Braughall Papers, Circular from Dublin Committee to the Former Delegates to the Catholic Convention, 27 Dec. 1794; Bishop Patrick Plunkett, Navan, to Thomas Braughall, 6 Jan. 1795; *DEP*, 30 Dec. 1794.

9. *DEP*, *passim*, Jan.–Feb. 1795; *Jnl H.C. Irl.*, XVI, *passim*, Jan.–March 1795.

10. Blaquiere to Lord Hawkesbury, 18 Jan., 19 Feb. 1795, quoted in McDowell, *Age of Imperialism*, p.485.

11. Marquis of Downshire to John Reilly and others, Jan.–Feb. 1795 (Downshire Papers, D607/C/68/72/75).

12. J. Pollock to Lord Westmorland, 15 Apr. 1795 (PRONI, ENV 5/HP/8/1. Co. Down); Thomas Hussey to Edmund Burke, 29 Jan. 1795, in *Burke Corr.*, VII, p.125.

13. *Parl. Reg. Irl.*, XV, pp.133; *DEP*, 28 Feb. 1795.

14. *DEP*, 28 Feb. 1795; Feb.–Apr. 1795, *passim*.

15. *Parl. Reg. Irl.*, XV, pp.133–54, 165ff.; *DEP, N. Star*, March–April 1795.
16. F[rancis] H[iggins] to [Govt.], 29 Mar., 10, 13, 14 Apr. 1795 (KAO, Camden Papers, MS U840/0143/1); Grattan to Burke, 15 Apr. 1795, in *Burke Corr.*, VII, p.323.
17. Grattan's 'Reply' to Catholics of Dublin, *DEP*, 14 March 1795; George Knox to Lord Abercorn, 20, 23, 27 March 1795 (PRONI, ENV. 5 HP/7/1, Co. Donegal [IBI / 6 /15–6,20]).
18. *Parl. Reg. Irl.*, XV, pp.11–13, 71–82; O'Brien, *op. cit.*, pp.131–2.
19. *DEP*, 14 March, 3 April 1795; Burke to Hussey, 21 March 1795 in *Burke Corr.*, VII, p.213.
20. *DEP*, 2 April 1795; *N. Star*, 26 March 1795; *FDJ*, 26 March 1795.
21. *DEP*, 9, 14 April 1795; *N. Star*, 13 April 1795.
22. Burke to Hussey, 18 May 1795, in *Burke Corr.*, VIII, p.245; *Parl. Reg. Irl.*, XV, pp.216, 221, 264–70.
23. Elliott, *Tone*, p.249.
24. *DEP*, March–April 1795, *passim*; for Co. Antrim meeting, see *DEP*, 2 April 1795.
25. One of Fitzwilliam's first dispatches from Dublin to Whitehall concerned Defender violence in Cos Meath, Westmeath, Longford and Cavan (PRO[L.], H.O 100/56, fol. 58); 'Copy of Printed Handbill posted up in different Parts of Co. Sligo, April 29, 1795' (PRO[L.], H.O. 100/57/225–6).
26. Portland to Camden, 26 March 1795.
27. *Idem.*
28. Burke to Hussey, 13 March 1795, in *Burke Corr.*, VIII, pp.193–5.
29. Camden to Portland, 3, 4 Jan. 1797 (PRO[L.], H.O. 100/69/23, 29, 62 ff).
30. 'Memorial Addressed to the Lord Lieutenant from...Roman Catholic Noblemen and Gentlemen, etc.', January 1797, and 'Memorial Address of Roman Catholic Noblemen and Gentlemen to the King, etc.', March 1797 (Camden Papers, 071, 073, 074/1–4). See also *DEP*, 14 March 1797 and McNally to [Government], 12 February 1797 (Reb. Papers, 620/10/121/50) for possible reasons for such petitions at this time.

Chapter 16

1. 'What did *not* happen in the north is as important as what did in the south': R.F. Foster, *Modern Ireland, 1600–1972* (London 1988), p.279; see also Elliott, *Partners*, pp.125–30, 166, who argues for the partial success of Lake's campaign and the subsequent alteration of the United Irish movement.
2. William Drennan, *A Letter to His Excellency Earl Fitzwilliam, Lord Lieutenant etc., of Ireland* (Dublin 1795), p.18.
3. For the creation of United Irish societies outside Ulster, see McDowell, 'Proceedings of U.I.', pp.8, 40, 51; *BNL*, 3 Apr. 1792.
4. *N. Star*, 16 Jan. 1792.
5. Samuel McSkimmin, *Annals of Ulster from 1790 to 1798*, E.J. McCrum (ed.) (Belfast 1906), p.5; McDowell, *Public Opinion*, p.147.
6. McDowell, 'Proceedings of U.I. ', p.40; *N.Star*, 11 Jan., 1, 4 Feb. 1792; *BNL*, 21 Dec. 1792; McSkimmin, *Annals*, p.5.
7. *N. Star*, 20 Oct. 1792.

8. William Drennan to Samuel McTier, [Nov. 1791] (Chart, *Drennan Letters*, p.65).

9. See *N. Star*, 23 May, 23 June, 28 July, 7 Nov. 1792 for the resolutions of the Downpatrick, Larne, Ballinahinch, Ballyclare, Ballyeaston, Connor, and Kircubbin Volunteer corps.

10. For the Volunteer revival and the United Irish influence within it, see *N. Star*, 23 May, 23 June, 28 July, 7 Nov. 1792 (resolutions of the Downpatrick, Larne, Ballinahinch, Ballyclare, Ballyeaston, Connor and Kircubbin Volunteer corps); *Rep. Comm. Sec.*, pp.40–1; William Drennan to Samuel McTier, [?] Feb. 1793 (Chart, *Drennan Letters*, pp.128–9). For radical pronouncements by Irish freemasons, see *N. Star*, 16 Jan. 1793. For reform declarations passed by Presbyterian congregations, see *N. Star*, 28 Nov. 1792, 8 Jan.–30 Jan., 29 Jan. 1793.

11. See Curtin, 'Transformation of U.I.', pp.483–92.

12. Robert Johnston to John Lees, 8 May 1795 (KAO, Camden Papers, U840/0146/3).

13. Earl Camden to Duke of Portland, 25 July 1795 (Nat. Archives, Reb. Papers, 620/22//19).

14. Note on the History of the Constitution of the United Irishmen (TCD, Russell Corr., MS 868/1[N.4.2]/1).

15. Constitution of the Society of United Irishmen (Reb. Papers, 620/34/59).

16. Information of John Smith (alias Bird), 1795–6 (Reb. Papers 620/34/59).

17. Constitution of the Society of United Irishmen (Reb. papers, 620/24/59).

18. Andrew MacNevin to John Pollock, 9 May 1795 (Camden Papers, U840/0146/7); McSkimmin, *Annals*, p.29.

19. Robert Johnston to John Lees, 8 Aug. 1795 (Reb. Papers, 620/22/28); Earl Camden to Duke of Portland, 25 July 1795; Capt. — Johnson to John Lees, 2 July 1795 (Camden Papers, U840/0147/17). The following table presents United Irish membership returns in Ulster by county (Source: PRO[L.]), HO 100/62/333–4; Reb. Papers, 620/28/285, 297; 620/30/61):

County	Oct. 1796	Feb. 1797	May 1797
Antrim	15,000	20,940	22,716
Down	11,016	15,000	26,153
Armagh	1000	4500	17,000
Tyrone	4855	7500	14,000
Derry	3696	10,000	10,500
Donegal	2000	5050	9648
Monaghan	1000	3200	9020
Cavan		1000	6880
Fermanagh		2000	2000
TOTAL	38,567	69,190	117,917

20. Earl Camden to Duke of Portland, 25 July 1795.

21. Rotation of offices was a cherished principle of eighteenth-century civic republican theory; see J.G.A. Pocock, *The Machiavellian Moment* (Princeton 1975), pp.393–4; Caroline Robbins, *The Eighteenth-Century Commonwealth-*

man (New York 1968), pp.8–9; Gordon S. Wood, *The Creation of the American Republic, 1776–1787* (New York 1972), pp.140–41.

22. Ibid.; Andrew MacNevin to Thomas Pelham, 6 July 1795 (Camden Papers, U840/0148/2/1).

23. Information of John Edward Newell, 15 Apr. 1797 (PRO[L.], HO100/69/202–5).

24. 'The unfortunate Robert McCormick's Discoveries of the Plans and Views of the United Irishmen, so far as Known to Him, and the History of his Connections with Them' (PRONI, McCance Papers, D272/6).

25. Constitution of the Society of United Irishmen (Reb. Papers, 620/34/59).

26. *Rep. Comm. Sec.*, p.71.

27. MacNeven, *Pieces*, p.183.

28. Lecky, *Ire.* , IV, p.13.

29. Matthew Hood to Marquess of Abercorn, 20 Feb. 1797; John H. Gebbie (ed.), *An Introduction to the Abercorn Letters (as relating to Ireland, 1736–1819)* (Omagh 1972), p.346.

30. James Stewart to Abercorn, 3 Mar. 1797 (PRONI, Abercorn Papers, T. 2541/IB2/2/6).

31. William Torney to Col. — Johnson, 2 Sept. 1797 (BL, Pelham Papers, Add. MS 33105/73).

32. Information of John Edward Newell, 15 Apr. 1797, *op. cit.*

33. United Irish Committee Report 1796 (BL, Pelham Papers, Add. MS 33104/330).

34. United Irish handbill forwarded by Roger Parke to Col.— Cooper, 22 May 1797 (Reb. Papers, 620/30/144).

35. *Rep. Comm. Sec.*, p.79.

36. Information of Francis Higgins (Reb. Papers, 620/18/14); William Bristow to Dublin Castle, 24 May 1796 (ibid., 620/23/122); John Macarra to Gen. George Nugent, 8 Aug. 1797 (BL, Pelham Papers, Add. MS 33105/14–15); Andrew MacNevin to Thomas Pelham, 6 July 1795 (Camden Papers, U840/0148/2/1).

37. Information of John Smith (alias Bird), 1795–6 (Reb. Papers, 620/27/1); see also MacNevin to Pelham, 6 July 1795 (Camden Papers, U840/0148/2/1).

38. John Macarra to Gen. George Nugent, 8 Aug. 1797, *op. cit.*

39. Francis Higgins to Dublin Castle, 19 Aug. 1796 (Reb. Papers, 620/18/14).

40. Viscount Castlereagh to Thomas Pelham, 11 Nov. 1797 (BL, Pelham Papers, Add. MS 33105/204).

41. Information of Samuel Turner (PRO[L.], HO 100/70/339–49).

42. Earl Camden to Duke of Portland, 17 June 1797 (ibid., 100/69/397–9).

43. Francis Higgins to Dublin Castle, Jan. 1798 (Reb. Papers, 620/18/14).

44. Earl Camden to Duke of Portland, 17 June 1797.

45. For official returns for Antrim and Down, see above, n.16. For the Defender estimate, see McSkimmin, *Annals*, p.75.

46. Richard Annesley to Edward Cooke, 26 Mar. 1798 (Reb. Papers, 620/36/82).

47. These figures are offered by Elliott, *Partners*, p.206; Charles Dickson, *Revolt in the North: Antrim and Down in 1798* (Dublin 1960), p.155; Lecky, *Ire.*, IV, pp.416, 420; McSkimmin, *Annals*, p.78; Pakenham, *Year of Liberty*, pp.252, 259.

48. Dickson, *Revolt in the North*, p.129.

49. McSkimmin, *Annals*, pp.75, 87.

50. C.H. Teeling, *The History of the Irish Rebellion of 1798 and Sequel to the History of the Irish Rebellion of 1798* (first pub. 1876; Shannon 1972), pp.201–3.

51. Elliott claims about half of the organised United Irishmen rose in Antrim: see Elliott, *Partners*, p.206.

52. Report of Joseph Pollock on his examination of Robert Hunter, 29 Jan. 1799 (Reb. Papers, 620/7/74/5).

53. Thomas Addis Emmet, 'Part of an Essay towards a History of Ireland' in MacNeven, *Pieces*, p.77.

54. See Elliott, *Partners*, pp.244–50, 303–22.

55. See Fergus O'Ferrall, *Catholic Emancipation: Daniel O'Connell and the Birth of Irish Democracy, 1822–30* (Dublin 1985). O'Ferrall credits O'Connell with creating the first modern political party and pioneering Irish democracy. He nevertheless describes a tightly run, hierarchical organisation with little input from rank and file, an organisation akin to a modern political machine. The success and explicitly public character of the Catholic Association is in sharp contrast with the United Irish organisation. The republicans, however, proved to be far more willing and successful in adopting democratic practice.

Chapter 17

1. See Elliott, 'The Origins and Transformation of Early Irish Republicanism' in *Internat. Rev. Soc. Hist.*, XXIII (1978), pp.405–22; Elliott, *Partners*, pp.15–20, 39–50; Bartlett, 'Defenders', pp.373–94; Tom Garvin, 'Defenders, Ribbonmen and Others: Underground Political Networks in Pre-Famine Ireland' in *Past & Present*, XCVI (1982), pp.133–55; Nancy Curtin, *The United Irishmen and the Origins of Irish Republicanism, 1791–8*, forthcoming (Oxford 1993); Jim Smyth, 'Dublin's Political Underground in the 1790s' in G. O'Brien (ed.), *Parliament, Politics and People...*(Dublin 1989), pp.129–48; *idem*, 'Popular Politicisation, Defenderism and the Catholic Question' in Gough and Dickson (eds), *Ire. and the Fr. Rev.*, pp.109–16; David W. Miller (ed.), *Peep O'Day Boys and Defenders: Selected Documents on the County Armagh Disturbances, 1784–96* (Belfast 1990).

2. Sean Connolly, 'Catholicism in Ulster' in P. Roebuck (ed.), *Plantation to Partition: Essays in Ulster History in Honour of J.L. McCracken* (Belfast 1981), pp.168–9.

3. Cooke to Nepean, 8 Feb, 1793 (PRO[L.], HO100/34/243–4).

4. See for e.g. n.43 below.

5. Hobart to Nepean, 8 Oct. 1792 (HO100/38/11); W.H. Crawford, 'The Ulster Irish in the Eighteenth Century' in *Ulster Folklife*, XXVIII (1982), 25–33, and *idem*, 'Economy and Society in South Ulster in the Eighteenth-Century' in *Clogher Record*, VII (1975), pp.249–58; D. Miller, 'The Armagh Troubles, 1784–95' in Samuel Clarke and James S. Donnelly, jun. (eds), *Irish Peasants: Violence and Political Unrest, 1780–1914* (Madison, Wisconsin 1983), p.178, found the same process in Armagh.

6. William MacAfee, 'The Population of Ulster, 1630–1841: Evidence from Mid-Ulster' (Univ. of Ulster, D.Phil thesis 1987), pp.149–58 – though in Ireland, Connacht registered similar growth.

7. P.J. Duffy, 'Geographical Perspectives on the Borderlands' in Raymond Gillespie and Harold O'Sullivan (eds), *The Borderlands: Essays on the History of the Ulster-Leinster Border* (Belfast 1989), p.7. Such unusual population pressure on the land has also been recorded in a palaeoecological study of vegetational changes in County Tyrone (1969), showing potato cultivation to have spread over areas hitherto untilled; see M.J. O'Kelly, *Early Ireland* (Cambridge 1989), pp.232–3. See MacAfee, 'The Population of Ulster', pp.55, 92, for the predominance of Catholics on remoter, more barren areas; also W. Harris, *The Ancient and Present State of the County of Down* (Dublin 1744), pp.77–8, and Philip Dixon Hardy, *The Northern Tourist or Stranger's Guide to the North and North-West of Ireland* (Dublin 1830), pp.34, 37, 59.

8. J.H. Andrews, *Plantation Acres: an Historical Study of the Irish Land Surveyor* (Belfast 1985), p.13.

9. Thomas Pelham to the Duke of York, 14 Nov. 1796; BL, Add. MS 33, 113/66–9; *The Distress'd State of Ireland Considered; More particularly with Respect to the North* (Dublin 1740); D. McCourt, 'Surviving Openfield in County Londonderry' in *Ulster Folklife*, IV (1958), pp.19–28; E.A. Currie, 'Field Patterns in County Derry' in *Ulster Folklife*, XXIX (1983), pp.70–80.

10. Raymond Gillespie, *Colonial Ulster: the Settlement of East Ulster, 1600–1641* (Cork 1985), p.140; Katharine Simms, 'Gaelic Lordships in Ulster in the Later Middle Ages' (Univ. of Dublin, Ph.D. thesis 1976), p.655; H.F. Hore (ed.), 'Marshal 'Bagenal's Description of Ulster, Anno 1586', *UJA*, II, 1st ser. (1854), pp.149–50.

11. Thomas Ó Fiaich, 'Art Mac Cooey and his Times', *Seanchas Ardmhacha*, VI, 2 (1971), 239–43.

12. C.H. Teeling, *History of the Irish Rebellion* (Shannon 1972), pp.103–4, 115.

13. Westmorland to Pitt, 20 Oct. 1792; (PRO[L.], HO/100/34/220); T.B. Howell, *State Trials*, XXV, pp.754, 757, 761.

14. Edward MacLysaght, *Irish Families* (Dublin 1957), pp.70, 72, 157–8, 311, and *idem, Supplement to Irish Families* (Dublin 1964), p.145.

15. Thomas Lane to Downshire, 12 Oct. 1799 (PRONI, D 607/G/200).

16. See list in PRO(L.), HO/100/34/93–8; also in Tone, *Life*, I, pp.456–61, and F. Plowden, *An Historical Review of the State of Ireland*, London (2 vols, 1803), II, pp.220–4.

17. Peadar Livingstone, *The Monaghan Story* (Enniskillen 1980), p.170; R.R. Madden, *Antrim and Down in '98* (Glasgow, n.d.), p.12.

18. Rev. Brendan McEvoy, 'Father James Quigley', *Seanchas Ardmhacha*, V (1970), pp.247–8.

19. Westmorland to [Dundas], 17 Nov. 1792 (HO/100/38/72–85).

20. Elliott, *Partners*, pp.40–1; Westmorland to [Dundas], 31 Dec. 1792 (HO/100/42/27–28).

21 Westmorland to Dundas, 24 May and 3 July 1793 (HO/100/43/319–20 and 100/44/204); Thomas Bartlett, 'An End to the Moral Economy: the Irish Militia Disturbances in 1793', *Past & Present*, XCIX (1983), pp.205, 210.

22. Pitt to Westmorland, 10 Nov. 1792 (HO/100/38/381); Westmorland to Pitt, 3 Nov. 1792 (Nat. Archives, Westmorland Corr., I, 68); see also *F. Jnl*, 8 Sept. 1792.

23. Keogh to Burke, 26 July 1792 (HO/100/38/266v).

24. See Miller, *Peep O'Day Boys*, pp.133, 139; *F. Jnl*, 6 Apr. 1790.
25. C. Blake Dillon to Baron Dillon, 21 May 1793 (HO/100/46/47g); Hobart to Nepean, 8 Oct. 1792 (HO/100/38/11–19); *F. Jnl*, 5, 16, 21 Mar. 1793.
26. *F. Jnl*, 10 Sept. 1791, commenting that more had been tried for murder in Armagh in previous three years than in entire country over last fifty years.
27. *F. Jnl*, June–July 1789.
28. See *Defence of the Sub-Committee of the Catholics of Ireland from the Imputations Attempted to be Thrown on that Body...of Supporting the Defenders* (Dublin 1793), reproduced in Tone, *Life*, I, p.478, for identification of April 1792 as the date when the new breed of Defenderism emerged.
29. Notably, J.S. Donnelly, jun., 'Propagating the Cause of the United Irishmen', *Studies*, LXIX (1980), pp.5–23; Curtin, *United Irishmen*, notably chaps 4–5; Elliott, *Tone*, pp.219–20.
30. BL, Add MSS 38, 759 /37v, unsigned lengthy narrative, June 1797.
31. TCD, Sirr Papers, MSS 868/1/100; this document is now more accessible and legible in Woods, *Russell* pp.69–70.
32. 'On the Manner of Conducting the Election of Delegates' in Edward Byrne's circular letter, 26 May 1792 (HO/100/34/60); Elliott, *Tone*, pp.190; also Westmorland Corr. I, 55, copy of printed instructions for the elections, annotated 'bought in a shop in Derry...there at the behest of the P.P.'.
33. See Extracts of information from R. Longfield, Oct. 1792 (HO/100/38/361–5); on the mobilisation of ordinary Catholics by the Committee's campaign.; also HO/100/34/220, on the expectations raised by it.
34. Tone, *Life*, I, pp.176, 479–81; *BNL*, 28 Aug. 1798.
35. Westmoreland to Pitt, 20 Oct. 1795 (HO/100/34/220v).
36. Westmorland to —, 17 Nov. 1792 (HO/100/38/72–85); also ibid. fn.373, his letter to Pitt, 20 Oct. 1792.
37. J. Sweetman, *A Refutation of the Charges Attempted to be Made against the Secretary of the Sub-Committee of the Catholics of Ireland, Particularly that of Abetting the Defenders* (Dublin 1793); T.B. Howell, *State Trials*, XXV, pp.750–84, trial of James Bird, Roger Hamill, Casimir Delahoyde, Patrick Kenny, Bartholomew Walsh, Matthew Read and Patrick Tiernan, 23 April 1794. Unlike other newspapers, reports on the Defenders are rare in the *Northern Star*.
37. *Rep. Comm. Sec.*, pp.37–8.
38. Elliott, *Tone*, pp.197–200.
39. PRONI, D272/1: Black Book, 1798; Notebook of D. Browne, *c.*1797 (Reb Papers 620/54/7); Rev. James O'Laverty, *An Historical Acccount of the Diocese of Down and Connor Ancient and Modern* (5 vols, Dublin 1878–87), II, p.417.
40. Madden, *Antrim and Down*, p.13.
41. Miller, *Peep O'Day Boys*, ch. v; *F. Jnl*, 6 June 1789, 6 Apr. 1790, 6 Oct. 1791.
42. Sirr Papers, MS 868/1/100; Woods, *Russell*, pp.69–70.
43. Information enclosed in Lord Bayhem to Dundas, 25 July 1792 (HO/100/34/66–7).
44. Tone, *Life*, I, p.183; *N. Star*, 29 Aug. 1792.
45. See O'Laverty, *Down and Connor*, I, p.164 and Keogh, to [Richard Burke], 26 July 1792 (HO/100/38/267), calling him 'a crack'd brain'd Priest, who has been goaded to a degree of lunacy'.
46. Keogh to [Richard Burke], 26 July 1792 (HO/100/38/267).

47. Tone, *Life*, I, pp.170–5; see his letters in *N. Star*, 14, 28 July and *BNL*, 28 Aug. 1792, also the Committee's address to the Defenders, based on the visit to Rathfriland, in *BNL*, 24 Aug. 1792.

48. Elliott, *Tone*, p.221.

49. Tone, *Life*, I, p.164.

50. See various correspondence HO/100/37/251–3, 100/38/3, 31–41, 69, 94; HO/42/21/159, 138, 435–42, 42/22/153, 169, 385; and A.A.E., C.P.A. 583/119, for French complaints about the Irish buying up all the arms in London.

51. *Rep. Comm. Sec.*, p.37.

52. William MacAfee, 'The Population of Ulster', pp.173–4.

53. Richard White to Nepean, 8 Apr. 1793 (HO/100/46/59).

54. Samuel McSkimmen, *Annals of Ulster* (Belfast 1849), pp.114–5; Curtin, *United Irishmen*, pp.182–3.

55. Castlereagh to Portland, 3 June 1799 (HO/100/87/5–7).

56. Madden, *Antrim and Down*, p.98.

57. Ibid., pp.172–3.

58. See Examination of Dan McFadden, 15 Jan 1799 (Reb. Papers, 620/46/18); Elliott, *Partners*, pp.245–7.

59. Browne, Notebook (Reb. Papers, 620/54/7).

60. Reb. Papers, 620/5/47; Bird's information: HO/100/62/141; BL, Add. MSS 33,105/14–15: evidence given by Dr John McCarra to Gen. Nugent, 8 Aug. 1797; O'Laverty, *Down and Connor*, II, pp.416–7.

61. Lord Altamont to —, 29 Nov. 1796 (620/26/82); Patrick Hogan, 'The Migration of Ulster Catholics to Connaught, 1795–96', *Seanchas Ardmhacha*, IX (1979), pp.286–301.

62. Camden to Portland, 6 Aug. 1796 (HO/100/64/168–72); Elliott, *Partners*, pp.107–8.

63. Information enclosed in Cooke to Pelham, 30 July 1796 on Cuthbert (HO/100/62/141); Ralph Fletcher to Pelham, 3 Apr. 1802, on Magennis (H0/42/65). The divisions within the United Irish Society are developed more fully in Eliott, *Partners*, ch. 5.

Chapter 18

1. W. Richardson, *The History of the Origins of the Irish Yeomanry* (Dublin 1801); Curtin, 'Transformation of U.I.'.

2. Edward Cooke to Gen. Nugent, 25 July 1796 (National Army Museum, Nugent Papers, MS 6807/174 f.147).

3. Elliott, *Tone*, p.250.

4. Knox to [?Pelham], 25 June 1796 (Nat. Archives, Reb. Papers, 620/23/202).

5. 37 Geo. III, *c*.2.

6. Yeomanry Office to Abbot, 31 Oct. 1801 (PRO[L.], Colchester Papers, 30/9/124/227).

7. Nugent to Castlereagh, 24 June 1798 (Nugent Papers, MS 6807/174, 473–5ff.).

8. 'Yeomanry Plan', 22 Sept. 1796 (PRO[L.], HO100/61/112).

9. *Jnl H.C. G.B.*, LX, app. 1, p.517.

10. Hart to Littlehales, 29 Aug. 1803 (Nat. Archives, SOC, 1025/34).
11. Camden to Portland, 22 Sept. 1796 (PRO[L.], HO100/61/112).
12. Richardson, *Irish Yeomanry*, p.29.
13. Camden to Pelham, 3 Oct. 1795 (PRONI, T755/218–9).
14. *Cobbet's Parliamentary History*, XXXI, p.90; J.E. Cookson, 'The English Volunteer Movement of the French Wars, 1793–1815: Some Contexts' in *Historical Journal*, XXXII, 4 (1989), pp.867–91.
15. Portland to Camden, 29 Sept. 1796 (PRO[L.], HO100/62/200).
16. Leinster to Camden, 25 Sept. 1796 (KAO, Camden Papers, U840/0182/4).
17. Leinster to Camden, 8 Nov. 1796 (Camden Papers, U840/0130/A).
18. Pelham to Downshire, 2 Oct. 1796 (PRONI, Downshire Papers, D607/D/213).
19. *DNB*, 'Charlemont'.
20. Camden to Portland, 3 Sept., 22 Sept. 1796 (PRO[L.], HO100/62/208–14, HO100/66/106–9.
21. Richardson to Wolfe, 26 Sept. 1796 (Reb. Papers, 620/25/118).
22. Ibid.
23. *A List of the Officers of the Several District Corps. of Ireland…26 Jan. 1797* (Dublin 1797).
24. P. Ó Snodaigh, 'Volunteers, Militia, Orangemen and Yeomanry of County Roscommon' in *Irish Sword*, XII (1975–6); 'Militia and Yeomanry of County Wexford' in *The Past*, XIV (1983).
25. Knox to Pelham, 22 May 1797 (PRONI, T755/5/72A).
26. Pelham to Knox, 14 June 1797 (NLI, MS 56, f.88).
27. Ibid.
28. Camden to Charlemont, 22 Nov. 1796, *Charlemont MSS* (HMC 1894), II, p.289.
29. P.C. Stoddart, 'Counter-Insurgency and Defence in Ireland, 1790–1805' (Unpublished D. Phil., Oxford 1972).
30. H. Senior, *Orangeism in Ireland and Britain, 1795–1836* (London 1966).
31. *Loyal Songs no. 2 as sung in all the Orange Lodges of Ireland* (Dublin n.d. [*c.*1800]) – copy in BL (11622.d.2).
32. Camden to Portland, 3 Sept. 1796 (PRO[L.], HO100/62/208–14).
33. Fitzwilliam to Portland, 26 Jan. 1795 (PRO[L.] HO100/56/161–5).
34. Ditto to do, 16 Feb., 25 Feb. 1795 (PRO[L.], HO100/51/251–8, HO100/51/329).
35. Camden to Portland, 12 Apr. 1795 (PRO[L.], HO100/57/115–7).
36. *Parl. Reg. Irl.*, XVII, p.13.
37. 'J.W.' to Cooke, 13 Aug. 1796 (Reb. Papers, 620/36/227).
38. Ibid., 28 Sept. 1796.
39. Camden to Pelham, 13 Aug. 1796 (PRONI T155/3/57–8).
40. Camden to Downshire (n.d. [*c.*Aug. 1796]) (PRONI, Downshire Papers, D607/D/142).
41. Camden to Waterford, 14 Sept. 1796 (Camden Papers, U840/0174/15).
42. Richardson to Abercorn, 22 Feb. 1796 (PRONI, Abercorn Papers, T2541/1B/6/5).
43. Knox to Pelham, 28 May 1797 (PRONI, T755/5/101).
44. PRO(L.), HO100/124/153, 16 Apr. 1798; 'Notes on the Defence of Ireland',

25 Apr. 1798 (PRO[L.], HO30/66/211).

45. Stephen Gwynn, *Henry Grattan and his Times* (London 1939), p.369.
46. Wickham to Castlereagh, 14 Aug. 1803 (*Castlereagh Corr.*, IV, pp.294–8).
47. Michael Banim, *The Croppy Boy* (Dublin 1828).

                                       Chapter 19

1. *Rep. Comm. Sec.*, app. dcccxxxviii.
2. Ibid., app. dccccviii, dccccxxv.
3. McDowell, *Age of Imperialism*, p.389.
4. McDowell, 'Personnel of U.I.'. Fifty-five of the names listed were from out-side Dublin, spread across twenty-four counties.
5. At least fifty (21 per cent) of the Catholic Convention's 233 delegates were United Irishmen. Four of the presiding ten-man sub-committee were mem-bers, and Tone was Secretary.
6. Jim Smyth, 'Popular Politicisation, Defenderism and the Catholic Question' in Gough & Dickson, *Ire. and the Fr. Rev.*, pp.109–16.
7. Elliott, *Partners*, pp.xvi, 96.
8. Elliott, *Tone*, p.256.
9. Curtin, 'Transformation of U.I.'. This path-finding article has established beyond doubt the continuity between the so-called 'first' and 'second' soci-eties.
10. Ibid., p.470.
11. Elliott, *Tone*, p.256.
12. Ibid., pp.257, 343. This is also implied in Tom Dunne, *Theobald Wolfe Tone, Colonial Outsider: an Analysis of his Political Philosophy* (Cork 1982).
13. Elliott, *Partners*.
14. *Rep. Comm. Sec.*, app. dccclxxxi; Edward Boyle to Edward Cooke (enclosure), 25 April 1797 (Nat. Archives, Reb. Papers, 620/30/61); anonymous, 6 May 1797 (ibid., 620/37/29).
15. Information from Nicholas Maguan, *Rep. Comm. Sec.*, app. dccclix–dccclxvii.
16. Peter Tesch, 'Ulster Presbyterianism in the 1790s' (University of Dublin, Ph.D. thesis, in progress).
17. Andrew Newton to —, 19 June 1797 (Reb. Papers, 620/31/114).
18. Information of James McGuckin, Aug. 1798 (Reb. Papers, 620/3/32/13).
19. Camden to Portland (enclosure re Turner's information), 9 Dec. 1797 (PRO[L.], HO/100/70/339–48).
20. Elliott, *Partners*, p.166.
21. *Rep. Comm. Sec.*, app. dccclxxxix.
22. This is the assumption in the most readable and influential narrative of the rebellion: Pakenham, *Year of Liberty*.
23. For the complex political and social situation in Wexford, see Kevin Whelan, 'Politicisation in County Wexford' in Gough and Dickson, *Ire. and the Fr. Rev.*, pp.156–78; for an assessment of the extent of United Irish organisation there, see L.M. Cullen, 'The 1798 Rebellion in County Wexford: United Irishman Organisation, Membership, Leadership' in Whelan (ed.), *Wexford: History and Society* (Dublin 1987), pp.248–95.
24. Pakenham, *Year of Liberty*, pp.90, 105, 112 and 194. The claim is repeated in

Elliott, *Partners*, p.199.

25. Graham, 'The Organisation of the Dublin United Irishmen, 1794–8' (University of Dublin Ph.D. thesis, in progress).

26. Francis Higgins to Cooke, 30 Jan. 1798 (Reb. Papers, 620/36/226).

27. Thomas Reynolds, jun., *The Life of Thomas Reynolds* (London 1839), p.184.

28. 'J.W.' to Cooke, 13 Mar. 1798 (Reb. Papers, 620/10/121/96).

29. Memoire; or, Detailed Statement of the Origin and Progress of the Irish Union: Delivered to the Irish government, by Messrs. Emmet, O'Connor, and McNevin, p.13 (Reb. Papers, 620/44/1).

30. *Rep. Comm. Sec.*, app. dccccxxviii.

31. Pakenham, *Year of Liberty*, pp.106 and 125.

32. Annesley to Cooke, 21 Mar. 1798; anon., 17 May 1798, Higgins to Cooke, 20 May 1798; information of McConkey, 6 June 1798; anon., 25 June 1798; information of Blackham, 25 June 1798; (Reb. Papers, 620/36/40; 620/37/97; 620/18/14; 620/38/67; 620/38/232; 620/38/234).

33. Pakenham, *Year of Liberty*, p.119.

34. Samuel Sproule to John Lees, 14 May 1798; information of Reynolds, undated (Reb. Papers, 620/51/40; 620/51/251).

35. For 'Lord Edward's curious state of paralysis', see Pakenham, *Year of Liberty*, p.119.

36. Sproule to Lees, 14 May 1798 (Reb. Papers, 620/51/40).

37. Pakenham, *Year of Liberty*, p.126.

38. Ibid., p.111.

39. Thomas Boyle to Cooke, 10 Mar. 1798; information of Denis Ryan, undated (Reb. Papers, 620/18/3; 620/51/145; 620/52/145).

40. Sproule to Lees, 21 May 1798; 'J.W' to Cooke, 23 May 1798 (Reb. Papers, 620/51/23; 620/10/121/156).

41. Higgins to Cooke, 25 May 1798 (Reb. Papers, 620/18/14); Musgrave, *Rebellions*, p.214.

42. Musgrave, *Rebellions*, pp.211–3.

43. Ibid., p.213.

44. NLI MS 637, p.210.

45. Ibid., p.435.

46. Pakenham, *Year of Liberty*, p.124.

47. J.T. Gilbert, *Documents Relating to Ireland, 1795–1804* (rep. Shannon 1970), p.131.

Chapter 20

1. The 'official press' is represented by the *Moniteur* and the *Rédacteur*; the anti-English press of 1797–8 by the *Journal des Côtes d'Angleterre*, Lemaire's *Patriote Français* and the *Journal des Défenseurs de la Patrie*; the Girondin press by the *Annales Patriotiques*, the *Sentinelle*, the *Bulletin des Amis de la Verité*, the *Républicain*, the *Chronique de Paris*, the *Chronique du Mois*, the *Bouche de Fer*, the *Bien Informé*, Brissot's *Patriote Français* and Lebrun's *Journal Général de l'Europe*; the Jacobin press by the *Journal de la Montagne*, the *Journal des Hommes Libres*; the Anglo-French press by Cox's *Courrier de l'Europe*; the popular press by the *Feuille du Jour*, the *Journal de Paris* and others such as

the *Ami des Lois*, the *Courrier de l'Europe*, the *Mercure Français*, the *Messager des Relations Extérieures*, the *Mercure Universel* and the *Mercure National*.

2. Arthur Young's *Travels* were published in Paris in Year VIII (1799–1800), but extracts from it had already been used to explain the Whiteboys (*Journal des Côtes d'Angleterre*, 5, 8 *nivôse* VI).

3. *Bien Informé*, 13 *thermidor* VI (1 August 1798).

4. *Moniteur*, 3 *brumaire* VIII (24 October 1798).

5. The first edition of the *Bien Informé* appeared on 3 September 1797 (17 *fructidor* V). Published by the Cercle Social, its contributors included Nicolas de Bonneville, Thomas Paine and Louis Sébastien Mercier. According to *Patriote Français* it was a journal 'whose every page records the victories of liberty and justice, and whose incomparable editor is one of the veterans of the Revolution' (no. 248, 8 *prairial* V).

6. *Moniteur*, 28 February 1792.

7. *Sentinelle*, no. 881, 2 *frimaire* VI (22 November 1797).

8. *Patriote Français*, no. 957, 24 March 1792.

9. *Journal Général de l'Europe*, no. 227, 3 February 1792.

10. *Bulletin des Amis de la Vérité*, no. 4, 3 March 1792.

11. *Journal des Hommes Libres*, no. 146, 27 March 1793.

12. *Journal Général de l'Europe*, no. 229, 5 February 1792.

13. *Mercure Français*, 13 October 1793.

14. *Moniteur*, 1 December 1792.

15. *Chronique de Paris*, no. 159, June 1792; *Bulletin des Amis de la Vérité*, no. 4, 3 March 1793.

16. *Journal Général de l'Europe*, no. 45, 4 August 1791.

17. *Courrier de l'Europe*, no. 41, 24 May 1792.

18. *Chronique de Paris*, no. 148, 26 May 1792 and no. 152, 30 May 1792; *Annales Patriotiques*, no. 150, 30 May 1792; *Patriote Français*, no. 1026, 1 June 1792.

19. *Annales Patriotiques*, no. 172, 20 June 1792.

20. *Bulletin des Amis de la Vérité*, no. 8, 7, 1792.

21. *Courrier de l'Europe*, no. 38, 9 November 1792; *Patriote Français*, nos 1194, 1195, 1198, 16, 17 and 20 November 1792; *Journal des Hommes Libres*, no. 17, 18 November 1792.

22. *Journal des Hommes Libres*, no. 28, 29 November 1792.

23. *Bulletin des Amis de la Vérité*, no. 44, 13 February 1793, and no. 49, 18 February 1793; *Journal des Hommes Libres*, no. 105, 14 February 1793.

24. *Journal des Hommes Libres*, no. 110, 19 February 1793.

25. *Bulletin des Amis de la Vérité*, nos 62 and 63, 2 and 3 March 1793; *Journal des Hommes Libres*, no. 123, 4 March 1793.

26. *Journal des Hommes Libres*, no. 17, 17 January 1793.

27. *Journal des Hommes Libres*, no. 44, 1 February 1793; no. 46, 14 February 1793; no. 61, 1 March 1793.

28. *Patriote Français*, no. 1306, 10 March 1793.

29. M. Dorigny, 'Le Cercle Social' in A. Soboul, *Dictionnaire historique de la Révolution française* (Paris 1989).

30. *Journal de la Montagne*, no. 55, 18 *nivôse* II; *Annales Patriotiques*, no. 468, 25 *germinal* II.

31. Jackson's trial was covered in *Annales Patriotiques*, no. 170–1, 20 and 21 *prair-*

ial II.

32. *Journal des Hommes Libres*, no. 74, 29 *frimaire* V.
33. *Sentinelle*, no. 11, 16 *messidor* III.
34. See, for example, reports on the trial and execution of James Weldon (*Sentinelle*, no, 228–9, 18 and 19 *pluvôse* IV), which prompted the comment from the *Annales Patriotiques*: 'Mr Pitt is following in the footsteps of Robespierre' (no. 142, 22 *pluvôse* IV [11 February 1796]). Reports on the trial also detailed the Defenders' use of oaths and catechisms (*Sentinelle*, no. 228, 18 *pluvôse* IV [7 February 1796]).
35. *Annales Patriotiques*, no. 245, 6 *fructidor* III.
36. *Journal des Hommes Libres*, no. 44, 29 *brumaire* V (19 November 1796); *Sentinelle*, no. 515, 30 *brumaire* V (20 November 1796).
37. *Sentinelle*, no. 504, 19 *brumaire* V (9 November 1796).
38. *Annales Patriotiques*, no. 20, 20 *brumaire* V (10 November 1796).
39. *Sentinelle*, no. 553, 8 *nivôse* V (28 December 1796).
40. *Ami des Lois*, nos 514 and 515, 19 and 20 *nivôse* V (10 January 1797).
41. *Ami des Lois*, no. 516, 21 *nivôse* V (10 January 1797).
42. *Ami des Lois*, no. 670, 26 *prairial* V (10 June 1797).
43. *Ami des Lois*, no. 718, 16 *thermidor* V (3 August 1797).
44. Almost all newspapers regularly covered this kind of material, some of it dedicated to the Council of Five Hundred or the Council of Elders: for example, the *Descente en Angleterre* of Mittié, which was staged in Paris in the autumn of 1797, and again in both Paris and Bordeaux during 1798.
45. *Patriote Français*, no. 60, 30 *brumaire* VI.
46. *Ami des Lois*, no. 835, 8 *frimaire* VI (26 November 1797).
47. *Rédacteur*, no. 856, 1 *floréal* VI (19 April 1798).
48. Letter from Thomas Muir and Citizen Molet du Passy published in *Ami des Lois*, no. 896, 9 *pluvôse* VI (28 January 1798).
49. 'Citizen Pinard, jeweller manufacturer and retailer, has badges of Irish union in the form of the Ossian harp with silver strings, and the Erin go Bragh in the form of broaches; both based on models sent to the legislature, and worn by fine Irish women, the generals of the United Irishmen and the generals of the armée d'Angleterre' (*Bien Informé*, no. 324, 5 *thermidor* VI).
50. *Bien Informé*, no. 142, 22 January 1798; no. 147, 27 January 1798.
51. *Bien Informé*, no. 208, 9 *germinal* VI (29 March 1798).
52. *Rédacteur*, no. 946, 1 *thermidor* VI (19 July 1798).,
53. *Bien Informé*, no. 194, 15 March 1798; no. 279, 20 *prairial* VI (8 June 1798).
54. *Bien Informé*, no. 212, 13 *germinal* VI (2 April 1798).
55. *Bien Informé*, no. 235, 6 *floréal* VI (25 April 1798).
56. *Bien Informé*, no. 245, 16 *floréal* VI (5 May 1798).
57. *Bien Informé*, no. 309, 20 *messidor* VI (8 July 1798).
58. The *Bien Informé* and the *Messager des Relations Extérieures* were bitter rivals: a report on the *Messager* of 2 *messidor* VI (20 June 1798) noted 'this new journal exhibits all the marks of genuine royalism...and attacks the *Bien Informé*', cited in F.A. Aulard, *Paris pendant la réaction thermidorienne et sous le Directoire* (5 vols, Paris 1898–1902), iv.
59. 'Erin go Bragh' (in the *Bien Informé* of 2 *messidor* VI [20 June 1798]), and the 'Chant funèbre pour Lord Edward Fitzgerald' in *Bien Informé*, no. 295, 6

messidor VI (24 June 1798).

60. *Bien Informé*, no. 323, 4 *thermidor* VI (22 July 1798).
61. *Ami des Lois*, no. 1066, 1 *thermidor* VI (19 July 1798).
62. *Ami des Lois*, no. 1090, 25 *thermidor* VI (12 August 1798).
63. *Ami des Lois*, no. 1090, 25 *thermidor* VI (12 August 1798).
64. *Bien Informé*, no. 335, 16 *thermidor* VI (3 August 1798).
65. *Bien Informé*, no. 346, 27 *thermidor* VI (14 August 1798).
66. *Ami des Lois*, no. 1119, 23 *fructidor* VI (9 September 1798).
67. *Ami des Lois*, no. 1089, 24 *thermidor* VI (11 August 1798).
68. *Moniteur*, 2 *messidor* VI (20 June 1798).
69. *Patriote Français*, no. 368, 4 *vendémiaire* VIII (25 September 1798).
70. The same is true for Napper Tandy's landing on the island of Rutland, and the naval encounter on Lough Swilly.
71. *Moniteur*, no. 310, 10 *thermidor* VI (28 July 1798); for the trial see *Ami des Lois*, no. 1088, 22 *thermidor* VI (9 August 1798).
72. *Bien Informé*, no. 405, 6 *brumaire* VII (26 October 1798).
73. *Bien Informé*, no. 415, 16 *brumaire* VII (6 November 1798).
74. *Moniteur*, no. 81, 21 *frimaire* VII (11 December 1798).
75. *Bien Informé*, no. 451, 21 *frimaire* VII (11 December 1798).
76. *Ami des Lois*, no. 1219, 27 *frimaire* VII (17 December 1798).
77. *Bien Informé*, no. 480, 21 *nivôse* VII (10 January 1798).
78. *Bien Informé*, no. 485, 26 *nivôse* VII (15 January 1798).
79. *Patriote Français*, no. 406, 12 *brumaire* VII (2 November 1798).
80. *Ami des Lois*, nos 1203–14, 10–22 *frimaire* VII (1–12 December 1798).
81. *Correspondance des Représentants du Peuple*, no. 42, 12 *brumaire* VII (December 1798).

Chapter 21

1. T.W. Tone, *An Argument on Behalf of the Catholics of Ireland* (Dublin 1791), p.3.
2. Cited in W. Bailie, 'Rev. Samuel Barber, 1738–1811, National Volunteer and United Irishman' in J. Haire (ed.), *Challenge and Conflict: Essays in Presbyterian History and Doctrine* (Antrim 1981), p.82.
3. *Rep. Comm. Sec.*, pp.67, 71, 74.
4. *N. Star*, 1 June 1795.
5. *Rep. Comm. Sec.*, p.72.
6. I have used the 1777 Dublin edition of *The Complete Works of M. de Montesqieu Translated from the French* (4 vols). 'The Spirit of Laws' is in vol. I. My treatment is greatly influenced by S. Deane, 'The Irish Enlightenment', lecture delivered to the Eighteenth-Century Ireland Society, Drumcondra, Spring 1991.
7. Dying declaration of William Michael Byrne, Reb. Papers, 620/39/109.
8. Tone, *Life*, I, p.51.
9. J. Larkin (ed.), *The Trial of William Drennan* (Dublin 1991), p.40.
10. A. O'Connor, *The State of Ireland* (Dublin 1798), p.28.
11. *Rep. Comm. Sec.*, p.72.
12. *Drennan Letters*, p.228.

13. Bartlett, 'Defenders', pp.373–94.
14. *Ibid.*, p.385.
15. *Ibid.*, p.394.
16. *Ibid.*, p.376.
17. [A. O'Connor], *Beauties of the Press* (London 1800), p.34.
18. *Ibid.*, p.171.
19. Forster Archer to —, 6 Dec. 1797 (Reb. Papers, 620/33/123).
20. Information of John Smyth (Reb. Papers, 620/54/7).
21. McDowell, 'Personnel of U.I.', pp.12–53. See also *FDJ*, 24 Apr. 1798.
22. 'An Account of the Numbers of Persons Surrendering themselves in the City of Dublin...from 29 June–9 September 1798' in *Jnl H.C. Irl.*, append. dccc-cxlvi–lix.
23. *The Speech of the Right Honourable John Earl of Clare...19 February 1798* (Dublin 1798), p.33; Larkin, *Drennan Trial*, p.51.
24. Denis Browne (Westport) to —, 6 June 1793 (PRO[L.], HO100/44/115–8).
25. J. Alexander, *Some Account of the First Apparent Symptoms of the Late Rebellion...* (Dublin 1800), p.19.
26. Leonard McNally to Edward Cooke, 12 Sept. 1795 (Reb. Papers 620/10/121/27).
27. — Dillon (Athlone) to Edward Cooke, 14 Feb. 1795 (Nat. Archives, SOC 30/159).
28. Edward Newenham (Limerick) to Thomas Pelham, 31 May 1797 (Reb. Papers, 620/30/257).
29. S. Grimes (ed.), *Dublin in 1804* (Dublin 1980), p.18.
30. Walter Bermingham to Edward Cooke, 24 Dec. 1796 (Reb. Papers, 620/26/153).
31. *FLJ*, 2–6 Mar. 1793.
32. *DEP*, 21 Mar. 1797.
33. Cited in McDowell, *Age of Imperialism*, p.353.
34. S. Davies, 'The *Northern Star* and the Propagation of Enlightened Ideas' in *Eighteenth-Century Ireland*, V (1990), pp.143–52; R. Cole, *Irish Booksellers and English Writers, 1740–1800* (London 1986), p.17.
35. Woods, *Russell*, p.112.
36. A. O'Connor to C. Fox, n.d. (Reb. Papers, 620/ 15/3/8); Musgrave, *Rebellions*, p.155.
37. *Rep. Comm. Sec.*, p.12.
38. *FDJ*, 2 Jan. 1798.
39. *FDJ*, 2, 9 Jan. 1798. For an earlier example of a political clampdown (on a hawker of political ballads), see *DEP*, 20 Oct. 1794.
40. Transcript of the trial of Fr John Brookes (Reb. Papers, 620/41/66).
41. John Sweeney's papers (Reb. Papers, 620/48/47).
42. M.H. Thuente, *The United Irishmen and the Development of Irish Literary Nationalism* (Syracuse, forthcoming).
43. Cited in McDowell, *Age of Imperialism*, p.366.
44. Richard Nevill to Edward Cooke, 10 Dec. 1797 (Reb. Papers, 620/33/139).
45. Maurice Tracey (Baltinglass) to Thomas Pelham, 26 May 1797 (Reb. Papers 620/30/198).
46. *Saunder's Newsletter*, 14 Dec. 1797.

47. R. Darnton and D. Roche (eds), *Revolution in Print: the Press in France, 1775–1800* (Berkeley 1989); J. Landes, 'More than Words: the Printing Press and the French Revolution' in *Eighteenth-Century Studies*, XXV (1991), pp.85–98; R. Darnton, *Edition et sédition: l'univers de la littérature clandestine au XVIIIe siècle* (Paris 1991).

48. O. Smith, *The Politics of Language, 1791–1819* (Oxford 1984).

49. *Union Doctrine or Poor Man's Catechism* (Dublin 1798), p.6.

50. Address to the Grand Jury of County Kerry, 18 March 1799 (RIA MS 12/10/11).

51. *FDJ*, 3 Mar. 1796. See also *Some Reflections on the Late and Critical Disturbances in Ireland* (Dublin 1798), p.5.

52. Andrew MacNevin (Carrickfergus) to —, 9 July 1795, in Digest of Evidence on the United Irishmen (PRO[L.], HO/100/58/190).

53. Musgrave, *Rebellions*, p.155.

54. *N. Star*, 15 July 1796.

55. *Union Doctrine*, p.5.

56. *The Cry of the Poor for Bread* (Dublin 1795), copy in Reb. Papers, 620/18/14.

57. T. Paulin, *Minotaur: Poetry and the Nation State* (London 1992), p.167.

58. Abraham Shackleton (Ballitore) to Joseph Williams, Cole Alley, Dublin, 29 Nov. 1792 (NLI, Shackleton Papers, uncat. coll.).

59. J. Little, 'A Diary of the French Landing in 1798' in *Anal. Hib.*, XVI (1948), p.122.

60. John Beresford to Lord Auckland, 4 Sept. 1796, in *Beresford Corr.*, II, p.128.

61. Lecky, *Ire.*, III, pp.441–2. For other references to prophecies, see Reb. Papers 620/54/126; 620/57/52; *Press*, 2 Nov. 1797.

62. J. Adams, *The Printed Word and the Common Man: Popular Culture in Ulster, 1700–1900* (Belfast 1987), p.89.

63. *A Discourse on the Rise and Fall of Anti-Christ, wherein the Revolution in France and the Downfall of Monarchy in this Kingdom are Distinctly Pointed out, Delivered at London in the Year 1701 by Robert Fleming* (Belfast 1795), p.v. (copy in Reb. papers, 620/22/63).

64. *Christ in Triumph Coming to Judgement* (Strabane 1795), p.3 (copy in Reb Papers, 620/29/8).

65. R. Bloch, *Visionary Republic: Millennial Themes in American Thought, 1756–1801* (Cambridge 1991).

66. General Whyte to Edward Cooke, 17 March 1793 (PRO[L.], HO/100/43/103).

67. Woods, *Russell*, pp.66–7.

68. *Saunders Newsletter*, 10 Dec. 1797; George Holdcroft (Kells) to John Lees (Dublin), 7 Apr. 1796 (Reb. Papers, 620/23/73); *Press*, 5, 14 Dec. 1797.

69. C. Jackson, *A Narrative of the Sufferings and Escape of Charles Jackson…* (London 1798), pp.22–3.

70. Thuente, *United Irishmen*.

71. *N. Star*, 2 Sept. 1796.

72. T. Handcock, 'A Narrative of the Battle of Enniscorthy' (NLI MS 16,232, p.116).

73. — to Edward Cooke, 29 May 1798 (Reb. Papers, 620/37/211A).

74. T.A. Emmet, 'Part of an Essay Towards a History of Ireland' in MacNeven,

Pieces, p.77. See also J.S. Donnelly, 'Propagating the Cause of the United Irishmen' in *Studies*, LXIX (1980), pp.5–23.

75. *Press*, 20 Jan. 1798.

76. Adams, *Printed Word*, p.6.

77. *DEP*, 11 June 1791.

78. Tone, *Life*, I, p.545.

79. B. McDermott (ed.), *The Catholic Question in Ireland and England, 1798–1822: the Papers of Denys Scully* (Dublin 1988), p.6.

80. *FDJ*, 3 Mar. 1796.

81. J. Burk, *History of the Late War in Ireland with an Account of the United Irish Association* (Philadelphia 1799), pp.45–6.

82. Musgrave, *Rebellions*, p.117; Dexter Club (Reb. Papers, 620/31/2); Shoe Club (Reb. Papers, 620/34/58); Strugglers (Burk, *History*, p.44); Cold Bone Club (NLI MS 1429); Real United Traders (Reb. Papers, 620/24/171); Clady Club (Reb. Papers, 620/34/59); Shamrock Club (Musgrave, *Rebellions*, p.113).

83. *FDJ*, 5, 8 Mar. 1796.

84. Robert Day's charge to the Kilmainham Quarter Sessions, 12 Jan. 1796, in *FDJ*, 26 Jan. 1796.

85. *FDJ*, 5 Jan. 1796.

86. *Freeman's Journal*, 19 Mar. 1796.

87. Thomas Boyle to —, 13 Apr. 1797 (Reb. Papers, 620/18/3).

88. John Smith to —, 16 June 1797 (SOC, 11/3086).

89. Caesar Colclough (Duffry Hall) to —, 18 Jan. 1799 (Reb. Papers, 620/56/62).

90. Little, 'Diary', pp.64–5, 67. For other references to confraternities, see Reb. Papers, 620/26/64; 620/32/77; 620/31/180; 620/56/14.

91. L. Hyland, Bovagh, to Lord Glentworth 8 Dec. 1796 (Reb. Papers, 620/26/105); *N. Star*, 18 Jan. 1796; Reb. Papers, 620/23/53; Jim Smyth, *Men of No Property* (London 1992), *passim*.

92. *Saunder's Newsletter*, 2 June 1797; A. Cole-Hamilton (Beltrim Castle) to —, 24 Mar. 1796 (Reb. Papers, 620/25/53).

93. R. McHugh (ed.), *Carlow in '98: the Autobiography of William Farrell* (Dublin 1949), p.23.

94. *FLJ*, 20–3 July 1770; 13–16 Mar. 1776.

95. *Wexford People*, 3 July 1909; M. Byrne, *Memoirs* (Paris 1863), I, p.223; Reb. Papers, 620/11/138/43; 620/13/168/3; SOC, 1804, 1026/17, 1027/2.

96. Byrne, *Memoirs*, I, p.94.

97. *The Tryal of William Byrne of Ballymanus* (Dublin 1799), p.19.

98. *Address of the County Committee of Dublin City to their Constituents, 1 Feb. 1798* (Dublin 1798), p.3 (copy in Reb. Papers, 620/42/14).

99. K. Whelan, 'Politicisation in County Wexford and the Origins of the 1798 Rebellion' in Gough and Dickson, *Ire. and the Fr. Rev.*, p.174; E. Hay, *History of the Insurrection of the County of Wexford* (Dublin 1803), app., p.xxvi.

100. K. Whelan, 'The Catholic Community in Eighteenth-Century County Wexford' in T. Power and K. Whelan (eds), *Endurance and Emergence: Catholics in Ireland in the Eighteenth Century* (Dublin 1990), pp.129–70.

101. Letter of Robert Jephson, cited in C. Maxwell, *Dublin Under the Georges, 1714–1890* (London 1938), p.108.

102. Anne, Countess of Roden (Dublin) to Harriett Skeffington (Belfast), 21 Feb.

1793 (PRONI, D 562/2563).

103. Alexander, *Symptoms*, p.22.

104. *FDJ*, 3 May 1798.

105. *FLJ*, 5–8 Aug. 1795.

106. Henry Echlin (Balbriggan) to —, 17 May 1798 (Reb. Papers, 620/37/95).

107. *Rep. Comm. Sec.*, p.6. See also S. McSkimin, *Annals of Ulster* (Belfast 1849), pp.37–9; *Press*, 21 Dec. 1797; Froude, *Ire*, III, pp.217–8.

108. *FLJ*, 31 Aug.–4 Sept. 1782. For similar examples, see *FLJ*, 21–5 Aug. 1773; 28–31 Aug. 1782; 20–4 Sept 1783; 24–7 Sept. 1783.

109. *FLJ*, 27–30 May 1795.

110. Information of — Sheridan, 21 Apr. 1795, Digest on the United Irishmen (PRO[L.], HO/100/58/189).

111. A. Newton (Coagh) to Thomas Pelham 15 Aug. 1796 (Reb. Papers 620/24/ 120).

112. Benjamin Chapman (Trim) to Lord Shelburne (Bowood), 25 Apr. 1797 (Michigan University Library, Ann Arbor, Shelburne Papers).

113. J. E. Walsh, *Sketches of Ireland Sixty Years Ago* (Dublin 1849), p.110.

114. *Letters from a Gentleman in Ireland to his Friend at Bath* (Cork 1798), p.9.

115. *Robert Day's Charge to Kilmainham Quarter Sessions*, 12 Jan. 1796; *FDJ*, 28 Jan. 1796.

116. *DEP*, 23 June 1791.

117. *FLJ*, 16–19 Feb. 1791; See also *FLJ*, 2–6 May 1788, 23–6 Feb. 1791; *DEP*, 23 June 1791.

118. *FLJ*, 3–7 Oct. 1789; Grimes, *Dublin in 1804*, p.28.

119. T. Brennan, *Public Drinking and Popular Culture in Eighteenth-Century Paris* (Princeton 1988).

120. *FLJ*, 13–16 Mar. 1793; Froude, *Ire.*, III, p.122.

121. *Address of the County Committee of Dublin City*, pp.2–3.

122. *To the Friends of the Union of the County of Meath* (Trim 1797) (copy in Rep. Papers, 620/54/37); *To the United Men of Ireland* (Dublin 1797) (copy in Reb. Papers, 620/54/40).

123. Musgrave, *Rebellions*, p.232; *Diary of Robert Day*, 1829, p.163 (RIA MS 12/W/ 16).

124. *Granias lamentation* [Ballad re Armagh expulsions] (copy in SOC 1797, 30/46).

125. Reb. Papers, 620/39/10.

126. James Laffan (Kilkenny) to —, 1 Oct. 1804 (PRO[L.], HO/100/122/340–2).

127. P. Burke, *Popular Culture in Early Modern Europe* (London 1978); K. Whelan, 'An Underground Gentry? Catholic Middlemen in Eighteenth-Century Ireland' in J. Donnelly and K. Miller (eds), *Popular Culture in Ireland* (forthcoming).

128. I do not have space to discuss this crucial issue here. For the broader context, see L. Colley, *Britons: Forging the Nation, 1707–1837* (Yale 1992).

129. Spencer Hoey (Drogheda) to J. Forbes (Kildare Street), 1 July 1788, in M. Corcoran (ed.), 'Three Eighteenth-Century Drogheda Letters' in *Louth Arch. Soc. Jn.*, XXII (1989), p.31.

130. *FLJ*, 11–14 July 1792.

131. James Caulfield, *Advice to the Roman Catholic Clergy of the Diocese of Ferns, 12 April 1803* (Wexford 1803), p.3.

Chapter 22

1. Madden, *U.I.*, 2nd ser., II, pp.190–4.
2. The most recent estimation of the number of United Irish *émigrés* to the United States has been made by Michael Durey in 'Irish Deism and Jefferson's Republic: Denis Driscol in Ireland and America, 1793–1810' in *Éire-Ireland*, XXV (Winter 1990), pp.56–76. See also his earlier essays, 'Thomas Paine's Apostles: Radical *Émigrés* and the Triumph of Jeffersonian Republicanism' in *William and Mary Quarterly*, XLIV (October 1987), pp.661–88; 'Transatlantic Patriotism: Political Exiles and America in the Age of Revolutions' in Clive Emsley and James Walvin (eds), *Artisans, Peasants, and Proletarians: 1760–1860* (London 1985), pp.7–31.
3. In addition to the work of Madden and Durey on the United Irishmen in America, see David N. Doyle, *Ireland, Irishmen, and Revolutionary America* (Dublin 1981); Maurice J. Bric, 'Ireland, Irishmen, and the Broadening of the Late Eighteenth-Century Philadelphia Polity' (unpublished Ph.D. thesis, John Hopkins University 1991); Edward Carter, 'A Wild Irishman Under Every Federalist Bed: Nativism in Philadelphia, 1789–1806' in *Pennsylvania Magazine of History and Biography*, XCIV (July 1970), pp.331–41; J.J. St Mark, 'The Red Shamrock: United Irishmen and Revolution, 1795–1803' (unpublished Ph.D. thesis, Georgetown University 1975); Harvey Strum, 'Federalist Hibernophobes in New York, 1807' in *Éire-Ireland*, XVI (Winter 1981), pp.7–13; Rex Syndergaard, 'Wild Irishmen and the Alien and Sedition Acts' in *Éire-Ireland*, IX (Spring 1974), pp.14–24; Richard Twomey, 'Jacobins and Jeffersonians: Anglo-American Radical Ideology, 1790–1810' in Margaret and James Jacob (eds), *The Origins of Anglo-American Radicalism* (London 1984), pp.284–99.
4. The often contentious terms and contradictory assumptions of Irish historiography are discussed by J.R. Hill, 'Popery and Protestantism, Civil and Religious Liberty: the Disputed Lessons of Irish History, 1690–1812' in *Past and Present*, CXVIII (February 1988), pp.96–129; Francis G. James, 'Historiography and the Irish Constitutional Revolution of 1782' in *Éire-Ireland*, XVIII (Winter 1983), pp.6–16; Donal MacCartney, 'The Writing of History in Ireland, 1800–1830' in *IHS*, X (1957), pp.347–62. On the writing of Irish history in America, see Martin J. Burke, 'The Politics and Poetics of Nationalist Historiography' in Cecil Barfoot (ed.), *The Politics of Literature and the Literature of Politics* (Amsterdam, Rodopf, forthcoming).
5. John Burk, *History of the Late War in Ireland, with an Account of the United Irish Association from the First Meeting in Belfast, to the Landing at Killala* (Philadelphia 1799).
6. [John Burk], *The Trial of John Burk, Late of Trinity College, for Heresy and Blasphemy* (Dublin 1794). On Burk, see Edward A. Wyatt, *John Daly Burk: Patriot, Playwright, Historian* (Charlottesville: Historical Publishing Company 1936); Joseph Shulim, *John Daly Burk: Irish Revolutionist and American Patriot* (Philadelphia 1964). The significance of Burk's clandestine political activities in Dublin has been recently re-evaluated by Michael Durey, 'Irish Deism and Jefferson's Republic', pp.61–4.
7. In addition to Shulim and Wyatt, Burk's historical writing, in particular the

History of Virginia, is discussed by Richard Beale Davis, *Literature and Society in Early Virginia, 1608–1840* (Baton Rouge 1973), pp.202, 205, 218–20, 230–1. On his theatrical pieces, see Martin J. Burke, 'Why Not Columbia's Rising Fame by Sung: Irish-American Playwrights and Republican Theatricals in the New Nation' in Robert Welch (ed.), *Anglo-Irish Literature: International Perspectives* (London 1991).

8. Among the more provocative pieces of his literature is William Cobbett's *Detection of a Conspiracy Formed by the United Irishmen, with the Evident Intention of Aiding the Tyrants of France in Subverting the Government of the United States* (Philadelphia 1797). See as well Fennos' treatment of the events of 1798 and his attacks upon the 'wild Irishmen' in his *Gazette of the United States*, then published in Philadelphia. The details of this war of words are covered in Edward C. Carter, 'A Wild Irishman Under Every Federalist Bed', and in Rex Syndergaard, 'Wild Irishmen and the Alien and Sedition Acts'.

9. John Burk, *History of the Late War*, pp.13–16, 119–30.

10. Ibid., pp.130–2, 136–40.

11. On MacNeven's life and career, see Madden, 'Memoir of William James MacNeven' in *U.I.*, 2nd ser., II, pp.209–88; Deasmumhan Ó Raghailaigh, 'William James MacNeven' in *Studies*, XXX (June 1944), pp.247–59.

12. Madden, 'MacNeven'; Ó Raghailaigh, 'MacNeven'. See also Sean O'Donnell, 'Irish-American Scientists' in *Éire-Ireland* XV (Summer 1979), pp. 106–9; and 'Early American Science: the Irish Contribution' in *Éire-Ireland*, LXVIII (Spring 1983), pp.134–6.

13. This campaign is analysed in detail in Harvey Strum, 'Federalist Hibernophobes in New York, 1807'.

14. MacNeven, *Pieces*, pp.i–ii, xi–xii.

15. Ibid., pp.xvi, xxii–xxiii, 303–5. Among those 'impartial' texts were James Gordon, *History of the Rebellion in Ireland in the year 1798...* (London 1803); John Jones, *An Impartial Narrative of Each Engagement which Took Place between His Majesty's Forces and the Rebels during the Irish Rebellions* (Dublin 1800); and Musgrave, *Rebellions*.

16. MacNeven, *Pieces*, pp.i–xxiii.

17. On Emmet, see Madden, *U.I.*, 2nd ser., II, 'Memoir of Thomas Addis Emmet', pp.1–208; Thomas P. Robinson 'The Life of Thomas Addis Emmet' (unpublished Ph.D. thesis, New York University 1955).

18. Emmet, 'Towards the History of Ireland' in MacNeven, *Pieces*, pp.1, 13–14.

19. Ibid., pp.78–9.

20. Ibid., pp.119–25, 131–44.

21. William Sampson, *Memoirs of William Sampson...* (New York 1807). On Sampson, see Madden, 'William Sampson' in *U.I.*, 2nd ser., II, pp.335–88.

22. Sampson, *Memoirs*, pp.iii–iv, 4–5, 15, 19.

23. Ibid., pp.30, 202–11.

24. Ibid,. pp.30–6, 69, 119, 193, 211.

25. Miles Byrne, *Some Notes of an Irish Exile of 1798* (Dublin n.d.), p.41; Madden, *U.I.*, 2nd ser., II, p.99.

26. Ibid., pp.30–6, 69, 119, 193, 211, 277. Letter xxxii of the *Memoirs* is entitled 'A Brief Review of Irish History'.

27. William Sampson, *History of Ireland* (New York 1841). Sampson's edition is of William Cook Taylor's *History of the Civil Wars in Ireland*.
28 Miles Byrne, *Some Notes...*, p.41; Madden, *U.I.*, 2nd ser., II, p.99.

INDEX